Educational Experience as Lived

"Not only is this an important book, it is also a necessary book. William Pinar is one of the major curriculum theorists of the past forty years. While he launched the reconceptualization of curriculum studies, subsequent events have shown that he has set the scholarly direction for the field in the 21st Century."
Terrance R. Carson, University of Alberta, Canada

In this volume William F. Pinar enacts his theory of curriculum, detailing the relations among knowledge, history, and alterity. The introduction is his intellectual life history, naming the contributions he has made to understanding educational experience. Through his portraits of educational experience as lived—encompassing study as the center of educational experience, his conceptions of disciplinarity and internationalization, reactivating the past to find the future, the gendering and racialization of U.S. school reform, the technologization of education, and the educational project of subjective and social reconstruction—Pinar threads the relations among knowledge, history, and alterity.

William F. Pinar is Professor and Canada Research Chair at the University of British Columbia. He has also served as the St. Bernard Parish Alumni Endowed Professor at Louisiana State University, the Frank Talbott Professor at the University of Virginia, and the A. Lindsay O'Connor Professor of American Institutions at Colgate University. The former President of the International Association for the Advancement of Curriculum Studies and the founder of its U.S. affiliate, the American Association for the Advancement of Curriculum Studies, Pinar received, in 2000, the LSU Distinguished Faculty Award and a Lifetime Achievement Award from the American Educational Research Association.

World Library of Educationalists Series

Thinking and Rethinking the University
The selected works of Ronald Barnett
Ronald Barnett

The Politics of Race, Class and Special Education
The selected works of Sally Tomlinson
Sally Tomlinson

Lessons from History of Education
The selected works of Richard Aldrich
Richard Aldrich

Knowledge, Power, and Education
The selected works of Michael W. Apple
Michael W. Apple

Education Policy and Social Class
The selected works of Stephen J. Ball
Stephen J. Ball

Race, Culture, and Education
The selected works of James A. Banks
James A. Banks

In Search of Pedagogy Volume I
The selected works of Jerome Bruner, 1957–1978
Jerome S. Bruner

In Search of Pedagogy Volume II
The selected works of Jerome Bruner, 1979–2006
Jerome S. Bruner

Reimagining Schools
The selected works of Elliot W. Eisner
Elliot W. Eisner

Reflecting Where the Action Is
The selected works of John Elliot
John Elliot

The Development and Education of the Mind
The Selected Works of Howard Gardner
Howard Gardner

Constructing Worlds through Science Education
The selected works of John K. Gilbert
John K. Gilbert

Making Sense of Learners Making Sense of Written Language
The Selected Words of Kenneth S. Goodman and Yetta M. Goodman
Kenneth S. Goodman and Yetta M. Goodman

Learning, Curriculum and Life Politics
The selected works of Ivor F. Goodson
Ivor F. Goodson

Education and the Nation State
The selected works of S. Gopinathan
S. Gopinathan

Educational Assessment, Evaluation, and Research
The selected works of Mary E. James
Mary E. James

Teaching, Learning and Education in Late Modernity
The selected works of Peter Jarvis
Peter Jarvis

Education, Markets, and the Public Good
The selected works of David F. Labaree
David F. Labaree

Politics, Policies and Pedagogies in Education
The selected works of Bob Lingard
Bob Lingard

A Life in Education
The selected works of John Macbeath
John Macbeath

Overcoming Exclusion
Social Justice through Education
Peter Mittler

Learner-Centered English Language Education
The selected works of David Nunan
David Nunan

Educational Philosophy and Politics
The selected works of Michael A. Peters
Michael A. Peters

Encountering Education in the Global
The selected works of Fazal Rizvi
Fazal Rizvi

Landmarks in Literacy
The Selected Works of Frank Smith
Frank Smith

Corporatism, Social Control, and Cultural Domination in Education: From the Radical Right to Globalization
The selected works of Joel Spring
Joel Spring

The Curriculum and the Child
The selected works of John White
John White

The Art and Science of Teaching and Learning
The selected works of Ted Wragg
E. C. Wragg

China through the Lens of Comparative Education
The Selected Works of Ruth Hayhoe
Ruth Hayhoe

Multiculturalism in Education and Teaching
The selected works of Carl A. Grant
Carl A. Grant

Educational Experience as Lived: Knowledge, History, Alterity
The Selected Works of William F. Pinar
William F. Pinar

Educational Experience as Lived: Knowledge, History, Alterity

The Selected Works of William F. Pinar

William F. Pinar

Routledge
Taylor & Francis Group
NEW YORK AND LONDON

First published 2015
by Routledge
711 Third Avenue, New York, NY 10017

and by Routledge
2 Park Square, Milton Park, Abingdon, Oxon OX14 4RN

Routledge is an imprint of the Taylor & Francis Group, an informa business

Library of Congress Cataloging-in-Publication Data
Pinar, William F.
[Works. Selections]
Educational experience as lived : knowledge, history, alterity : the selected writings of William F. Pinar / William F. Pinar.
pages cm. — (World library of educationalists)
Includes bibliographical references and index.
1. Education—Curricula—Philosophy. 2. Education—Philosophy.
3. Pinar, William F.—Influence. I. Title.
LB1570.P5523 2015
375′.001—dc23
2014028778

ISBN: 978-1-138-80499-9 (hbk)
ISBN: 978-1-315-75259-4 (ebk)

Typeset in Sabon
by Apex CoVantage, LLC

Printed and bound in the United States of America by Publishers Graphics, LLC on sustainably sourced paper.

CONTENTS

ACKNOWLEDGMENTS

First and foremost I express my gratitude to my exceptional editor at Routledge—Naomi Silverman—without whose editorial encouragement and acumen this volume would not exist.

My thanks to Peter Taubman for introducing me to the work of Robert Musil (chapter 16), to Petra Munro Hendry for encouraging my study of Jane Addams (chapter 17) and Ida B. Wells (chapter 10), to Terry Carson, Nicholas Ng-A-Fook, and Teresa Strong-Wilson for their comments on chapter 4, to José María García Garduño for his critique of chapter 7, and to Nicholas Ng-A-Fook for alerting me to the work of Ben Williamson (chapter 6).

My thanks to those who have taught me and studied with me. It has been my privilege to participate in the conversation you have stimulated.

PREFACE

> What is so important about the relation between power and knowledge for our historical present?
>
> Colin Koopman[1]

I came of intellectual age in the era of New Criticism, the close reading of literary texts, attentive to their internal structures, meanings, dynamics. I kept the training in close reading but not that tradition's disinterest in reader response, authorial intention, politics, and history. These I threaded into a theory of curriculum as complicated conversation with those present and absent, contemporaries of course but also with the dead and those not yet born. Like a compelling conversation, curriculum can have a life of its own. In my conception, the teacher becomes even more indispensable when freed from objectives and outcomes. The key interlocutor, the educator is engaged in ongoing study, in solitude, with others.

My B.S. in Ed. degree was in English, but I studied history, philosophy, and music as well. In graduate school I supplemented studies in education with coursework in the English Department. My doctoral dissertation recorded those early efforts to associate ideas from these disciplines to the academic study of education. The year after graduating with the Ph.D., I linked these with studies in consciousness, informed by my Zen practice, too severed (my practice, not Zen) from everyday life I decided. Finding my way each day, amidst knowledge, history, and alterity, was the needle I knew I had to thread, and by the mid-1970s autobiography had become my stitch.

Those early autobiographical experiments remained focused on "texts," especially those of Virginia Woolf, as I attempted to portray what "study" could be, namely ongoing ethical engagement with alterity. The chapters in this volume are a series of studies in which I labor to understand what is at stake in the historical and biographical present—themselves intersecting categories as History is also often personal—through understanding the "text," after poststructuralism expansively depicted as persons, events, literatures. There are chapters focused on Jane Addams, Frantz Fanon, George Grant, Robert Musil, and Ida B. Wells, as well as on Ralph Tyler, Roger Simon, and Joe Kincheloe. Each individual life is also allegorical, as each personifies ideas—even ideals—and so I invoke concepts[2] to entitle the chapters, emphasizing, as Luxon does (in her study of Foucault and Freud) that such "exemplarity" enacts "the dilemma of the Foucauldian individual: that she must believe in certain values while accepting the impossibility of their realization."[3] Any appeal to exemplarity ought not obscure, she continues, "Foucault's insistence on relationships irreducible to the persons involved."[4] While Foucault may have fled—for a while—the human subject to concentrate on the historical conditions which structure subjectivity, I underscore their interrelation.

After sketching my intellectual life history and where and when it took place, in chapter 1 I turn to a central category in my life's work: study. Not test preparation, "study" is an ongoing engagement with alterity, with what and whom I don't know and perhaps can't understand, at least not initially and perhaps never fully. Study is the medium not only of knowledge but of subject formation, as one comes to form as a person through what one experiences when studying texts of various kinds, including everyday life.

Study is—as I point out in chapter 2—mythic and historical as well as individual and spiritual. Study invites us to teach and learn from others, including students and colleagues working worldwide. Seeking clarification of colleagues' and students' intellectual histories and present circumstances requires us to study our own, as I point out in chapter 3. While the nation is often the geo-political context in which our work is undertaken, its influence is sometimes insidious, as I note in chapter 4. Insidious can be the cultural consequences of technology, as chapter 5 underlines. It now structures school reform. That reform can take us teachers where we hadn't anticipated—namely out of the picture—is a concern I raise in chapter 6. Out of the picture is precisely where those who formulated the so-called basic principles of curriculum and instruction have gone, as I document in chapter 7. In chapter 8 I incorporate instruction within an expansive conception of curriculum as complicated conversation, through which study is articulated, extended, often reconstructed through dialogical encounter. That conversation occurs in solitude and in social settings like classrooms, but decidedly in specific places, the subject of chapter 9. Place is geographical and biospheric yes, but it is also historical, the site of disappearance and emergence, sometimes due to teaching, as I appreciate in chapter 10. The struggle to emerge from the past requires us to return to it, as I insist in chapter 11. From the past one can return temporally restructured, not stuck in the mud of the present, perhaps even capable of discipline, although not the kinky kind I describe in chapter 12. Not only study can be fetishized, so can identities, as I complain in chapter 13. Identity politics substitutes righteousness for remembrance, but fidelity to the dead means not only indignation but dwelling between hope and despair, as I lament in chapter 14. The tragedy of triumph—if the subjective sides of decolonization are ignored—leaves one wretched, trapped between masks and inwardness, a challenge not only for the historically emergent—as I elaborate in chapter 15—but for those caught in decline, as we see in chapter 16. In chapter 17 I compose an ode to individuality and its reconstruction through public service: educational experience as lived.[5] "Becoming historical," I note in chapter 18, constitutes the cosmopolitan cause of curriculum, as it is the alterity of History that can enable us to excavate non-coincidence with the present wherein we might answer the question Koopman asks. In that riddle we live as modernity is enclosed passage out of the present.

Notes

1 2013, 36.

2 "Concepts get their lives," Lear (2006, 37–38) reminds, "through the lives we are able to live with them."

3 2013, 184.
4 Ibid.
5 "Søren Kierkegaard," Martin and Barresi (2006, 192) remind,

> regarded by many as the founder of existentialism, is famous for his rejection of abstract philosophy, particularly Hegel's theories, on the grounds that life cannot be represented adequately within a conceptual system. The core of human existence is passion, which implies that human existence is not primarily thinking, but living. Most important, passion involves living in a condition of extreme inwardness in which a person embraces all of the contradictions in his or her being.

As I know from my studies of Jane Addams (reprinted in this volume, chapter 17), Laura Bragg, and Pier Paulo Pasolini (Pinar 2009), such inwardness (see also chapter 16, this volume) radiates outward.

Bibliography

Koopman, Colin. 2013. *Genealogy as Critique: Foucault and the Problems of Modernity.* Bloomington: Indiana University Press.
Lear, Jonathan. 2006. *Radical Hope: Ethics in the Face of Cultural Devastation.* Cambridge, MA: Harvard University Press.
Luxon, Nancy. 2013. *Crisis of Authority. Politics, Trust, and Truth-Telling in Freud and Foucault.* Cambridge: Cambridge University Press.
Martin, Raymond and Barresi, John. 2006. *The Rise and Fall of Soul and Self. An Intellectual History of Personal Identity.* New York: Columbia University Press.
Pinar, William F. 2009. *The Worldliness of a Cosmopolitan Education: Passionate Lives in Public Service.* New York: Routledge.
Toews, John. 2008. *Becoming Historical: Cultural Reformation and Public Memory in Early Nineteenth-Century Berlin.* New York: Cambridge University Press.

INTRODUCTION[1]

Commentary

To introduce the collection I sketch my intellectual history—where and with whom I studied, what disciplines and concepts informed my research—and how my research has contributed to the complicated conversation that is the academic field of curriculum studies. In contrast to those educationists prepared in the social sciences, my own training was in the humanities, studies in American and English fiction as well as in literary theory and criticism. That training in close reading, theory, and criticism remains the methodology by which I conduct curriculum research.

Reference

Pinar, William F. 2009. The Primacy of the Particular. In *Leaders in Curriculum Studies: Intellectual Self-Portraits,* edited by Leonard Waks and Edmund C. Short (143–152). Rotterdam and Tapei: Sense Publishers.

> As I get older, time gets shorter every day, one needs to hurry.
>
> Teresa de Lauretis[2]

By my count, I have made seven contributions to curriculum studies. First is the concept of *currere*, the infinitive form of the noun curriculum. I invoked it first during the 1970s to denote a shift from curriculum defined as syllabus (or objectives or outcomes, or from any of its conceptualizations as a static entity, implied by the noun) to curriculum conceived as the educational experience of "complicated conversation."[3] *Currere*—and the autobiographical method[4] I devised to understand curriculum as educational experience—initiated what became, in fifteen years, an entire sector of curriculum studies scholarship.[5] Extolling the centrality of educational experience in understanding curriculum precipitated my participation in what turned out to be a shift in the field's fundamental idea of itself: from a field focused on curriculum development to one devoted to understanding curriculum. My theorizing of the field's *Reconceptualization*[6]—contribution number 2—informs my present studies of disciplinarity and internationalization.[7]

In December 1981 (in the public library of Berkeley, California, where I was visiting my then five-year-old son Gabriel), I theorized curriculum as gender text,[8] thereby establishing *queer theory* in education, *avant la lettre*. That I count as contribution number 3. Twenty years later, informed by queer theory, I reconfigured *anti-racist education* from a preoccupation with attitudes (tolerance, for instance) to subjective reconstruction through academic knowledge, theorizing the gender of racial politics and violence in America by juxtaposing lynching and interracial prison rape.[9] That is contribution number 4. In that 2001 synoptic textbook, and in the genealogy of whiteness that followed, I demonstrated that curriculum development is an intellectual not bureaucratic undertaking.[10] Reconceptualizing curriculum development counts as contribution number 5.

Contributing to my queering of race was my earlier elaboration of *place* as a category in understanding curriculum, now a concept common not only in contemporary curriculum studies. Theorizing place began as an effort to contextualize the curricular challenges posed by living—as I did for twenty years—in the American South.[11] While continuing to emphasize the singularities the intersections of history and culture create, in recent years I have also acknowledged *place* as biospheric.[12] This reconstruction of place as planetary animates my current effort to reconstruct humanism.[13] Introducing the conception of place constitutes contribution number 6.

Since 2000 I have initiated an intellectual and organizational movement known as the *internationalization of curriculum studies*, establishing (with help, of course) the International Association for the Advancement of Curriculum Studies, its U.S. affiliate, the American Association for the Advancement of Curriculum Studies, editing the international handbook of curriculum research.[14] With funding from the Social Sciences and Humanities Research Council of Canada, I have been enabled to study the intellectual histories and present circumstances of five nationally distinctive curriculum studies fields: Brazil, China, India, Mexico, and South Africa. Now I turned my attention (again) to Canada, focusing on the life's work of George Grant.[15]

The Past in the Present

I was born in Huntington, West Virginia, on August 27, 1947. In 1953 we moved to Pennsylvania (first to Emporium in the northwest corner, then to Pittsburgh); in 1955 we moved to Ohio (Westerville, a suburb of Columbus). I received a solid introduction to the various school subjects, taught by often animated and dedicated teachers. It was during my senior year (1964–1965) at Westerville High School that I glimpsed—in an honors government class taught by Mrs. Sarah Ott—what a multi-referenced complicated conversation curriculum could be. The main referents of that course were the texts—among them Heilbroner's *The Worldly Philosophers*—and the World History class Mrs. Ott had taught two years before. (Each of us had been invited as a consequence of our work with her in that earlier class.) Mrs. Ott was a superb teacher: erudite and engaging.

After graduation, I studied at a small conservatory of music in Columbus where I was a performance major: alto saxophone was my primary instrument, piano my minor. During my freshman year, Professor William Kuhre lured me to the liberal arts with his provocative teaching of freshman composition and American literature, a year-long course featuring, during spring term, J.D. Salinger's *Catcher in the Rye*. I transferred first to Otterbein College, then to Ohio State, where I studied history, enjoying individual attention in an honors program under the supervision of Professor Mary Young, a distinguished historian of American Indian policy, whom I would later meet—this time as a colleague—at the

University of Rochester. Back in Columbus, in 1966, I too aspired to become a historian, but when graduate school was dropped as a category of deferment from military service—an issue urgent to those of us opposed to the Vietnam War—and public school teaching remained eligible, I switched to English, a subject more in demand in the public schools, and one to which I had already been drawn.

The political chaos of those years was mirrored in my psychological life. Adrift in turbulence, I fastened upon academic study as providing opportunities to understand the reality around me while mooring me. As provocative and influential as reading William Appleman Williams was, the major intellectual event in my undergraduate life was philosophical not historical, namely existentialism and phenomenology, subjects I studied with Professor Lee Brown in Ohio State's Department of Philosophy. At first I was drawn to Kierkegaard, then Nietzsche, but I settled on Sartre. Especially his fiction (*Nausea*) forced me to confront the question: how shall I live? Like Pasternak's Zhivago, I embraced subjectivity as politically precious in an unjust world lacerated by violence. Nineteen sixty-eight was a violent year, indeed.

In my senior year—fall 1969—I enjoyed an opportunity to believe again in meaningful public service, thanks to Professor Donald R. Bateman,[16] who permitted me to join his experimental urban education program. There I was introduced to Freire while working in the inner city of Columbus, where I tutored (in twin towers off I-70 East that remain visible today), then taught at Roosevelt Junior High School. I chose—those were days when teachers still enjoyed some measure of academic freedom—Richard Wright's *Black Boy* and Eldridge Cleaver's *Soul on Ice* for my six-week sojourn with black inner-city eighth-graders. Somehow I was offered a job that spring, probably due to the influence of Professor Bateman. Despite this opportunity and my subsequent enrollment in Ohio State's M.A. program—that summer I took Professor Paul R. Klohr's 860 course on curriculum development—I chose to leave Ohio to accept a position as Teacher of English at the Paul D. Schreiber High School in Port Washington, on Long Island, New York.

While there only two years, teaching at Schreiber was an imprinting experience. Intellectually impressive, the Department of English faculty purchased paperbacks we could distribute to students according to the course we chose to teach. Teaching four classes during a nine-period day, I offered six-week-long electives of my own devising, including one on existentialist literature. Students were academically strong: most went to university, many to Ivy-League schools. I chose to teach the one small non-college-bound group. Whatever their class location, many Schreiber students were estranged: the year was, after all, 1969. Drugs were widespread, but mostly recreational: few "dropped out." I became close to several students, among them Betsy Bernhard and Kenny Schatz, and with two other first-year teachers—Marilyn Baldauf and Gail Starkman—while admiring other colleagues from a distance. My students were skeptical but played along; indeed, a few became enthusiastic about "working from within."[17] One night a week I traveled to Teachers College to attend a seminar offered by Professor Dwayne E. Huebner, to whose work Paul Klohr had introduced me. Huebner's scholarship influenced me deeply, and some two decades later, with his encouragement, I published his essays as *The Lure of the Transcendent*.

The other curriculum theorist who influenced me most as a graduate student—Klohr and Bateman were supervising directed readings during my time on Long Island teaching—was James B. Macdonald.[18] Later, Kliebard's critiques of Tyler and analyses of the field's failings—specifically its atheoretical and ahistorical character—proved decisive in my efforts to find my way in a field falling apart.[19] As a resident Ph.D. student in 1971, I supervised English student teachers while taking courses in education, English, and Psychology. In the English Department, I studied 20th-century British and Irish literature with Professors Morris Beja and John Muste. In the Psychology Department, I studied psychopathology and participated in a Tavistock group, not so very different from the National Training Lab (NTL) encounter group work I had undergone earlier. I was determined to link the experiential with the intellectual, and these academic studies juxtaposed with psychological experiments (such as Tavistock and NTL) helped me to focus on what was at stake. In my Ph.D. dissertation research I theorized a humanities curriculum that cultivated self-formation through the juxtaposition of academic study, solitude, and encounter group experience.

Klohr met with me regularly to discuss what we were reading. (We met over lunch, a tradition I continued with my own Ph.D. students.) He questioned, challenged, and encouraged me, acting as a supportive skeptic. He became my intellectual father, and I never tired of listening to him. For thirty-five years after I graduated I returned to him at his home at 420 Walhalla in Columbus. Traveling from first Rochester, then from Baton Rouge, and finally from Vancouver, I would not miss an opportunity to spend several days with my beloved Paul.

Many of Paul's students adored him, and each of us—I know several still today—learned something unique from our relationship with him. I took from him his keen interest in theoretical developments, including those outside the field of education. Still I remember his palpable excitement upon discovering Michael Polanyi's *Personal Knowledge* and, later, Richard J. Bernstein's *The Restructuring of Social and Political Theory*. From him I came to experience curriculum studies as a dramatic and ongoing intellectual event. While the public school provided the primary site for engagement with curriculum studies, education has never been for me an institutional problem to be solved, but, rather, a provocative phenomenon to be understood. Other Klohr students concluded otherwise. That was, in part, the man's pedagogical genius, his capacity—through focused conversation drawing upon his erudition, exercising his pedagogical discernment—to draw out the originality of each student. How I have worked—much more clumsily—to do the same with mine!

After the Ph.D. was conferred in 1972, I took a job at the University of Rochester. There I met Madeleine Grumet, Janet L. Miller, and Peter Taubman.[20] Each influenced me deeply, including in feminist theory and gender studies. Madeleine joined me in the study of autobiography[21] in teacher education, extending its theoretical elaboration through phenomenology and psychoanalysis, traditions she mastered and melded in her *Bitter Milk*.[22] From the university's point of view, Madeleine was my doctoral student, but the truth was that I was hers.

Janet Miller and I collaborated on the establishment of what would become the Bergamo Conference (the conference of the Reconceptualization of curriculum studies) and on *JCT* (the journal of the Reconceptualization). I dedicated to Janet the collection[23] subtitled *Twenty Years of JCT*, but these acknowledgements hardly capture the complexity of her contribution to curriculum studies.[24] Both Bergamo and *JCT* continue today.

Peter Taubman introduced me to the work of Foucault, as he embraced his first translated works, specifically *The Archeology of Knowledge*, which Peter employed in his critique of gender essentialism. Recently, with Foucauldian detail and theoretical sophistication he has detailed the calamity that is U.S. school reform.[25] During the 1990s Peter introduced me to the cinema of Pier Paolo

Pasolini and the 1906 novel *Young Torless* by Robert Musil. Each[26] has remained central to my intellectual life; I composed a biographical sketch of Pasolini to personify the worldliness of a cosmopolitan education (2009). I glossed Musil's novel[27] and am now portraying Musil as a public pedagogue.

At Rochester I enjoyed proximity to great scholars, among them historians Christopher Lasch, Eugene Genovese, and Elizabeth Fox-Genovese, the great Dickens scholar George H. Ford, and philosopher Lewis White Beck. Beck—with whom I chatted over Saturday lunches at the Faculty Club—kindly advised me in my readings in autobiography. But the most formative intellectual influence during those years—the early 1970s—was Virginia Woolf, whose novels I had studied as a graduate student at Ohio State. Now it was not only her fiction but her life that preoccupied me; I reread Quentin Bell's biography several times. Her stream-of-consciousness method inspired me to dwell upon sensory detail in the method of *currere*, her feminist courage inspired what would become, later, my own gendered struggles, and her central position in the Bloomsbury Group inspired my inchoate conception of what an academic community might mean.

While Woolf was the most formative, she was not the only influence. I was reading psychoanalytic theory (especially object relations theory: Chodorow 1978) and phenomenology as I tried to imagine a future for the field after Tyler. My early pieces[28] testify to my efforts to theorize curriculum as structured by the intersections among autobiography, history, and culture.

During my first years at Rochester my relationship with Paul Klohr intensified. I wrote him every day. He helped me plan the 1973 Rochester Conference—inaugurating the Reconceptualization—and participated in the event.[29] The summer after we spent a week together on upstate New York's Keuka Lake, rowing and reading and talking, my own micro-moment of Bloomsbury. While it was Don Bateman who had introduced me to the intellectually serious study of education it was Paul Klohr whom I loved. His stories fascinated me: his childhood, his undergraduate days studying German in Indiana, working afterward as a high-school teacher in Illinois interrupted by World War II, his graduate school days studying with Harold Alberty at Ohio State, his initial faculty appointment at Syracuse University, his stint as curriculum coordinator of the Columbus Public Schools, as Head of Ohio State's Laboratory School (and his excruciating experience of its demise at the hands of right-wing demagogues), his subsequent service in the Dean's office at Ohio State's College of Education, and the final phase of his career as a professor. Equally important (and inseparable from these discussions) was our ongoing reflection on the nature and function of curriculum studies, including its history, its relationship with schools, its possible futures. To think about these topics required, Paul always asserted, knowledge not only of the field itself, but of related disciplines, especially social theory and philosophy, which Paul read constantly. Aside from my parents, Paul is the major influence in my life.

It was during my early years at Rochester that I fastened onto autobiography as a means to recast curriculum study. Neo-Marxists would misunderstand the autobiographical emphasis as bourgeois narcissism rather than a relocation of the political project in which many of us had engaged during the 1960s. Others would detach autobiographical study from the curriculum, morphing it into "narrative inquiry." From the phenomenological I moved—as did many others—to post-structuralist understandings of subjectivity and society, influenced by Foucault (at first through Peter Taubman), then later by Derrida and Deleuze (at first through the brilliant Jacques Daignault and Clermont Gauthier, who began attending Bergamo in the early 1980s, later inspired by my LSU colleague Denise Egéa-Kuehne and the great Ted Aoki, who also made a similar journey from phenomenology to poststructuralism[30]). Only in recent years have I recoiled from what now seems to me an excessive textualism in post-structuralism. But I get ahead of myself.

Certain that the consolidation of the intellectual gains made during the Reconceptualization required institutionalization, I took on the chairmanship of the Department of Curriculum and Instruction at Louisiana State University in 1985, hiring a number of new Ph.D.s to institutionalize the Reconceptualization.[31] Those were heady days—LSU was a hospitable and intellectually stimulating place, Bergamo was reaching its apex (at one late 1980s conference 453 presentations were listed)—and I began to chronicle the Reconceptualization. That project threatened to overwhelm me, and so I invited three former doctoral students[32]—William Reynolds, Patrick Slattery, and Peter Taubman—to join me in what became *Understanding Curriculum*. I had hoped to publish a series of readers to accompany *Understanding Curriculum* (illustrating each of the discourses), but I managed to find time to produce only six of the planned eleven.[33]

After *Understanding Curriculum* I devoted myself to race studies. Becoming committed to an African American man—on November 10, 2013, Jeff Turner and I were married after 18 years of being together—and living in Louisiana provided existential stimulus for renewing my study of race I had first undertaken as an undergraduate. Never losing the self-reflexive impulse autobiographical study habitualized, I then turned my attention to whiteness, resulting in the most intellectually experimental of my works.[34] There I juxtaposed Noah—the mythological inception of racial servitude in Genesis 9:23—with Daniel Paul Schreber, the infamous late-nineteenth German judge whose memoirs Freud used to devise his theory of paranoia as disavowed homosexual desire in theorizing whiteness as the "curse of the covenant."

I have always studied subjectivity as a passage to (as well as a retreat from) the world; during these first years of the new millennium my engagement with curriculum studies scholars worldwide multiplied. What became the project of internationalization started by accident; in 1993 I had represented the United States at a UNESCO conference on curriculum worldwide held in Santiago, Chile. In Oslo, Norway, in 1995, I represented U.S. curriculum studies in what (I learned later) was supposed to be a "face-off" with Wolfgang Klafki, the great German theorist of *Didaktik*. (The confrontation never occurred.) Back in Baton Rouge, Bill Doll, Donna Trueit, and I organized two international conferences, one in 1999 on philosophy of education (taking advantage of a world meeting in nearby New Orleans) and in 2000 a Conference on the Internationalization of Curriculum Studies, drawing scholars from every continent and thirty-plus countries. On the final morning I offered to meet with those interested in founding an international association. Not expecting much interest, I had reserved a room holding 15, but 150 showed up! Working during the year with representatives from each continent, I helped inaugurate the International Association for the Advancement of Curriculum Studies (www.iaacs.org). IAACS' first triennial meeting was held in 2003 in Shanghai, China; the second in 2006 in Tampere, Finland; the 2009 meeting took place in Cape Town, South Africa; the 2012 in Rio de Janeiro, Brazil. The 2015 meeting is scheduled for Ottawa.

During that same academic year I worked with U.S. colleagues to form the American Association for the Advancement of Curriculum Studies, an IAACS affiliate. After its inception in 2001, I persuaded the general membership to authorize three interrelated undertakings: 1) the formation of a journal—edited by Alan A. Block—focused on the intellectual production of the field, 2) a Commission on the State of Curriculum Studies in the United States—directed by Madeleine R. Grumet—that would survey the institutional circumstances of the field and provide recommendations for administrators, and 3) a Canon Project to institutionalize attentiveness to the intellectual history of U.S. curriculum studies.

It was what Janet Miller[35] has termed the "worldliness" of curriculum studies that persuaded me to leave LSU after twenty years to accept the Canada Research Chair in curriculum studies. In Canada I have been able to pursue—with federal funding and free of homeland security preoccupations—complicated conversation among nationally distinctive curriculum studies fields in Brazil, China, India, Mexico, and South Africa.[36]

Now sitting in my sixties, I am clear that my intellectual life was structured first by my parents, Frederick Eugene Pinar (1920–1988), an aeronautical engineer, and Malinda Brooke (1917–1982), a night-club singer and regional radio personality. From Dad I internalized the injunction that "understanding" was the most important thing in life; from Mom I learned that pleasure was paramount. With these twin and often opposing dispositions embedded in me, I have been driven to understand the reality around and within me. I have sought pleasure well outside the confines of the bourgeois life for which I was conditioned by school and society. Despite its appearance as a quiet scholarly life (finally, now it is), my life has been intense, dramatic, and very full. Imprinted by my parents and our post–World War II experience—haunted by economic and political catastrophes, driven by the intensity of seeking pleasure because death was imminent, overwhelmed with love of country in a brief period of post-war triumph and relief quickly turning to alarm and the enduring emergency that was the Cold War—and by their distinctive presence (my parents' own singular adaptations of these historical realities mixed with their psychic and genetic inheritances), and, later, with the help of friends and the intimacy of lovers (in my life, intermixed categories), I have found passages through the labyrinth that has been my life, compelled to understand, and thereby participate—often with intense pleasure—in the reconstruction of the reality in which we are embedded.

Notes

1 Originally (in Waks and Short 2009) entitled "The Primacy of the Particular" (quoted from Flores 2006, 64), this phrase summarizes my ongoing inquiry; it specifies the subjective link among my seven contributions to curriculum studies. It also acknowledges my appreciation for those individuals named here who have been so significant to me over the years. Prominent among these is my mentor Professor Paul R. Klohr, who died that summer. I composed this self-portrait in his shadow.

2 1994, 306.

3 Implied by the verb; see Pinar et al. 1995, 848.

4 To understand educational experience autobiographically, I suggested (juxtaposing Freud and Sartre), one might work regressively (re-experiencing the past), progressively (imagining the future), analytically (understanding what one had discovered regressively and progressively), synthetically (acting in the world).

5 See Pinar et al. 1995, chapter 10.

6 Central to the organizational infrastructure of the movement was my founding of the Bergamo conference and the journal JCT: see Pinar et al. 1995, chapter 4. In the mid-1990s a dissident group separated from Bergamo and formed the Curriculum and Pedagogy group, with its own journal. As offshoots, any genealogy would register their lineage in my efforts during the 1970s to create disciplinary infrastructure.

7 See Pinar 2007a, 2010, 2011a, 2011b, 2014a, in press-a.

8 Pinar 1998, 2013a.
9 Pinar 2001.
10 Pinar 2006a, 2006b.
11 Pinar 1991.
12 Pinar 2007b, 9.
13 Pinar 2009; Said 2004.
14 Pinar 2003, 2014a.
15 Pinar 2013b, 2013c, 2014b.
16 See 1974.
17 See Pinar 1994.
18 See Macdonald 1995.
19 See Pinar 2000 (1975).
20 I enjoyed the company of other astonishing doctoral students during my time at Rochester (1972–1985), among them Stephen DeMocker, Bonnie Meath-Lang, Ronald Padgham, JoAnne Pagano, Meredith Reininger, William Reynolds, and Sandra Wallenstein. My colleagues are memorable, too: philosopher Robert Osborn provided friendship and constant questioning, Eleanore Larson was wise and quietly encouraging, Bill Lowe was skeptical but supportive. Dean James Doi funded the 1973 Conference that inaugurated the Reconceptualization. I hired Philip Wexler in 1981; during our time together jogging and parenting Philip taught me social theory.
21 Pinar and Grumet 2006 (1976).
22 See Grumet 1988.
23 Pinar 1999.
24 See Miller 2005.
25 See Taubman 2009.
26 See Pinar 2009, 99–142; 2002.
27 See Pinar 2006c.
28 In 1975, reprinted in 2000.
29 Klohr 1974; Pinar in press-a.
30 See Pinar and Irwin 2005.
31 Among these were Eric Chapel (from the University of Alberta where he had worked with Ted Aoki), Jacques Daignault (from the University of Québec), William E. Doll, Jr., Cameron McCarthy and Leslie Roman (both from the University of Wisconsin-Madison where they had worked with Michael Apple), and Tony Whitson (who had his doctorate at the University of Rochester with Philip Wexler). Other colleagues followed, among them Ron Good—jointly appointed to the Department of Physics—a close friend and constant critic of my interest in psychoanalysis. Professor Petra Munro Hendry animated my interest in Jane Addams as she elaborated a theory of feminist curriculum history. In addition to being colleagues and friends in the Department of Curriculum and Instruction, Petra and I worked together in Women's and Gender Studies. There I met remarkable colleagues outside education, among them English Professor Elsie Mitchie, who brought Kaja Silverman to my attention. Central to that period were my friendships with Bill Doll, Mary Aswell Doll, Marla Morris, and Donna Trueit. I have before acknowledged Bill's importance to me (2006b, xiv–xv); we've been friends since 1976, having known each other in upstate New York, south Louisiana, and now the Pacific Northwest where we have once again worked together, as he and Donna Trueit have served as visiting professors at the University of British Columbia. I was privileged to provide the introduction to the "selected works" volume (Trueit 2012).
32 Reynolds and Taubman had taken their doctorates with me at the University of Rochester, Patrick at LSU. There are many remarkable Ph.D. students who graduated from LSU during my time there (1985–2005), among them Brian Casemore, Toby Daspit, Susan Edgerton, Brenda Hatfield, Nicole Guillory, Wen-Song Wu, Laura Jewett, Doug McKnight, Marla Morris, Anthony Molina, Nicholas Ng-A-Fook, Anne Pautz, Patrick Slattery, Donna Trueit, Hongyu Wang, and Ugena Whitlock.
33 See 1991 (with Kincheloe); 1992 (with Reynolds); 1993 (with Castenell); 1998b, 1998c, 1999, 2005 (with Irwin).

34 See Pinar 2006a.
35 2005, 249.
36 Each of these projects is reported in book form: Pinar 2010, 2011a, 2011b, 2014c, in press-a, in press-b.

Bibliography

Bateman, Donald R. 1974. The Politics of Curriculum. In *Heightened Consciousness, Cultural Revolution, and Curriculum Theory*, edited by William Pinar (54–68). Berkeley, CA: McCutchan.

Bell, Quentin. 1972. *Virginia Woolf: A Biography*. New York: Harcourt Brace Jovanovich.

Castenell, Jr., Louis A. and Pinar, William F. eds. 1993. *Understanding Curriculum as Racial Text: Representations of Identity and Difference in Education*. Albany: State University of New York Press.

Chodorow, Nancy J. 1978. *The Reproduction of Mothering*. Berkeley: University of California Press.

de Lauretis, Teresa. 1994. Habit changes. *Differences* 6 (2+3), 296–313.

Flores, Juan. 2006. Reclaiming Left Baggage. In *Identity Politics Reconsidered*, edited by Linda Martín Alcoff, Michael Hames-García, Satya P. Mohanty, and Paula M. L. Moya (53–68). New York: Palgrave Macmillan.

Grumet, Madeleine R. 1988. *Bitter Milk*. Amherst: University of Massachusetts Press.

Heilbroner, Robert L. 1961. *The Worldly Philosophers*. New York: Simon & Schuster.

Huebner, Dwayne. 1999. *The Lure of the Transcendent*. [Edited by Vikki Hillis. Collected and introduced by William F. Pinar.] Mahwah, NJ: Lawrence Erlbaum.

Kincheloe, Joe L. and Pinar, William F. eds. 1991. *Curriculum as Social Psychoanalysis: The Significance of Place*. Albany: State University of New York Press.

Klohr, Paul R. 1974. Reflections on the Conference. In *Heightened Consciousness, Cultural Revolution, and Curriculum Theory*, edited by William Pinar (166–173). Berkeley, CA: McCutchan.

Macdonald, Bradley J. ed. 1995. *Theory as a Prayerful Act: The Collected Essays of James B. Macdonald*. [Introduction by William F. Pinar.] New York: Peter Lang.

Miller, Janet L. 2005. *The Sound of Silence Breaking and Other Essays*. New York: Peter Lang.

Musil, Robert. 1955 (1906). *Young Torless*. [Preface by Alan Pryce-Jones.] New York: Pantheon Books.

Pinar, William F. ed. 1974. *Heightened Consciousness, Cultural Revolution and Curriculum Theory*. Berkeley, CA: McCutchan.

Pinar, William F. 1991. Curriculum as Social Psychoanalysis: On the Significance of Place. In *Curriculum as Social Psychoanalysis: Essays on the Significance of Place*, edited by Joe L. Kincheloe and William F. Pinar (167–186). Albany: State University of New York Press.

Pinar, William F. 1994. *Autobiography, Politics, and Sexuality: Essays in Curriculum Theory 1972–1992*. New York: Peter Lang.

Pinar, William F. ed. 1998a. *Queer Theory in Education*. Mahwah, NJ: Lawrence Erlbaum.

Pinar, William F. ed. 1998b. *Curriculum: Toward New Identities*. New York: Garland.

Pinar, William F. 1998c. *The Passionate Mind of Maxine Greene*: "*I Am Not Yet.*" London: Falmer.

Pinar, William F. ed. 1999. *Contemporary Curriculum Discourses: Twenty Years of JCT*. New York: Peter Lang.

Pinar, William F. ed. 2000 (1975). *Curriculum Theorizing: The Reconceptualization*. Troy, NY: Educator's International Press.

Pinar, William F. 2001. *The Gender of Racial Politics and Violence in America: Lynching, Prison Rape, and the Crisis of Masculinity*. New York: Peter Lang.

Pinar, William F. 2002. Robert Musil and the Crisis of European Culture in America. In *Curriculum Visions*, edited by William E. Doll, Jr. and Noel Gough (102–110). New York: Peter Lang.

Pinar, William F. ed. 2003. *International Handbook of Curriculum Research*. Mahwah, NJ: Lawrence Erlbaum.
Pinar, William F. 2004. *What is Curriculum Theory?* Mahwah, NJ: Lawrence Erlbaum.
Pinar, William F. 2005. A Lingering Note. In *Curriculum in a New Key*, edited by William F. Pinar and Rita L. Irwin (1–85). Mahwah, NJ: Lawrence Erlbaum.
Pinar, William F. 2006a. *Race, Religion and a Curriculum of Reparation*. New York: Palgrave Macmillan.
Pinar, William F. 2006b. *The Synoptic Text Today and Other Essays: Curriculum Development after the Reconceptualization*. New York: Peter Lang.
Pinar, William F. 2006c. Literary Study as Educational Research. In *Doing Educational Research*, edited by Kenneth Tobin and Joe L. Kincheloe (347–377). Rotterdam and Taipei: Sense Publishers.
Pinar, William F. 2007a. *Intellectual Advancement through Disciplinarity: Verticality and Horizontality in Curriculum Studies*. Rotterdam and Tapei: Sense Publishers.
Pinar, William F. 2007b. Introduction: A Queer Conversation, Toward Sustainability. In *Queering Straight Teachers*, edited by Nelson M. Rodriguez and William F. Pinar (1–12). New York: Peter Lang.
Pinar, William F. 2008. Introduction to George S. Tomkins' *A Common Countenance: Stability and Change in the Canadian Curriculum* (xi–xxiv). Vancouver, Canada: Pacific Educational Press.
Pinar, William F. 2009. *The Worldliness of a Cosmopolitan Education*. New York: Routledge.
Pinar, William F. ed. 2010. *Curriculum Studies in South Africa*. New York: Palgrave Macmillan.
Pinar, William F. ed. 2011a. *Curriculum Studies in Brazil*. New York: Palgrave Macmillan.
Pinar, William F. ed. 2011b. *Curriculum Studies in Mexico*. New York: Palgrave Macmillan.
Pinar, William F. 2013a. Strict Discipline. *International Journal for the Historiography of Education* 3 (1), 94–101.
Pinar, William F. 2013b. The First Task of Thought in Our Time. *Critical Literacy: Theories and Practices* 7 (1), 1–16.
Pinar, William F. 2013c. Modernity, Technology, Nationality. *Critical Literacy: Theories and Practices* 7 (2), 3–19.
Pinar, William F. ed. 2014a. *The International Handbook of Curriculum Research*. New York: Routledge.
Pinar, William F. 2014b. On the Teachings of George Grant. *Critical Studies in Education* 55 (1), 8–17.
Pinar, William F. ed. 2014c. *Curriculum Studies in China*. New York: Palgrave Macmillan.
Pinar, William F. in press-a. That First Year. *In The Dignity of the Calling*, edited by Andrew Kemp. Charlotte, NC: Information Age Publishing.
Pinar, William F. ed. in press-b. *Curriculum Studies in India*. New York: Palgrave Macmillan.
Pinar, William F. and Grumet, Madeleine R. 2006 (1976). *Toward a Poor Curriculum*. Troy, NY: Educator's International Press. [Originally published by Kendall/Hunt.]
Pinar, William F. and Reynolds, William M. eds. 1992. *Understanding as Phenomenological and Deconstructed text*. New York: Teachers College Press.
Pinar, William F., Reynolds, William M., Slattery, Patrick, and Taubman, Peter M. 1995. *Understanding Curriculum*. New York: Peter Lang.
Sartre, Jean-Paul. 1964. *Nausea*. [Trans. Lloyd Alexander.] New York: New Directions.
Taubman, Peter M. 2009. *Teaching by Numbers: Deconstructing the Discourse of Standards and Accountability in Education*. New York: Routledge.
Trueit, Donna. ed. 2012. *Pragmatism, Postmodernism, Complexity Theory: The Fascinating Imaginative Realm of William E. Doll, Jr*. New York: Routledge.
Waks, Leonard and Short, Edmund C. eds. 2009. *Leaders in Curriculum Studies: Intellectual Self-Portraits* (203–217). Rotterdam and Tapei: Sense Publishers.
Woolf, Virginia. 1925. *Mrs. Dalloway*. New York: Harvest.
Woolf, Virginia. 1955 (1927). *To the Lighthouse*. New York: Harcourt, Brace & Company.

CHAPTER 1

STUDY

Commentary

Study—not teaching—is the site of education. In contrast to cramming, study is self-paced and its end unknown; it supports subjective and social reconstruction[1] threaded through academic knowledge and everyday life, between "popular and erudite knowledge."[2] In contrast to the anonymity and utility of "information"—currency in a "knowledge economy"—academic knowledge—especially in the humanities and the arts—bears the mark of its composer, his or her time and place. Knowledge can speak to you, as it incorporates the specificity of its origins, even the lived experience of its creator.[3] Intrinsically important, as Michael F. D. Young[4] appreciates, knowledge is dated—is (as Tyson Lewis[5] suggests)—a "remnant." As a form of witness,[6] study encourages historicity and foreshadows the future. Solitary even as it informed by and shared with others—"perhaps in study," Block[7] suggests, "sufferings may be shared"—study does not disavow, despite secularization, its religious and ethical subtexts. These animate and singularize its potential and promise as a "form of life."[8]

Bibliography

Block, Alan A. 2007. *Pedagogy, Religion, and Practice: Reflections on Ethics and Teaching*. New York: Palgrave Macmillan.

Lewis, Tyson E. 2013. *On Study. Giorgio Agamben and Educational Potentiality*. New York: Routledge.

Muller, Johan. 2000. *Reclaiming Knowledge: Social Theory, Curriculum and Education Policy*. London: Routledge.

Pinar, William F. 2004, June. The Problem with Curriculum and Pedagogy. *Journal of Curriculum and Pedagogy*, 1 (1), 21–24.

Pinar, William F. 2012. *What Is Curriculum Theory?* 2nd edition. New York: Routledge.

Said, Edward. 2004. *Humanism and Democratic Criticism*. New York: Palgrave Macmillan.

Simon, Roger I. 2005. *The Touch of the Past: Remembrance, Learning, and Ethics*. New York: Palgrave Macmillan.

Strong-Wilson, Teresa. 2007. *Bringing Memory Forward*. New York: Peter Lang.

Young, Michael F. D. 2008. *Bringing Knowledge Back In: From Social Constructivism to Social Realism in the Sociology of Education*. London: Routledge.

Study, like prayer, is a way of being—it is an ethics.

Alan A. Block[9]

The academic field of education is so very reluctant to abandon social engineering. If only we can find the right technique, the right modification of classroom organization, teach according to "best practices," if only we have students self-reflect or if only we develop "standards" or conduct "scientific" research, then students will learn what we teach them.

Social engineering—the enormously influential early-twentieth-century American Edward L. Thorndike called it, simply, "human engineering"[10]—appears to assume that education is like an automobile engine: if only we make the right adjustments—in teaching, in learning, in assessment—it will hum, transport us to our destination, the promised land of high test scores, or, for many of us on the educational Left, a truly democratic society.

America's historic preoccupations with business and religion have provided cultural support for such a view of mind, a view profoundly anti-intellectual in consequence, as historian Richard Hofstadter[11] has famously documented. The business-minded—encapsulated in the concept of entrepreneur—are interested in designing effects on situations that can be profitable. In this sense, social engineering is the complement of capitalism. The religiously-minded mangle the present by disavowing it (the best is yet to come), employing religious rituals (such as prayer) to manipulate present circumstances. Protestantism and capitalism are infamously intertwined,[12] perhaps most savagely in the American South.[13]

Social engineering has structured much of American intellectual life. It has structured, some allege, that American philosophical movement known as pragmatism, thanks in part to William James' construal of the significance of thought as emphasizing its effects on situations.[14] Pragmatism's progressive formulation of social engineering has been eclipsed, as we are painfully aware, by political conservatism, intent on side-stepping culture and history by focusing on "learning technologies" such as the computer.[15] If only we place computers in every classroom, if only school children stare at screens (rather than at teachers, evidently), they will "learn," will become "competitive" in the "new millennium." Information is not knowledge, and without ethical and intellectual judgment—which cannot be programmed into a machine—the Age of Information is an Age of Ignorance.

In 1938 the first Department of Curriculum and Teaching was established in the United States (at Teachers College, Columbia University). This historic mistake—the conjunction of curriculum with teaching—institutionalized social engineering at the site of the teacher. In so doing, the field set itself up for the eclipse of institutionally-led curriculum development and the politics of scapegoating, vividly obvious in *No Child Left Behind* and *Race to the Top*, wherein teachers are held responsible for student learning. Despite its very different politics, progressive education also inflated the role of the teacher in the process of education, suggesting that role could be socially and economically transformative.

Adjusting the inflated status of pedagogy in curriculum studies will be difficult but necessary labor. To contribute to that project, I focus here on the concept of "study," relying on the work of Robert McClintock and Alan A. Block. The former provides a history and analysis of its place in humanism; the latter locates this lost tradition in Judaism. I suggest that one form of contemporary curriculum research, resulting in a "new" synoptic text, can also contribute to the resuscitation of this lost tradition. Like teaching or instruction or pedagogy, study, too, should be a subsidiary concept in curriculum studies.[16]

The Lost World of Study

The word study connotes zealous striving.

Anna Julia Cooper[17]

Robert McClintock begins his argument for study against instruction with attention to Montaigne who, McClintock tells us, engaged himself in an ongoing project of "self-education."[18] A process, study is also a place (as McClintock makes explicit in his essay's title); for Montaigne, that place was his study wall to which he appended sayings—(McClintock quotes one from Lucian)—stimulating the process of his self-formation through the creation of a "self-culture," stimulating self-reflection as he went about his daily life.[19] Sayings appended to the wall, McClintock theorizes, stimulated his "self-formation."[20]

As if anticipating the Marxist misunderstanding of autobiography as narcissism,[21] McClintock points out that study is not only a private project. For Montaigne, he notes, education was a never-ending "heightening" of "consciousness," an unceasing cultivation of judgment.[22] Like Seneca, McClintock observes, Montaigne worried that relying on teachers for one's education could replace one's self-engaged labor of discovery with passivity.[23] "Authoritative" instruction can discourage thinking, McClintock notes.[24] Undermining altogether the authority of the teacher can as well.

Montaigne was hardly alone in preferring study to instruction. McClintock names Erasmus as a second example. "[I] shall not refuse any task," McClintock quotes him as saying, "if I see that it will be conducive to the promotion of honest study."[25] He justified his editorial labor—recall that Erasmus edited both pagan and Christian classics—as providing readers with important literature for personal study. His writing—McClintock cites *The Handbook of the Christian Knight*—aimed to support readers' self-formation and self-possession. Teaching and learning might disseminate knowledge, McClintock notes, but study enables "understanding."[26]

Self-formation specifies no "standards" or "best practices," as the paths of study are numerous.[27] Study follows not from uncritical compliance with instructions, but from an aspiration to assert "control" over the shifting conjunctions between self and circumstances.[28] While I disclaim the aspiration for "control," I embrace study's capacity to contest conformity.[29] The final phrase of McClintock's sentence—pointing to the conjunctions between self and circumstances—acknowledges the historicity and cultural situatedness of the "self."[30]

It is through study that we "impose" our character upon our roles in life, McClintock asserts.[31] For me, this verb is too voluntarist and even essentialist: after Lacan we must acknowledge that any Rortyian reinvention of ourselves is limited, and occurs, yes, through acts of "will," but, as well, through waiting, withdrawing, dissimulation. Certainly I share McClintock's sense that there is an ethical, even (we might say) ontological call to "be here," in Sartre's sense of "*engagé*," in Grumet's call for us to embrace relationality and attachment.[32] But the imagery of "impose"[33] lacks subtlety and complexity; perhaps it is too "masculinist."

McClintock's notion of study is expansive; it is by no means limited to the official curriculum. The student draws upon "nature," "faith," and "reason" as these speak to his "situation," enabling him to convert the contingencies of time, place, and circumstance into "achieved intention."[34] The echoes of the early Sartre are loud here; if we dwell on the aesthetics rather than the gender of "achieved intention" we can appreciate the creative, singular, and social sense of study. In the "art"[35] of study, McClintock explains, all of culture can, potentially, become educational—if one studies, that is.

In this ancient tradition, study is the site of education. Not instruction, not learning, but study constitutes the process of education, a view, McClintock tells us, grounded in "individuality," "autonomy," and "creativity."[36] (The three are, I suggest, inter-related.) Again sounding like the early Sartre, McClintock emphasizes the significance of our "particularity," that we become more than we have been influenced to be, that we (here he anticipates Rorty) refashion ourselves by engaging "freely" and "creatively" our circumstances.[37]

Such a statement recalls certain strands of the progressive tradition, although not its confidence that we can teach freedom for creativity, let alone for individuality and autonomy. Rather, from the point of view of study, self-formation follows from our individual reconstruction of what is around and within us; this capacity for selection, for focus, for judgment, McClintock suggests, is the great mystery to be solved.[38] This is, I submit, the mystery that autobiography purports not to solve, but to portray and complicate.[39]

McClintock has a faith in an "inward" almost "inborn" capacity for judgment that directs us to that to which we "attend."[40] It is a faith I do not, but would like to, share. But the point to which this faith is in service I endorse, namely that education is only "incidentally" a function of teaching and learning, that it is, necessarily, a "zig-zag" and "self-directed" process of intellectual experimentation by means of which the individual's capacity for judgment is cultivated and takes, perhaps, a "transcendent" turn.[41] Questions of transcendence aside (certainly for many in the West there is the "lure"[42] of that), here McClintock risks solidifying the self, overstating its force and autonomy while understating the interwoven relations among self-formation, society, and the historical moment.

McClintock quickly complicates this naïve view of the structure and force of the self by citing Eros, the "expectant" and "fecund force" that "stimulates" one's "craving urge."[43] He associates Eros not with Freud but with Plato, but the two merge in his choice of words to describe eroticism and its life-structuring influence, namely an "insatiable, polymorphous teleology."[44] Joseph Schwab, too, linked Eros with study, with liberal education more specifically: "Not only the means, however, but also the ends of liberal education involve Eros. For the end includes not only knowledge gained but knowledge desired and knowledge sought."[45] Block's analysis suggests that such desire is expressed educationally through study.

Study as a Prayerful Act

> Study . . . is a prayerful act.[46]
>
> Alan A. Block

Alan Block has Joseph Schwab, not James B. Macdonald,[47] in mind when he characterizes "engagement in study [as] engagement in prayer."[48] Block argues that Schwab believed that even the point of assessment was to provoke study. While an act of faith, prayer—and the conception of study to which faith is allied—is not a "cause" in hopes of a future "effect," a disavowal of this world in hopes of a better deal in a future one. Rather, within the rabbinical tradition, Block argues, "study, like prayer, is a stance we assume in the world."[49] As such, "study, like prayer, is a way of being—it is an ethics."[50] It does not repudiate the mundane; prayer "sacralizes the mundane. So, too, does study."[51]

Like prayer, then, study is a spiritual discipline. It is an intellectual discipline as well, but not one that leads to confidence about cause-effect relationships in human affairs. "In prayer and in study," Block writes, "we acknowledge that our knowledge will never suffice and that what we undertake in the classroom is merely a hint of all that exists outside it."[52] Echoing Dwayne Huebner, Block regards "prayer and study [as] emanat[ing] from the silence of awe and wonder."[53]

Block is working in Jewish not Christian traditions. To appreciate Schwab's notion of "deliberation," Block situates the concept in "the traditional Jewish pedagogical methods of the Yeshiva, itself, perhaps, based in ancient Jewish exegetical traditions."[54] In the yeshivah, "study [is] institutionalized . . . as a performative act carried out by the students' participation, [and] the learning space is shaped by the intensity and quality of the ongoing exchange of its students."[55] Such complicated conversation is simultaneously intellectual and spiritual. "At the center of Judaism," Block argues, "is the love and study of text—of Torah. This study is not theoretical but practical, not reverential but critical: At the center of Judaism is practical study."[56] Does our field's emphasis upon teaching disclose its Christian rather than Jewish character? Is the "lost world of study" a victim of Christian culture's aggressivity?[57]

Because "study is the equivalent of prayer," Block continues, "the classroom must be considered a sacred place."[58] But this is not a place severed from the world: "For the Rabbis, study must be related to the practical—to the continued striving for a holiness that can only be realized in our daily lives in this world."[59] This is no instrumentalist conception of the practical, however. "Study is central," Block explains, "but it must be practical as well, and its practice must lead only to ethical living."[60] For me, study stipulates no outcomes.

Technologies of Attention

> When we study we must actively pursue—to draw toward us—not only what is under study but the context in which and from which that study has been drawn.[61]
>
> Alan A. Block

In both Jewish and Christian traditions, ethical living requires redemption of the self. For McClintock, such self-redemption is secular. Its ends and means merge in study. Animated by Eros, intellectual interest would seem to be McClintock's guide to study: he characterizes intellectual interest as the student's "essential power," his capacity for "attention."[62] "Intellectual interest" has a long history in curriculum theory—Kilpatrick, for one, linked "present interests" with the formulation and execution of educational projects—but now the notion seems to me too vulnerable to consumerist chimera, detached, too often, from Eros—let alone from "wider social life"[63]—rendering it merely a distraction. I, too, had faith in it as a "compass," as my early autobiographical experiments testify.[64] The word is mine; we can pause to consider its problems by focusing on McClintock's word: "attention."

What is at stake is the status of "intellectual interest" and McClintock's version of it ("attention") is the extent to which they are reliable as guides or, to change metaphors, "rudders" to study. Jonathan Crary argues that pragmatists were swimming against the historical current when they emphasized the agency of "attention." For William James, attention is, in Crary's words, "inseparable from the possibility of a cognitive and perceptual immediacy in which the self ceases to be separate from a world of objects, even if a stabilization of those objects can never occur."[65] For James, attention has ethical significance:

> The practical and theoretical life of the whole species, as well as of individual beings, results from the selection which the habitual direction of their attention involves. . . . Each of us literally chooses, by his ways of attending to things, what sort of a universe he shall appear to himself to inhabit.[66]

In James' underscoring of the creative agency implicit in sustained attention, we can discern the pragmatic antecedent embedded in McClintock's embrace of study.

James' emphasis on the autonomy of attention occurs, Crary points out, when technologies and institutions, including the school, are being designed to command the attention of mass populations.[67] Crary implies that James was consciously contradicting the influential work of William B. Carpenter, work done in the 1870s in which attention is described as an element of subjectivity to be externally shaped and controlled:

> It is the aim of the Teacher to fix the attention of the Pupil upon objects which may have in themselves little or no attraction for it. . . . The habit of attention, at first purely automatic, gradually becomes, by judicious training, in great degree amenable to the Will of the Teacher, who encourages it by the suggestion of appropriate motives, whilst taking care not to overstrain the child's mind by too long dwelling upon one object.[68]

Pedagogical regulation paralleled other disciplinary forms of self-regulation and self-control in the nineteenth century.[69]

Certainly Dewey attributed to the teacher a key role in enabling children to discover, articulate, and expand their interests and thereby direct their attention. (Even conservative critics of progressivism—invested in exaggerating the excesses of child-centeredness—acknowledge this point.[70]) Dewey brooked little confidence in what Kliebard characterizes as the metaphor of growth, wherein "the curriculum is the greenhouse where students will grow and develop to their fullest potential under the care of a wise and patient gardener."[71] For McClintock, the teacher's purpose is "hortatory" rather than didactic, to "incite" the students' "passion" for study.[72] McClintock locates the decisive turn from study to instruction with Comenius, but I leave McClintock's historical narrative for your private study. Suffice to say that its end appears definitive: study has now "disappeared."[73]

Instead of study, we have "learning" tied tightly to assessment and instruction. Even "curriculum"—presumably the content of learning—mutates to a means to the end that is assessment. Once learning described what a person accomplished as a result of serious study, but now, as McClintock observes, learning is a consequence of teaching.[74] The psychology of learning enjoys an inflated status in educational research not because it enables students to study, but because it enables instructors to devise effective strategies of teaching.[75] I would add that, because "learning" limits study to what is taught, it performs the dirty work of accountability, that cover for the closure of academic—intellectual—freedom in contemporary classrooms in the United States.

Study persists, McClintock acknowledges, but in the traditions of "curriculum and instruction" and "instruction and learning," that is, as "how to" treatises outlining short-cuts to good grades. Like Crary, McClintock locates these technologies historically; they structure the "disciplinary society," the "governmentality of the self," the mass production of docile workers and uncritical consumer-citizens.[76] Curriculum limited to instruction and linked to learning and assessment structure national systems of education.[77] As McClintock appreciates, accountability schemes ensure students'—and, I would add, teachers'—"servility."[78]

If curriculum were conjoined with study, the question is no longer, McClintock suggests, the "impossible" one of objectives.[79] If curriculum did not coincide with instruction, the question would no longer be what strategies—or "best practices"—I should employ to ensure students learn of the curriculum and of the "standards" the curriculum institutionalizes. If curriculum were not conjunctive with pedagogy (even the "critical" kind), "transformation" would not be the teacher's responsibility. Rather, teachers might ask themselves the more "restrained" question of what opportunities for study are appropriate for particular students.[80] McClintock's view here seems to invoke the curriculum metaphor of travel.[81]

McClintock is critical of the child-centered curriculum as insufficiently child-centered. The problem with the child-centered curriculum, he writes, is that its "subterfuge" instruction disrespects the "sobriety" of the student's interests.[82] Working with children's interests toward those of the school subjects—Dewey's basic pedagogical idea—is disingenuous, McClintock complains; in fact, the work of the teacher would not be instruction, but to engage each student's capacity for study.[83] Sounding phenomenological for the moment, McClintock suggests that in a school devoted to study, not instruction, students will focus on their "real" intellectual difficulties.[84]

Perhaps McClintock is working here with both metaphors of growth and travel, as he envisions schools as providing opportunities to study academic subjects that enable their "practical" and "worldly" employment by students animated by curiosity.[85] Certainly that is part of what I mean when I endorse, in *What Is Curriculum Theory?*, connecting academic knowledge to society and subjectivity. It is reminiscent—although McClintock shows no signs of Schwab—of Schwab's notion of the "practical," at least as Alan Block situates the concept within rabbinical traditions.

McClintock connects this conception of study with demographic and character-structure shifts in the West, a reading of which leads him, near the end of the essay, to become slightly sanguine about the future of study. Proliferating and unregulated encounters are important to his analysis; we can surmise that he would be excited by the educational potential of the Internet and the appearance of cyberculture. I suspect he would be less so today, given the surveillance, commercialization, bullying, and stunted social development submersion in screens signifies.

That McClintock is writing at the end of the 1960s (before we knew that it was the end) is evident in his suggestion (referencing Marcuse and his own work in progress *Eros and Education*[86]) that nearly everywhere, it seems, "coercive" authority is being replaced by "erotic" authority, and "manipulation" replaced by "erotic attraction."[87] While acknowledging that a society permeated with Eros will not necessarily be a good society, he does speculate that such a society will offer "boundless" opportunities.[88] He ends optimistically, suggesting that the prospects for study seem favorable.[89]

Ah, the remembrance of things past! The prospects for study could hardly be worse; perhaps these circumstances explain why this remarkable essay has been largely overlooked.[90] Because the metaphor of production[91] has triumphed, "instruction"—linked to learning and tied to assessment—replaced "study" as the complement of curriculum. That had already occurred by 1938 when the first Department of Curriculum and Teaching was established at Teachers College, Columbia University. The calamity was capped with Tyler's pithy *Principles of Curriculum and Instruction*: "Procedures of Curriculum and Instruction" would have been a more honest title and they are (as I point out in chapter 7) not his. Whatever Tyler's intentions, the conclusion is horrifyingly plain—*No Child Left Behind* and *Race to the Top*—wherein teachers are held responsible for student learning as measured by standardized examinations. The scapegoating politics of school deform represent deferred and displaced versions of racism and misogyny, as I argue in *What Is Curriculum Theory?*, but that is another story. Here I want to focus not upon our victimhood, but upon our culpability.

It is a culpability for which we were set up by our predecessors, and not only by Franklin Bobbitt, W.W. Charters, and Ralph Tyler. As noted earlier, John Dewey's pragmatist predecessor—William James—was, as David Simpson argues, "consequence oriented," concerned with the "practical cash value" of experience.[92] The significance of experience—of thought, action, and event—tended to be reduced to its effect on a particular situation. Simpson insists that James' "faith in instrumentalism" provided a "green light" for applied social science with its emphasis upon measuring outcomes quantitatively.[93] While not especially interested in statistics, the progressives positioned schools as a means to an end: social reconstruction. If schools could be structured democratically, American society could be reconstructed toward economic and social equality.

Even those who reject progressivism—Kieran Egan is, perhaps, the most startling example, given his earlier reliance on it[94]—reinstall some version of social engineering. "The trouble is," Egan writes—sounding for the moment like Diane Ravitch[95]—"that schools can be quite good institutions when they concentrate on intellectual education, but they are less good at developing the whole person or producing good citizens or ensuring parenting skills."[96] It has been clear for at least a century that the schools are not so "good" at "intellectual education." Is not that one reason why progressivism—certainly the child-centered wing of it—became (remains) compelling for so many: that "intellectual education" does not speak to many children, and, in failing to engage children's interests, alienates them, leaving many a child "behind"?

Perhaps persuaded by our own educational experience, egged on by politicians and parents and, perhaps, by our own megalomania, we teachers (and teacher educators) imagined we could—if only we taught this way or organized the curriculum that way or assessed authentically—produce literate and docile workers, or self-reflective and politically engaged citizens, well, name your outcome. We have known for a long time that, in fact, if human conduct could be regularized and rendered predictable, then the costly and ongoing "scientific" research mounted in the social sciences would have by now succeeded.[97] Of course, as Kieran Egan points out, authoritarianism works (at least for a while, sometimes a long while, as the Soviet example suggests):

> Unless the school has enormous power and authority over children, which in a democracy we are unwilling to allow, the dominant values and behavioral norms will be those the children bring to the school and against which any competing values and norms of the teachers' will be largely helpless.[98]

This is the political point of accountability, of course, to force teachers to force children—especially those "left behind" by forty-years of right-wing assault on them—to accept "new" norms: docility, dependence, and an unquestioning trust of authorities.

Conclusion

> Education is a private engagement in a public world for the redemption of both.[99]
>
> Alan A. Block

Instrumental rationality is to blame, I can hear you say, not pedagogy. You are right: instrumental rationality *is* to blame. There has been much criticism of it in the curriculum studies literature for a long time.[100] Even the concept of study can fall victim to it, as numerous study guides document. Moreover, teaching can be theorized and practiced in intriguing, even magical, ways, as the pedagogy of Ted Aoki, for one, documents.[101] While teaching can be theorized non-instrumentally does not the very concept tempt us to think we can, at the minimum, influence, or more optimistically—or is it arrogantly?—produce, certain effects or consequences?

While numerous so-called "study guides" do not exactly promise "effects," e.g. good grades, they do employ instrumental rationality, evident, for instance, in the title of the textbook used in Louisiana State University's College Study course: *Keys to Success in College, Career, and Life.*[102] Relying on Gardner's "multiple intelligences" concept, the authors include chapters on "Reading and Studying: Focusing on Content," "Listening, Memory, and Note Taking: Taking In, Retaining, and Recording Information," and "Test Taking: Showing What You Know." But the success to which this "how-to" manual holds the keys is not only academic; there are chapters as well on "Self-Awareness," "Relating to Others," and "Wellness and Stress Management." Foucault would have a field day.

The concept of study is hardly immune to instrumental rationality, self-governmentality, and bureaucratization. But what the sustained disciplinary attention to instruction or teaching or pedagogy (either the critical or conventional kinds) accomplished was to set intellectual and political traps for the teacher. Power and responsibility accompany the command of attention. It becomes the teacher upon whom the student depends in order to learn: that is the intellectual trap. And it is the teacher who becomes responsible for student learning: that is the political trap.

What the conjunctive relationship between curriculum and teaching, between curriculum and instruction, between curriculum and pedagogy invites, then, is an inflation of the claims and liabilities of the teacher (whether these be, after Egan and Ravitch, "intellectual" or "academic" education or, after the progressives, social reconstruction or workplace utility) that deludes both parents and politicians (not to mention students and teachers) that the locus of responsibility—the very site of education—is the teacher, not the student. The truth is, of course, quite different: teachers provide educational opportunities; students are responsible for taking advantage of them.[103]

Study is the site of education, McClintock reminds us.[104] While one's truths—academic knowledge grounded in lived, that is, subjective and social experience—cannot be taught, McClintock underscores they can be acquired through the struggle of study, for which every individual has the capacity, but not necessarily the will[105] (or the circumstances, I add). That is the truth that parents, and those politicians who exploit their anxieties over their children's future, cannot bear to face or, at least, acknowledge. It is the truth we must face and acknowledge. The first step in doing so is forcing the teaching genie back into the bottle. If we have a future, it will come to us through study.

Notes

1 Pinar 2012, 207.
2 Muller 2000, 13.
3 "Bringing memory forward," Strong-Wilson (2008, 4) explains, "is a particular application and re-visiting of *currere* as social autobiography."
4 2008, 23.
5 2013, 12, 44.
6 Simon 2005, 104. "[B]earing witness to our readers," Simon (2005, 107) notes, "can itself constitute an act of study."
7 2007, 192.
8 Lewis 2013, 94.
9 2004, 2.
10 1922, 1.
11 1962.
12 Weber 2002 (1930).
13 See Kincheloe and Pinar 1991; Pinar 2001.
14 See Simpson 2002, 98–99.
15 And, most recently, eclipsed by appropriation. Progressive concepts are now in the employ of a vocationalism so totalizing our ancestors would faint: see Williamson 2013.
16 My thanks to Kevin Franck for emphasizing this point. He did so at the paper's presentation at the 2004 Curriculum and Pedagogy conference.
17 Quoted in in Lemert and Bhan 1998, 312. The religious connotation of study is implied here.
18 1971, 161.
19 Ibid.
20 Ibid.
21 For an especially egregious example, see Carlson 2002, 56.
22 1971, 161.
23 1971, 162.
24 Ibid.
25 Quoted in 1971, 162.
26 1971, 162.
27 See 1971, 164–165.
28 1971, 165.

29 Despite Freud's insight, many in the West fantasize they can control themselves and their circumstances. As Dewey implied, democratization of society requires democratization of the self. In both, "control" is a casualty. See Trueit 2012, 85.
30 For an intellectual history of the concept, see Martin and Barresi 2006.
31 1971, 165.
32 See Grumet 1988.
33 1971, 165.
34 Ibid.
35 Ibid.
36 1971, 167.
37 Ibid.
38 Ibid.
39 See Pinar 1994.
40 1971, 168.
41 Ibid.
42 See Huebner 1999.
43 1971, 169.
44 Ibid.
45 Schwab 1978, 109; quoted in Block 2004, 131.
46 Block 2004, 2.
47 See 1995.
48 2004, 2.
49 Ibid.
50 2004, 2.
51 2004, 3.
52 Ibid.
53 Ibid.
54 2004, 11.
55 Halbertal and Halbertal 1998, 459.
56 2004, 58.
57 For a compelling account of the aggressivity—specifically, the anti-Semitic aggressivity—of Christian culture, including its secular expressions, see Morris (2001).
58 2004, 83.
59 Ibid.
60 2004, 84.
61 2004, 81.
62 1971, 169.
63 1918, 12.
64 See Pinar 1978.
65 1999, 61.
66 1950 (1890), 424; quoted in Crary 1999, 62.
67 1999, 63.
68 Carpenter 1886, 134–135; quoted in Crary 1999, 63.
69 See Bederman 1995; Doll 1993, 2002.
70 See Ravitch 2000, 172.
71 Kliebard 2000 (1975), 84.
72 1971, 176, 177.
73 1971, 179.
74 Ibid.
75 Ibid.
76 1971, 180.
77 See 1971, 182.
78 1971, 183.
79 1971, 187.
80 McClintock 1971, 187.

81 Kliebard 2000 (1975), 85.
82 1971, 189.
83 Ibid.
84 1971, 190.
85 Ibid.
86 Here again McClintock is reminiscent of Schwab. See Schwab's "Eros and Education" in 1978. I can find no evidence McClintock completed the book.
87 1971, 202.
88 1971, 203.
89 1971, 204.
90 It is the opening piece in a landmark issue of *Teachers College Record*, with important essays by Maxine Greene, Lawrence Cremin, Philip Phenix, and Douglas Sloan, among others. Tyson Lewis (2013, 12–15) acknowledges the significance of McClintock's seminal essay.
91 Kliebard 2000 (1975), 84.
92 Simpson 2002, 98.
93 2002, 98–99.
94 See Egan 1990.
95 The pre-reformed Ravitch (2000), that is.
96 2002, 147.
97 Bauman (1978) is hardly the first but worth remembering.
98 2002, 135.
99 2001, 37.
100 See, for instance, Macdonald 1995.
101 In his pedagogical performances, recorded in his numerous conference presentations, Aoki teaches shrewdly but humbly. In his essays, I could find no evidence that he imagined he could produce "effects" as a consequence of his pedagogical moves. As an explicit topic, Aoki characterizes teaching as "in-dwelling" between curriculum-as-plan and curriculum-as-experience. It is a "mode of being." He is consistently critical of teaching as "doing" and as producing "outcomes" (see Pinar and Irwin 2005).
102 Carter, Bishop, and Kravits 2003.
103 True, public-school-age students are not "responsible"—as age-of-consent laws make explicit—in the senses that adults are. And obviously teachers can enable students'—especially young children's—study. But, despite the nonsense, parents, not to mention psycho-social, economic, and political conditions, structure (even if they do not fully determine) the child's capacity to study. There is, centrally, the problem of the curriculum (see Pinar 2004b). Teachers' liability is, in matter of fact, limited.
104 See 1971, 170.
105 See 1971, 169.

Bibliography

Bauman, Zygmunt. 1978. *Hermeneutics and Social Science*. New York: Columbia University Press.

Bederman, Gail. 1995. *Manliness and Civilization: A Cultural History of Gender and Race in the United States, 1880–1917*. Chicago: University of Chicago Press.

Block, Alan A. 2001. Ethics and Curriculum. *JCT* 17 (3), 23–38.

Block, Alan A. 2004. *Talmud, Curriculum, and the Practical: Joseph Schwab and the Rabbis*. New York: Peter Lang.

Carlson, Dennis. 2002. *Leaving Safe Harbors: Toward a New Progressivism in American Education and Public Life*. New York: Routledge.

Carpenter, William B. 1886. *Principles of Mental Physiology*. London: Kegan Paul.
Carter, Carol, Bishop, Joyce, and Kravits, Sarah Lyman. 2003. *Keys to Success in College, Career, and Life*. Upper Saddle River, NJ: Prentice Hall.
Crary, Jonathan. 1999. *Suspensions of Perception: Attention, Spectacle, and Modern Culture*. Cambridge, MA: MIT Press/an October Book.
Doll, Jr., William E. 1993. *A Post-Modern Perspective on Curriculum*. New York: Teachers College Press.
Doll, Jr., William E. 2002. Ghosts and the Curriculum. In *Curriculum Visions*, edited by William E. Doll, Jr. and Noel Gough (23–70). New York: Peter Lang.
Egan, Kieran. 1990. *Romantic Understanding: The Development of Rationality and Imagination, Ages 8–15*. New York: Routledge.
Egan, Kieran. 2002. *Getting It Wrong from the Beginning: Our Progressivist Inheritance from Herbert Spencer, John Dewey, and Jean Piaget*. New Haven, CT: Yale University Press.
Grumet, Madeleine R. (1988). *Bitter Milk: Women and Teaching*. Amherst: University of Massachusetts Press.
Halbertal, M. and Halbertal, T.H. 1998. The Yeshiva, in *Philosophers on Education*, edited by A.O. Rorty. New York: Routledge.
Hofstadter, Richard. 1962. *Anti-Intellectualism in American Life*. New York: Vintage.
Huebner, Dwayne. 1999. *The Lure of the Transcendent*. Mahwah, NJ: Lawrence Erlbaum.
James, William. 1950 (1890). *Principles of Psychology*. 2 vols. New York: Dover.
Kilpatrick, William Heard. 1918, October 12. The Project Method. *Teachers College Bulletin*, Tenth Series, No. 3. [Reprinted from *Teachers College Record*.]
Kincheloe, Joe L. and Pinar, William F. eds. 1991. *Curriculum as Social Psychoanalysis: The Significance of Place*. Albany: State University of New York Press.
Kliebard, Herbert. 2000 (1975). Metaphorical Roots of Curriculum Design. In *Curriculum Studies: The Reconceptualization*, edited by William F. Pinar (84–85). Troy, NY: Educator's International Press. [Also published in *Curriculum Theorizing: The Reconceptualists*, edited by Pinar (84–85). Berkeley, CA: McCutchan.]
Lemert, Charles and Bhan, Esme. eds. 1998. *The Voice of Anna Julia Cooper*. Lanham, MD: Rowan & Littlefield Publishers.
Lewis, Tyson E. 2013. *On Study. Giorgio Agamben and Educational Potentiality*. New York: Routledge.
Macdonald, Bradley J. ed. 1995. *Theory as a Prayerful Act: The Collected Essays of James B. Macdonald*. [Introduction by William F. Pinar.] New York: Peter Lang.
Martin, Raymond and Barresi, John. 2006. *The Rise and Fall of Soul and Self: An Intellectual History of Personal Identity*. New York: Columbia University Press.
McClintock, Robert. 1971, December. Toward a Place for Study in a World of Instruction. *Teachers College Record* 73 (2), 161–205.
Morris, Marla. 2001. *Holocaust and Curriculum*. Mahwah, NJ: Lawrence Erlbaum.
Pinar, William F. 1978. *Currere*: A Case Study. In *Qualitative Evaluation*, edited by George Willis (316–342). Berkeley, CA: McCutchan.
Pinar, William F. 1994. *Autobiography, Politics, and Sexuality: Essays in Curriculum Theory 1972–1992*. New York: Peter Lang.
Pinar, William F. 2004. *What Is Curriculum Theory*? Mahwah, NJ: Lawrence Erlbaum.
Pinar, William F. and Irwin, Rita L. eds. 2005. *Curriculum in a New Key: The Collected Works of Ted T. Aoki*. Mahwah, NJ: Lawrence Erlbaum.
Ravitch, Diane. 2000. *Left Back: A Century of Battles over School Reform*. New York: Simon and Schuster.
Schwab, Joseph J. 1978. *Science, Curriculum, and Liberal Education: Selected Essays*. [Edited by Ian Westbury and Neil J. Wilkof.] Chicago: University of Chicago Press.
Simpson, David. 2002. *Situatedness, or, Why We Keep Saying Where We're Coming From*. Durham, NC: Duke University Press.

Thorndike, Edward L. 1922. Measurement in Education. In *Twenty First Yearbook of National Society for the Study of Education*. Bloomington, IL: Public School Publishing.

Trueit, Donna. ed. 2012. *Pragmatism, Postmodernism, Complexity Theory: The Fascinating Imaginative Realm of William E. Doll, Jr.* New York: Routledge.

Weber, Max. 2002 (1930). *The Protestant Ethic and the Spirit of Capitalism*. [Trans. Talcott Parsons. With an introduction by Anthony Giddens.] New York: Routledge.

Williamson, Ben. 2013. *The Future of the Curriculum. School Knowledge in the Digital Age*. Cambridge, MA: The MIT Press.

CHAPTER 2

ALLEGORY

Commentary

Walter Benjamin's conception of the present as the living dialectic of past and future, Eiland and Jennings[1] inform us, is evident even in his early essay "Metaphysics of Youth," composed in 1913–1914. In it Benjamin depicts the present as "eternally having been,"[2] an idea I associate with allegory. "What we do and think," Eiland and Jennings[3] paraphrase, "is filled with the being of our ancestors—which, having passed away, becomes futural." Each day, they continue, quoting Benjamin, we enact the "unmeasured energies" of an ever-present past that only occasionally breaks "into the brightness of the day," a palimpsest brought from the shadows by "rare shafts of insight."[4] In this pre-War essay, Eiland and Jennings explain, the idea of "awakening youth" foreshadows Benjamin's later formulation of the "dialectical image as a momentary constellation of historical tensions, an emergent force field in which the now of recognition wakens from and to 'that dream we name the past'." What is at stake in this historicizing dialectic, they remind (quoting Benjamin),[5] is "the art of experiencing the present as waking world," what Benjamin will come to call "now time." Allegory testifies to the fact that "now" is temporal and multiply layered, that our extrication from this present moment is immanent within it, if, that is, our experience is educational.

References

Eiland, Howard and Jennings, Michael W. 2014. *Walter Benjamin. A Critical Life*. Cambridge, MA: Belknap Press of Harvard University Press.

Pinar, William F. 2012. *What Is Curriculum Theory?* (2nd edition, 49–62). Routledge.

> If Allegory had a middle name, it would be Antinomy.
>
> Angus Fletcher[6]

In the United States, we have suffered a history of curriculum development predicated primarily on functionality. Over the past century there have been several such formulations—each is associated with a key theoretician[7]—that link the curriculum to the economy and to society. Regarding both domains these links are future-bound, although curriculum conservatives—focused on the ancient languages and cultures—did survive in the U.S. through the 1920s,[8] resurfacing briefly and mostly rhetorically in the 1980s. To achieve these functional objectives, curriculum development became primarily procedural and systematized, starting with objectives and ending with assessment. In linking objectives to assessment, teaching was reduced to implementation.

Severed from schools by the Kennedy Administration's 1960s national curriculum reform, curriculum development as an academic specialization gave way to understanding curriculum.[9] Curriculum reform gave way to concern not with the intellectual content of the curriculum—as it tended to be in the 1960s national curriculum reform—but with so-called standards during the 1980s. The rhetorical preoccupation with standards gave way to accountability since *New Child Left Behind*.[10] Curriculum reform has been replaced by what is more precisely termed *school deform*, in which the centerpiece of the school—its curriculum—is rendered only a means to an ends: student scores on standardized tests.

While globalization has accelerated trends toward curricular standardization, it has hardly expunged what is distinctive in local, regional, and national life. Even the same curriculum concepts connote different realities given the distinctiveness of our national and regional situations, and in five studies—in Brazil, China, India, Mexico, and South Africa—I have portrayed this fact. While a curriculum of functionality driven by exams was instituted in post-Apartheid South Africa, for instance, it was perceived (at least at first) not as the handmaiden of international corporations and right-wing politicians (as in fact it is in the U.S.) but of democratization and black empowerment.[11] In Brazil, in the large cities, a tripartite jurisdictional structure (federal, state, municipal) not necessarily coordinated with itself, enables teachers opportunities for refashioning the curriculum according to their specific situations. This complexity of jurisdiction has contributed to a sophisticated curriculum field structured by a distinctive set of curriculum concepts, such as *enunciation* and the *quotidian*.[12] The history of curriculum studies in Mexico is tragically different, despite the heroic efforts of intellectually sophisticated scholars to rethink their circumstances.[13] In China, an ambitious curriculum reform is underway that reactivates cultural and historical knowledge in efforts to transform students' and teachers' lives in schools.[14] Legacies of colonialism in India provide challenges and, it turns out, opportunities for educators committed to children's spiritual and academic development.[15]

It is important to acknowledge national history and culture—and to also acknowledge that these are themselves contested concepts and realities—in order to understand school curriculum and the academic field that studies and develops it. Here I offer one way to recast curriculum development and design away from the realm of the procedural—that is, conceptualized as "principles" and steps to follow no matter where you are, no matter the historical moment—to ongoing forms of intellectual engagement with one's distinctive situation, however complex and contested that situation is, however tragic one's history, however stressful the present might be, however promising or horrifying the future looks. Such culturally sensitive, historically attuned curriculum development requires a different set of concepts and practices from those many know so well, e.g. objectives to be implemented through curriculum design and teaching for the sake of assessment. Instead of objectives to be assessed, we study the historical moment, including how the present becomes embodied in our individual subjectivities, and how we might study both through academic knowledge in conversation with those around us. I realize that such language derives from culturally specific traditions and addresses nationally specific situations, but that acknowledgment is part of the rationale for curriculum development, design, and research situated in and addressed to the particular, in part through studying larger circles of influence, including intellectual histories and present circumstances.

What I describe to you here is addressed less to the country where I work—Canada—than it is to the country of my birth and residence, the United States. Most recently the problems of political polarization and economic destabilization structure the present moment there. While each of these has its own history and complexity, I link both to what I discern as deeper interrelated problems of presentism and narcissism in American culture, themselves intertwined with the crisis of technoculture created by consumer capitalism.

While U.S. historian Christopher Lasch's portrait[16] of what he termed "the culture of narcissism" seems overdrawn, it is, in my judgment, largely accurate. "The intense subjectivity of modern work, exemplified even more clearly in the office than in the factory," Lasch observed, "causes men and women to doubt the reality of the external world and to imprison themselves . . . in a shell of protective irony."[17] Exhausted by an unrelenting daily psychological intensity and an acute, even physical, sense of threat, many retreat from a public sphere that no longer seems safe, let alone supportive or worthy of their emotional investments. In the apparent safety of private life, however, many discover no solace. "On the contrary," Lasch notes, "private life takes on the very qualities of the anarchic social order from which it supposed to provide a refuge."[18]

With no place left to hide, many retreat into—and, Lasch argues, become lost in—themselves. The psychoanalytic term for this personality disturbance is *narcissism*, not to be confused with being egotistical or selfish.[19] Recoiling from meaningful engagement in the world, the privatized self atrophies—Lasch uses the term *minimal* to denote that contraction of the self narcissism necessitates—and becomes disabled from distinguishing sharply between self and other. The past and future disappear in an individualistic obsession with psychic survival in the present. As Lasch suggests: "The narcissist has no interest in the future because, in part, he has so little interest in the past."[20] How might we teach to restore students' sense of temporality—a sharp sense of the past, enabling discernment of the present and foreshadowing of the future—to the complicated conversation that is the school curriculum? My answer is allegory, a concept enabling us to understand, and engage in, subjectively situated, historically attuned curriculum development and design.

Allegory—"in which the apparent sense of a thing or text is seen to signal some other, possibly very different sense"[21]—is an ancient concept. Etymologically, "allegory" means to "speak publicly in an assembly." This genealogy forefronts its pedagogical and communicative nature. A speech at once concrete and abstract, allegory tells a specific story that hints at a more general significance. Its characters are at once particular and symbolic, simultaneously historical and metahistorical, even mythological. Understanding curriculum allegorically self-consciously incorporates the past into the present, threaded through one's subjectivity.[22]

Allegory acknowledges academic knowledge as important for its own sake, even as it implies its educational significance. Allegory underscores that our individual lives are structured by ever widening circles of influence: from family through friends to our fellow citizens, all of whom personify culture, symbolize society, embody history. But allegory's movements are not only outward, they are inward, as allegory provokes reflection on, say, the sciences not only as specific academic disciplines with distinctive intellectual histories and present circumstances, but also as social, in the public interest. Science is subjective as well, however indirectly subjectivity is expressed.[23]

Study enables one to articulate the singularity of public forms, requiring one to discern their histories and present associations. Study, then, becomes sensible not in an "environment," the long-time term of preference for a social and behavioral science that has too often stripped History from its efforts to understand what it observes. Rather, study proceeds in situation. As Madeleine Grumet pointed out decades ago, "environment" implies a blank slate, without history and empty of human intention, while "situation" specifies how what we confront is filled by legacy, meaning, and aspiration.[24]

And while it is no metaphysical bedrock, nevertheless it is each of us—the "I"— who testifies to the reality within and around us. "[N]either transcendent nor in process of self-realization," David D. Roberts explains, each of us (as individuals, as collectivities) "is rather bound up with some specific situation that is historical."[25] I endorse the concept of allegory because it forefronts both History and questions of its representation as central to understanding self and society through school curriculum.

Historical facts are primary, but it is their capacity to invoke our imagination that marks them as allegorical. Their meanings are not confined to the past; they leak into our experience of the present. Those meanings are to be articulated, in solitude through study, with others in classrooms and online, but such facts cannot be definitive, as they do not belong to the present. Bringing the past into the present while rigorously refusing to conflate the two incurs that "creative tensionality"[26] inherent in a historical sensibility.[27] Such a sensibility enables us to be attuned to the specific while not losing sight of its antecedents and associations.

For Walter Benjamin, Rauch reminds, allegory was a "model to represent the historical moment in terms of how a text affects us as readers even though we cannot determine its meaning."[28] Such a model derived from Benjamin's conviction that the cultivation of historical sensibility depended in part on the literariness of language and "its redemptive or memorial capacity in rhetorical structures."[29] Those structures are aesthetic, but what accords them immediacy and meaning is their saturation by the subjectivity of those who study them, whether in solitude or in assembly. Through allegory we can build passages from the particularity of our situations to the alterity of others. For Benjamin, Rauch[30] suggests, history became accessible through allegory.

It is the reciprocity between subjectivity and history that structures allegory, which is why school curriculum guidelines, in general, ought not be more than guidelines. Subjectively situated, historically attuned teachers must be free to follow wherever their imaginations and instincts lead them, acutely aware of the disciplinary knowledge which structures their ongoing inquiry and testimony. Like speech, allegory is not only self-referential; it extends beyond itself to comment on, to connect to, what is past in the present. An allegory-of-the-present combines the uniqueness and authenticity that Benjamin associated with the "aura" of an individually crafted work of art with the tradition such subjectively saturated art incorporates. The teacher is in this sense an artist and complicated conversation is the teacher's medium.

Allegory, then, achieves significance through its "combinatory structure,"[31] through both its internal elements—how the story that is told *is* told—and its positioning in disciplinary, subjective, and social structures. Rauch thinks of these allegories as "hieroglyphs," as "fragmentary remnants of historic cultural context which is lost" the juxtaposition of which can create a "chaotic" image (Benjamin's "dialectical image") of one's "historical experience."[32] Teachers and students themselves can decide how much "chaos" and how much "continuity" is appropriate, intellectually, and in making learning psychologically manageable. As teachers know, intellectual labor is also an emotional undertaking.

Allegory begins in the teacher's study, where it is transposed into curriculum design, or less formally, teaching (not necessarily "lesson") plans, as with what we choose to start classroom dialogue. It might be helpful to the teacher to reflect on what her or his intentions are, but "objectives" are hardly primary concerns. What matters is the conversation. Allegory "ends" in what students make of such knowledge, a fate hardly removed from the province of the teacher but never definitively dependent on the teacher. Even the most creative and provocative lessons can fall flat, as anyone knows. Attempting to force students' engagement (let alone learning) becomes autocratic if not mediated by the subjective knowledge teachers have of the individuals in their classroom. Moreover, what students make of their study may not be known, and then only by the students themselves, for years. Specific "core standards" such those enforced by the Obama Administration[33]—with the expectation that these will then be learned by students because teachers have taught them—amount to magical thinking, an example of how denial and obfuscation have predominated in U.S. school reform since the 1983 *A Nation at Risk*.

What determines when juxtaposed elements that comprise the curricular "hieroglyph" stretch credulity? There are developmentally inflected logical relations between elements that cannot be violated at whim, but even apparently illogical relations can become credible when contextualized specifically. The great Weimar cultural critic Siegfried Kracauer pointed out:

> The more reality opens itself up to man, the more foreign to him the average world with its distorted conceptual petrifactions becomes. He recognizes that a boundless plentitude of qualities inhabits each phenomenon, and that each is subject to widely differing laws. But the more he becomes aware of the many-sidedness of things, the more it becomes possible for him to relate them to each other.[34]

In that first sentence, Kracauer is acknowledging what has become in our era a commonplace: that reality is socially constructed, a palimpsest layered by not immediately discernible traces of the past. Of course, that hardly means that reality is immaterial or always elusive—even if finally mysterious—but it does underline that everyday life is always not only what it seems, that ordinariness contains and expresses elements not on the surface, elements that, despite their apparent difference, could also be related to each other, although not necessarily due to contiguity.

Difference becomes intelligible within relations of resemblances, as Kaja Silverman specifies through the concept of *analogy*, that which "links us to other beings—what makes all of our stories part of the same great book. But analogy is also internal to our own being—what connects the person we were yesterday with the slightly different person we are today."[35] I emphasize that these two—sociality and subjectivity—are themselves sometimes analogous. As teachers, individuation denotes the developmental—and professional—undertaking of sculpting the specificity of our individuality, however informed it inevitably is by sociality, through academic study and pedagogical participation in the complicated conversation that is the curriculum. In so participating, Silverman makes clear, we

> connect our lives to many others—to lives that are over, and to lives that have not yet begun, as well as to those proximate to us in time and space. Rather than a self-contained volume, authorized by us, our history is only one chapter in an enormous and ever-expanding book, whose overall meaning and shape we cannot even begin to grasp, let along determine. . . . This volume is written from the inside, through the analogies we acknowledge and those we refuse.[36]

Working from within, specifying the singularity of situations through threading the needle that is our individual subjective experience, we can affirm resemblance through difference. Simultaneously abstract and concrete, past and present, such pedagogical labor is allegorical, efforts at communication informed by academic knowledge.

While undistorted and unconstrained speech may not be possible, communication through understanding is. As James W. Carey realized: "reality is brought into existence, is produced, by communication—by, in short, the construction, apprehension, and utilization of symbolic forms."[37] The reconstruction of reality is, in this sense, intellectual labor. We cannot know what intellectual labor will bring; like the future, serious and creative thought can be enigmatic, sometimes contradictory, often incalculable. While curriculum as complicated conversation in the service of social and self-reflective understanding will transform the present, it will not do so in predictable ways, certainly not according to politicians' too often self-serving and ideology-laden agendas.

Curriculum theory and the complicated conversation it supports seek the truth of the present, not its manipulation for job creation. Economics is an important curricular topic, but it becomes so in the name of understanding and critique, not entrepreneurship. Intellectual agency—not entrepreneurship—is our academic calling. Curriculum conceived as conversation invites students to encounter themselves and the world they inhabit and that inhabits them through academic study, through academic knowledge, popular culture, everyday experience: all threaded through their own lived experience. Forefronting test scores on standardized tests cuts this thread.

How does quantifying educational experience *end* educational experience? Even private "thought is predominately public and social," Carey reminds.[38] Standardized tests undermine those lived links between the spoken word (the classroom is by definition a public square) and inner conversation (carried on in rooms of one's own). When guided by a thoughtful, imaginative, and knowledgeable teacher (these are not specifiable behaviors!), connecting the two spheres—inner and public speech—supports subjective and social reconstruction. Why are these reciprocally related processes central to the education of the public? "Reality," Carey explains,

> must be repaired for it consistently breaks down: people get lost physically and spiritually, experiments fail, evidence counter to the representation is produced, mental derangement sets in—all threats to our models of and for reality that lead to intense repair work.[39]

Curricular standardization—especially when accomplished by standardized testing—is not repair work. By silencing subjectivity and ensuring cultural conformity, the standardized test-making industry and the politicians who fund it stop communication and enforce mimicry. The spontaneity of conversation disappears in the application of so-called cognitive skills to solve conceptual puzzles unrelated to either inner experience or public life. Censored in such curricula is that self-reflexivity dialogical encounter invites.

Under such political circumstances, the curricular task becomes the recovery of memory and history in ways that psychologically allow individuals to reenter politically the public sphere in privately meaningful and ethically committed ways. The public sphere becomes the "commons," not another place to plunder for profit. How can we substitute social and subjective reconstruction for economic exploitation in a historical moment consumed by the latter? The answer is not obvious or easy, but I suggest that by studying the past students might begin to extricate themselves from the present. The great Italian filmmaker and public intellectual Pier Paolo Pasolini understood:

> Now I prefer to move through the past, precisely because I believe that the past is the only force to contest the present; it is an aberrant form, but all the values that were the values which formed us—with all that made them atrocious, with their negative aspects—are the ones that are capable of putting the present into crisis.[40]

Subjective reconstruction requires reactivating the past in the present, rendering the present past. This is the regressive phase of the method of *currere*, the lived experience of curriculum.[41]

Such autobiographical labor is not only intrasubjective. It is allegorical as well, as it requires as it precipitates social engagement. Such complicated conversation within oneself and with others reinvigorates "the oral tradition, with its emphasis on dialogue and dialectic, values and philosophical speculation, as the countervailing culture to the technological culture of sensation and mobility."[42] Part of the project of *currere*—curriculum conceived as a verb, as embodied and personified—is to contradict presentism by self-consciously cultivating the temporal structure of subjectivity, insisting on the distinctiveness and simultaneity of past, present, and future, a temporal complexity in which difference does not dissolve onto a flattened never-ending "now," but is stretched as it is spoken, reconstructing the present as temporally and spatially differentiated. Presentism not only erases time but space as well, as place becomes nowhere in particular, cyberspace.[43] In the midst of such an ongoing, perhaps accelerating, cultural calamity, the education of the public requires, above all, the cultivation of historicality.

To enact curriculum conceived as subjectively situated, historically attuned conversation means associating academic knowledge with the individual him or herself, teaching not only what is, for instance, historical knowledge, but also suggesting its possible consequences for the individual's self-formation in the historical present, allowing that knowledge to shape the individual's coming to social form. Doing so is an elusive and ongoing threading of subjectivity through the social forms and intellectual constructs we discover through study, reanimating our original passions through acting in the world. "What we do in school in the classroom," Alan Block suggests, "is to forever pursue lost objects," and "this pursuit and effort is both a personal and a communal obligation."[44] In fact, he adds, addressing teachers directly, "until we find our own lost articles we ought not to undertake assisting others."[45] I suggest this search can also be conducted *through* assisting others.

The Future in the Past

> [E]very subject finds herself obligated to search for the future in the past.[46]
> Kaja Silverman

Procedures and principles remain important, but unless we can think our way through the structures of the present, we cannot find our way to the future. Reactivating the past reconstructs the present so we can find the future. In the United States, that means rejecting the Obama Administration's school reform initiative—the so-called *Race to the Top*—and encouraging teachers to engage in an ethics of intransigence.[47] They must appear to comply with federal and state guidelines, but, I suggest, professional ethics precedes politics. As Franz Rosenzweig reminds us from the past: "vocation is more primeval than condition."[48] That affirmation of our calling takes historically shifting, culturally specific, and subjectively situated forms. We share one planet, yes, and the cultivation of cosmopolitanism—tolerance of, even hospitality toward difference and dissent—is key to our survival as a species, but these require not curricular standardization but curricular differentiation, as working through the legacies of the past enables finding the future. "Working through," in Dominick LaCapra's cumbersome but clarifying definition,

> is in general an articulatory practice with political dimensions: to the extent one works through trauma and its symptoms on both personal and sociocultural levels, one is able to distinguish between past and present and to recall in memory that something happened to one (or one's people) back then while realizing that one is living here and now with openings to the future.[49]

It is such complicated conversation—acknowledging the trauma of historical experience while never ceasing to articulate its character and effects—that also reactivates the past in the present.

The key curriculum question—*what knowledge is of most worth?*—is animated by ethics, history, and politics. As such, it is an ongoing question, as the immediacy of the historical moment, the particularity of place, and the singularity of one's own individuality become articulated through the subject matter—history, poetry, science, technology—that one studies and teaches.

Expressing one's subjectivity through academic knowledge is how one links the lived curriculum with the planned one, how one demonstrates to students that scholarship can speak to them, how in fact scholarship can enable them to speak. No empty abstraction invoked to enforce compliance now for the sake of a time yet to come, the future is here and now. Finding the future in an era of pervasive presentism and narcissism is not obvious. In fact, the future will not be found in front of us at all, but in back of us. Reactivating the past reconstructs the present so we can find the future.

Notes

1 2014, 43.
2 2014, 44.
3 Ibid.
4 Quoted in 2014, 44.
5 See 2014, 44.
6 2012, 382.
7 See, for example, Jackson 1992.
8 See Ravitch 2000, 119.
9 For a sketch of the U.S. field's history, see Pinar 2014a.
10 See Ravitch 2010.
11 Pinar 2010.
12 Pinar 2011a.
13 Pinar 2011b.
14 Pinar 2014b.
15 Pinar in press.
16 See Lasch 1978.
17 1978, 102.
18 1978, 27.
19 See Lasch 1984, 18.
20 Lasch 1978, xvi.
21 Eiland and Jennings 2014, 18. Allegory was, Eiland and Jennings point out, "determinate" (2014, 18) for Walter Benjamin, the subject of their study.
22 As Kögler (1999, 174–175) explains:

> We are to reconstruct other meaning structures such that they retain their alterity; in this way, we may be able to achieve a measure of immediate unfamiliarity over against our own horizons, which previously had gone unquestioned. The foreign or unfamiliar features of earlier epochs and other cultures are therefore to be approached in such a way that their alterity does not disappear (or become "sublated"); rather, this alterity must serve as an anchor and a point of departure for a new self-understanding, within which we experience ourselves as other.

23 As histories of science document: see, for instance, Shapin 2010.
24 1978, 281.
25 1995, 7.
26 Aoki 2005 (1985/1991), 232.
27 Sometimes characterized as "historical consciousness": see Seixas 2004 and Simon 2005.
28 Rauch 2000, 186.
29 Ibid.
30 See 2000, 213.
31 Rauch 2000, 188.

32 2000, 231 n. 7.
33 Lewin 2010, July 21.
34 Kracauer 1995, 234.
35 Silverman 2009, 74.
36 2009, 65.
37 Carey 1992, 25.
38 1992, 28.
39 1992, 30.
40 Quoted in Rumble 1996, 58.
41 Rather than remembering the past from the perspective the present, the regressive phase invites one to re-experience what has occurred before, thereby reconstructing the subjective structures repression enforces. For more detail, see Pinar 2012, 45.
42 Carey 1992, 135.
43 See Chun 2006, 43.
44 Block 2009, 73.
45 2009, 77.
46 Silverman 2000, 49.
47 In contrast to "resistance" this concept includes dissimulation in acknowledgement of the politically inferior positions educators often occupy; see Pinar 2012, 238.
48 Mosès 2009 (1992), 29.
49 LaCapra 2009, 54.

Bibliography

Aoki, Ted T. 2005 (1985/1991). Signs of Vitality in Curriculum Scholarship. In *Curriculum in a New Key*, edited by William F. Pinar and Rita L. Irwin (229–233). Mahwah, NJ: Lawrence Erlbaum.

Block, Alan A. 2009. *Ethics and Teaching: A Religious Perspective on Revitalizing Education*. New York: Palgrave Macmillan.

Carey, James W. 1992. *Communication as Culture: Essays on Media and Society*. New York: Routledge.

Chun, Wendy Hui Kyong. 2006. *Control and Freedom: Power and Paranoia in the Age of Fiber Optics*. Cambridge, MA: MIT Press.

Eiland, Howard and Jennings, Michael W. 2014. *Walter Benjamin. A Critical Life*. Cambridge, MA: Belknap Press of Harvard University Press.

Fletcher, Angus. 2012. *Allegory. The Theory of a Symbolic Model*. [With a foreword by Harold Bloom and a new afterword by the author.] Princeton, NJ: Princeton University Press.

Grumet, Madeleine R. 1978. Songs and Situations. In *Qualitative Evaluation*, edited by George Willis (274–315), Berkeley, CA: McCutchan.

Jackson, Philip W. 1992. Conceptions of Curriculum and Curriculum Specialists. In the *Handbook of Research on Curriculum*, edited by Philip W. Jackson (3–40). New York: Macmillan.

Kögler, Hans-Herbert. 1999. *The Power of Dialogue: Critical Hermeneutics after Gadamer and Foucault*. Cambridge, MA: MIT Press.

Kracauer, Siegfried. 1995. *The Mass Ornament: Weimar Essays*. [Translated, edited, and with an introduction by Thomas Y. Levin.] Cambridge, MA: Harvard University Press.

LaCapra, Dominick. 2009. *History and Its Limits: Human, Animal, Violence*. Ithaca, NY: Cornell University Press.

Lasch, Christopher. 1978. *The Culture of Narcissism: American Life in an Age of Diminishing Expectations*. New York: Norton.

Lasch, Christopher. 1984. *The Minimal Self: Psychic Survival in Troubled Times*. New York: Norton.

Lewin, Tamar. 2010, July 21. States Embrace Core Standards for the Schools. Unusually Fast Action. U.S. Offers Yearly Goals, and a Deadline for a Share of $3 Billion. *New York Times* CLIX (55,108), A1, A3.

Mosès, Stéphane. 2009 (1992). *The Angel of History: Rosenzweig, Benjamin, Scholem.* [Trans. Barbara Harshav] Stanford, CA: Stanford University Press.

National Commission on Excellence in Education. 1983. *A Nation at Risk: The Imperative for Educational Reform.* Washington, DC: United States Department of Education.

Pinar, William F. ed. 2010. *Curriculum Studies in South Africa.* New York: Palgrave Macmillan.

Pinar, William F. ed. 2011a. *Curriculum Studies in Brazil.* New York: Palgrave Macmillan.

Pinar, William F. ed. 2011b. *Curriculum Studies in Mexico.* New York: Palgrave Macmillan.

Pinar, William F. 2012. *What Is Curriculum Theory?* 2nd edition. New York: Routledge.

Pinar, William F. Ed. 2014a. *The International Handbook of Curriculum Research.* New York: Routledge.

Pinar, William F. ed. 2014b. *Curriculum Studies in China.* New York: Palgrave Macmillan.

Pinar, William F. ed. in press. *Curriculum Studies in India: Intellectual Histories, Present Circumstances.* New York: Palgrave Macmillan.

Rauch, Angelika. 2000. *The Hieroglyph of Tradition: Freud, Benjamin, Gadamer, Novalis, Kant.* Madison, NJ: Fairleigh Dickinson University Press.

Ravitch, Diane. 2000. *Left Back: A Century of Battles over School Reform.* New York: Simon and Schuster.

Ravitch, Diane. 2010. *The Death and Life of the Great American School System: How Testing and Choice Are Undermining Education.* New York: Basic Books.

Roberts, David D. 1995. *Nothing but History: Reconstruction and Extremity after Metaphysics.* Berkeley and Los Angeles: University of California Press.

Rumble, Patrick. 1996. *Allegories of Contamination: Pier Paolo Pasolini's Trilogy of Life.* Toronto: University of Toronto Press.

Seixas, Peter. Ed. 2004. *Theorizing Historical Consciousness.* Toronto: University of Toronto Press.

Shapin, Steven. 2010. *Never Pure: Historical Studies of Science as if It Was Produced by People with Bodies, Situated in Time, Space, Culture, and Society, Struggling for Credibility and Authority.* Baltimore, MD: Johns Hopkins University Press.

Silverman, Kaja. 2000. *World Spectators.* Stanford, CA: Stanford University Press.

Silverman, Kaja. 2009. *Flesh of My Flesh.* Stanford, CA: Stanford University Press.

Simon, Roger I. 2005. *The Touch of the Past. Remembrance, Learning, and Ethics.* New York: Palgrave Macmillan.

CHAPTER 3

INTERNATIONALIZATION

Commentary

Distinguishing between internationalization—ethical engagement with difference—and globalization—neo-imperialism enforced through economic and educational standardization—I suggest that we can address the emergency of the present moment only if we are knowledgeable about the intellectual histories and present circumstances of the complicated conversation in which we are engaged.[1] I provide examples of these intellectual histories and present circumstances from a project I directed on curriculum studies in Brazil,[2] concluding with curriculum research in Canada.

References

Pinar, William F. 2007. *Intellectual Advancement through Disciplinarity: Verticality and Horizontality in Curriculum Studies*. Rotterdam and Taipei: Sense Publishers.

Pinar, William F. Ed. 2011. *Curriculum Studies in Brazil: Intellectual Histories, Present Circumstances*. New York: Palgrave Macmillan.

Pinar, William F. 2012. Disciplinarity and Internationalization. A Lecture Presented at the University of the State of Rio de Janeiro. Copyright William F. Pinar.

> Disciplines are now experiencing a legitimation crisis.[3]
>
> Mitsuhiro Yoshimoto

The academic field of education is regarded as an applied field, a field of practice rather than theory, dedicated to intervention in rather than contemplation of the world. Consequently, whatever the specialization—curriculum, instruction, administration, assessment—the disciplinary demand is to provide proposals for intervention, proposals organized to solve specific problems large and small, and often associated with broader visions of "improvement" in educational institutions. The state of emergency[4] of the world requires action now. Not often are we accorded opportunities for contemplation that, if we reflect on the matter, is no alternative but a prerequisite to intervention.

However pressed by present circumstances, we do spend time (alone and with each other) thinking about the problems to be solved, the vision to be articulated and translated into action. We read the relevant literature for its potential to help us act. The point, however, remains intervention, and not necessarily to make a contribution to an ongoing disciplinary conversation but to solve a problem. The point of scholarly publications in an applied field is to provide protocols for action. In an applied field, one's study is secondarily—sometimes even only incidentally—characterized as contributing to the academic field—the ongoing conversation—wherein the practical problem or broader vision is articulated. This applied character of research in education is in play when, as university faculty supervising graduate student research, we require reviews of the relevant literature. When students review the relevant literature they do so focused on the research they propose, scanning that literature for its potential for justifying the intervention the dissertation research is investigating. Precedents are indeed acknowledged, but the point is less contributing to the intellectual advancement of an academic discipline as much as it is to intervene in the world, from which the academic discipline is imagined as separate. Add to this applied disposition of the field the contemporary legitimation crisis to which Yoshimoto refers, and the demand for interdisciplinary, trans-disciplinary, post-disciplinary—anything *but* disciplinary—research becomes intelligible.

My point is that the applied character of curriculum studies can be strengthened by systematic attention to the field's intellectual history and present circumstances.[5] By strengthened I mean more sustained attention that is intellectually sophisticated, attention more capable of decoding the complexity of the problem one aspires to solve, the "real-world" dilemma that has prompted one's contemplation and deliberation. Remaining too focused on that "real-world" problem disguises the historical contingency of that situation, its genealogy, its complicity with what appears separate from it, "out there." We have known for decades now that we cannot sever the knower from the known, that our very capacity to discern dilemmas cannot be cut off from the disciplinary discourse that informs our discernment. To address problems in the world one must also understand them.[6]

Acknowledging the discipline-specific historical and international context in which one's topic becomes intelligible is the main means of disciplinarity.[7] Many have lamented—and more than a few have celebrated—the porous boundaries of curriculum studies, the vastness of its purview, the multiplicity of its discourses. It is a "big-picture" field, not one that focuses on knowing more about less. In a field as intellectually dynamic and diversified as curriculum studies, what we have in common, I suggest, is not necessarily the present but the past. To exercise expertise in a discipline obligates one to acknowledge the already-existing conversation in which one is presuming to participate. Our resistance to that rather obvious fact derives not only from the "state of emergency" we experience in the world, not only from our insistence that we study only what we want to study, relegating intellectual figures and traditions to opportunities for self-exploration and expression. Our resistance derives as well from political commitments[8] sometimes animated by historical injury and within disciplines by "paradigm wars"[9] and even, on occasion, intergenerational animosity.[10]

In certain cultures the significance of ancestors—and elders—can be spiritual as well as intellectual. Within the culture of the academic field of education, those who have gone before are regularly relegated to "shoulders on which we are standing,"[11] prosthetic props to our own accomplishments. Add to this narcissism a presentism that contains a confidence that "now" is almost always an improvement upon "then," a faith in "progress" often decried in the literature but reinstalled through our fascination with technology and "the new." In an applied field, ancestors become a list of names and publications dates following a sentence somehow summing up decades of variegated research.

While eschewing neither self-expressivity nor the educational significance of student interest nor ongoing ethical demands for intervention in the world, I am suggesting that both require a simultaneous engagement with the discipline-specific conversation in which self-expression and social activism become articulated and achieve intelligibility. That engagement—the cultivation of disciplinarity—can be institutionalized through sustained scholarly attention to the intellectual history and present circumstances of the field. Appreciating the significance of these two domains requires us to replace Schwab's syntactical and substantive structures of the disciplines.[12] Schwab's schema is more appropriate to the natural and social-behavioral sciences than it is to the humanities and the arts. I replace these two structures with two more appropriate to a discipline associated with the humanities and the arts and focused on the education of the public: curriculum studies.

The first of these disciplinary structures is verticality, by which I denote the intellectual history of the discipline. What ideas formulated in earlier eras inform one's own? Concepts have histories, histories that require acknowledgement and elaboration if the present usage of concepts is to have disciplinary resonance. Fifty years ago Huebner showed that the concept of learning—as it was widely and uncritically used in the field—effaced questions of politics, ethics, and culture, not to mention those associated with student interest and teachers' academic freedom. In a series of essays, Huebner argued that we must employ other concepts in order to advance our understanding of educational experience, among them conversation.[13]

Appreciating Huebner's work on the term as definitive, in *Understanding Curriculum* we tried to stuff the learning genie—and its complementary concept, instruction—back in the bottle by subsuming these within various discursive efforts to understand curriculum. Forty years after Huebner's crucial contribution, and inspired by another scholar of that generation—Robert McClintock—I have argued that "study"[14] is a more appropriate term for understanding educational experience, as it incorporates questions of agency and volition, interest and curiosity as well as interpellation and knowledge acquisition. Indeed, I have argued that "study"—not teaching or learning—is the site of education.

Like the discipline of intellectual history, verticality documents the ideas that constitute the complicated conversation that is curriculum studies. There is, of course, no one disciplinary conversation, no one collective history. Moreover, disciplinary conversation is hardly held in a soundproof room. Events outside the field—national history, cultural shifts, political events, even specific institutional settings—influence what we say to each other and to our colleagues in the schools. So while I define verticality as the intellectual history of the field, such history requires sustained attention to the external circumstances in which those ideas are generated.

The second disciplinary structure the cultivation of which can contribute to the field's intellectual advancement is horizontality: analyses of its present circumstances. Horizontality refers not only to the field's present set of intellectual circumstances—the concepts that structure disciplinary conversation now—but as well the social and political milieu which influences and, all too often, structures this set. Study of the "external" circumstances of the field complement ongoing attention to the field's intellectual history, as its history will configure the field's response to its present political and social circumstances. Horizontality and verticality are, then, intertwined disciplinary structures.

Disciplinarity informs internationalization. Over the past eight years, I studied curriculum studies in five nations by means of self-report and international dialogue. In the first phase of the project I interviewed the participating scholars regarding their intellectual life histories and subjective investments in their field, from which I prepared introductions to each. Interesting and important in itself, this phase of the project—"situating-the-self,"[15] as I summarized it—enables us to appreciate where the "other" is "coming from." In the second phase participating scholars composed essays sketching the intellectual history and present circumstances of curriculum studies in their respective countries, emphasizing their own engagement and research. In the third phase members of an International Panel questioned the participants regarding those essays; I summarized and commented on these exchanges, sharing these with the participants, asking them to critique and comment in the epilogue, the "final word." In the following section I provide a glimpse of what I learned about curriculum studies in Brazil. I conclude by returning considerations of disciplinarity home, to Canada.

Curriculum Studies in Brazil

> Why are we still so disciplinary?[16]
>
> Alice Casimiro Lopes

In South African curriculum studies, the concept of "agency" was inflected racially and politically, echoing a long history of struggle from slavery through Apartheid into the post-Apartheid present.[17] While hardly severed from History, in Brazil the concept (agency) seems more specific to efforts to understand curriculum, what Steve Fuller terms the "internal approach."[18] In "enunciation"—one of the key concepts in curriculum studies in Brazil—the agency of teachers is "always" on the "horizon" as a form of "political reinvention" enacted through "signification." Its discursive status underscores the symbolic sphere in which the curriculum can be reconstructed. As discursive, "agency" in Brazilian curriculum studies implies "translation." These concepts stand separate from, indeed, become subsumed in others, forming a "knowledge network," wherein the "agency of subjects" becomes central, expressed in "decisions" enacted "in the undecidable space of displaced structure."[19]

Agency becomes almost inevitable as the "creative tensionality"[20]—this phrase I import from Ted T. Aoki—demands decisions, an interpretation supported by Elba Siqueira de Sá Barretto's emphasis upon representation as a space of "in-between" the social and personal.[21] For Nilda Alves, agency appears through the "everyday lives of educative networks" which engage emotion and fantasy in creating classroom realities other than those prescribed officially.[22] This notion of "in-between" or "third space"[23] has a prominent position, and not only in curriculum studies in Brazil; it recalls still another key concept: hybridity. In such "in-between" or "third" moments are opportunities for "action" and "creations of new meaning."[24]

In Brazil, curriculum as *enunciation* endorses the unexpected in the classrooms, thereby locating agency at the core of everyday life in schools. Registering her disagreement with studies of the quotidian, however, Macedo reports that she devised the concept of "curriculum as enunciation" to "overcome the binary between formal and lived curriculum." In her conception of enunciation, the agency of teachers is "always" on the "horizon," although not with what Macedo regards as the naïve faith sometimes evident in "everyday life" research.[25] Enunciation emphasizes "signification of the world,"[26] linking discourse and material reality through meaning, a hybridized conception incorporating poststructuralism, hermeneutics, and cultural studies. In Macedo's formulation, "culture" becomes a "signification," an "*enunciation*," a "production, irregular and incomplete, with meaning and value."[27] So understood, culture is no static inheritance to be preserved or contested, as both movements are evident when students and teachers articulate what is hybrid in their "political reinvention" of academic knowledge. In Antonio Carlos Amorim's terms, curriculum becomes disfigured.[28] It is through the "destructured structure" of articulatory practice that the "agency of subjects" is performed. Enunciation recasts curriculum implementation as "translation."[29]

The concept of translation I embed in the concept of *eventfulness*, itself something of a hybrid term that forefronts (in my terms) the immanence of education, not its fragmentation into static binaries: process/product, subject/object, objective/outcome. For Inês Barbosa de Oliveira, the eventfulness of education is associated with the concept of "emergence" (for her, more a post-Marxist term than one associated with complexity theory)[30] that she defines as "emancipating the potential . . . in quotidian practices." Such emancipating practice is articulated by means of a "cosmopolitan rationality" that "transforms absences into presences." The future is thereby built from "plural and concrete possibilities discernible in the present," constructed "through individual and/or collective action."[31] While the terms are linked they are not interchangeable. Indeed, each accents reality distinctively, but each emphasizes movement, action, agency, what I might summarize (after John Dewey) as "subjective and social reconstruction." Curriculum may remain a complicated conversation, but underscored in Brazilian studies of the quotidian are its turbulence, intensity, its immanence.

Emphasizing "absence" and "emergence," Oliveira's conception of the quotidian provides the site of enunciation, translation, and hybridity. The quotidian is the sphere of the singular, denoting (simultaneously) site, time, action, what Oliveira summarizes as "makings/doings." Despite the phraseology, the intellectual debt here is as much to Marxism as it is to phenomenology, as Oliveira implies: "we understand each reality as a product of the singularities and specificities of subjects and circumstances that define them, constituting potential for social emancipation." That potential can be realized pedagogically, Oliveira's asserts, as "apprentices of the quotidian" become "holders of possible formal education contributions to the society's democratization."[32] I am struck by the association of emancipation with particularity, by the tacit acknowledgement that speech—in Macedo's formulation, enunciation—becomes the medium of movement. The singularity of the situation becomes the portal to its reconstruction, to, in Oliveira's terms, the "emergence" of what is "not yet." This is no radical particularism, however, as Oliveira also acknowledges the "common heritage of humanity" as inhering in the singularity of the quotidian.[33]

Differences seem sharper in proximity than from a distance. While present and no doubt magnified within Brazil itself, I am still struck—writing from not only geographical but intellectual distance—by the interrelatedness of these concepts. Despite the differences in intellectual traditions that inform them, despite differences in focus and emphasis, it seems to me that each of the concepts I have identified (among them enunciation, eventfulness, the quotidian) addresses the others. Indeed, each depends upon the others, while differences ensure boundaries (however porous) remain. In my reconstruction of curriculum studies in Brazil, enunciation becomes the "engine" of the everyday, as its articulation of what is and what is not yet marks the movement—the eventfulness—that everyday life portends. And because enunciation is not only the pronouncements of policymakers and administrators, but (especially) the actions of teachers and students (and the pressure of parents), located in the everyday world of the school, inflected by the world outside the school, the vibrant mélange that is social reality becomes restructured—and de-structured as both Macedo and Lopes emphasize—in endlessly hybrid forms. This ongoing composition of curriculum—spatial and, as Amorim emphasizes, durational, in his Deleuzian formulation a plane of sensation—promises no utopia, but it does fracture the hegemony of homogeneity.

Canonicity

> This productive character of cultural contact . . . articulates discontinuous and unequal elements, . . . thereby traversing the globalized structural crisis of our time, in our field, accomplishing the internationalization of curriculum studies.[34]
>
> Alicia De Alba

The internationalization of curriculum studies is work well underway. While there exists organizational infrastructure—the International Association for the Advancement of Curriculum Studies and affiliated national associations, the *International Handbook of Curriculum Research*[35]—intellectual infrastructure can be improved in many nations. Each nationally distinctive field could profit from the establishment of a canon, a coherent if always shifting sense of that field's intellectual history and present circumstances that, in de Alba's fine phrasing, "articulates discontinuous and unequal elements." Reparation requires remembering the past and reconstructing the present. That is the calling of canon formation.

In the context of Canadian curriculum studies—the field in which I now work—the proposal to construct a canon is, I submit, a *progressive* move. In Canada there is ongoing concern over cultural content, initially over British, now U.S., imports. Contesting U.S. intellectual hegemony was the "Canadianization" movement,[36] contesting U.S. professors' presence in Canadian universities (especially in administrative positions) and their privileging—specifically in the social sciences and humanities—of U.S. research in their course offerings. Persisting preoccupations with Canadian identity are then unsurprising, given these and continuing issues concerning the indigenous peoples, the "two solitudes," and the new immigrants. Add to these specifically Canadian issues more general cultural concerns accompanying advanced capitalism and information technology—epitomized, perhaps, in the work of George Grant[37]—and curriculum studies in Canada risks a self-dispersing presentism, preoccupied as the field is with efforts at reparation of past injustice, efforts that are not yet adequately incorporated into disciplinary history.[38] Installing a canon for Canadian curriculum studies[39] represents, then, ongoing reconstruction of the intellectual history and present circumstances of the field.

Speaking of their own field—area studies generally, Japanese studies specifically—Masao Miyoshi and D.H. Harootunian acknowledge that disciplinary mappings, depicting the chronologies of discourses, are especially "difficult to compile at a moment like ours where the central authority for evaluation has largely vanished from the arena of scholarship."[40] Many must welcome this absence, suggesting, perhaps, that it leaves the field unhampered, able to develop freely and creatively. "And yet," Miyoshi and Harootunian continue, "a total absence of attempts to sort out, interrelate, and map out ideas and analyses could result in a loss of critical scholarship, coherent reference, and articulate knowledge."[41] To put the matter more bluntly than they: without disciplinary history there is no discipline. Even jazz[42]—the quintessential musical instance of freedom, originality, and creativity—proceeds within specific musical histories, structural forms, and social relations, recalling the past as it invites the future into the present.

Who among us would disagree that the works of George Tomkins, Ted Aoki, and Cynthia Chambers are among the "basics" of Canadian curriculum studies knowledge? To the put matter conversely, who can claim expertise in curriculum studies without knowing these crucial figures and their work? Establishing a Canadian canon is the labor of each of us, working independently, emphasizing different elements. It could also be the labor the Canadian Association for Curriculum Studies. A committee could establish a more extensive annotated bibliography of key works. These could be linked on the association website with associated literature, enabling students of the field to ascertain what conversation has proceeded, where it is now, what could—should—be said next. We can think of this disciplinary architecture as one exemplary form of curriculum design.[43]

Despite our applied field's long-standing skepticism toward disciplinarity, despite the concept's conservative connotations, the cultivation of curriculum studies' disciplinarity—its structures of verticality and horizontality—is progressive labor compelled by present circumstances. It is labor each of us—as individual disciplinary specialists—is obligated to undertake. Such individual labor will be given focus and intensity by a collective canon project, a project appropriately undertaken institutionally—by our respective professional and scholarly associations—and by ourselves, as individuals and unaffiliated groups, not only where we work but worldwide. Quickly it becomes clear that in our time disciplinarity and internationalization proceed hand-in-hand.

Notes

1 See Pinar 2007.
2 See Pinar 2011.
3 Yoshimoto 2002, 369.

4 Discussing the George W. Bush Administration, Agamben (2005, 2, emphasis added) referenced "modern totalitarianism" as the

> establishment, by means of the state of exception, of a legal civil war that allows for the physical elimination not only of political adversaries but of entire categories of citizens who for some reason cannot be integrated into the political system. Since, then, the voluntary creation of a permanent state of emergency (though perhaps not declared in the technical sense) has become one of the essential practices of contemporary states, including so-called democratic ones.

Obviously the meanings differ, but they also overlap, as U.S. "school reform" has meant an ongoing assault on teachers, education professors, and now, indirectly, on students who are said to be lacking "grit." See *Economist* 2013, January 19–25, 81.

5 For one recent exemplary example, see Magrini 2014.

6 This is Foucault's project of problematization, as Colin Koopman (2013, 48) makes clear: "In sum, problematization functions to open up our problems in their full contingency and complexity in a way that makes them available for critical investigation." He emphasizes that "Foucaultian problematization specifically invites reconstruction" (2013, 21). Understanding the emergency of the moment is prerequisite to addressing it. Without theory there can be no practice.

7 With this term I am referencing the "complicated conversation" that is an academic discipline, not contemporary forms of ideological control, as theorized in Alice Casimiro Lopes (in Pinar 2011a, 178) or in Hardt and Negri (2000, 23):

> The society of control might thus be characterized by an intensification and generalization of the normalizing apparatuses of disciplinarity that internally animate our common and daily practices, but in contrast to discipline, this control extends well outside the structured sites of social institutions through flexible and fluctuating networks.

Obviously devotion to disciplinarity advancement could lead to "disciplinarity" in this negative and panoramic political sense, but instead I am here construing the uncritical embrace of student "interest" as an instance of commodification of intellectual labor that, like "commodity fetishism," effaces the labor that produced it. Student interest should be reciprocally related to the intellectual advancement of the academic discipline.

8 Chow (2002b, 112, 113) cautions

> those who see in cultural studies the critical potential for examining and transforming institutionalized intellectual disciplinarity itself, the necessity to mobilize against such foreclosures of that potential by many enthusiastic supports of 'curriculum-diversification' cannot be sufficiently emphasized. Otherwise, in the name of precisely sponsoring the 'marginal,' the study of non-Western cultures would simply contribute toward a new, or renewed, Orientalism.

9 Pinar et al. 1995, 63–65.

10 Pinar et al. 1995, 32, 210, 219.

11 Apple 2006, 204.

12 See Pinar et al. 1995, 161

13 See Huebner 1999.

14 See chapter 1, this volume.

15 Pinar 2010, 231.

16 Quoted in Pinar 2011a, 125.

17 Pinar 2010, 12.
18 Fuller (1993, 126) defines "the *internal* approach," as "devoted to charting the growth of knowledge in terms of the extension of rational methods to an ever-larger domain of objects," and in contrast to "the *external* approach, devoted to charting the adaptability of knowledge to science's ever-changing social arrangements."
19 Macedo, quoted in Pinar 2011a 182–184, 143–145.
20 Aoki 2005 (1991), 383. Alan Block (2010, 523) agrees: "I like to think of tension as a potentially generative state."
21 Quoted in Pinar 2011a.
22 Quoted in Pinar 2011a, 46, 48.
23 See Wang 2004.
24 See Pinar 2011a, 209–212.
25 Quoted in Pinar 2011a, 202–203.
26 See Lopes in Pinar 2011a, 11, 120, 126, 179.
27 Quoted in Pinar 2011a, 182.
28 See Pinar 2011a, 58.
29 See Pinar 2011a, 205.
30 See Trueit 2012.
31 Quoted in Pinar 2011a, 161–163
32 Quoted passages from Pinar 2011a, 206.
33 Ibid.
34 Quoted in Pinar 2011b, 66–67.
35 Pinar 2014.
36 See Cormier 2004.
37 See chapter 5, this volume.
38 See Ng-A-Fook and Rottman 2012.
39 I start with a Group of Three: George Tomkins, Ted Aoki, and Cynthia Chambers. Tomkins (2008) provides a history from which we can work through the past. While reissued, the book is dated—everyone's work is of course—and it requires supplementation and amplification. In his cosmopolitanism, his devotion to teaching and teachers, Aoki's work (see Pinar and Irwin 2005) reverberates throughout the contemporary Canadian field. It also provides a focused but panoramic portrait of the intellectual histories—especially those associated with phenomenology and post-structuralism—that inform much of the present intellectual scene. Cynthia Chambers (2003, 2004, 2008) configures the field through her comprehensive surveys of it, emphasizing indigenous knowledge, the ascendant domain of scholarship in the contemporary field (see, for instance, Ng-A-Fook and Rottman 2012).
40 Miyoshi and Harootunian 2002, 8.
41 2002, 9.
42 See Aoki 2005 (1990).
43 See Grimmett and Halvorson 2010.

Bibliography

Agamben, Giorgio. 2005. *State of Exception*. [Trans. Kevin Attell.] Chicago: University of Chicago Press.

Aoki, Ted. 2005 (1990). Sonare and Videre: A Story, Three Echoes and a Lingering Note. In *Curriculum in a New Key: The Collected Works of Ted T. Aoki*, edited by William F. Pinar and Rita L. Irwin (367–376). Mahwah, NJ: Lawrence Erlbaum.

Apple, Michael W. 2006. Afterword. In *Ideology, Curriculum, and the New Sociology of Education*, edited by Lois Weis, Cameron McCarthy, and Greg Dimitriadis (203–217). New York: Routledge.

Axelrod, Charles David. 1979. *Studies in Intellectual Breakthrough*. Amherst: University of Massachusetts Press.

Baszile, Denise Taliaferro. 2006. A Fire Inside: A Critical Meditation on the Importance of Freedom Dreams. *JCT* 22 (3), 7–25.

Block, Alan A. 2004. *Talmud, Curriculum, and the Practical: Joseph Schwab and the Rabbis*. New York: Peter Lang.

Block, Alan A. 2010. And They'll Say That It's a Movement. In *Curriculum Studies Handbook: The Next Moment*, edited by Erik Malewski (523–527). New York: Routledge.

Chambers, Cynthia. 2003. "As Canadian as Possible Under the Circumstances": A View of Contemporary Curriculum Discourses in Canada. In *International Handbook of Curriculum Research,* edited by William F. Pinar (221–252). Mahwah, NJ: Lawrence Erlbaum.

Chambers, Cynthia. 2004. Research that Matters: Finding a Path with Heart. *Journal of the Canadian Association for Curriculum Studies* 2 (1), 1–19.

Chambers, Cynthia. 2008. Where Are We? Finding Common Ground in a Curriculum of Place. *Journal of the Canadian Association for Curriculum Studies* 6 (2), 113–128.

Chow, Rey. 2002. Theory, Area Studies, Cultural Studies: Issues of Pedagogy in Multiculturalism. In *Learning Places: The Afterlives of Area Studies*, edited by Masao Miyoshi and D.H. Harootunian (103–118). Durham, NC: Duke University Press.

Clarke, Penney. 2011. *New Possibilities for the Past: Shaping History Education in Canada*. Vancouver: University of British Columbia Press.

Cormier, Jeffrey. 2004. *The Canadianization Movement: Emergence, Survival, and Success*. Toronto: University of Toronto Press.

Fuller, Steve. 1993. Disciplinary Boundaries and the Rhetoric of the Social Sciences. In *Knowledges: Historical and Critical Studies in Disciplinarity*, edited by Ellen Messer-Davidow, David R. Shumway, and David J. Sylvan (125–149). Charlottesville: University Press of Virginia.

Grimmett, Peter P. and Halvorson, Mark. 2010. From Understanding Curriculum to Creating Curriculum: The Case for the Co-Evolution of Re-Conceptualized Design with Re-Conceptualized Curriculum. *Curriculum Inquiry* 40 (2), 241–262.

Hardt, Michael and Negri, Antonio. 2000. *Empire*. Cambridge, MA: Harvard University Press.

Huebner, Dwayne E. 1999. *The Lure of the Transcendent*. Mahwah, NJ: Lawrence Erlbaum.

Koopman, Colin. 2013. *Genealogy as Critique: Foucault and the Problems of Modernity*. Bloomington: Indiana University Press.

Magrini, James M. 2014. *Social Efficiency and Instrumentalism in Education. Critical Essays in Ontology, Phenomenology, and Philosophical Hermeneutics*. New York: Routledge.

Miyoshi, Masao and Harootunian, D.H. eds. 2002. *Learning Places: The Afterlives of Area Studies*. Durham, NC: Duke University Press.

Ng-A-Fook, Nicholas. 2007, February 19. Personal communication.

Ng-A-Fook, Nicholas and Rottmann, Jennifer. eds. 2012. *Reconsidering Canadian Curriculum Studies: An Uncommon Countenance*. New York: Palgrave Macmillan.

Pinar, William F. ed. 2010. *Curriculum Studies in South Africa*. New York: Palgrave Macmillan.

Pinar, William F. ed. 2011a. *Curriculum Studies in Brazil*. New York: Palgrave Macmillan.

Pinar, William F. ed. 2011b. *Curriculum Studies in Mexico*. New York: Palgrave Macmillan.

Pinar, William F. ed. 2014. *International Handbook of Curriculum Research*. 2nd edition. New York: Routledge.

Pinar, William F. and Irwin, Rita L. eds. 2005. *Curriculum in a New Key: The Collected Works of Ted T. Aoki*. Mahwah, NJ: Lawrence Erlbaum.

Pinar, William F., Reynolds, William M., Slattery, Patrick, and Taubman, Peter M. 1995. *Understanding Curriculum*. New York: Peter Lang.

Seixas, Peter. ed. 2004. *Theorizing Historical Consciousness*. Toronto: University of Toronto Press.
Stanley, Darren and Kelly Young. eds. 2011. *Contemporary Studies in Canadian Curriculum: Principles, Portraits and Practices*. Calgary, Alberta, Canada: Detselig.
Tomkins, George S. 2008 (1986). *A Common Countenance: Stability and Change in the Canadian Curriculum*. Vancouver, Canada: Pacific Educational Press.
Trueit, Donna. ed. 2012. *Pragmatism, Postmodernism, Complexity Theory: The Fascinating Imaginative Realm of William E. Doll, Jr*. New York: Routledge.
Yoshimoto, Mitsuhiro. 2002. Questions of Japanese Cinema: Disciplinary Boundaries and the Invention of the Scholarly Object. In *Learning Places: The Afterlives of Area Studies*, edited by Masao Miyoshi and D.H. Harootunian (368–401). Durham, NC: Duke University Press.
Wang, Hongyu. 2004. *The Call from the Stranger on a Journey Home: Curriculum in a Third Space*. New York: Peter Lang.

CHAPTER 4

NATIONALISM

Commentary

Juxtaposing a 1974 publication with a 2001 one, I chart a shift in how nation, nationalism, and nationality are construed in the two. In the 1974 publication—a collection of papers presented at a conference at the Ontario Institute for Studies in Education—nationalism is treated skeptically, contextualized historically, and theorized as a portal to internationalism. In the 2001 essay—published prominently in the *Canadian Journal of Education*—nationalism is asserted uncritically, if as a negation of nationalism in the United States. In this essay Canadians are defined as not-Americans. What happens to self-critique and self-affirmation when identity is constructed through negation?

Reference

Pinar, William F. 2011. Nationalism, Anti-Americanism, Canadian Identity. In *Curriculum in Today's World: Configuring Knowledge, Identities, Work and Politics,* edited by Lyn Yates and Madeleine Grumet (31–43). London: Routledge.

> Yet there is much to be said for approaching the question of Canada's identity from the outside.
>
> Jill Conway[1]

"If anything offers the possibility for community and commonality in this era of multiplicity and difference," Cynthia Chambers suggests, "it is the land that we share."[2] The land—"deeply ingrained in Canada's national psyche"[3]—to which Chambers is referring is Canada, not North America generally, and the "we" she invokes references Canadians, not North Americans generally. It is a plural pronoun complicated, as Chambers is keenly aware, by Canadian history, specifically its status as a colony displacing indigenous peoples: the First Nations, Métis, and Inuit. Displacement characterizes the genesis of all nations comprising North America.[4] Conway concludes[5] the sentence quoted above as rationalizing her study of Canadian identity as one instance of the general problem of colonial cultures.[6]

Conway judges one of the "worst" consequences of European colonization as psychic.[7] Indeed, as Fanon[8] knew, colonial cultures are not only political and historical facts, they are psychic facts, among them (Conway underlines) the consequences of severance from the originary culture, in Canada's case three originary cultures: indigenous, French, and British. Such separation constitutes, she suggests, a psychic loss that not only deprives colonial (and colonized) peoples of "creativity on their own terms" but of identity itself, about which they are left "confused" and "uncertain."[9] John Ralston Saul believes Canada remains "emotionally and existentially hampered by its colonial insecurity."[10] Do "insecurity" and "confusion" and "uncertainty" characterize Canadian identity? Has proximity to the United States provided occasions to contradict these conditions, intensifying an Anglophone Canadian nationalism defined by negation?[11]

Despite differences in its emphases—Canadian peacekeeping vs. American militarism, Canadian multiculturalism-as-mosaic vs. the American melting pot[12]—does the depiction of Canada in Canadian curriculum studies also convey nationalism by implying "exceptionalism"?[13] If, like Americans, Canadians also emphasize their difference from others, especially differences from its neighbor to the South, does the Canadian identity become overdetermined by what it is not? By emphasizing identity by negation, does Canadian identity vitiate self-critical encounter? By rereading two publications separated by almost thirty years[14] I suggest initial answers to these questions.

1974

> Canada has not escaped some of the excesses of nationalism.
>
> Geoffrey Milburn and John Herbert[15]

In 1974 the Ontario Institute for Studies in Education (OISE) published a collection of essays entitled *National Consciousness and the Curriculum: The Canadian Case*. In their introduction, Milburn and Herbert cite two developments during the preceding decade that have "significantly" altered Canadian public opinion regarding issues of Canadian culture.[16] The first is a greater awareness of what they call the Canadian habit of "dependency"; the second is a "greater appreciation of the uniqueness of the Canadian experience."[17] That the second follows from the first is evident in the Milburn and Herbert assertion[18] that U.S. "domination" of Canada has been "much more extensive" than British or French; it pervades "every aspect" of Canadian life.[19] That view—that Canada is dominated[20] by the United States—becomes the ground against which the figure of mid-twentieth-century Anglophone Canadian nationalism emerges.

This element of Anglophone Canadian nationalism is evident in Milburn and Herbert's assertion that "separation" from the American "colossus" is what drives those seeking a Canadian "identity."[21] So conceived, Canadian identity is not derived from internal features but, rather, becomes a tactic to create distance through difference from the "colossus." Milburn and Herbert were not alone in acknowledging this motive. Canadian political scientist Peter Regenstreif proclaimed: "Canada was founded first and foremost as an essentially defensive reaction—primarily against the United States."[22] What are the consequences of constructing an identity as "defensive reaction"?

Internally Canadian identity bifurcates into French and British, that duality fractured further by the presence of the First Nations, other indigenous peoples, and the arrival of new immigrants.[23] As Philip Resnick suggests, "Canada is made up of three founding peoples, not two."[24] Canadian identity is, then, not "single,"[25] as the country is a "multination state."[26] In addition to multiculturalism, regionalism prevails,[27] despite Tomkins' complaint that in the curriculum the "great regional and cultural diversity" of Canada has been "ignored."[28] Has alterity—as Nature or culture or region or the "American colossus"—functioned as a series of constitutive exteriors, resulting in the designation of "survival"[29] as the central and ongoing national thematic?[30]

The conflation of physical[31] with political and cultural survival is evident in the Milburn and Herbert observation that school textbooks in Québec have "preached" the doctrine of "*survivance*."[32] In Québec, this "siege mentality"[33] has meant an ongoing struggle for cultural survival, but the resistance (the so-called "Quiet Revolution") it expressed was focused more on Anglophone Canada than it was on the United States. Indeed, Québec nationalism included "openness" to—on occasion "admiration" of—the United States.[34] With their nationalism structured by anti-Americanism, Anglophone Canadians were "unprepared for a Québec nationalism which was not based on a similar set of rejections."[35] Indeed, efforts to construct a pan-Canadian identity, Kymlicka concludes, have failed among the Québécois.[36]

Survival is prominent in Margaret Atwood's controversial[37] thematic guide to Canadian literature for schools, entitled *Survival*.[38] In Atwood's analysis of North American writing, Lipset notes, she suggests that the symbol for the United States is "the Frontier," connoting "a place that is *new*, where the old order can be discarded."[39] The central image for Canada, Atwood concludes, is "Survival, *la survivance*, hanging on, staying alive."[40] For Tomkins, the term has "clear negative connotations" in that "survival" implies resistance to "hostile" or "alien forces."[41] Those include Nature[42] and the United States. Vickers[43] acknowledges that for many the survival of Canada depends on accenting differences from the United States.

Curriculum reform followed Hodgetts'[44] landmark *What Culture? What Heritage?* As Tomkins[45] notes, this widely read report on the state of civic education concluded that Canadian history was taught in narrow even pedantic ways that failed to ignite student interest. Never mind, as Resnick[46] asserts, that "Canadian history is pretty dull stuff . . . when compared to that of countries like the United States or France with revolution in their blood." Hodgetts found that (in Tomkins' words) "many pupils expressed an active dislike for Canadian studies, and more than a few indicated a preference for American history, about which they often claimed to be more knowledgeable."[47] (Hodgetts[48] blamed the dullness of Canadian history not only on Canadian schoolteachers, but on their university professors as well.) Hodgetts' study marked the "the birth of the formal Canadian Studies movement,"[49] institutionalized in March 1970 by the establishment of the Canada Studies Foundation, dedicated to improving the quality of Canadian studies at the elementary and secondary school levels.

At one point—two decades ago[50]—Canadian Studies were judged as having failed to become important, presumably, Vickers suggested, because the study of "things Canadian" was imprinted with its founders' nationalism that has "seriously constrained" subsequent generations of scholars in theorizing Canadian experience "as we actually live it."[51] In her early 1990s assessment, Jill Vickers[52] judged Canadian Studies to be a "largely incoherent" field held together only by the legacies of its founding fathers' nationalism and anti-Americanism.

The implication that Canada is defined as much by its differences from the United States as it is by its own internal distinctiveness[53] also surfaces in a reflection Tomkins[54] makes regarding the "Americanization" of the Canadian curriculum. On this occasion he dates "Americanization" to the mid-1950s, when, he reports, it displaced the old "imperial curriculum" in Anglophone Canada. His point is that Americanization provoked the "demand for more Canadian content."[55] The associated public school curriculum development project, Tomkins[56] emphasizes, was "in no sense" like the U.S. curriculum reform. In contrast, Canada-centered curriculum reform was to be "teacher-based": indeed, Tomkins reassured his readers that "from the beginning, the 'top-down' or 'teacher-proof' approach to curriculum reform that has characterized so much of the American efforts of the 1960s has been rejected."[57] Once again Canadian distinctiveness is defined as difference from the United States.

"Canadian national consciousness"[58]—summarizing what Regenstreif[59] saw as "evidence of intensifying Canadian nationalism"—was reflected,[60] in part, by a "growing number" of Canadian teachers becoming concerned about the teaching of Canadian Studies in the nation's schools.[61] Richler[62] acknowledges "1970" as dating "a new sense of self-awareness in Canada," when "the spirit of nationalism was rampaging over the land." Canadian nationalism, he acknowledges, has "its murky underside, anti-Americanism," which he judges as "sometimes justified."[63] Starting from the American Revolution, anti-Americanism appears to ebb periodically, but as refracted through the 1974 collection, it appears as not only a constant but animating force and not only in the Canadian Studies movement.

While the 1974 OISE publication never confronts how anti-Americanism affects Canada's capacity for self-critique and self-understanding, it does problematize nationalism by scrutinizing historical, political, cultural (including gendered) elements. I wonder how contributors to that OISE publication would judge another publication that appears almost 30 years later, wherein such problematization is nowhere in evidence, wherein Canada nationalism is, simply, asserted. To that publication I turn next.

2001

> While Canadians can't seem to agree on what they are, they have no trouble at all agreeing on what they're not.
>
> Dennis Sumara, Brent Davis, and Linda Laidlaw[64]

The source for the distinctions Sumara, Davis, and Laidlaw[65] draw between Canada and the United States turns out to be academic meetings; they report finding themselves "taken aback" by the "virulent" exchanges they have witnessed at U.S. meetings. The modest size of this data set was not discouraging. To account for the differences they noticed between Canadian and U.S. conferences, Sumara, Davis, and Laidlaw[66] point to how Canadian cultural myths are expressed in Canadian curriculum studies. Disclaiming any essentializing or reifying intentions, they do not posit a "quintessential" Canadian identity.[67] While positing such an identity is politically impossible in contemporary Canada, historically Great Britain was the marker of exactly the "quintessential" identity of Anglophone Canada; in Québec, nationalists accented French language and culture as the "quintessential markers" of identity.[68]

While theory is not "determined" by its national setting, it is, presumably, "dependent,"[69] and Sumara, Davis, and Laidlaw propose the idea of "ecological postmodernism"[70] to depict this dependency.[71] Such a phrase points to the ways "humans" tend to "adapt" to new situations and "reinterpret" the past.[72] Apparently associated with a Deweyan[73] conception of reconstruction,[74] more so than with postmodern celebrations of difference, uncertainty, and unintelligibility,[75] this conception turns out to be not only not American but, indeed, anti-American. Sumara, Davis, and Laidlaw assert that Canadians are "not overbearing . . . totalizing . . . monolithic . . . unified . . . static": Canadians are "not Americans."[76] In contrast to America's "inward-looking nationalism" and "outward-looking imperialism," Sumara, Davis, and Laidlaw continue, Canada is characterized by "peace-keeping, not policing."[77]

Although American influences were, we are told, "ever-present" in the classroom[78] and on school library shelves,[79] evidently they never took hold, as the two countries are presented as opposites. Canada was constructed not through violent revolution and the genocide of indigenous peoples but through "conflict, co-operation, and conciliation."[80] Because the Canadian nation was formed by "stitching together" various cultural differences, curriculum studies scholars in Canada appreciate that "meanings" and "identities" are not "discovered," nor can they be "fully represented."[81] Would nationalists in Québec and the First Nations agree?

Unlike the Americans, Sumara, Davis and Laidlaw[82] continue, Canadians are circumspect in their representation of identity. In contrast to the monolithic American identity, they explain, Canadian identity is "not unified," but "shifts."[83] Consequently, curriculum studies in Canada can be characterized as a form of "ecological postmodernism,"[84] a phrase that declines any dissociation between the biological and the phenomenological. Rejecting grand narratives,[85] the Canadian "sensibility"[86] expresses "deep commitments" to the layering of history, the inability of language to represent experience, and the complexity of translation. Sumara, Davis, and Laidlaw[87] remind us that understanding curriculum is "always rooted" in the local. Among the four "challenges" Cynthia Chambers[88] sets for Canadian curriculum theorists is to "write from this place" and "write in a language of our own," devising "interpretive tools that arise from and fit for this place."[89] That implies, as Chambers[90] reminds, attention to "borders," but not only what lies beyond them, but what they divide within, e.g. the "local."

Conclusion

> [T]his [current] wave of Canadian nationalism is greater than at any time since the 1960s.
>
> Cynthia Chambers[91]

This juxtaposition of "then and now"[92] reveals one of those "shifts" Sumara, Davis and Laidlaw reference. In the 1974 collection, there is a strong self-consciousness of nationalism's problematic character, its dissonance with Canadian cosmopolitan ideals, prominently among them the embrace of difference.[93] Nationalism, Herbert and Milburn concluded, is a "fuzzy, unclear, and sometimes dangerous concept."[94] Despite this distrust of nationalism, there was "sympathy" for the construction of a Canadian "identity," provided that identity is one face of a coin the other side of which is "world community."[95] For Herbert and Milburn, the "thirst" for Canadian identity and the "desire" for "international understanding" (based on "equality" and "interdependence") must be balanced.[96] In these concepts—"thirst" and "desire"—is foreshadowed Tomkins' acknowledgement of the "psychic significance"[97] of curriculum questions. That psychic significance becomes, for Herbert and Milburn, focused on self-knowledge, on using national consciousness as a "liberating force."[98] In this conception, the national becomes the portal to the international. Physical survival portends social sensitivity, an attunement to place that Chambers elaborates in indigenous terms.[99]

In the 2001 essay Canadian nationalism is no longer problematic, no longer a provocation to self-knowledge or a portal to internationalism.[100] Its anti-Americanism is not problematized but simply performed. "Self-doubt"—what Resnick[101] suggests is the "dominant motif in Canadian political culture"—is nowhere in evidence. Indeed, the essay smacks of the "self-boosterism and proselytism" that Resnick[102] associates with the United States. Rather than Canadian identity defined by internal difference—the originary Indigenous and Francophone populations juxtaposed with British and subsequent immigrants, especially from East and South Asia—it is defined by what Canadians are not: Americans. Such identity-by-negation recalls Regenstreif's characterization of Canada as a "defensive reaction."[103] "Instead of liberty, individualism, achievement, and optimism," he told the OISE conference, "Canada institutionalized authority, order, ascription, and a certain pessimism."[104] Given the substitution of self-accolades for self-knowledge in the 2001 statement, perhaps Conway's observation holds true then and now: "The anti-American myth operates to divert the critical gaze firmly to the south, leaving starling unanimity in a society that protests with correctness that in other respects it is not conformist."[105]

After chronicling a series of issues on which Canadians assume they have a better record than the United States (including the livability of cities and the environmental policies of the provinces/states), Kymlicka finds "striking" how quickly Canadians "overlook any such embarrassing facts that contradict their preferred self-image."[106] That "Canadians differ profoundly from Americans"[107] need not be summarized by stereotypes: that in itself contradicts Canadian claims for appreciating diversity. Canada is an ongoing fact created in history and still under construction culturally and politically. In his claim that Canadians resemble Europeans more than they do Americans, Resnick[108] may underestimate the growing significance of the other continents—especially Asia—to Canadian society (both in terms of immigrants and economically and politically), but in historical terms his point stands.[109]

"A new model of nationalism for the twenty-first century," Resnick[110] proposes, "may yet turn out to be a version of 'nationalism lite'." Reminiscent of Hodgetts'[111] "low-key patriotism," this playful phrase performs what it depicts, a nationalism that does not take itself entirely seriously. It is, however, also serious, as Resnick[112] specifies that "such nationalism seeks to be open to other cultures and nations, to a level of political and economic integration beyond the nation-state, to a global/cosmopolitan dimension of identity." Such a nationalism would then seem to be an internationalism as well.

Despite resemblances with the United States, Canada seems to me in no danger of disappearing. In *Lament for a Nation,* George Grant[113] predicted that Canada would become totally immersed in the political realities of continental economic integration, a prediction many worried would be confirmed by the implementation of Free Trade. In Vickers'[114] judgment, that fear was contradicted by the ongoing "vitality" of both French- and English-Canadian cultures, as well as the "dynamic movements" of immigrant cultures and the "revival" of the cultures and languages of the First Nations. Lipset[115] points to high, not popular, culture, finding that

> the vitality of the creative arts north of the border is striking. The country is producing world-class novelists, playwrights, dancers, painters, and other artists in numbers never before witnessed. Canadian complaints about being ignored by American reviewers no longer hold; they now pay considerable attention to the Canadian cultural scene.

American attention may not always be welcomed, especially if it becomes aggravated with envy, of oil reserves for instance. But sensible skepticism—wariness of sleeping with an "unruly elephant"[116]—can deteriorate into paranoia unless linked to facts. Recall George Grant's[117] invocation of Canadian "self-restraint" as prerequisite to the "good life" (in contrast, he thought, to the American "emancipation of the passions"). That restraint might well extend to expansive, if reductive, summaries of national difference.

Pride in country seems an appropriate state of mind, especially when it does not mask internal problems but prompts efforts to solve them. Grant's embrace of Canadian nationalism, he insisted, was not "anti-American," but "simply a lack of Americanism."[118] Such patriotism—certainly I have expressed my own[119]—is what Saul[120] characterizes as "the positive form of nationalism," e.g. "self-confidence and openness and to a concept of the public good." In contrast is "negative nationalism," fueled by fear and anger and a desperate conviction that one nation's rights exist by comparison with those of another nation."[121] Such bifurcation obliterates the particularity patriotism aspires to preserve.

For this American student of Canada, the point is to study not only differences and similarities between the two nations, but, as Aoki appreciated, to "dwell in tensionality in the realm of the between, in the tensionality of differences."[122] As that great Canadian curriculum theorist sagely observed, the very concept of "identity" risks "reducing our life reality to an abstracted totality of its own, pretending to wholeness."[123] That pretense obscures the tensioned lived landscape of difference *and* similarity, the "common ground"[124] that is Canada.

Notes

1 1974, 71.
2 1999, 147.
3 White 2007, 11.
4 Genocide is the more accurate term for the fate of the First Nations: in what is now the United States, the population fell from 5 million to 250,000 by the late nineteenth century (Saul 2005, 29). Lipset (1990, 176) acknowledges that "the record is clear that the native peoples have been better able to survive in Canada than in the United States" (see, too, Ng-A-Fook 2007). Carr and Lund (2007, 1) take a harsher view, alleging that "Canada has long been a welcome home to the KKK and numerous

other hate groups"; they juxtapose "slavery" with the "colonialism [sic] of First Nations and other peoples." The 1876 *Indian Act*, restated in 1920 by Duncan Campbell Scott, Superintendent of Indian Affairs, was "to continue until there is not a single Indian in Canada that has not been absorbed into the body politic and there is no Indian question and no Indian Department" (Chambers 2006b, 6). Forced assimilation was to be accomplished, in part, by removing "aboriginal children from their families and communities and [sending them] to church-run residential schools to remove their native languages and cultures" (Carson 2005, 7).

5 See 1974, 71.

6 The ironic echo of this epigraph is that I—an American working in Canada—am in this instance the "alienated outsider" (Chambers 1999, 139). That is both liability and opportunity. (In acting on the latter no doubt I reveal the former.) If, as Lipset (1990, xiii) suggests, that "knowledge of Canada or the United States is the best way to gain insight into the other North American country," then every American (not just those working in Canada) is well-advised to study Canada. I suspect there will be Canadians who will judge my study as presumptuous if not impertinent. For a history of efforts to exclude Americans from academic (especially administrative) posts in Canadian universities see Cormier (2004). The Canadianization movement did increase the numbers of Canadians working in Canadian universities (2004, 193); as well it influenced federal immigration policy (2004, 159, 170, 187–188).

7 1974, 72.

8 1967; see chapter 15.

9 1974, 72.

10 2005, 32.

11 Anglophone Canadian nationalism, Kymlicka (see 2003, 377) notes, was also a reaction against Québec separatism, which was not necessarily anti-American. Nor did Québec nationalism share Anglophone Canada's reverence for the land (White 2007, 13). While early Québec was, like its British counterpart, counter-revolutionary, it was settled before the French Revolution and (given its conservative clerical cast: Tomkins 1981, 158) was skeptical of it. But its mid-twentieth-century nationalism did not necessarily involve anti-Americanism (Vickers 1994, 361). Not every nationalism can be decoded as compensatory, aggravated by international threat and devoted to the suppression of internal difference. In that same 1974 OISE collection, Max van Manen (1974, 13) points out that "for a colonized people, such as the natives of Angola, nationalism may hold the promise of decentralization of power (away from the imperial country), local autonomy, and self-determination." Kanu (2003, 68, 76) also references African "anti-colonial nationalism." Of course, anti-colonial nationalism has itself hardly always been utopic; African genocides and ongoing corruption cannot be attributed entirely to "neocolonialism" (Kanu 2003, 76; see Sekyi-Out 1996).

12 While not mistaken, the "mosaic/melting pot" distinction is, Kymlicka suggests, overdrawn. He points out that while the United States does not endorse multiculturalism at the federal level, lower levels of government, such as states or cities, often do. "If we look at state-level policies regarding the education curriculum, for example, or city-level policies regarding policing or hospitals," he (2003, 371) points out, "we shall find that they are often indistinguishable from the way provinces and cities in Canada deal with issues of immigrant ethnocultural diversity." Lipset (1990, 218) believes that "particularistic demands by minorities have led to increased institutionalization of multiculturalism on both sides of the border." Within Canada, he reports, "a backlash against the mosaic concept is occurring" (1990, 187) and immigrant groups often doubt the sincerity of Canada's commitment to multiculturalism, which they deride as rhetorical (Kymlicka 2003, 377). While its multiculturalism may not be distinctive from the United States and other Western democracies, Canada is the only country to have constitutionalized its commitment in section 27 of the Canadian Constitution (Kymlicka 2003, 375).

13 If, like the United States, Canada imagines itself as exceptional (as, around landscape, it did before the 1960s: O'Brian and White 2007, 5), that in itself would not be exceptional. There are, for example, multiple exceptionalisms, including Japanese (Yoshimoto 2002, 374), South African (Muller 2000, 3), and Jewish (Gollaher 2000, 9, 31). The landscape narrative Canadian artists (most conspicuously the Group of Seven: see note 31) expressed was not uniquely Canadian, as John White (2007, 26–27) points out; it was shared with the artists working in the United States and Europe. While Canadian claims to exceptionality due to its affirmation of diversity may be overstated, Kymlicka (2003, 375) allows that Canada's constitutional protection of diversity (see note 12) points to diversity's emphasis within national narratives (including Québec but excluding the First Nations, who continue to insist on ethnic, not civic, criteria for inclusion). While the United States has granted self-government treaty rights to American Indians and regional autonomy and language rights to Puerto Rico while making multicultural accommodations to immigrant groups, Kymlicka points out that these are "peripheral" to American self-perception; they are not considered as "defining" features of the American identity or its national character (2003, 375).

14 While I use years as subheadings, I realize that these two publications are by no means representative of Canadian curriculum studies during those years. They do, however, provide glimpses of how specific Canadian curriculum studies scholars reconstructed nationalism "then" and "now." The inflated role "there" (the United States) plays in the construction of "here" (Canada) seems to have only intensified during the period, as evidenced by references to other (and not only curriculum) scholarship. Before the forefronting of the American "colossus," it had been Great Britain and the Commonwealth that constituted the "there" that blurred the singularity of the "here" (see Chambers 1999, 139). Cavell (1994, 76–77) reminds that Canadian culture is often depicted as a function of place, alternately defined as "landscape," "geography," "archipelago," or "North" (a "Canadian analogy to the idea of West" in the United States: O'Brian and White 2007, 3). This assumption (one shared by Cynthia Chambers: see 2006b, 5), Cavell points out, follows from Northrop Frye's "Conclusion" to the first edition of *A Literary History of Canada*, wherein he suggests that the question of Canadian identity is not so much "Who am I?" as "Where is here?" (quoted in 1994, 77). Cavell complains that Frye's conception of "place" is abstract, devoid of the social.

15 1974, 4.

16 1974, 5.

17 Ibid.

18 1974, 6.

19 Canadian fears regarding domination by the United States did not start in the 1960s. Tomkins (1974, 18) reminds: "Concern [in Canada] about American books reached a peak in 1847 when it found that half of the books used in the schools came from the United States." Indeed, "concern" escalates on occasion to "repulsion" (1974, 18; see also Tomkins 1981, 159, 162). But, Tomkins (1981, 162) concludes, "it would be a mistake to assume that the cultural content of Canadian curricula was American dominated, at least before 1960." If not, then why was Canadian fear sometimes so pronounced? American strong-arming of the Canadian government during the Cuban missile crisis would seem to provide one answer, although George Grant (2005 [1965], 12) insists the majority of Canadians approved. Indeed, the event evidently helped bring down the Diefenbacker government.

20 As Tomkins (1981, 157) notes, "The ascription of 'influence,' whether in historical or other terms, is notoriously difficult and carries with it the further danger of violating the research canon that correlation is not to be equated with causation." If "influence" is difficult to assess, can "domination" be any easier? Milburn and Herbert reference no data. Is proximity (see Tomkins 1981, 163) equivalent to threat? In this 1974 publication, not one example is given of the American "domination"

of Canada. Given significant policy differences—including over multiculturalism, gay marriage, the U.S. invasion of Iraq (Resnick 2005, 85)—such "domination" would appear not to be political. While there may well be "hazards of sleeping with an elephant" (Potter 2005, xxxviii), the threat may come more from inside, than outside, Canada. In his analysis of George Grant's *Lament for a Nation*, Andrew Potter (2005, lxiii) argues that Grant demonstrated the "most important fault-line" in Canadian federal politics is not between the political left and right or between the French and the English, but "between those who favor an independent Canada and those who desire every closer continental integration." Grant (2005 [1965]) himself suggested that the "central problem for nationalism in English-speaking Canada has always been: in what ways and for what reasons do we have the power and the desire to maintain some independence of the American Empire?"

21 1974, 6.

22 1974, 54.

23 See Gunew 2004, 5; Renaud 1974, 37; Haig-Brown 2008, 13.

24 2005, 17.

25 Milburn and Herbert 1974, 7; see Chambers 2003, 245.

26 Kymlicka 2003, 382.

27 See Tomkins 1974, 16; Chambers 2003, 221; Hodgetts 1968, 84.

28 1974, 23.

29 The climate has been viewed favorably, as during the 1890s, when Canadian nationalist George Parkin embraced the "northernness" of the country, an attitude evident in the Canadian national anthem "the true north strong and free." Due to its northern climate, Parkin was confident that Canada would have no "Negro problem" nor would it "attract the vagrant population of Italy and other countries of Southern Europe." Indeed, climate was claimed as "fundamental political and social advantage which the Dominion enjoys over the United States" (quoted passages in Tomkins 1974, 19). This valorization of "the North" was not left in the past; Conway (1974, 78) comments that besides anti-Americanism, Canada's most powerful mythology is the "mystique" of the North, with its associated celebration of "wilderness" as a "source of power" (O'Brian and White 2007, 4).

30 Chambers 1999, 141; 2003, 245.

31 Survival was of course physical, but it was also gendered, specifically masculine (see Conway 1974, 76). Supplementing gender was spirituality, as Conway (1974, 77) suggests that what was tested in the wilderness was not only one's masculinity but one's spirituality, itself informed by European values. Like masculinity, spirituality and culture can function defensively, including in the Canadian curriculum (see Tomkins 1986, 34, 35). Conflations of landscape, nationality, and spirituality show up in Canadian painting as well, specifically in the work of the Group of Seven (see Conway 1974, 77; Pente 2009, 118–124; White 2007, 20). Conway emphasizes human insignificance before nature, and reminds us that not only gendered or cultural elements are in play in the dynamics of survival: so, too, are commercial concerns (1974, 77; see, also, White 2007, 24), a point emphasized by Teresa Strong-Wilson (2010) in her questioning of "reverence" to depict Anglophone Canada's relationship to the land (see note 11). Hodgetts (1968, 86) phrase—"amorphous attachment"—implies a more complex attitude. Chambers (1999, 140) references this Conway essay, as she does the Milburn-Herbert collection (see Chambers 1999, 142).

32 1974, 7.

33 Resnick 2005, 13.

34 Vickers 1994, 361.

35 Vickers 1994, 360.

36 See Kymlicka 2003, 377.

37 See Dean 1994, 158–159.

38 See Tomkins 1986, 269.

39 Lipset 1990, 60.

40 Ibid.
41 Tomkins 1981, 158.
42 Lipset 1990, 21.
43 1994, 353.
44 See 1968.
45 1974, 23.
46 2005, 21.
47 Tomkins 1986, 328.
48 See 1968, 99.
49 Tomkins 1986, 327.
50 See Lorimer and Goldie 1994, 3.
51 Vickers 1994, 353.
52 1994, 357.
53 See Vickers 1994, 353.
54 1981, 165.
55 Ibid.
56 1974, 24.
57 1974, 26.
58 Milburn and Herbert 1974, 8.
59 1974, 55.
60 The expression of Canadian nationalism was reflected not only in curriculum reform. Sweeny (1994, 342–343) points out that in the 1960s and 1970s "the principal economic problem was not the concentrated Canadian corporate sector, but American imperialism," an "ahistorical, neo-nationalist discourse" that enabled the "tacit political alliance" between the Liberal and New Democratic parties in the 1970s, an alliance that "sanctioned a substantially increased role for the federal government." Sweeny cites federal energy policy, including the creation of Petro-Canada, as evidence. Centralization, then, was accomplished under the guise of anti-Americanism; it was "the Canadian bourgeois which has gained the most from the increased role according the federal government in the economic life of the country" (Sweeny 1994, 343).
61 See Milburn and Herbert 1974, 8; Tomkins 1974, 18. Teachers may not have been only "reproducing" dominant ideology (as reproduction theorists have simplistically and obsessively insisted), they may have also been resisting those foreign influences (from Europe as well as from the United States) that Tomkins (1981, 159) suggests followed the 1960s replacement of church with state control. Tomkins (1981, 159) notes the receptivity of Québec educators specifically to American progressive ideas, anticipating his later emphasis on British Columbia, Ontario, and the prairie provinces (see Pinar 2008, xv). Mid-1960s Canadian nationalism forefronted "francophone nationalism" (Tomkins 1981, 164), which was not (as noted earlier) necessarily anti-American.
62 1974, 106.
63 Ibid.
64 2001, 147.
65 2001, 145.
66 Ibid.
67 2001, 146.
68 Resnick 2005, 33.
69 Sumara, Davis, and Laidlaw 2001, 146.
70 2001, 45.
71 Like the "lynchpin" theory, "ecological postmodernism" may also make a "virtue out of Canada's lack of strong identity" (Richardson 2002, 66). Rather than mediating between the United States and the United Kingdom (between North America and Europe, in Resnick's [2005, 97] revision), this updated "lynchpin" theory attends to the "co-evolutions" of "humans" and "the-more-than-human world"

(Sumara, Davis, and Laidlaw 2001, 148). The idea of Canada as a "postmodern version of the nation-state" dates to a June 1991 article in *The Economist* (see Kymlicka 2003, 368). Andrew Potter (see 2005, lx) dates the concept similarly, but attributes it to journalist Robert Fulford and the literary theorist Linda Hutcheson. The "ecological" half of the Sumara-Davis-Laidlaw formulation does seem new, evoking not only the contemporary concern with climate change but as well the "mythological relationship Canadians have developed with the land," if ignoring the fact that "for the first 100 years of the country's development it was a mythology expressed in the language of technology, domination, and development" (Potter 2005, lix).

72 Sumara, Davis, and Laidlaw 2001, 147.

73 1920, 183.

74 "Adaptation" implies dependency, even conformity, as the dictionary records. The biologistic tendency in this assertion is implied too by the use of the term "humans" and by splitting "adaptation" from "reinterpretation." In a cultural and/or political analysis, the two would be conjoined, as reinterpretation reconstructs the situation, especially as it is informed by new knowledge, the "superiority of discovery of new facts and truths to demonstration of the old" (Dewey 1920, 31). Nowhere is the theoretical throughline between U.S. progressivism and postmodernism articulated with more clarity than in Doll (1993). See also Trueit 2012.

75 Lather 2007, 76.

76 Sumara, Davis, and Laidlaw 2001, 147.

77 Ibid.

78 As Tomkins' canonical study of Canadian curriculum makes clear, the educational similarities between the two countries are at least as numerous as the differences (see Pinar 2008). The Sumara-Davis-Laidlaw casting of the United States as the opposite of Canada is contradicted by others (Vickers 1994, 353; Wein 1994, 380). Lipset (1990, 212) puts it this way: "Regardless of whether one emphasizes structural factors or cultural values, Canada and the United States continue to differ considerably. . . . At the same time, the two resemble each other more than either resembles any other nation." Resnick (2005) disagrees, emphasizing resemblances between Canada and Europe.

79 Sumara, Davis, and Laidlaw 2001, 157

80 2001, 153.

81 2001, 150.

82 2001, 154.

83 2001, 154–155.

84 2001, 150.

85 2001, 157.

86 2001, 158.

87 2001, 159. "Always" rooting scholarship in the local seems a universalism, does it not? In the United States, "place"—with its local elements—has been an important concept (see Pinar 1991), emphasizing the specificities of local histories and cultures.

88 2006a, 30.

89 The last of the four challenges—mapping the field—Chambers (2003) has also accomplished. For me "mapping" includes "vertical" or historical as well as "horizontal" or contemporary elements (see chapter 3, this volume), including the updating of Tomkins (1986 [2008]) whose work—along with Chambers' oeuvre and others'—could be considered (as I suggested at the close of chapter 3) canonical in Canadian curriculum studies.

90 2006b, 6, 13.

91 2006b, 7.

92 A phrase I've used before: see Pinar 2007.

93 Chambers 2003, 238.

94 1974, 143.

95 1974, 144.

96 Ibid.
97 Tomkins 1986, 440.
98 Herbert and Milburn 1974, 147.
99 See 2008. Chambers (2006b, 12) laments the under-emphasis of native peoples in Canadian curriculum studies. That seems corrected in more recent studies (Ng-A-Fook and Rottman 2012).
100 While there is yet no text that updates Tomkins' canonical curriculum history, there are clues to the transition between the two historical moments (as refracted through these two publications). One such clue comes in George Richardson's study of the Province of Alberta's *Program of Studies*. Discussing the transition from the 1981 to the 1991 programs, Richardson (2002, 78) counts four "seismic shocks to Canada's national identity," among them a receding significance of British influence, growing concern over "the exact nature of Canada's relationship with the United States," the "emergence of French Canadian nationalism," as well as "the rapidly changing demographic composition of the nation." Richardson observes no "them-us" characteristic of modern nationalism, but, rather, a national identity that was "ambiguous and uneasy." These adjectives do not apply to Sumara, Davis, and Laidlaw's 2001 statement, wherein the binary "we-they" structures Canadian identity.
101 2005, 89.
102 2005, 91.
103 See 1974, 54. In Canadian literature the "sister concept" of "survival" is "victim" (Chambers 1999, 143), a pairing traceable to Atwood and critiqued subsequently by several scholars (see Dean 1994, 158; Vickers 1994, 360). Does victimhood risk morphing into a smug self-pity when conflating the threat of "Nature" with the "American colossus"? Perhaps in the Sumara-Davis-Laidlaw piece, but not in Canadian literature generally, as Chambers (1999, 143) reports: "These writers and theorists have reconfigured the margins, the place of survival, as a topos filled with life worth living and at certain times worth talking and writing about." Indeed, there is no evidence of victimhood or self-pity in the Canadian Chancery in Washington, D.C. There, "victim" becomes "adversary." Constructed to caricature the "faux-classicism" of the U.S. capitol's architecture, the Chancery challenges American imperialism (Cavell 1994, 89). In addition to the architectural parody performed by the classical "folly" (1994, 90)—in which neo-classical columns are miniaturized, forming a circle whose ends do not meet—the inclusion of Bill Reid's sculpture "The Spirit of Haida Gwai" completes this Canadian expression of contempt. That sculpture—figuring a canoe filled with animal and human passengers mythologically related to Canada's First Nations—gestures to Emanuel Leutze's famous painting of George Washington crossing the Delaware. The prow of the sculptural canoe is pointed toward the Capitol. Cavell (1994, 95) suggests that "Reid's sculpture identifies that space [the Canadian Chancery, not the U.S. Capitol] as a site of resistance." To a Canadian sensibility the Chancery may express "resistance," but to this American one that word seems (as noted above) an understatement.
104 1974, 54. Marshall McLuhan was even more critical, Vickers (1994, 360) reminds, calling Canada a "stagnant stream" and (changing metaphors) a "mental vacuum" full of "terrible social cowardice." These judgments express a temper tantrum, not a considered judgment.
105 Conway 1974, 78.
106 Kymlicka 2003, 365.
107 Resnick 2005, 84.
108 Ibid.
109 Terry Carson (2010) points out that the recurring question of Canada's identification with the United States and with Europe remains an open one, personified today (March 2010) in the persons of Prime Minister Stephen Harper (representing the economic and political continentalism George Grant worried would dissolve Canadian national distinctiveness and, eventually, sovereignty) and Liberal leader

Michael Ignatieff (representing Canada's European association). As Hodgetts (1968, 120) pointed out, the study of Canadian history remains key to appreciating these issues. While I endorse its strengthening in the schools (and in Canadian curriculum studies), "history is," Resnick (2005, 37) notes, "no more a unifying force in Canada." He cites a 2001 survey of history teachers in secondary schools in English Canada and Québec that found "a striking difference in what each cohort held to be important" (Resnick 2005, 38; see Hodgetts 1968, 71, 76, 80–81, 112 n. 7). While history may be no force for national political unification, it would (more modestly) advance Canadian curriculum studies as it would make less likely the substitution of simplistic stereotypes for complex facts.

110 2005, 47.

111 1968, 76.

112 2005, 47.

113 See 1968. Grant's critique of technology is the subject of chapter 5.

114 1994, 33.

115 1990, 221.

116 O'Brian 2007, 27.

117 2005 (1965), 35.

118 2005 (1965), 34.

119 Pinar 2009, 45–55.

120 2005, 245.

121 Ibid.

122 Aoki 2005 (1987), 354.

123 Ibid.

124 Chambers 2008, 125.

Bibliography

Aoki, Ted. 2005 (1987). Revisiting the Notions of Leadership and Identity. In *Curriculum in a New Key: The Collected Works of Ted T. Aoki*, edited by William F. Pinar and Rita L. Irwin (349–355). Mahwah, NJ: Lawrence Erlbaum.

Carr, Paul R. and Lund, Darren E. 2007. Introduction: Scanning Whiteness. In *The Great White North? Exploring Whiteness, Privilege and Identity in Education*, edited by Paul R. Carr and Darren E. Lund (1–15). Rotterdam/Boston/Tapei: Sense Publishers.

Carson, Terry. 2005. Beyond Instrumentalism: The Significance of Teacher Identity in Educational Change. *Journal of the Canadian Association for Curriculum Studies* 3 (2), 1–8.

Carson, Terry. 2010. Personal communication.

Cavell, Richard A. 1994. Theorizing Canadian Space: Postcolonial Articulations. In *Canada: Theoretical Discourse*, edited by Terry Goldie, Carmen Lambert, and Rowland Lorimer (75–194). Montreal: Association for Canadian Studies.

Chambers, Cynthia. 1999. A Topography for Canadian Curriculum Theory. *Canadian Journal of Education* 24 (2), 137–150.

Chambers, Cynthia. 2003. "As Canadian as Possible under the Circumstances": A View of Contemporary Curriculum Discourses in Canada. In the *International Handbook of Curriculum Research*, edited by William F. Pinar (221–252). Mahwah, NJ: Lawrence Erlbaum.

Chambers, Cynthia. 2006a. "The Land is the Best Teacher I Ever Had": Places as Pedagogy for Precarious Times. *JCT: Journal of Curriculum Theorizing* 22 (3), 27–37.

Chambers, Cynthia. 2006b. "Where Do I Belong?": Canadian Curriculum as Passport Home. *Journal of the American Association for the Advancement of Curriculum Studies* 2. Available online at http://www.uwstout.edu/soe/jaaacs/vol2/chambers.htm

Chambers, Cynthia. 2008. Where Are We? Finding Common Ground in a Curriculum of Place. *Journal of the Canadian Association for Curriculum Studies* 6 (2), 113–128.

Conway, Jill. 1974. Culture and National Identity. In *National Consciousness and the Curriculum: The Canadian Case*, edited by Geoffrey Milburn and John Herbert (71–87). Toronto: Ontario Institute for Studies in Education, Department of Curriculum.
Cormier, Jeffrey. 2004. *The Canadianization Movement: Emergence, Survival, and Success*. Toronto: University of Toronto Press.
Dean, Misao. 1994. Canadian "Vulgar Nationalism" in the Postmodern Age. In *Canada: Theoretical Discourse*, edited by Terry Goldie, Carmen Lambert, and Rowland Lorimer (153–166). Montreal: Association for Canadian Studies.
Dewey, John. 1920. *Reconstruction in Philosophy*. New York: Henry Holt and Company.
Doll, Jr., William E. 1993. *A Post-Modern Perspective on Curriculum*. New York: Teachers College Press.
Fanon, Frantz. 1967. *Black Skin, White Masks*. [Trans. Charles Lam Markmann.] New York: Grove Weidenfeld.
Gollaher, David L. 2000. *Circumcision*. New York: Basic Books.
Grant, George. 2005 (1965). *Lament for a Nation*. [40th anniversary edition.] Montreal and Kingston: McGill-Queen's University Press.
Gunew, Sneja. 2004. *Haunted Nations: The Colonial Dimensions of Multiculturalisms*. London: Routledge.
Haig-Brown, Celia. 2008. Taking Indigenous Thought Seriously: A Rant on Globalization with Some Cautionary Notes. *Journal of the Canadian Association for Curriculum Studies* 6 (2), 8–24.
Herbert, John and Milburn, Geoffrey. 1974. Nationalism and the Curriculum. In *National Consciousness and the Curriculum: The Canadian Case*, edited by Geoffrey Milburn and John Herbert (143–147). Toronto: Ontario Institute for Studies in Education, Department of Curriculum.
Hodgetts, A.B. 1968. *What Culture? What Heritage? A Study of Civic Education in Canada*. Toronto: Ontario Institute for Studies in Education.
Kanu, Yatta. 2003. Curriculum as Cultural Practice: Postcolonial Imagination. *Journal of the Canadian Association for Curriculum Studies* 1 (1), 67–81.
Kymlicka, Will. 2003. Being Canadian. *Government and Opposition* 38 (3), 357–385.
Lather, Patti. 2007. *Getting Lost: Feminist Efforts toward a Double(d) Science*. Albany: State University of New York Press.
Lipset, Seymour Martin. 1990. *Continental Divide: The Values and Institutions of the United States and Canada*. New York: Routledge.
Lorimer, Rowland and Goldie, Terry. 1994. Introduction to *Canada: Theoretical Discourse*, edited by Terry Goldie, Carmen Lambert and Rowland Lorimer (1–8). Montreal: Association for Canadian Studies.
Muller, Johan. 2000. *Reclaiming Knowledge*. London: Routledge.
Ng-A-Fook, Nicholas. 2007. *An Indigenous Curriculum of Place: The United Houma Nation's Contentious Relationship with Louisiana's Educational Institutions*. New York: Peter Lang.
Ng-A-Fook, Nicholas and Rottmann, Jennifer. Eds. 2012. *Reconsidering Canadian Curriculum Studies: An Uncommon Countenance*. New York: Palgrave Macmillan.
O'Brian, John. 2007. Wild Art History. In *Beyond Wilderness: The Group of Seven, Canadian Identity, and Contemporary Art*, edited by John O'Brian and Peter White (21–37). Montreal and Kingston: McGill-Queen's University Press.
O'Brian, John and White, Peter. 2007. Introduction. To *Beyond Wilderness: The Group of Seven, Canadian Identity, and Contemporary Art*, edited by John O'Brian and Peter White (3–6). Montreal and Kingston: McGill-Queen's University Press.
Pente, Patti Vera. 2009. The Hidden Curriculum of Wilderness: Images of Landscape in Canada. *Journal of the Canadian Association for Curriculum Studies* 7 (1), 111–134.
Pinar, William F. 1991. Curriculum as Social Psychoanalysis: On the Significance of Place. In *Curriculum as Social Psychoanalysis: The Significance of Place*, edited by Joe L. Kincheloe and William F. Pinar (167–186). Albany: State University of New York Press.

Pinar, William F. 2007. Curriculum Leadership Then and Now. In *Approaches to Educational Leadership*, edited by William Smale and Kelly Young (110–125). Calgary, Alberta: Detselig.

Pinar, William F. 2008. Introduction to George S. Tomkins' *A Common Countenance: Stability and Change in the Canadian Curriculum* (xi–xxiv). Vancouver, Canada: Pacific Educational Press.

Potter, Andrew. 2005. Introduction to the 40th Anniversary Edition of George P. Grant's *Lament for a Nation*. Montreal and Kingston: McGill-Queen's University Press.

Ray, Douglas. 1974. Canadian Studies Are Overrated. In *National Consciousness and the Curriculum: The Canadian Case*, edited by Geoffrey Milburn and John Herbert (33–36). Toronto: Ontario Institute for Studies in Education, Department of Curriculum.

Regenstrief, Peter. 1974. Some Social and Political Obstacles to Canadian National Consciousness. In *National Consciousness and the Curriculum: The Canadian Case*, edited by Geoffrey Milburn and John Herbert (37–41). Toronto: Ontario Institute for Studies in Education, Department of Curriculum.

Renaud, Andre. 1974. Indians in White Culture Curricula and Society. In *National Consciousness and the Curriculum: The Canadian Case*, edited by Geoffrey Milburn and John Herbert (37–41).Toronto: Ontario Institute for Studies in Education, Department of Curriculum.

Resnick, Philip. 2005. *The European Roots of Canadian Identity*. Peterborough, Ontario: Broadview Press.

Richardson, George H. 2002. *The Death of the Good Canadian: Teachers, National Identities, and the Social Studies Curriculum*. New York: Peter Lang.

Richler, Mordecai. 1974. Nationalism and Literature in Canada. In *National Consciousness and the Curriculum: The Canadian Case*, edited by Geoffrey Milburn and John Herbert (105–117). Toronto: Ontario Institute for Studies in Education, Department of Curriculum.

Saul, John Ralston. 2005. *The Collapse of Globalism: And the Reinvention of the World*. Toronto: Viking Canada.

Sekyi-Otu, Ato. 1996. *Fanon's Dialectic of Experience*. Cambridge, MA: Harvard University Press.

Strong-Wilson, Teresa. 2010. Personal communication.

Sumara, Dennis, Davis, Brent, and Laidlaw, Linda. 2001. Canadian Identity and Curriculum Theory: An Ecological, Postmodern Perspective. *Canadian Journal of Education* 26 (2), 144–163.

Sutherland, Neil. 1986. Foreword to George S. Tomkins' *A Common Countenance* (x–xiv). Scarborough, Ontario Canada: Prentice Hall. [Reissued in 2008 by Pacific Educational Press, Vancouver.]

Sweeny, Robert C. H. 1994. The Staples as the Significant Past: A Case Study in Historical Theory and Method. In *Canada: Theoretical Discourse*, edited by Terry Goldie, Carmen Lambert and Rowland Lorimer (327–349). Montreal: Association for Canadian Studies.

Tomkins, George. 1974. National Consciousness, the Curriculum, and Canadian Studies. In *National Consciousness and the Curriculum: The Canadian Case*, edited by Geoffrey Milburn and John Herbert (15–29). Toronto: Ontario Institute for Studies in Education, Department of Curriculum.

Tomkins, George. 1981. Foreign Influences on Curriculum and Curriculum Policy Making in Canada: Some Impressions in Historical and Contemporary Perspective. *Curriculum Inquiry* 11 (2), 157–166.

Tomkins, George S. 1986. *A Common Countenance: Stability and Change in the Canadian Curriculum*. Scarborough, Ontario, Canada: Prentice-Hall. [Reissued in 2008 by Pacific Educational Press. References are the 1986 edition.]

Trueit, Donna. ed. 2012. *Pragmatism, Postmodernism, Complexity Theory: The Fascinating Imaginative Realm of William E. Doll, Jr*. New York: Routledge.

Van Manen, Max M. J. 1974. Notes on the Concept of Nationalism in the Curriculum. In *National Consciousness and the Curriculum: The Canadian Case*, edited by Geoffrey Milburn and John Herbert (11–14). Toronto: Ontario Institute for Studies in Education, Department of Curriculum.

Vickers, Jill. 1994. Liberating Theory in Canadian Studies. In *Canada: Theoretical Discourse*, edited by Terry Goldie, Carmen Lambert, and Rowland Lorimer (351–371). Montreal: Association for Canadian Studies.

Wein, Sheldon. 1994. American and Canadian Justice. In *Canada: Theoretical Discourse*, edited by Terry Goldie, Carmen Lambert, and Rowland Lorimer (373–391). Montreal: Association for Canadian Studies.

White, Peter. 2007. Out of the Woods. In *Beyond Wilderness: The Group of Seven, Canadian Identity, and Contemporary Art*, edited by John O'Brian and Peter White (11–20). Montreal and Kingston: McGill-Queen's University Press.

Yoshimoto, Mitsuhiro. 2002. Questions of Japanese Cinema: Disciplinary Boundaries and the Invention of the Scholarly Object. In *Learning Places: The Afterlives of Area Studies*, edited by Masao Miyoshi and D. H. Harootunian (368–401). Durham, NC: Duke University Press.

CHAPTER 5

TECHNOLOGY

Commentary

Reviewing details of the life of the great Canadian public intellectual George Grant, I summarize key elements of his critique of technology and modernity. Technology for Grant is a form of idolatry, substituting materiality for spirituality, distracting us from dialogical encounter—subjective presence through face-to-face communication—and diverting us into screens where we are forced to comply with programs created by commercial entities with profit, not freedom, in mind. While no technophobe, Grant was clear that in modernity faith in technology had replaced the religious kind, severing us from historic spiritual aspirations for human excellence.

Reference

Pinar, William F. 2013. The First Task of Thought in Our Time. Critical Literacy: Theories and Practices 7 (1), 1–16. Copyright William F. Pinar.

> The first task of thought in our era is to think what technology is.[1]
>
> George Grant

One of Canada's greatest public intellectuals[2], George Grant was born on 13 November 1918, two days after the armistice. His father, William, a historian who had lectured at Oxford University and written a "controversial history"[3] of Canada for use in Ontario high schools (1914), had volunteered for active service and had been seriously injured in France. "My father," George Grant would write, "was a Nova Scotian, who had grown up in Kingston, Ontario, and was essentially a very gentle, strong scholar, who I think, above all, was ruined by the First World War. He was ruined physically; he was terribly wounded. For these people, who had grown up in the great era of progress, to meet the holocaust of the trenches was terrible."[4] William Grant grew embittered over the pointless slaughter of the First World War, the first war structured by technology.[5]

Like his father, George Grant studied history. He won the history medal at Queen's University, where, William Christian[6] tells us, "he was drawn to grand themes, rather than to the minutiae of historical research." That same disposition surfaced later at Oxford, where he'd gone on a Rhodes scholarship to study law. While at first he welcomed the intellectual discipline this new subject demanded, soon enough Grant judged law "tiresome" due to its focus on "detail" and "its indifference to broader questions."[7]

After service as an Air Raid Precautions warden during the German bombing of London, Grant returned to Canada in February 1942 suffering from a nervous breakdown and tuberculosis. Much of the next year he spent in recovery. In 1943 he published a pamphlet, *Canada—An Introduction to a Nation*, and in 1945 *The Empire, Yes or No*? Returning to Oxford after the war, he left law to study theology, earning extra money by writing historical articles on Canada for Chambers' *Encyclopedia*. "Before I became a philosopher," he reflected years later, "I studied history and still think very much as an historian."[8] The history to which Grant was increasingly drawn, Christian[9] clarifies, "reflected his early predispositions to the philosophy of history." That subject became personified in his doctoral dissertation, a study of the Scottish Presbyterian theologian John Oman.

While attending meetings of C.S. Lewis's Socratic Club, Grant met Sheila Allen, an English student and fellow pacifist, whom he married in the spring of 1947. The two returned to Canada where Grant had accepted a position teaching philosophy at Dalhousie University in Halifax. He spent the next thirteen years there, during which time the Grants had six children. Grant found Dalhousie a "congenial place," Potter[10] reports, but he felt he was in Halifax on the periphery of North American life. In 1961 he accepted a professorship in the department of religion at McMaster University in Hamilton, Ontario, near Toronto.

During the 1950s Grant was studying philosophy and history, first Nietzsche, then Sartre, then Heidegger. He had also undertaken the study of Freud and Weber. By 1962, Christian[11] reports, when Grant delivered a CBC radio lecture on the C.G. Jung, he had begun to focus on Nietzsche. Grant's central insight between the time he wrote *Philosophy in the Mass Age* in 1959 and *Time as History* a decade later, was that the contemporary conception of history was very different from the ancient one, wherein time had been regarded as the "moving image of eternity."[12] Now history had become a totalizing process within which all events are subsumed.[13] The world, in David D. Roberts' phrase, is "nothing but history."[14] Even historicists like Marx and Hegel had imagined some end toward which history was moving, and in so doing had conferred a broader significance upon individual events. But now the utter contingency of history had stripped particularity of any general (mythic or religious) importance, as history had become "nothing but this freakish concatenation of lies, errors, and self-serving actions."[15] Roberts' descriptors could have well been Grant's, as Grant inveighed against the economic and political integration of the North American continent, threatening, indeed ending (he felt sure), Canada's political autonomy.[16]

In its political contingency, that event[17] involved the United States, but more generally, Grant argued, Canada's capitulation was another "realization of the technological dream," e.g. "universalization and homogenization."[18] Associated with modernity itself, and with the United States specifically as modernity's most "expressive manifestation,"[19] technology had become not just one optional *mode d'être*, but the only way of life on earth. Technology had become, in Emberley's[20] succinct summary of Grant's understanding of the term,[21] "a philosophy of reason as domination over nature, a politics of imperial, bureaucratic administration, a public discourse of efficiency, and a sociology of adjustment and equilibrium." Canada's "collapse," Grant[22] asserted, "stems from the very character of the modern era." That era, the so-called age of "progress," contiguous with the rise of capitalism, science, and the "conquest of nature," contrasted sharply with ancient Greece, Grant[23] emphasized. That genesis of the North American present became the contrast to which Grant juxtaposed the present. As science achieved hegemony, Grant[24] felt sure, "there is no place for local cultures."

How did this happen? How did the local become subsumed in the global, and how has the global become technological? In the West, Grant answered, there had been a "close relation" between technology and political liberalism, by which he meant the "belief that man's essence is his freedom."[25] That belief in a "truly liberal society," Grant[26] reminded, has been linked historically to the progress of science. In something like a sleight of hand, political liberalism installed legal and social homogeneity[27] in order to guarantee individual diversity, something primarily private and psychological, and expressed through the consumption of goods. As Grant[28] puts the matter: "the purpose of action becomes the building of the universal and homogenous state—the society in which all men are free and equal and increasingly able to realize their concrete individuality." Significant, and this is the crucial difference Grant draws between the ancient (Greek) world and the contemporary secular world, is that the realization of individuality is not spiritual or moral or intellectual, but psychologistic, and it is fused with technological development. "As we push towards the goal we envisage," Grant[29] cautioned, "our need of technology for its realization becomes ever more pressing." In U.S. school reform, this has translated into the deafening demand for "what works" in classrooms, a restated behaviorism quantified in students' standardized test scores. Just as learning disappears into numbers on tests, moral striving is recast as increases in productivity that are dependent upon technological advancement.[30] No longer conceived as laboratories for democracy, in the U.S. schools are dismissed as antiquated "bricks-and-mortar" institutions, now to be privatized, then virtualized, as increasingly the curriculum is moved online.[31]

Problem-solving is no longer construed as a moral imperative—as the intellectual labor of judgment informed by knowledge and wisdom—but, rather, applying relevant information, devising a technological fix. No longer public, morality becomes a matter of privately held "values," for Grant, equivalent to commodities, statements of personal preference, often ornamental, sometimes self-servingly instrumental. Whatever their function, "values" were to be confined to the private sphere[32] where one was, presumably, free to do what one wanted. The public sphere[33] was no longer the civic square but, rather, the marketplace, the site where one purchased whatever one valued.

> As for pluralism, differences in the technological state are able to exist only in private activities: how we eat; how we mate; how we practice ceremonies. Some like pizza; some like steaks; some like girls, some like boys; some like synagogue, some like the mass.[34]

From Grant's perspective, it seems to me, the insistence on "gay rights"—especially the right to public affirmations of private commitments, as in gay marriage—risks the relegation of homosexual desire to the status of yet another "lifestyle." In so doing, recognition normalizes desire. Difference becomes another possibly entertaining instance of the same.

The division between private and public was blurred by technology, then dismissed in theoretical terms as a "binary." There remains among some, however, an ongoing lament for the loss of privacy, under stress for centuries given the emphasis upon confession in Christianity, a compulsion for self-disclosure secularized in psychoanalysis, and popularized in less time-consuming psychotherapies and self-help groups. The confessions that had before been private—confined to priests, psychotherapists, or trustworthy friends—are now exhibited openly online, risking not only reputations (also an increasingly archaic concept) but the fluidity of subjectivity as well, as now the inner life has a point only inasmuch it can be posted in public. The technological opportunity for exhibitionism and surveillance coupled with an uneasiness over privacy[35] threatens the disappearance of private life. While it may not be the cause, technology could be a consequence of what Heidegger called *das Man*, the public man in conformity with his or her fellows.[36] That dispersion of an individuated subjectivity—leaving what Lasch[37] termed a minimal self—reassembles as *das Man*, even when we are women and have secrets. As Kleinberg notes, in a different but related context: "In the interest of uniformity and complete systematic understanding, publicness invents responses that make all cases conform to one rule, one logic, and thus removes all differentiation."[38] This obliteration of internal differentiation and external distinctiveness accompanies globalization, itself materialized through technological innovation.

As technology ensures social conformity, it dissolves individuality. Avatars substitute for selves. Without internal subjective complexity, external multiplicity fades as material fact and moral challenge. Presumably the site of freedom, the Internet presents new opportunities for imperialism. It is under the "banner of freedom and a liberating modernization," Grant[39]points out, that this new-style "imperialism" is justified to the public.[40] This "expansionist practicality"[41] has become a common faith, and not only in America, so that to "think outside this faith is to make oneself a stranger to the public realm."[42] The technological era is a time, Grant charges, during which "nobility and wisdom have been exchanged for a pale belief in progress."[43]

"Pale"[44] here is probably not a play on racialization, although to non-European listeners, especially to the descendants of the victims of imperialism it might seem so, if inadvertently. Rather, the word conveys the stripped-down, naked (as in "vulgar" and "brutal": Grant's words) "drive to an unlimited technological future, in which technical reason has become so universal that it has closed down on openness and awe, questioning and listening."[45] These prerequisites and processes of education, of curriculum as complicated conversation, depend upon the cultivation of non-coincidence, one subspecies of which is disidentification. In a period of narcissism, boundaries blur, and not only between self and other, but among social and political phenomena. Technology restructures political liberalism so that it conflates instrumentalism with action, exhibitionism with communication, image with reality.[46] How can I use technology as the subject of a sentence? To do so acknowledges, in Nusselder's phrasing, "technology as *volition*."[47] In Grant's terms, technology materializes the human will to power, precipitating the "violence of an undirected willing of novelty."[48] As Grant appreciated:

> When men are committed to technology, they are also committed to continual change in institutions and customs. Freedom must be the first political principle—the freedom to change any order that stands in the way of technological advance. Such a society cannot take seriously the conception of an eternal order that stands in the way of technological advance.[49]

When transcendence is recast as the production of novelty—new products, new ideas, always the "new"—the future is foreclosed and what matters is now.

Our Civilizational Destiny

> Surely the deepest alienation must be when the civilization one inhabits no longer claims one's loyalty.
>
> George Grant[50]

Not in the remembrance of things past or as risks taken in the name of the future, social action is replaced by proceduralism, in our field conveyed simplistically in the so-called Tyler Rationale, wherein the implementation of objectives is constantly evaluated, creating a self-referential set of culs-de-sac reiterating what is already. Because proceduralism leads nowhere but where one began, the objectives-evaluation axis tends toward intensification, creating, in Raymond Callahan's famous phrase, a cult of efficiency. A technological society, Potter summarizes, is one that pursues the systematic application of reason to the invention of tools and methods for enhancing freedom by making all activity more efficient.[51] "Freedom's great achievement was that it allowed modern technology to appear," Grant acknowledged, and "technology's great achievement was that it allowed freedom to flourish."[52] In the private sphere, freedom is recast as choice of consumer goods; in the public sphere it converts to control, the demand that freedom flourish so that whatever is profitable occurs. In new products and increased productivity, technology and capitalism conflate. At the same time, in its tendency toward intensification, technology undermines freedom and efficiency, submerging us in minutiae, tying us to the present moment, an interminable present in which we become preoccupied with the next sensation, a next "hit" of communication or information,[53] focused on the expectation that in the next moment "something" will happen, something will stimulate.

Technology is, then, no set of tools supplementary to our way of life. For Grant, Potter explains, "technology is a way of apprehending the world, it is a mode of existence that transforms the way we know, think, and will."[54] Nature becomes, in Heidegger's famous phrase, a "standing reserve" (or *Bestand*), a source of energy or resources for future use. As Krauss points out, "*Bestand* implies orderability and substitutability; objects will necessarily lose their autonomy."[55] The system or way of thinking that enframes the world as "standing reserve" Heidegger calls *Gestell*; this is, Grant was sure, our "civilizational destiny."[56] It is not only Nature that is wasted in this technology of thinking, it is human nature[57] itself. "Powerful and value-laden," Potter states, summarizing Grant's view, technology

> will come to dominate our consciousness and constrain our very sense of "freedom" and our sense of the possibilities for thought and for action. It

enslaves us even while it appears to liberate, giving us a fragmented and atomized society that is heavily dependent on the impersonal and alienating institutions of mass society.[58]

No one who has lived through the financial events of 2008 or the European crisis of 2011–2012 can doubt our dependency on "impersonal" and "alienating institutions of mass society." Significantly, one recent response to these was an improvisational, anti-institutional "Occupation of Wall Street," a reference one supposes less to previous occupations (of the Rhineland after the First World War, for instance) than to the "impersonal" (as in "having no personal reference or connection")[59] character of the financial system.[60]

Minus a subjectively coherent civic subject—the consumer is dispersed along fused planes of need, mood, possession—resistance becomes quixotic. Given our subsumption in the "technological sensorium,"[61] resistance (with its implication of a force separate from "us" that can in fact be "resisted") dissipates as a concept and social practice. Instead we have anther "reality" TV show, this one (Occupy Wall Street) with poor lighting and inadequate accommodation. Quoting Marshall McLuhan, Arthur Kroker points out:

> If, indeed, we are now "looking out" from inside the technological sensorium; and if, in fact, in the merger of biology and technology which is the locus of the electronic age, "we" have become the vanishing points of technique, then a way had to be discovered for breaching the "invisible environment" within which we are now enclosed.[62]

Kroker's choice of "breaching" seems especially apt, as it specifies not "push back," as "resistance" implies, but non-coincidence,[63] however internalized that "environment" has become within subjectivity.

As would Ted Aoki[64] decades later, George Grant, Emberley points out, did not overlook the "moral promise and concrete achievements of modern technology."[65] Many of these are familiar—increased food production, advances in medicine, convenience of communication—if with consequences, including poisoning by pesticides, preservatives and genetic modification, pills and practices that kill as they cure, and connectivity condensed to the constancy of information transmission as we stare at screens, not at each other or the world from which, evidently, we are now disembedded.[66] "Canadians in particular," Grant wrote, "felt the blessing of technology in an environment so hard that to master it needed courage. But conservatism must languish as technology increases."[67] By "conservatism" Grant meant not the "defense of property rights and chauvinism," but the "right of the community to restrain freedom in the name of the common good."[68] Those phrases meant something rather different to the Nazis, who, during the 1920s, enlisted technology to dazzle unemployed German youth.[69]

Technological achievements imply, Emberley notes, the "extension of individual freedom."[70] In its everyday practical sense, Grant thought of his wife's housekeeping chores, in Christian's description, her "relationship" with the "wonderful American machines that relieved her of drudgery, and therefore let her live a freer life than was possible even a hundred years before."[71] While machines have been employed for millennia,[72] what is different now—and this was evidently reflected in Grant's thinking (at least in the 1970s)—was that "never before had human beings defined and understood themselves primarily as free. George [Grant] recognized this as an authentic phenomenon and agreed that such freedom was a genuine good for human beings."[73] But not only, as Grant was clear that freedom represents danger as well as opportunity.

Grant was quite clear—since his father's First World War injury, since the 1940 London bombing raids he had endured on site—that the freedom technology affords is also the opportunity to do what is morally wrong. Of course machines make for "convenience" and yes they free people to do other things. But do they render us *more* free? Does not "freedom" depend upon subjective non-coincidence with what is and the self-conscious cultivation of the capacity to critique, to reflect, to act independently of what is? Convenience comes with consequences, Grant knew.

Open access—made possible by those information technologies devised and disseminated after Grant's death—would seem to represent an instance of "non-coincidence" and an increased capacity for critique and insight. The case for open access is made nowhere more succinctly than by John Willinsky who importantly links the development with its antecedents:

> The public library has long been a beacon of self-directed and deeply motivated learning on the part of common readers. It is not only a vital cornerstone of democracy, but a public site of quiet solace, intellectual inquiry, and literary pleasures. To increase public access to online research and scholarship would add a great deal to what has emerged over the last decade on the Internet as a wired and virtual public library, providing people with an opportunity to explore a new world of ideas that they may have only suspected existed.[74]

Opportunity yes, but one, it bears repeating, that depends upon the curiosity and capacity of the person, assuming online access is available to him or her.

Let us consider another apparently progressive—again referencing Grant's association of technology with the extension of freedom—consequence of online access. The so-called Arab Spring of 2011 was enabled, many thought, by the information technologies and social media. Research by Navid Hassanpour questions that assumption. "Full connectivity in a social network sometimes can hinder collective action," Hassanpour concluded.[75] While Twitter posting, texting, and Facebook wall-posting may have disseminated calls to protest and facilitated the actual organization of protest events, it also communicated caution, delay, and confusion as in "I don't have time for all this politics, did you see what Lady Gaga is wearing?"[76] Specifically, after President Hosni Mubarak shut down the Internet and cellphone service on 28 January 2011, Hassanpour found that protests *increased*, not only in Cairo but throughout Egypt. The number of actual protestors participating had not increased, but the number of protest events had. Hassanpour terms this phenomenon a "localization process." He explains:

> The disruption of cellphone coverage and the Internet on the 28th exacerbated the unrest in at least three major ways. It implicated many apolitical citizens unaware of or uninterested in the unrest; it forced more face-to-face communication, i.e., more physical presence in the streets; and finally it effectively decentralized the rebellion on the 28th through new hybrid

communication tactics, producing a quagmire much harder to control and repress than one massive gathering in Tahrir.[77]

I am reminded of Harold Innis' insistence on orality as central to democratic dialogue. While orality can occur online, it is made more difficult without physical presence and nonverbal communication. Hassanpour is thinking of the "normalization" effect of being "connected." In an interview he suggested that "we become more normal when we actually know what is going on—we are more unpredictable when we don't—on a mass scale and that has interesting implications."[78]

Canadians' commitment to technology was not initially, Grant suggests, an expression of the will to power, the insistence on clearing any obstacles to economic development. Instead, as Atwood also argued, Canadians' commitment was associated with survival in a harsh land. But what permitted physical survival, Grant warned, threatened cultural survival. In particular, the conservation of tradition is threatened by technology's limitless expansiveness. Grant points to the particularities of one's homeland to which citizens have loyalty and in which they take pride. Such particularities come to cultural distinctively forms through time, but history—traditional education is predicated on the preservation of culture—becomes dissolved by the presentism technology installs and is codified in the "new social sciences."[79] "When men are committed to technology," Grant appreciated, "they are also committed to continual change in institutions and customs. Freedom must be the first political principle—the freedom to change any order that stands in the way of technological advance."[80] Freedom, then, is the opportunity to do whatever is possible.

School reform in the United States—always forefronting technology in the classroom, not always a form of pedagogy but outright profiteering[81]—has been rationalized in recent years as reparation. It was especially the poor U.S. schools that were alleged to be failing, and it was, presumably, in the service of leaving no child behind that George W. Bush installed accountability schemes that deformed educational institutions into businesses. Recalling our long-standing faith[82] in technological development to address hunger, ease labor, and build wealth, Grant admonishes: "One must never think about technological destiny without looking squarely at the justice in those hopes."[83] Now that faith in technology as the driver of justice is no longer so simple or strong, as we are faced—Grant was writing in the mid-1980s here—with technologically produced crises of overpopulation and life-threatening pollution. Documenting "the determining power of our technological representation of reality," Grant notes, "the political response to these interlocking emergencies has been a call for an even greater mobilization of technology. More technology is needed to meet the emergencies which technology has produced."[84] This paradox was evident to the influential right-wing German intellectual Ernst Jünger, who, in 1931, observed: "The history of inventions also raises ever more clearly the question of whether a space of absolute comfort or a space of absolute danger is the final aim concealed in technology."[85] Technology enables the extension of life as it threatens the extinguishing of the species.

"Much of the new technology upon which we are going to depend to meet these crises," Grant predicted, "is technology turned towards human beings." Self-mastery must accompany mastery of nature. Self-mastery implies the "mastery of other people," requiring, he suspected, "the proliferation of new arts and sciences directed towards human control, so that we can be shaped to live consonantly with the demands of mass society."[86] The neurosciences might qualify as an academic instance of Grant's prediction. The information technologies provide another, as they create the illusion of "connectivity" while increasing isolation[87] and constraining one to the social networks to which, within which, one is "connected." The constancy of being connected reorganizes time around disclosure—of one's whereabouts, what one's feeling, "news" now as minutiae—and the presentism of a narcissistic age is sounded by cell phones demanding to be answered. Never mind the effects of being constantly connected to employers.

Grant's example is not cellphones—he died before they metastasized—but the medical profession, whose "proliferating power," he asserted, functions to tighten "social control."[88] Sounding like Foucault, he points to the profession's alignment with law enforcement and government in addressing the problems of the "psyche," increasingly, he notes, focused on physiology as well as behavior. The aggressive prescription of pharmaceuticals for complaints mild and severe prove the prescience of the philosophy professor from Halifax. Technology, he pronounced, "is the pervasive mode of being in our political and social lives."[89]

Now humanity stares at screens. The sleight-of-hand achieved in Grant's analysis is that he—we—could somehow stand outside technology. Rather, we abstract the term technology from the totality as an analytic device, to enable us to speak about a totality from which we cannot actually separate but with which we can choose not to coincide completely. Grant's strategy seems to be one of mobility, as he moves from one to another instance of technology's pervasiveness, as if he were skipping like a stone on the surface of the pond, knowing he would sink should he stop. Movement is propelled by thinking, including out loud, "witnessing" one might say in the Christian tradition. "If protest cannot go further than witnessing," Paras suggests in a different but related context, "it is because the twentieth century has revealed the dangers of theorizing solutions."[90]

Indeed, the instrumentalism of technology is not confined to "external objects"—like the computer, which, anticipating C. A. Bowers,[91] Grant will mention—but it also structures "systems of organization and communication as bureaucracies and factories."[92] Efficiency and rationalization accomplish homogeneity as time accelerates, flattening its own structures—past, present, future—into an apparently eternal now, yet always almost new, "marking, among other things, the priority of the values of disruption and interference over those historically establishing continuity."[93] "[H]ow far," Grant asks,

> will the race be able to carry the divided state which characterizes individuals in modernity: the plush patina of hectic subjectivity lived out in the iron maiden of an objectified world inhabited by increasingly objectifiable beings. . . . Is there some force in man which will rage against such division: rage not only against a subjectivity which creates itself, but also against our own lives being so much at the disposal of the powerful objectifications of other freedoms?[94]

This is the question Alice Miller posed in the context of child abuse.[95] How can the abused survive when love and violence are fused?

Conclusion

> What is worth doing in the midst of this barren twilight is the incredibly difficult question.
>
> George Grant[96]

While no technophobe,[97] George Grant understood that technological progress transforms the human spirit as it severs the "new social controls" from "traditional moralities and politics."[98] Because it is simultaneously universalizing and homogenizing, technology's intensification of immediacy and efficiency erases heterogeneity: cultural, political, subjective.[99] Whatever "difference" remains becomes commodified, incorporated into a system of exchange recalculating its value as eccentricity or pathology or sentimentality. Whatever the economic benefits (and, as 2008 reminded, they are hardly uniform or predictable), technology, Grant argued, is a universal tyranny, destined to eradicate the historic aspirations of the Western world and particularly its North American experiments. "The unfolding of modern society," Grant wrote, "has not only required the criticism of all older standards of human excellence, but has also at its heart that trust in the overcoming of change which leads us back to judge every human situation as being solvable in terms of technology."[100] And, Grant added: "What makes the drive to technology so strong is that it is carried on by men who still identify what they are doing with the liberation of mankind."[101]

George Grant knew that submergence in the technological present requires not resistance but reconstruction and in its historical sense. Such reconstruction requires becoming aware, as Emberley summarizes, of "traces of practices, understandings, ways of life, and lived-experience which are pre-technological in our cultural and political legacy."[102] Grant knew that one could not escape technology, but one could, again in Emberley's words, find one's way "between local parochialism on the one hand and the deracinated life of the modern universal and homogenous state on the other."[103] As in Weimar Germany—whose dissolution was followed by arguably the first "modern universal and homogenous state"—finding passage between provincialism and an incapacitating deracination, demands, as Emberley notes, "attentiveness and courage."[104] After all, "in no society," as Grant was keenly aware, "is it possible for many men to live outside the dominant assumptions of their world for very long."[105] We cannot live outside them, but as educators, like Grant, we can decline to coincide with them.

"We thought we could pick and choose, as in a supermarket," Christian reminds, summarizing Grant's dismissal of the technology-is-neutral argument, that it is only a tool we can use (or not) according to our convenience.[106] That thought is itself technological, affirming, however inadvertently, our demotion to "standing reserve," Heidegger's concept.[107] At first we thought "only nature would be subject to human will," but "ourselves not."[108] But we are not exempt from our prostheses' power over us, Grant knew, as we have "bought a package deal of far more fundamental novelness than simply a set of instruments under our control. It is a destiny which enfolds us in its own conception of instrumentality, neutrality and purposiveness."[109] As we disappear into the technoculture we created and which now recreates us as its subjects, technology surpasses our capacity to grasp it. "We apprehend our destiny by forms of thought which are themselves the very core of that destiny," Grant lamented.[110] As if conscious of the idolatry technology insinuates, Grant challenged us to "understand our technological destiny from principles more comprehensive than its own."[111] For Grant, "Thought is steadfast attention to the whole."[112]

Grant did not imagine that "the whole" could be grasped, intellectually or otherwise. It was one's relationship to that which exceeds understanding that absorbed Grant's attention in his final years. He reaffirmed his Christian faith as he reasserted his contempt for the cult of convenience, whether exercised in academics or abortion. I suspect it was his anti-abortion arguments—and perhaps his somewhat strange obsession with the controversial French writer Louis-Ferdinand Céline—that have contributed to his present obscurity. For me it is Grant's courage that remains, expressed through his insightful critiques and searing laments. Grant formulated and followed his convictions, always engaged with his countrymen and the historical moment, seeking the timeless truth he discerned as lodged within the particularities of each. He followed his thought, his attention to the whole, wherever it led him, at whatever cost to his worldly status. He lamented his nation and took on technology, not due to personal quirkiness—although there was that—but in fidelity to an ancient conception of justice and truth.

"To put the matter in a popular way," Grant wrote, "justice is an unchanging measure of all our times and places, and our love of it defines us."[113] It was the love of justice—no contract, as his critique of John Rawls underscores—that attunes us to "the whole," that demands attention and duty. It is our love of justice, Grant insisted, that inspires us to exceed what technology has made of us. It is in fact our calling to "understand our technological destiny from principles more comprehensive than its own."[114] What principles could be "more comprehensive" than *those* principles—calculation, instrumentality, obsession—that the technological imperative installs? By the end of his life, Grant felt he had found it. The primary principle was love, which Grant conceived as "consent to the fact that there is authentic otherness."[115] On Tuesday the 27th of September 1988, George Grant died. His critique of technology remains with us, a testimony to the capacity of thought to exceed what is, including those idols whose vassals Grant suspected we have become.

Notes

1 Grant (1998 [1974], 1).

2 "A political philosopher who spent his most productive years teaching in a department of religion," Andrew Potter (2005, ix) summarizes, "George Grant is probably best known today as the father of English-speaking Canadian nationalism." For Robin Lathangue (1998, vii) a "public intellectual," for the distinguished American sociologist Seymour Martin Lipset (1990, 36) Grant was "Canada's most distinguished conservative intellectual." It is the adjective "conservative" that requires clarification, as the term connotes for Grant a different set of political preoccupations than it does in the United States. "The truth of conservatism," Grant (1966 [1959], 108) wrote, "is the truth of order and limit, both in social and personal life. But obviously conservatism by itself will not do. For it can say nothing about the overcoming of evil, and at its worst implies that certain evils are a continuing necessity." Even at this stage—the late 1950s—Grant (1966 [1959], 109) appreciated the concept's appropriation: "Yet to express conservatism in Canada means *de facto* to justify the continuing rule of the businessman and the right of the greedy to turn all activities into sources of personal gain."

3 Trained in history at Queen's University, William Grant lectured in colonial history at Oxford from 1906 until 1910; he then returned to teach history at Queen's. Among his publications were a biography of his father (1905), a controversial history of Canada for use in Ontario high schools (1914) and *The Tribune of Nova Scotia: A Chronicle of Joseph Howe* (1915; see Christian 2001 [1995], viii).
4 Quoted in Christian (2001 [1995], viii–ix).
5 Harold Innis' biographer Alexander John Watson (2007, 426) positions Grant in a generational cohort of "profound figures . . . whose gestation period was between the end of the First and Second World Wars." In addition to Innis and Grant, Watson adds Innis' political economist colleague C. B. Macpherson, classics scholar A. E. Havelock, the great literary critic and public intellectual Northrop Frye, and Marshall McLuhan.
6 Christian (2001 [1995], ix).
7 Ibid.
8 Quoted in Christian (2001 [1995], x).
9 Christian (2001 [1995], x).
10 Potter (2005, xxx).
11 Christian (2001 [1995], xiii).
12 Christian (2001 [1995], xiv).
13 "Our interest in history as a study is directly related to our belief that we are historical beings," Grant (2001 [1969], 10) argued: "Indeed, in modern thought the idea of history is everywhere. . . . Even reason, which was traditionally conceived as transcending all development, has been given its history."
14 Roberts (1995, 60).
15 Ibid. While not a key category for Grant, allegory could be said to structure Grant's *oeuvre*, as he grapples with questions of meaning, contingency, and history. "The enchantment of our souls by myth, philosophy or revelation," he observed, "has been replaced by a more immediate meaning—the building of a society of free and equal men by the overcoming of chance" (1969, 138). Any overarching—for Grant it is eternity—meaning of our lives disappears in modernity's conflation of "freedom" with "will" (Grant 1969, 142). While Emberley (2005 [1994], lxxvii) employs "meditation" to describe Grant's *Lament for a Nation*, it is clear the term resonates with the doubleness of allegory:

> A meditation raises the reader from what is familiar and near, to a level in which the recollection of experiences and understandings reveals what is most enduring in our human existence. It demands that we reflect on the tension between our particular historical existence and the greater whole of which we are a part. A meditation closes by returning its participants to the familiar and near, having disclosed how they are necessarily invested with what is highest and most enduring.

This is precisely what is lost to a world wherein there is "nothing but history." It is this world allegory inscribes (see Pinar 2012, 50).
16 See Grant (2005 [1965], 4).
17 It had been the fall of the Progressive Conservative government in 1963 and its replacement by the Liberal party and the new Prime Minister Lester Pearson's willingness to accept nuclear warheads and generally accommodate the Americans that provided the political provocation for George Grant's *Lament for a Nation*. It was the "shabby" treatment of John G. Diefenbaker—of whom Grant was critical—by the "Canadian elite" that fueled, Potter (2005, xvi) suggests, Grant's "seething, focused anger." See also Grant (2005 [1970], lxxi).
18 Grant (2005 [1970], lxxii).
19 Emberley (2005 [1994], lxxx).
20 Ibid.

21 Detlev J.K. Peukert (1992, 81–82) provides a more detailed definition; for him "modernity" refers

> to the form of fully fledged industrialized society that has been with us from the turn of the century until the present day. In an economic sense, modernity is characterized by highly rationalized industrial production, complex technological infrastructures and a substantial degree of bureaucratized administrative and service activity; food production is carried out by an increasingly small but productive, agricultural sector. Socially speaking, its typical features include the division of labor, wage and salary discipline, an urbanized environment, extensive educational opportunities and a demand for skills and training. As far as culture is concerned, media products dominate; continuity with traditional aesthetic principles and practices in architecture and the visual and other creative arts is broken, and is replaced by unrestricted formal experimentation. In intellectual terms, modernity marks the triumph of Western rationality, whether in social planning, the expansion of the sciences or the self-replicating dynamism of technology, although this optimism is accompanied by skeptical doubts from social thinkers and cultural critics.

22 Grant (2005 [1965], 52).
23 Grant (2005 [1965], 52 n. 15).
24 Grant (2005 [1965], 53).
25 Grant (1966, iv).
26 Grant (1998 [1974], 2).
27 Potter (2005, xxiv) points out that Grant's divination of technology as a universal homogenizing force is reflected in the mainstream social sciences from the 1950s to the 1970s.
28 Grant (1969, 33).
29 Ibid.
30 See Grant (1969, 34).
31 As the school as educational institution is dismantled in the United States, professional educators are no longer required; the curriculum is moved online and assignments are monitored by underpaid checkers. In this regard, "school reform" is a subspecies of ongoing profit-driven corporate restructuring, downgrading professionals into interchangeable parts, easily replaced and paid accordingly. One hundred years ago the top executive of a business firm typically earned no more than 20 times the average wage of its workers. In the United States today that multiple has risen to 200, Cohen (2009, 30, 33, 34) reminds. The same greed drives the privatization of public schools in the United States today, as public funds are diverted from school children and their teachers into the pockets of profiteers (see Saul 2011).
32 The private sphere of freedom is also where thought is relegated. "In capitalist democracy," Grant (1986, 10) notes, "differences about practice are seen as important, while theoretical differences are seen as people's private business. It is of the very nature of 'technology' that this should be the case."
33 Many (among them Habermas) attribute a normative dimension to the public sphere as it housed the liberal idea of public discussion of different viewpoints. With Herf (1984, 24 n. 17), "I am using the term in a strictly descriptive sense to refer to a forum in which politics is discussed without all points of view necessarily being represented." In a public-sphere-as-market, politics becomes "retail" and public dialogue devolves into advertising (as McLuhan, in 1974, pointed out: see Cavell 2002, 186), often of the "false" kind. The point is private accumulation, not sacrifice for the common good, these last two concepts that are incomprehensible in the public sphere as market.
34 Grant (1969, 26).
35 Two (sometimes overstated) threats to contemporary society—terrorists and child predators—have rendered retreat from the public sphere suspect.

36 For Heidegger, Kleinberg (2005, 15) points out, *das Man* is an "essential structure" of *Dasein* because it is what accords *Dasein* its "values, norms, and practices." While the "basis for all shared practices," Kleinberg (2005, 16) continues, "it is [also] the locus of conformity wherein the individual *Dasein* loses itself in the anonymity of shared practices." The "rationality" and "universal principles" of the present age strengthen the "grip" of "das Man," Kleinberg (2005, 16) explains, "obscuring" the character, indeed the ontology, of *Dasein*. The materialization of that "rationality" is, in part, technology. Charles Larmore (2010, 142), in contrast, contests the idea that being authentic requires us to be "independent of what conventions and borrowed models have made of us." For him, authenticity turns on the self's relationship to itself (see 2010, 173).

37 See Lasch (1984).

38 Kleinberg (2005, 16).

39 Grant (1969, 26–27).

40 "Our modern way of looking at the world hides from us the reality of many political things," Grant (1969, 72–73) argues, "but about nothing is it more obscuring than the inevitable relation between dynamic technology and imperialism." In his *Lament for A Nation*, Grant (2005 [1965], 9, n. 1) had defended his use of the phrase "American Empire" by noting that "an empire does not have to wield direct political control over colonial countries." Indeed, decades before the "retreat of the state" argument (see Strange 1996), George Grant (2005 [1965], 42) knew that "by its very nature the capitalist system makes of national boundaries only matters of political formality." Is this prescience in part an acknowledgement of Empire as a "non-place," as Hardt and Negri (2000, xiv) later suggest, as "characterized fundamentally by a lack of boundaries; Empire's rule has no limits." To guarantee "justice . . . for all peoples," Hardt and Negri (2000, 11) continue, "the single power is given the necessary force to conduct, when necessary, 'just wars' at the borders against the barbarians and internally against the rebellious." But all violence is not directed elsewhere, as "the totalizing social processes of Empire" (2000, 10) ensure that standardization—leaving no child behind—will be enforced at home. Grant (1969, 73) discerned an "inevitable relation between dynamic technology and imperialism." There is also blowback (although Grant never uses this term associated with 9/11; I am associate it here with social disintegration) in "the practical tumult of the technological society" (Grant 1998 [1974], 88).

41 This is Grant's (1969, 28) phrase.

42 Grant (1969, 28).

43 Grant (1969, 24).

44 In addition to its racialized connotation, "pale" can also point to the absence of the specificity of relationality. Martin Buber, Axelrod (1979, 63) notes, employed the term "alien place" to reference social structures "emptied themselves of their relational content." So-called "interactive" behaviors may be more sensorimotor than affectional in nature, disembodied and imagistic: online.

45 Grant (1969, 24). Is there anyplace to hide? Forty years ago Grant (1969, 24) named "art and sexuality," but I suspect he might today exclude these as well, given their commodification. "Repressive desublimation" (for a succinct summary see Savran 1998, 34–36) was a key concept in his time. Grant (2001 [1969], 26) associated desublimation with the human will and the emancipation of passion; Marcuse argued that desublimation could also be "repressive." But that politically reactionary consequence is outstripped by the confidence many express in electronic media, that an "electronic enlightenment will overcome the old anal rationality of print and speech" (Grant 2001 [1969], 49). Grant may be referencing McLuhan here, who thought not only linear rationality but nationalism itself had been a "product of print" (Cavell 2002, 186).

46 Recall that Lasch links the culture of narcissism with the United States and the latter decades of the twentieth century. Technologism is not confined to our time, but,

in Peukert's analysis (see 1992, 241–242), was prominent in the Weimar Republic and its dissolution. Especially unbridled capitalism undermines democracy, replacing questions of common good with private gain, and converting technology into extensions of desire, the unleashing of passion without its reconstruction into public service. It all happened once before, in the Weimar Republic.

47 Nusselder's (2009, 23).
48 Grant (2001 [1969], 56).
49 Grant (2005 [1965], 71).
50 Grant (1969, 76).
51 Potter (2005, xliii).
52 Grant (1998 [1974], 3).
53 "'Information' is about objects," Grant (1986, 24) points out, "and comes forth as part of that science which summons subjects to give us their reasons." In its very nature it is "homogenizing" (1986, 24).
54 Potter (2005, xliii).
55 Krauss (2007, 30).
56 Quoted in Potter (2005, xliii).
57 Silverman (2009, 107) recalls a 1945 Heidegger presentation ("What Are Poets For?") to a small group of listeners, in which he that suggested that what "threatens" humanity "with death, and indeed with the death of his own nature, is the unconditional character of mere willing in the sense of purposeful self-assertion in everything." Such instrumental—technological—rationality has come to dominate thinking, now reduced to everyday calculation of self-interest, dignified in academic disciplines such as economics. Applied economics assumes, Coyle (2007, 124) asserts, "rational and self-interested behavior by individuals."
58 Potter (2005, xlv).
59 *Webster's New Collegiate Dictionary*, p. 575.
60 Potter (2005, xlv) points out that Grant's analysis of technology as "universalizing" and "homogenizing," dissolving "all particularity" remains uppermost in today's anti-globalization activism, concerned that the "culturally uniformity that has swept through North America will soon extend to the rest of the planet."
61 As Kroker (1984, 60) points out:

> [B]ecause we live now, fully, within the designed environment of the technological sensorium. . . . We now take our 'environment' with us in the form of technical 'extensions' of the human body or senses. The technostructure is both the lens through which we experience the world, and, in fact, the 'anxious object' with which human experience has become imperceptibly, almost subliminally, merged.

62 Kroker (1984, 61).
63 As a structure enabling subjective reconstruction, non-coincidence (see Pinar 2011, 158 n. 13) is the space of freedom, wherein—I'm recalling Potter's phrasing quoted earlier in the main text—thought and action can occur. It is the space of non-coincidence that study can cultivate.
64 Also informed by Heidegger, Aoki's analysis of technology merits a separate section, but suffice to say here that he concludes his essay by recounting a case in which life itself depends on technology. "Carol," Aoki (2005 [1987], 157) informs us, "has been for 12 years a child of haemo-dialysis technology. She and her three siblings have been sustained by a dialysis machine at the University of Alberta Hospital. . . . She recently wrote of her experiences with technology: 'We acknowledge our indebtedness to technology; we refuse to be enslaved by technology'." In another essay, Aoki (2005 [1993], 292) reflects: "As I contemplate my relationship to technology, I affirm that it is both a blessing and a burden." Whatever his intentions, these terms—"blessing" and "burden"—convey Christian connotations, interesting in

light of Grant's acknowledgement that technology, however it has undermined hierarchies and ended parochialism, cannot communicate spirituality (see Emberley 2005 [1994], lxxxi).

65 Emberley (2005 [1994], lxxxi).

66 Richard Cavell (2002, 170) points out that it was Marshall McLuhan who "sought to convey the notion that the world around us, and the lived experience of it, had become artifactual through the effects of media, such that nature could be said to have collapse into culture." This seems to me more like an acknowledgement of pervasive narcissism than it does historical or empirical fact. With climate change, for instance, nature isn't collapsing into culture, but vice versa.

67 Grant (2005 [1965], 73).

68 Grant (2005 [1965], 63).

69 See Pinar (2012, 172).

70 Emberley (2005 [1994], lxxxi).

71 Christian (1996, 177).

72 Mary Bryson (2004, 240), too, notes that "everyday cultural practices have always-already been mediated by artifacts."

73 Christian (1996, 177).

74 Willinsky (2006, 113).

75 Quoted in Cohen (2011, August 29, B3).

76 Cohen (2011, August 29, B3).

77 Quoted in Cohen (2011, August 29, B3).

78 Ibid.

79 Grant (2005 [1965], 78). In the 1970s—before U.S. school reform became a juggernaut—I noticed officials in schools wearing buttons that said simply "Change Agent!" What change was advocated, and for what purpose? These were left unaddressed: change was important for its own sake. Later, when they were addressed—the change demanded was numerical: test scores—the academic culture of schools was undermined.

80 Grant (2005 [1965], 71).

81 See, for instance, Saul (2011, December 13, A1) and Spring 2012.

82 "It is hard indeed," Grant (1966, vi) observes in another context, "to overstate the importance of faith in progress through technology to those brought up in the main stream of North American life. It is the very ground of their being. The loss of this faith for a North American is equivalent to the loss of himself and the knowledge of how to live."

83 Grant (1986, 15).

84 Grant (1986, 16).

85 Jünger ([1931], in Kaes, Jay, and Dimendberg 1995, 371).

86 Grant (1986, 16).

87 Ling (2008, 3) argues that "mobile communication . . . supports better contact within the personal sphere, sometimes at the expense of interaction with those who are co-present," but in doing so, supports "social cohesion" (2008, 5). Ling's study is of cellphone use; Keller (2012, June 11, A19) reports that online sites—Facebook in particular—leave many "lonely, and narcissistic and actually ill."

88 Grant (1986, 16).

89 Grant (1986, 17).

90 Paras (2006, 85).

91 Bowers (2000, 22) worries that "computers lead us to substitute decontextualized ways of thinking about the world for the sensory encounters with the natural world that intertwine our lives." Such dissociation occurs not only vis-à-vis natural world, but within culture as well. "[T]he the electronic 'community'," he argues, "is populated by individuals who are free both of the moral constraints and the wisdom contained in the intergenerational narratives of the cultural group" (Bowers 2000, 46). Grant (1986, 26) notes that "computers . . . exclude certain forms of

community and permit others." Such intergenerational isolation spells narcissism, implied in Bowers' (2000, 47) observation that: "Just as data should be viewed as a degraded from of knowledge, computer-mediated communication should be viewed as a degraded form of symbolic interaction—one that reinforces the rootless individual who is comfortable with the expressions of self-creation that the computer industry finds profitable to encourage." Concerning education specifically, Bowers (2000, 111) cites evidence from the mid-1990s questioning the positive correlation between technology and learning. Despite the evidence, that faith remains unbroken and aggressively promoted, as in the U.S. schools are privatized and curriculum moved online (Spring 2012).

92 Grant (1986, 19).

93 Ronell (2003, 97). Discussing the work of Paul de Man, Ronell (2003, 98) suggests that "technology's essence is disclosed in its moments of breakdown . . . the fact that 'l'effet machinal' is responsible for effects of meaning generated by sheer contingency, elements of uncontrol and improvisation." Such disruption—the "technicity of a power failure" (Ronell 2003, 97)—denotes, one might say, "the experience of permanent parabasis" (Ronell 2003, 99). Can this be an experience of ecstatic self-departure . . . a desubjectivizing rupture [producing] a medused effect, terrorizing and petrifying the other[?]" (Ronell 2003, 193) asks, underwriting "the radical vulnerability of the psychologically uninsured" (Ronell 2003, 209)? Probably such "rupture" underwrites nothing.

94 Grant (1969, 142).

95 After achieving access to her childhood experience through painting, Alice Miller abandoned any concept of pedagogy, asserting that all pedagogies serve the needs of adults, not of children; she substitutes the concept "support" (Capps 1995, 8). Interesting in light of Grant's later critique of abortion, Miller is critical of opponents of abortion, who, she points out, substitute abstract conceptions of life for "lived life," thereby distracting our attention away from the need to work toward the protection of the right of already-born children to a life without parental violence. Instead of making parental abuse a criminal offence, "pro-life" advocates want to illegalize abortion. Miller points out as well that those who oppose abortion are often supporters of "traditional" childrearing practices (what she terms "poisonous pedagogies"), characterized by abusive ideas such as "spoil the rod and spare the child." These people exhibit no commitment to protect the children they insist be born from parental, social, and economic violence. They say they "love" the unborn child, but to claim to "love" without at the same time condemning traditional childrearing practices discloses the same confusion of love and cruelty that these "old-fashioned" childrearing practices themselves reproduce (see Capps 1995, 19).

96 Grant (1969, 78).

97 In contrast to Freud, for instance, who, Elsaesser (2009, 93) reminds us, was a "notorious technophobe, who, according to his son, hated both the radio and the telephone. . . . Freud's obdurate refusal to have anything to do with cinema . . . is well documented." While "refusal" is not an option for many of us, the great man's contempt for technology was no eccentricity.

98 As Emberley (2005 [1994], lxxxi–xxxiii) points out.

99 "[I]n its profound past form," (Grant 1986, 24) reminds, "heterogeneity" was an "expression of autochthony."

100 Grant (1969, 34).

101 Grant (1969, 27).

102 Emberley (2005 [1994], lxxxiv).

103 Ibid.

104 Ibid.

105 Grant (2005 [1965], 41).

106 Christian (1996, 358).

107 Contemplating computer technology twenty-five years ago, Ted Aoki (2005 [1987], 153) sounds a little like George Grant:

> How, then, is this essence (of computer technology) revealed? It is revealed as an enframing, the ordering of both man and nature that aims at mastery. This enframing reduces man and beings to a sort of 'standing reserve,' a stock pile of resources to be at hand and on call for utilitarian ends. . . . But by so becoming, man tends to be forgetful of his own essence, no longer able to encounter himself authentically. Hence, what endangers man where revealing as ordering holds sway is his inability to present other possibilities of revealing. In this, it is not computer technology that is dangerous; it is the essence of computer technology that is dangerous.

Aoki's distinction reminds us that it is the way of being technology invites that threatens revelation and that it is our responsibility to decline the invitation. Still, the threat is "revealed" through the machine, apparently only harmless if not in fact helpful, and in that misrecognition our "inability to present other possibilities of revealing" becomes installed (like a virus). That means that, as Grant—and later C.A. Bowers (1995, 12; 2000, 8)—knew, computer technology is indeed "dangerous."

108 Christian (1996, 358).
109 Ibid.
110 Grant (1986, 32).
111 Quoted in Christian (1996, 358).
112 Grant (1998 [1974], 84).
113 Quoted in Christian (1996, 354).
114 Quoted in Christian (1996, 358).
115 Quoted in Christian (1996, 359).

Bibliography

Aoki, Ted T. 2005 (1986/1991). Teaching as Indwelling Between Two Curriculum Worlds. In *Curriculum in a New Key: The Collected Works of Ted T. Aoki*, edited by William F. Pinar and Rita L. Irwin (159–165). Mahwah, NJ: Lawrence Erlbaum.

Aoki, Ted. T. 2005 (1987). Toward Understanding Computer Application. In *Curriculum in a New Key: The Collected Works of Ted T. Aoki* edited by William F. Pinar and Rita L. Irwin (151–158). Mahwah, NJ: Lawrence Erlbaum.

Aoki, Ted T. 2005 (1990). *Sonare* and *Videre*: A Story, Three Echoes and a Lingering Note. In *Curriculum in a New Key: The Collected Works of Ted T. Aoki*, edited by William F. Pinar and Rita L. Irwin (367–376). Mahwah, NJ: Lawrence Erlbaum.

Autio, Tero. 2006. *Subjectivity, Schooling, Society: Between and Beyond German Didaktik and Anglo-American Curriculum Studies*. Mahwah, NJ: Lawrence Erlbaum.

Axelrod, Charles David. 1979. *Studies in Intellectual Breakthrough*. Amherst: University of Massachusetts Press.

Banchero, Stephanie and Simon, Stephanie. 2011, November 12–13. My Teacher is an App. *Wall Street Journal*, C1–C2.

Barnard, Anne. 2013, February 1. As Arab Spring's Glow Fades and Turmoil Rises Unsettling Questions. *New York Times*, A10.

Barriga, Frida Díaz. 2003. Main Trends of Curriculum Research in México. In *International Handbook of Curriculum Research*, edited by William F. Pinar (457–469). Mahwah, NJ: Lawrence Erlbaum.

Bowers, C.A. 1995. *Educating for an Ecologically Sustainable Culture*. Albany: State University of New York Press.

Bowers, C.A. 2000. *Let Them Eat Data: How Computers Affect Education, Cultural Diversity and the Prospects of Ecological Sustainability*. Athens: University of Georgia Press.
Bryson, Mary. 2004. When Jill Jacks In: Queer Women and the Net. *Feminist Media Studies* 4 (3), 239–254.
Callahan, Raymond E. 1962. *Education and the Cult of Efficiency*. Chicago: University of Chicago Press.
Capps, Donald. 1995. *The Child's Song: The Religious Abuse of Children*. Louisville, KY: Westminster John Knox Press.
Cavell, Richard. 2002. *McLuhan in Space: A Cultural Geography*. Toronto: University of Toronto Press.
Christian, William. 1995. Introduction to George Grant's *Time as History* (vii–xli). Toronto: University of Toronto Press.
Christian, William. 1996. *George Grant: A Biography*. Toronto: University of Toronto Press.
Christian, William. 2001 (1995). Editor's Introduction: George Grant's Nietzsche. George Grant's *Time as History* (vii–xli). Toronto: University of Toronto Press.
Cohen, Daniel. 2009. *Three Lectures on Post-Industrial society*. [Trans. William McCuaig.] Cambridge, MA: The MIT Press.
Cohen, Noam. 2011, August 29. In Unsettled Times, Media Can Be a Call to Action, or a Distraction. *New York Times*, B3.
Coyle, Diane. 2007. *The Soulful Science: What Economists Really Do and Why It Matters*. Princeton, NJ: Princeton University Press.
Cusset, François. 2008. *French Theory: How Foucault, Derrida, Deleuze, & Co. Transformed the Intellectual Life of the United States*. [Trans. Jeff Fort.] Minneapolis: University of Minnesota Press.
Dewey, John. 1910. *How We Think*. Boston: D.C. Health & Co.
Dewey, John. 1920. *Reconstruction in Philosophy*. New York: Henry Holt and Company.
Dewey, John. 1962 (1934). *A Common Faith*. New Haven, CT: Yale University Press.
Elsaesser, Thomas. 2009. No end to *Nosferatu* (1922). In *Weimar Cinema*, edited by Noah Isenberg (79–94). New York: Columbia University Press.
Emberley, Peter C. 2005 (1994). Foreword to the Carleton Library Edition of *Lament for a Nation* by George Grant (lxxviii–lxxxv). Montreal and Kingston: McGill-Queen's University Press.
Epstein, Jason. 2010 (March 11). Publishing: The Revolutionary Future. *New York Review of Books*, 4, 6.
Foster, Thomas. 2005. *The Souls of Cyberfolk: Posthumanism as Vernacular Theory*. Minneapolis: University of Minnesota Press.
Gouldner, Alvin W. 1970. *The Coming Crisis of Western Sociology*. New York: Basic Books.
Grant, George. 1966. Introduction to *Philosophy in the Mass Age* (iii–ix). Toronto: Copp Clark Publishing.
Grant, George. 1966 (1959). *Philosophy in the Mass Age*. Toronto: Copp Clark Publishing.
Grant, George. 1969. *Technology & Empire*. Toronto: Anansi.
Grant, George. 1986. *Technology and Justice*. Toronto: Anansi.
Grant, George. 1995 (1969). *Time as History*. [Edited and with an introduction by William Christian.] Toronto: University of Toronto Press.
Grant, George. 1998 (1974). *English-Speaking Justice*. Toronto: Anansi.
Grant, George. 2001 (1969). *Time as History*. Toronto: University of Toronto Press.
Grant, George. 2005 (1965). *Lament for a Nation*. [40th anniversary edition.] Montreal and Kingston: McGill-Queen's University Press.
Grant, George. 2005 (1970). Introduction to the Carleton Library Edition of *Lament for a Nation* (lxix–lxxvi). Montreal and Kingston: McGill-Queen's University Press.

Gutek, Gerald L. 2006. George S. Counts and the Origins of Social Reconstructionism. In *Social Reconstruction: People, Politics, Perspectives*, edited by Karen L. Riley (1–26). Greenwich, CT: Information Age Publishing.

Hardt, Michael and Negri, Antonio. 2000. *Empire*. Cambridge, MA: Harvard University Press.

Herf, Jeffrey. 1984. *Reactionary Modernism: Technology, Culture, and Politics in Weimar and the Third Reich*. Cambridge: Cambridge University Press.

Hofstadter, Richard. 1996 (1965). *The Paranoid Style in American Politics and Other Essays*. Cambridge, MA: Harvard University Press.

Kaes, Anton, Jay, Martin, and Dimendberg, Edward. eds. 1995. *The Weimar Sourcebook*. Berkeley: University of California Press.

Keller, Bill. 2012, June 11. Wising Up to Facebook. *New York Times*, A19.

Kimmel, Michael S. 1996. *Manhood in America: A Cultural History*. New York: Free Press

Kleinberg, Ethan. 2005. *Generation Existential: Heidegger's Philosophy in France, 1927–1961*. Ithaca, NY: Cornell University Press.

Kracauer, Siegfried. 1995. *The Mass Ornament: Weimar Essays*. [Translated, edited, and with an introduction by Thomas Y. Levin.] Cambridge, MA: Harvard University Press.

Krauss, Rosalind. 2007. Who Comes after the Subject? In *The Life & The Work: Art and Biography*, edited by Charles G. Salas (28–33). Los Angeles, CA: Getty Publications.

Kroker, Arthur. 1984. *Technology and the Canadian Mind: Innis/McLuhan/Grant*. Montreal: New World Perspectives.

LaCapra, Dominick. 2004. *History in Transit: Experience, Identity, Critical Theory*. Ithaca, NY: Cornell University Press.

Larmore, Charles. 2010. *The Practices of the Self*. [Trans. Sharon Bowman.] Chicago: University of Chicago Press.

Lasch, Christopher. 1978. *The Culture of Narcissism: American Life in an Age of Diminishing Expectations*. New York: Norton.

Lasch, Christopher. 1984. *The Minimal Self: Psychic Survival in Troubled Times*. New York: Norton.

Lathangue, Robin. 1998. Introduction to George Grant *English-Speaking Justice* (vii–xxi). Toronto: Anansi.

Levin, Thomas Y. 1995. Introduction to *The Mass Ornament: Weimar Essays* by Siegfried Kracauer (1–30). Cambridge, MA: Harvard University Press.

Lilla, Mark. 2010, May 27. The Tea Party Jacobins. *New York Review of Books*, 53–56.

Ling, Rich. 2008. *New Tech, New Ties: How Mobile Communication is Reshaping Social Cohesion*. Cambridge, MA: The MIT Press.

Lipset, Seymour Martin. 1990. *Continental Divide: The Values and Institutions of the United States and Canada*. New York: Routledge.

Macdonald, James B. 1995. *Theory as a Prayerful Act*. New York: Peter Lang.

McKnight, Douglas. 2002. *Schooling, the Puritan Imperative, and the Molding of the American National Identity*. Mahwah, NJ: Lawrence Erlbaum.

Nusselder, André. 2009. *Interface Fantasy: A Lacanian Cyborg Ontology*. Cambridge, MA: The MIT Press.

Paras, Eric. 2006. *Foucault 2.0: Beyond Power and Knowledge*. New York: Other Press.

Perlstein, Daniel. 2000. "There is no escape . . . from the ogre of indoctrination": George Counts and the Civic Dilemmas of Democratic Educators. In *Reconstructing the Common Good in Education: Coping with Intractable Dilemmas*, edited by Larry Cuban and Dorothy Shipps (51–67). Stanford, CA: Stanford University Press.

Peukert, Detlev J.K. 1992. *The Weimar Republic: The Crisis of Classical Modernity*. [Trans. Richard Deveson.] New York: Hill and Wang.

Pinar, William F. 2000 (1975). Sanity, Madness and the School. In *Curriculum Theorizing: The Reconceptualization,* edited by William F. Pinar (359–383). Troy, NY:

Educator's International Press. (Originally published in *Curriculum Theorizing: The Reconceptualists* [359–383]. Berkeley, CA: McCutchan.)

Pinar, William F. 2001. *The Gender of Racial Politics and Violence in American: Lynching, Prison Rape, and the Crisis of Masculinity*. New York: Peter Lang.

Pinar, William F. 2011. *The Character of Curriculum Studies: Bildung, Currere, and the Recurring Question of the Subject*. New York: Palgrave Macmillan.

Pinar, William F. 2012. *What Is Curriculum Theory?* [Second edition.] New York: Routledge.

Pinar, William F. and Grumet, Madeleine R. 2006 (1976). *Toward a Poor Curriculum*. Troy, NY: Educator's International Press. [Originally published by Kendall/Hunt.]

Potter, Andrew. 2005. Introduction to the 40th Anniversary Edition of George P. Grant's *Lament for a Nation* (ix–lxviii). Montreal and Kingston: McGill-Queen's University Press.

Roberts, David D. 1995. *Nothing but History: Reconstruction and Extremity after Metaphysics*. Berkeley and Los Angeles: University of California Press.

Robinson, Marilynne. 2010. *Absence of Mind: The Dispelling of Inwardness from the Modern Myth of the Self*. New Haven, CT: Yale University Press.

Romero, Simon. 2012, August 13. Argentina's New Literary Tradition—Pensions for Aging Writers. *New York Times*, A5.

Ronell, Avital. 2003. *Stupidity*. Urbana and Chicago: University of Illinois Press.

Saul, John Ralston. 2005. *The Collapse of Globalism: And the Reinvention of the World*. Toronto: Viking Canada.

Saul, Stephanie. 2011, December 13. Profits and Questions at Online Charter Schools. Parents Get to Choose, but Standards Slip and Scores Suffer. *New York Times*, A1, A18–A19.

Savran, David. 1998. *Taking It a Like a Man: White Masculinity, Masochism, and Contemporary American Culture*. Princeton, NJ: Princeton University Press.

Seixas, Peter. 2011. Assessment of Historical Thinking. In *New Possibilities for the Past: Shaping History Education in Canada*, edited by Penney Clark (139–153). Vancouver: University of British Columbia Press.

Silverman, Kaja. 2009. *Flesh of My Flesh*. Stanford, CA: Stanford University Press.

Smith, David Geoffrey. In press. *Wisdom Responses to Globalization: The Pedagogic Context*. In the International Handbook of Curriculum Research, edited by William F. Pinar. New York: Routledge.

Spring, Joel. 2012. *Education Networks: Power, Wealth, Cyberspace, and the Digital Mind*. New York: Routledge.

Strange, Susan. 1996. *The Retreat of the State: The Diffusion of Power in the World Economy*. Cambridge: Cambridge University Press.

Sztajn, Paola, Confrey, Jere, Wilson, P. Holt, and Cynthia Edgington. 2012, June–July. Learning Trajectory Based Instruction: Toward a Theory of Teaching. *Educational Researcher* 41 (5), 147–156.

Taba, Hilda. 1932. *The Dynamics of Education. A Methodology of Progressive Educational Thought*. [With a foreword by William Heard Kilpatrick.] New York: Harcourt, Brace and Company.

Taba, Hilda. 1945. General Techniques of Curriculum Planning. In the National Society for the Study of Education, *American Education in the Post War Period: Curriculum Reconstruction*. Forty-fourth Yearbook, Pt. 1 (1945), Ch. 5, 12, 267.

Taba, Hilda. 1962. *Curriculum Development: Theory and Practice*. New York: Harcourt, Brace & World.

Taubman, Peter M. 2009. *Teaching by Numbers: Deconstructing the Discourse of Standards and Accountability in Education*. New York: Routledge.

Taubman, Peter M. 2011. *Disavowed Knowledge*. New York: Routledge.

Toews, John. 2004. *Becoming Historical: Cultural Reformation and Public Memory in Early Nineteenth-Century Berlin*. New York: Cambridge University Press.

Tomkins, George S. 2008 (1986). *A Common Countenance: Stability and Change in the Canadian Curriculum*. Vancouver, Canada: Pacific Educational Press.
Tröhler, Daniel. 2011. *Languages of Education. Protestant Legacies, National Identities, and Global Aspirations*. New York: Routledge.
Tyler, Ralph W. 1949. *Basic Principles of Curriculum and Instruction*. Chicago: University of Chicago Press.
Wapner, Paul. 2010. *Living Through the End of Nature: The Future of American Environmentalism*. Cambridge, MA: The MIT Press.
Watson, Alexander John. 2007. *Marginal Man: The Dark Vision of Harold Innis*. Toronto: University of Toronto Press.
Weaver, John A. 2010. The Posthuman Condition: A Complicated Conversation. In *Curriculum Studies Handbook: The Next Moment*, edited by Erik Malewski (190–200). New York: Routledge.
Webster's New Collegiate Dictionary. 1975. Springfield, MA: G. & C. Merriam Company.
Weitz, Eric D. 2007. *Weimar Germany: Promise and Tragedy*. Princeton, NJ: Princeton University Press.
Willinsky, John. 2006. *The Access Principle: The Case for Open Access to Research and Scholarship*. Cambridge, MA: MIT Press.
Zaretsky, Eli. 2004. *Secrets of the Soul: A Social and Cultural History of Psychoanalysis*. New York: Alfred A. Knopf.

CHAPTER 6

REFORM

Commentary

Juxtaposing China's contemporary curriculum reform—as I glimpsed it in a recently completed project in China—with Ben Williamson's vision of the future of curriculum, I underscore the significance of context in understanding curriculum. China's reform follows decades of authoritarian pedagogy formulated in the Soviet Union and enforced in China; the reform draws on U.S. progressivism (Dewey in particular) as well as on ancient Chinese traditions of Confucianism, Taoism, and Buddhism.[1] Williamson[2] employs some of the same language as do the Chinese reformers but toward the commercialization of the curriculum. Does the future Williamson foresees for curriculum in the West foreshadow the future of China's reform?

Bibliography

Pinar, William F. ed. 2014. *Curriculum Studies in China: Intellectual Histories, Present Circumstances.* New York: Palgrave Macmillan.

Williamson, Ben. 2013. *The Future of the Curriculum. School Knowledge in the Digital Age.* Cambridge, MA: The MIT Press.

> Curriculum is the intellectual center of schooling and its main message system.
>
> Ben Williamson[3]

In China's curriculum reform—as I glimpsed it through the essays of Zhang Hua, Zhang Wenjun, Chen Yuting, Kang Changyun, Cong Lixin, Ma Yunpeng, Zhou Huixia, and Liu Jian[4]—the status of student is shifting.[5] Relying on their essays and a book by Ben Williamson on the future of curriculum, I will sketch the context[6] of this shift, its enactment of ethical conviction in China, and its corporatization in the West. The juxtaposition of the two—the repositioning of students in China and the West—can contribute, I trust, to our appreciation of how crucial context is to understanding curriculum.[7]

In China

> The curriculum should enable students to build strong bodies and healthy mental qualities, to develop healthy aesthetic tastes and life styles, and to become a new generation with aspiration, ethics, literacy, and discipline.
>
> Zhou Huixia[8]

While more complex than I can indicate here, elements of the context in which China's curriculum reform is occurring can be glimpsed—can it not?—by referencing "Kairov's pedagogy," the Chinese version of which has been called the "special epistemology of instruction" (SEI), as elaborated by Professor Wang Cesan. Wang had argued that "teachers teach students to mainly learn ready-made knowledge in order to know the world and develop themselves." Students do not construct knowledge, he insisted; students, in Wang's words, "must be ready to receive ready-made knowledge from textbooks by teachers' instruction."[9] This view means, Zhang Hua has observed,[10] "that teachers play the dominant roles and students must be obedient in the instructional process."

One hundred years ago[11] U.S. progressives decried this hierarchical pedagogical relationship as authoritarian, inappropriate for classrooms conceived as laboratories for democracy.[12] Progressives lost this argument to curriculum conservatives by the 1950s as anxieties over the Cold War and racial integration became recast as curriculum reform.[13] The concepts progressives had advanced—and that sound somewhat similar in contemporary curriculum reform in China[14]—have come back to haunt progressives in the West, as I will show momentarily. The context—historical, national, cultural—is of course considerably different and that fact is, I submit, crucial.

"Like most Chinese students," Kang Changyun[15] confides, "I strove to take a seat on the examination train when it was my turn. Unfortunately, I didn't do well enough to go to a good university." It took "courage" to try again, but try Kang did, this time doing well enough to be admitted to the early childhood education program at Shandong Normal University. In Kang's essay—published in *Curriculum Studies in China*—we follow his journey through graduate school, his participation in the 2001 curriculum reform as expressed through his work at the Beijing Normal University Press. It concludes with his reflections on the textbook and its changing status in the ongoing reform. Kang's story is specific but references an experience shared—in singular ways—by others, scholars and students alike. While not necessarily the linchpin, textbooks' shift in status—from one taught nationwide to several, from the authoritative text to one of several sources of curricular knowledge—allegorizes[16] the scale and site of China's curriculum reform.

That site, I suggest, is subjectivity, evident in the commitment of Zhang Hua[17] to "root" curriculum and classroom practice in "each student's and teacher's personality, their individuality, creativity, and basic human rights, and a social ideal of democracy." Zhang Hua continues to study and participate in the "bottom-up" reform of curriculum and teaching in China, determined to support students' self-reflective engagement with a "curriculum of life-inquiry" and teachers' capacities to "create curriculum" as they regain "professional dignity" through "autonomy." Integral to that theoretically informed practical work, Zhang Hua points out, is the formulation of a distinctive Chinese curriculum theory based on Confucianism, Taoism, and Buddhism.[18]

"Every week," Zhang Hua explains, "I go to schools to listen to the schoolteachers. I base my study in schools on the pedagogy of listening. And this echoes my theoretical thinking." Contesting the "technical" orientation of curriculum reform—the objectives-outcomes sequence—constitutes a "next step" for the field to take, Zhang Hua suggests, but his own next steps "focus on the question of children and cultures. The former is toward the dignity of the human being; the latter is toward the dignity of culture. The connection of the two is the cause of 'neo-enlightenment' in China. This is my life's work."[19] This is a strong statement of ethical conviction key to the educator's code of conduct.

While among its most visible and important advocates, Zhang Hua is not alone in affirming the centrality of students in China's curriculum reform. Chen Yuting also affirms that students—and teachers—are now encouraged to reposition themselves from "followers" to "creators." She pointed to "a new form of curriculum called research-based study, emphasizing students' cooperation and problem-solving." Chen continued: "The purpose of a research-based subject is to pay attention to problems in social, economic, scientific, and technological life, so as to develop students' abilities to solve problems and experience synthetically and to cultivate their humanistic spirit and scientific literacy through the process of self-exploration and practice." Acknowledging the ironies of a top-down reform that encourages teachers' and students' agency, Chen Yuting remains resolved: "We all must collaborate with each other so as to surpass ourselves in the process of becoming creators, not followers."[20]

Pledging itself to improving the status of students, Zhang Wenjun reported, the government of China undertook a reform entitled "For the Development of Every Student, for the Revival of the Chinese Nation." The new curriculum, Zhang Wenjun[21] explained, "aimed at moral and values development, social responsibility, basic knowledge, skills for lifelong learning, creativity, physical and psychological well-being, healthy aesthetic tastes, and healthy life styles," acknowledging that "only a student-centered, democratic curriculum" can encourage more creative talents to compete with other countries in a "knowledge economy" in an era of "globalization." In this last phrase—linking student-centeredness to economic competition—this reform sounds close to the curriculum now being advocated in the West, as we will see.

Others focus on the educational elements that accrue when students are positioned as central to curriculum. China's curriculum reform, Zhou Huixia[22] reports, encourages students to demonstrate "creativity, practical skills, scientific and artistic skills, and environmental awareness." Students, she continued, should learn the "fundamental knowledge, skills, and methods for life-long learning." Moreover, Zhou continues, the curriculum should enable students "to become a new generation with aspiration, ethics, literacy, and discipline." Accompanying this expansive aspiration is the acknowledgement that children develop intelligence from, she writes, "their life and learning experience." No longer conceived as an isolated exercise, intelligence enables us to address—as we are addressed—by everyday life.[23]

Curriculum content, Zhou[24] continues, emphasizing the centrality of students in the reform, "should attend to students' interests and experience." The Comprehensive Practical Activity component—which included information technology (IT) education, inquiry-based studies, community service and social practice, and labor-skill education—was added "to enhance students' creativity and practical skills, to strengthen the connection between schooling and social development, to end schools' divorce from society, and to cultivate students' social responsibility." It deemphasized "passive learning, rote memorizing, and mechanical training while encouraging students' active participation, inquiry, and practice." The "classroom format," Zhou summarizes, "is shifting from teacher-centered to student-centered in which teachers are facilitators."

"Respecting students by helping teachers emphasize student inquiry," Liu Jian[25] reports, requires teachers to "face unknown knowledge together with the students in their classrooms, listening to the voices of children, learning the unique characteristics of children's thinking, observing the process of their learning, realizing the uniqueness of each child consciously, and profoundly comprehending the essence of 'respecting students' and 'student-oriented development'." These crucial concepts have far-reaching implications. "First of all," Liu Jian wrote, "how do we ensure that each student will live a decent happy life?" "Second," he asked, "how do we contribute—through exerting a gentle and subtle influence—to students' sense of responsibility?" "Third, how do we encourage students to think independently, critically and creatively?" When the curriculum enables the actualization of these aspirations—happiness, responsibility, critical and creative thinking—"we are indeed making the greatest contribution to humankind."[26]

In these affirmations of the centrality of students to China's curriculum reform one hears profound appreciation for the dignity of the individual student, expressed in the conviction—at once ethical and professional—that curriculum can contribute to the realization of each student's potential. That potential includes intelligence, practical skills, creativity, and social development. No atomized individual—as sometimes advanced in the West—this conception of the student is in the service of national development, understood in civic, cultural, and economic terms. And in Liu Jian's formulation, such national development can also be a contribution to the development of humanity. This cosmopolitan cause requires, it seems to me, concentration on the student as a singular embodiment of China's history, culture, and aspiration. That cause is degraded if national development becomes conflated with economic development, and, correspondingly, education as only preparation for economic activity. This degradation of the student—from one who studies to one who prepares for future economic activity—is what is occurring in the West.

In the West

> Consuming is learning and learning is consuming.
>
> Ben Williamson[27]

While what is occurring in the West can hardly be contained in one book, *The Future of the Curriculum: School Knowledge in the Digital Age* does convey key concepts in contemporary efforts to technologize the school curriculum in service of economic development. These concepts can sound (at least in English) chillingly close to those advanced in China's curriculum reform. While the historical and cultural context differs, Williamson's work can serve as a cautionary note to China's curriculum reformers. Can China's scholars and teachers chart their own distinctive course? Or will efforts to reactivate ancient Chinese culture and incorporate elements of twentieth-century U.S. progressivism be appropriated by the contemporary corporate determination to "profitize" the education of children?

Curriculum reform, Ben Williamson[28] acknowledges, requires "political change" and "changing what teachers and children do[29] in schools." It is not obvious what *teachers* will "do" in what he terms "cybernetically distributed . . . learning," as such learning, he[30] tells us, will be "interest-based, peer-to-peer, just-in-time participatory learning." Structured by technology, the "prototypical curriculum" of the future will be, he continues, "a more 'open source' process" than a "fixed product," as illustrated in the "wiki" layout: "open authorship, collective editing, and collaborative production." Where are teachers positioned in this "open, collective, collaborative production"?[31]

The answer is implied in his choice of words, as that last word—"production"—seems to suggest an exclusively economic structuring of classroom activity. The examples he gives are almost always financed by companies, not publics.[32] Where is acknowledgement of curriculum as complicated conversation, wherein students and teachers together engage their own distinctiveness as inheritors of their country's cultures? In the curriculum of the future—as conceived by technology corporations and summarized by Ben Williamson—technology replaces subjective presence.[33]

Because "know-how" is alleged to be "now more important" than "know-what,"[34] Williamson[35] reports that curriculum is replaced by "learning,"[36] and "knowledge"[37] by "skills." Evidently students need know nothing except how to do what is demanded of them in their future jobs, although if "knowledge" is quickly "outdated"—which Williamson[38] asserts—it is not obvious how "skills" could escape the same fate. The concept of curriculum reappears, however, as Williamson[39] references Howard Gardner's "multiple intelligences" theory, with its endorsement of a "'student-curriculum' brokerage system" that would "match students' profiles, goals, and interests to particular curricula and styles of learning, a task," Williamson adds, "for which interactive technology seemed to offer considerable potential."[40] If student "profiles, goals, and interests" do not "match" Chinese (or American) history and culture, for example, evidently students will not be asked to study these.

History and culture could be the key casualties in "centrifugal[41] schooling," and even the school seems threatened with extinction. Schools, Williamson[42] complains, institutionalize "structured hierarchical relationships," a "static print culture," and pedagogies of "old-style transmission" that don't align with our "networked era" of "interactivity" and "hypertextuality." Erudition, expertise, even intellectuality itself seem dinosaurs in this brave new world. Face-to-face engagement—dialogical encounter—is another one of those antiquated elements schools perversely preserve. Without human presence, meeting-places—such as schools—are indeed superfluous. Everything can be moved online.[43]

"Competence," Williamson[44] declares, becomes the "technical descriptor" of the child's soul." That term—with its long history in the West[45]—contracts in the curriculum of the future, shedding its spiritual, social, even psychic dimensions, except insofar as these offer value in the marketplace. The emphasis on "human capital" to be invested in the economy, Williamson writes, constitutes a "clear case of purposeful identity formation."[46] One of Williamson's[47] "prototypical examples" of the curriculum of the future—High Tech High—forefronts students' future employability in its motto "flexible learning = flexible labor."[48] Such a curriculum, he continues, encourages in children the "creativity required for nonlinear thinking and generating new ideas," exactly what, he claims, "business culture values."[49] With the forefronting of such "business culture," Williamson[50] continues, "commercial activities" will "structure" the school curriculum, and "determine" whether children can access to technology. In the West, then, creativity is no longer important in itself. Nor is academic knowledge. Nor are students, except insofar as they can be converted into "human capital" to fund "commercial activities."

Inquiry, we are told, not academic knowledge, comprises the curriculum of the future. The "task" teachers face in the "inquiry classroom," Williamson[51] explains, is to "listen" and "respond . . . flexibly and fluidly to their interests and questions." The "ideal pedagogy," he emphasizes, is a "responsive form of interactionism."[52] He adds: "Students need to be made to be inquiring." The repressive force of this regime is disclosed in that last sentence. So there can be no mistake, Williamson[53] repeats that "future of the curriculum is subject to a new[54] form of professional psychological expertise that acts to shape students as creative souls through reshaping curriculum." Ethical engagement with students studying knowledge of most worth is replaced with regimes of manipulation.[55]

In this "new" regime, institutional hierarchies of authority are inadequate to accomplish "learning." Manipulation is psychic as well as behavioral.[56] Students, Williamson[57] makes clear, are to be "shaped" as "inner-focused individuals whose own self-responsibility, competence, and well-being—their deep inner soul, interior life, and habits of mind—have been fused to the political objective of economic innovation."[58] Fusion facilitates porous psychic boundaries that open the private sphere—interiority and the very site of subjectivity—to its occupation by others. Fooled into thinking the world corresponds to his ideas of it, the psychically fused person coincides with "communities." In such cultures of narcissism, technology dissolves the differences boundaries protect, as Williamson[59] appreciates: "mass self-communication . . . prioritizes 'my time' over 'prime time'."[60] Alterity is replaced by a hall of mirrors, a "DIY[61] self-driven culture."[62]

There is, however, no "self," at least we have understood that term to denote an ongoing site of subjectivity, wherein experience occurs and wherein it can be reconstructed as educational. The actual embodied experience of the material world is replaced by virtual experience, e.g. staring at screens that stare back. Or, as Williamson writes: "learning" is recast by digital media culture as a "lifestyle choice" not an "institutionalized process."[63] Totalization and malleability are the main things, not specific (let alone lasting) influences of family or intellectual provocation through academic study and dialogical encounter in complicated conversation. Let's make this easy. Students who study will morph into "self-fashioning digital learning identities," Williamson reports, a configuration that "links young people more forcefully to changing working circumstances where the emphasis is on workers who can continually improve themselves, upskilling and retraining as changing job descriptions require."[64] Crucial to this reconfiguration of the student from soul, citizen, daughter, or son is the virtuality of the Internet, which dissolves material actuality: tradition, history, embodied psychic coherence. Those "digital learning identities" required by "centrifugal schooling" are in fact "'cyborg' identities," Williamson appreciates, "hybrids of humans with information technologies, which connect the bodies and minds of young people into the disembodied and deterritorialized spaces of the Internet."[65] From somewhere specific—home, family, school—students are transported to nowhere where "they" no longer exist. In the West, repositioning students as central in curriculum reform means not only the displacement of teachers, of curriculum as sustained study of knowledge of most worth, it provides passage to cyberspace where students themselves no longer exist, as Williamson notes, "disembodied . . . hybrids of humans."

Conclusion

> Chinese scholars have the proven capability to engage in dialogue worldwide and to reflect critically on the curriculum development experience and lessons learned from the West. We will not blindly follow or uncritically accept.
>
> Kang Changyun[66]

After decades of Kairov's pedagogy, after centuries of examination-focused schooling, and given China's commitment to the economic improvement of its citizens, what Williamson describes may sound appealing to certain reformers in China. In his vision of the future of curriculum in the West, teachers are indeed removed from their central position in the classroom, as students are repositioned onto online curriculum that appears to encourage "conversation," a practice one might imagine I could endorse. I do understand curriculum as complicated conversation, but if that conversation is predicated primarily on a conception of the student as homo economicus[67] I am inalterably opposed. This is schooling in service to corporate capitalism, not to the education of the human subject.[68] Motive matters: are student central in curriculum due to ethical conviction or due to their incorporation into commercialized virtual "learning spaces"? The former emphasizes the formation of a person, the latter the preparation of an employee.

In the West, ethical conviction disappears into economic development. Children are commodified into opportunities for profit, not as the subjects of professional commitment, as spiritually significant in themselves. In the West corporatization occurs now through technologization. Technology eviscerates subjectivity in its substitution of virtual for actual experience, with its stunting of social sensitivity and embodied expression. Orality—with its emphasis upon the cultivation of the public expression of subjective presence—can be supplemented but never replaced by technology. In the West, Williamson's work represents the cutting edge of corporatization, indeed the end of public education by its incorporation by mammoth corporations.[69] Machines substitute for substance, online sequences for dialogical encounter and subjective presence. Corporate employees not academic specialists will develop curriculum and evaluate its consequences. As corporate employees, teachers are demoted from public to domestic servants, subservient to company policy not committed to truth telling and the education of children as human beings. Students in Williamson's world are, first and finally, future employees.[70]

But today[71] we are not in the West, we are in China, with its comprehensive curriculum reform calling for recasting the teacher-student relationship. No doubt the relationship needs recasting, but I caution you to beware your enthusiasms, as they may take you farther than you at first foresaw. Few of you, I suspect, endorse without qualification Williamson's world of curriculum structured by technology, in which students and teachers seem to share almost equal footing, and where academic knowledge is replaced by skills pertinent to future employment. In China's curriculum reform, history and culture couple with contemporary concerns, and the nation remains primary. Can capitalism incorporate the humanistic and civic concerns that animate China's contemporary curriculum reform? Can China's curriculum scholars and schoolteachers chart their own distinctive course? That is the challenge you face. The outcome the world awaits.

Notes

1 See Pinar 2014.
2 See Williamson 2013.
3 2013, 15.
4 See Pinar 2014
5 Not for the first time. The May Fourth Movement—"a watershed event between traditional China and modern China" (Zhang 2014, 31)—and the 1922 Curriculum Reform reflected and presaged shifts in the status of students. See also Zhang and Gao 2014.
6 The concept of "context" connotes a divide between, say, curriculum and its circumstances, that can obscure how interrelated the two can be. Collingwood (2002, 62) points out "that the history of political theory is not the history of different answers given to one and the same question, but the history of a problem more or less constantly changing, whose solution was changing with it." Context reconfigures curriculum itself, so that the same concepts connote different meanings at different moments and in different places.
7 By "context" I am referencing "intellectual histories" and "present circumstances," terms I have employed in their almost self-evident senses. In one study (Pinar 2013), for instance, I reported the "news"—literally summarizing stories taken mostly from *The New York Times*—to depict "present circumstances" and excerpting a recent *Handbook of Curriculum Studies* as disclosing "intellectual histories." There can be less self-evident depictions of these concepts if we borrow Walter Benjamin's argument that works of art contain auratic elements that can activate what is latent in everyday life. In his 1914–1915 essay "The Life of Students," Benjamin suggested that "history rests concentrated, as in a focal point," as "elements of the ultimate condition . . . are deeply embedded in every present in the form of the most endangered, excoriated, and ridiculed creations and ideas" (quoted in Eiland and Jennings 2014, 365). In this view *The New York Times* and the *Handbook of Curriculum Studies* could obscure as much as reveal "present circumstances" and "intellectual histories." We teachers might listen carefully to our students, not for the right answers or even to diagnose misconceptions, but for clues to what we ourselves cannot apprehend.
8 Zhou 2014, 136.
9 Zhang 2014, 48.
10 Zhang 2014, 49.
11 In 1900, Eiland and Jennings (2014, 24) remind, "the Swedish educational theorist and suffragist Ellen Key had declared the twentieth century 'the century of the child'." U.S. progressives were determined to make that prediction come true, creating "child-centeredness" as a key curriculum conception.
12 The phrase is associated with John Dewey, who may have formulated the idea after his move from the University of Michigan to the University of Chicago, where the Laboratory School represented "a principal outlet" for his emerging educational philosophy (see Levine 2007, 79). "For Dewey," Levine (2007, 79) summarizes,

the reconstruction of society and the reconstruction of education were aspects of the same process. The capacity to solve social problems required intellectual habits needed to perceive problems, identify their features, and entertain in imagination diverse options for their solution. In order to promote such habits at all levels of learning, Dewey maintained that new forms of teaching were needed, forms in which curiosity and imagination were awakened through direct encounter with puzzling experiences.

13 For details see Pinar 2012, 102–132.
14 Indeed, Zhang Hua has associated the 2001 reform with the 1922 reform, itself associated with the influence of John Dewey. See Zhang 2014.
15 Kang 2014, 83.
16 In allegory, "the apparent sense of a thing or a text is seen to signal some other, possibly very different sense" (Eiland and Jennings 2014, 18).
17 Quoted in Pinar 2014, 14.
18 The emergence of these interwoven commitments becomes evident in his life history. At 18 years-of-age, Zhang Hua became a middle-school teacher in his hometown of Laiwu, where he worked for four years. There he "watched, participated, and experienced students' agony" as they suffered through "school regimes of competition and examination." Students from the "disadvantaged" classes—"most were peasants' descendants"—suffered the most. "That's why I have been engaged in national curriculum reform" (quoted in Pinar 2014, 15).
19 Quoted passages in Pinar 2014, 16.
20 Chen 2014, 81.
21 Zhang Wenjun 2014, 119.
22 Zhou 2014, 136.
23 While the context is considerably different, this association of intelligence and educational experience with everyday life is an important concern of many curriculum scholars in Brazil. See Alves 2011.
24 Zhou 2014, 137.
25 Quoted in Pinar 2014, 12.
26 Quoted in Pinar 2014, 12–13.
27 2013, 98.
28 2013, 6.
29 I flag the choice of verbs as it recapitulates the behaviorism of twentieth-century curriculum development—evident in "Tyler's Rationale" (see chapter 7)—as it ignores the canonical curriculum question of "what knowledge is of most worth." As we will see, "knowledge" is one casualty of curriculum reform in the West, if in the name of "student-centeredness."
30 2013, 8.
31 Ibid.
32 Only *New Basics*: during 2000–2004, he reports, in more than fifty schools in Queensland, Australia, received support from the state government of education (see Williamson 2013, 13). *Enquiring Minds* (EM) was a curriculum R&D project conducted during 2005 and 2009 by the non-profit organization Futurelab in the city of Bristol in the United Kingdom, with funding from Microsoft Partners in Learning. *Enquiring Minds*, Williamson (2013, 62) tells us, "endorses" a "collaborative inquiry pedagogy" drawing from "children's everyday cultures mediated through networked technologies." *Tech High* (HTH) was originally launched in 2000 as a single charter school by a coalition of San Diego, California, business leaders (see Williamson 2013, 12). *Opening Minds* was initiated by the Royal Society for Arts, Manufactures and Commerce (RSA) in the United Kingdom (see Williamson 2013, 13). *Quest to Learn* (Q2L) is a school for "digital kids" that opened in New York City in 2009. A second school was opened in Chicago in 2011. Both receive support and funding from the John T. and Catherine D. MacArthur Foundation,

as did the Williamson book (see Williamson 2013, 14). At one point Williamson (2013, 34) suggests that curricular materials will be "digitized" and "offered freely" to children and their teachers, but given corporations' obligations to shareholders (never mind to the inflated salaries of top management), I am skeptical, although never underestimate the potentials of malefic generosity. "Learning activities have become consumer goods in themselves," Williamson (2013, 97–98) admits, "purchased within a marketplace where learning competes with those of leisure and entertainment." Unless "purchased" is being used metaphorically here, skepticism seems obligatory.

33 Recall—in chapter 5—that George Grant had characterized technology as a form of idolatry, mistaking materiality for spirituality. In the "curriculum of the future," it appears there is no one left to confuse the two.

34 2013, 20.

35 2013, 21.

36 Life itself is replaced by learning, as in the future, Williamson (2013, 95) tells us, as "learning" becomes a "whole way of life," both "continuous" and "nonstop." Unsurprisingly, subjectivity's coincidence with "learning" requires, Williamson observes, a "total pedagogy," a phrase reminiscent of characterizations of prisons as "total" institutions (Pinar 2001, 981ff). Total pedagogy involves, Williamson (2013, 96) explains, "continuous disposition to be trained for the requirements of an entire life in a process that is permanently open." In other words, *I am always available to learn whatever you want me to learn.* In political terms, this is—need I point out?—total subjugation, slavery that is voluntary although in the future it is the psychic—rather than physical—incapacity to escape that condemns humanity to imprisonment, complete incorporation within the grammar of capitalism: technology (Kroker 1984, 119).

37 "Knowledge," Williamson (2013, 28) explains, is recast as "thematic, modularized, connective, boundary-free, hybrid, and generic; learning is reconfigured as competence, thinking, problem solving, and 'learning to learn'." Is the matter of the Holocaust "hybrid" and "generic"? Actually, in the future the question cannot occur, as no one remembers anything, except skill is required to complete the task at hand.

38 2013, 21.

39 2013, 23.

40 Private business—not parents or publics—seems to be the driving force in these ventures. Williamson (2013, 23) tells us that the "negotiable" and "flexible" curriculum proposed by Gardner was "realized" in *Opening Minds*, launched as a pilot project in the United Kingdom in 1999 by the Royal Society of Arts, Manufactures and Commerce (RSA). By early 2012, Williamson (2013, 25) continues, over two hundred schools had incorporated "some form" of Opening Minds' "competencies curriculum." Infectious it would seem.

41 In "centrifugal schooling," Williamson (2013, 7) explains, "learning" is "decentered, distributed, and dispersed," not "narrowly centered, channeled, and canalized." Its "keywords are 'networks,' 'connections,' and 'decentralization,' as a family of related centrifugal terms." Appealing in the context of authoritarianism, in a culture of narcissism and presentism (Pinar 2011, 132–133; 2012, 4, 225–227)—the case in North America certainly and in Europe to an extent as well—such dispersion of curricular focus and dissipation of academic knowledge ensures students' ignorance of the past and their inability to imagine a collective future, except perhaps their own financial futures.

42 2013, 33.

43 "The School of Everything," Williamson (2013, 41) reports, "is a simple Web platform that allows anyone who has something they can teach to link up with anyone who would like to learn it." Alchemy anyone?

44 2013, 73.

45 See Martin and Barresi 2006.
46 2013, 102. In his discussion of Erving Goffman's "dramaturgy," Alvin Gouldner (1970, 383) distinguishes between functionalism (and its conception of human beings and their activities as having "use-values") and Goffman's social theory with its conception of human beings "solely" as "exchange values." This complete commodification of the self is, in the curriculum of the future, no sign of social crisis—as it was for Gouldner—but an accepted reality to be institutionalized in online curriculum.
47 2013, 49.
48 The usurpation of this concept—flexibility—is not futural but occurred in the past: see Tirado 2011.
49 2013, 50.
50 2013, 52.
51 2013, 73.
52 Ibid.
53 2013, 75.
54 I flag this adjective to point out how such rhetoric revolves around assertions of "the new," a key and continuing false promise of "reform" in the West. What seems "new" in China's curriculum reform is ancient culture: Buddhism, Confucianism, Taoism. While worried by capitalism's capacity to convert anything into currency for exchange, I am heartened by the effort in China to find its future through the past.
55 The "design" of technologies by "learning scientists," Williamson (2013, 81) explains, is a "method for 'designing people' through 'engineering' particular forms of learning, actions, and dispositions." Since the early twentieth-century social efficiency movement, the American school as been imagined as the means to another ends, a production line producing whatever aim or "objective"—efficient workers, democratic citizens—policy-makers planned. Then limited to the world of work or the public life of citizenship, here the scope of control—and the confidence to enforce it—seems limitless.
56 And pharmaceutical, as nearly one in five high school age boys in the United States and 11 percent of school-age children over all have received a medical diagnosis of attention deficit hyperactivity disorder, according to data from the U.S. Centers for Disease Control and Prevention. Approximately two-thirds of those with a current diagnosis, Schwarz and Cohen (2013, A1) report, receive prescriptions for stimulants like Ritalin or Adderall, which can "drastically improve the lives of those with A.D.H.D. but can also lead to addiction, anxiety and occasionally psychosis." Even more U.S. children will be prescribed medication in the near future, Schwarz and Cohen (2013, A1, A11) continue, as the American Psychological Association plans to change its definition of A.D.H.D. to allow more people to receive the diagnosis and treatment. A.D.H.D. is depicted as resulting from abnormal chemical levels in the brain that impair a person's impulse control and attention skills. Either through pharmaceutical, psychic, or behavioral intervention, then, students *will* enter the online curriculum of the future.
57 2013, 83.
58 "Fused" signals the collapse of intellectual and political independence and the evisceration of the subjectivity that sustain these. The structural space of non-coincidence (Pinar 2011, 8) is prerequisite to subject-formation and that subjectivity that enables independent thought and action. In these passages one also observes the appropriation of the language of inwardness by cultures of capitalism, converting what is intrinsically and subjectively important into commodities with exchange value.
59 2013, 86.
60 The great Canadian political economist and communications theorist Harold Innis understood eighty years ago that "communication" would become compulsory in an industrial—now technological—era, replacing contemplation and sustained

study, each of which requires solitude. Constant compulsory communication ensures encapsulation within context, not non-coincidence with it.

61 DIY means "do-it-yourself (DIY) self-shaping" (2013, 99).
62 2013, 108.
63 Ibid.
64 2013, 109–110.
65 2013, 110.
66 Kang 2014, 94.
67 That that conception of human being as essentially an economic creature structures the curriculum of the future Williamson (2013, 112) makes crystal clear: "Students are encouraged to think, feel, and act upon themselves psychologically as inner-focused persons with mental and emotional habits of mind and states of well-being that are to be sculpted in order to support an economy of creativity and innovation."
68 In *The Character of Curriculum Studies*, I review this Western—and specifically German—sense of the human subject, complicating it with postcolonial, international, and historical studies. In *Curriculum Studies in China*, Lixin Cong references German influences in Chinese educational thought; I wonder if traces of these surface in the present reform. Consider Walter Benjamin's interest, as a young man, in educational reform. As Eiland and Jennings (2014, 39) remind, nineteenth-century German thought from Schlegel and Novalis to Nietzsche "roots" Benjamin's idea of "awakening youth." They point out that "the project of youth culture was for him never limited to the program of school reform but sought a revolution in thinking and feeling. Meaningful institutional change could take place only in the wake of cultural transformation" (2014, 39). For Benjamin, Eiland and Jennings (2014, 39) emphasize, youth was imagined as the breaking wave of a "new humanity" and a "radical new seeing" (Benjamin, quoted in Eiland and Jennings 2014, 39). What technology portends, at least as Williamson foresees, is regressive restoration of oligarchy with its installation of vassals—virtualized, staring at screens—stripped of humanity. There is no "awakening" or "seeing" only submersion in the networks computer programs proclaim. "The digital network," Mejias (2013, 3) appreciates, "is a particularly delusive technological determinant because it is a mechanism for disenfranchisement through involvement."
69 It is political process as well, of course: see Pinar 2013.
70 And employers, Zhang Wenjun pointed out. Fewer of those of course, and all confined to the (in)corporation.
71 This chapter was presented as a keynote address at a conference on Repositioning Students in China's Curriculum Reform, 22 March 2014, Hangzhou Normal University, Hangzhou, China.

Bibliography

Alves, Nilda. 2011. Everyday Life in Schools. In *Curriculum Studies in Brazil*, edited by William F. Pinar (43–53). New York: Palgrave Macmillan.

Chen, Yuting. 2014. From Follower to Creator: The Past, Present and Future of the School as a Reform Subject. In *Curriculum Studies in China*, edited by William F. Pinar (69–82). New York: Palgrave Macmillan.

Collingwood, R. G. 2002. *An Autobiography*. [Introduced by Stephen Toulmin.] Oxford: Clarendon Press.

Eiland, Howard and Jennings, Michael W. 2014. *Walter Benjamin: A Critical Life*. Cambridge, MA: Belknap Press of Harvard University Press.

Gouldner, Alvin W. 1970. *The Coming Crisis of Western Sociology.* New York: Basic Books.

Kang, Changyun. 2014. The Question of the Textbook in Curriculum Reform: An Autobiographical Account. In *Curriculum Studies in China*, edited by William F. Pinar (83–94). New York: Palgrave Macmillan.

Kroker, Arthur. 1984. *Technology and the Canadian Mind: Innis/McLuhan/Grant*. Montreal: New World Perspectives.

Levine, Donald N. 2007. *Powers of the Mind: The Reinvention of Liberal Learning in America*. Chicago: University of Chicago Press.

Martin, Raymond and Barresi, John. 2006. *The Rise and Fall of Soul and Self. An Intellectual History of Personal Identity*. New York: Columbia University Press.

Mejias, Ulises Ali. 2013. *Off the Network: Disrupting the Digital World*. Minneapolis: University of Minnesota Press.

Pinar, William F. 2011. *The Character of Curriculum Studies*. New York: Palgrave Macmillan.

Pinar, William F. 2012. *What Is Curriculum Theory?* [Second edition.] New York: Routledge.

Pinar, William F. 2013. *Curriculum Studies in the United States*. New York: Palgrave Macmillan.

Pinar, William F. Ed. 2014. *Curriculum Studies in China: Intellectual Histories, Present Circumstances*. New York: Palgrave Macmillan.

Schwarz, Alan and Cohen, Sarah. 2013, April 1. More Diagnoses of Hyperactivity Causing Concern. *New York Times*, A1, A11.

Tirado, María Concepción Barrón. 2011. Professional Education in Mexico at the Beginning of the Twenty-First Century. In *Curriculum Studies in Mexico: Intellectual Histories, Present Circumstances*, edited by William F. Pinar (181–206). New York: Palgrave Macmillan.

Watson, Alexander John. 2007. *Marginal Man: The Dark Vision of Harold Innis*. Toronto: University of Toronto Press.

Williamson, Ben. 2013. *The Future of the Curriculum. School Knowledge in the Digital Age*. Cambridge, MA: The MIT Press.

Zhang, Hua. 2014. Curriculum Studies and Curriculum Reform in China: 1922–2012. In *Curriculum Studies in China*, edited by William F. Pinar (29–67). New York: Palgrave Macmillan.

Zhang, Hua and Gao, Zhenyu. 2014. Curriculum Studies in China: Retrospect and Prospect. In the *International Handbook of Curriculum Research*, edited by William F. Pinar (118–133). [Second edition.] New York: Routledge.

Zhou, Huixia. 2014. The Development of Curriculum Ideologies and the Present Circumstances of Curriculum Studies in China. In *Curriculum Studies in China*, edited by William F. Pinar (129–141). New York: Palgrave Macmillan.

CHAPTER 7

MISREPRESENTATION

Commentary

Tyler's Rationale[1] is not Tyler's. Hilda Taba claimed co-authorship in her 1962 book but had evidently forgotten that she had referenced the famous four questions in her 1932 book, a sophisticated theoretical study of which Tyler was evidently ignorant. Presenting information without reference is the definition of plagiarism, but that term has proved too strong for some readers. Is *misrepresentation* more manageable?

In popularizing proceduralism, Tyler contributed to the field's substitution of instrumentalism for the contemplation and critique that curriculum can invite. Walter Benjamin had critiqued instrumentalization of modern education as "the perversion of the creative spirit into the vocational spirit"[2] as it severs the academic disciplines from the very "idea of knowledge,"[3] as a "community of learning"[4] structured, I suggest, as complicated conversation. In the proceduralism vocationalism installs, even reading becomes degraded "as a concatenation of subskills leading to comprehension. Reading [becomes] an exact procedure."[5] Does the ahistorical anonymity of proceduralism ensure misrepresentation?

Bibliography

Block, Alan A. 1995. *Occupied Reading*. New York: Garland.

Eiland, Howard and Jennings, Michael W. 2014. *Walter Benjamin. A Critical Life*. Cambridge, MA: Belknap Press of Harvard University Press.

Pinar, William F. 2013, May. Plagiarism and the Tyler Rationale. *Journal of the American Association for the Advancement of Curriculum Studies* 9 (1), 1–13.

Taba, Hilda 1932. *The Dynamics of Education*. London: Kegan Paul, Trench, Trubner & Co.

Taba, Hilda. 1962. *Curriculum Development: Theory and Practice*. New York: Harcourt, Brace & World.

Tyler, Ralph W. 1949. *Basic Principles of Curriculum and Instruction*. Chicago: University of Chicago Press.

> Education being an evolving process, the sequences of its experiences and their contents are at least partly determined by the process itself. They cannot be fully seen or outlined in advance.
>
> Hilda Taba[6]

"Tyler lore," Craig Kridel and Robert Bullough, Jr., tell us, "describes a lunch occasion in the 1930s when 'Mike' Giles, Hilda Taba, and Tyler were discussing curriculum development and the 1949 Rationale's legendary questions were conceived by Tyler and written on a napkin."[7] Tyler may have recorded those questions on a napkin during lunch with Hilda Taba and "Mike" Giles, but he did not "conceive" them. The "1949 Rationale" is one version of an idea that was in circulation for decades, referenced, for instance, in *The Twenty-Sixth Yearbook of the National Society for the Study of Education*.[8] I am not the first to notice that the "Tyler Rationale" is credited incorrectly.[9] Daniel Tanner and Laurel Tanner blame the error on readers. "Unfortunately," they write, "it is sometimes erroneously portrayed as one man's version."[10] Is the error readers' responsibility only?

It is true that in his 1949 *Basic Principles of Curriculum and Instruction,* Ralph W. Tyler never claims authorship of the four questions he presents. "This small book attempts to explain," he tells us in his introductory remarks, "a rationale for viewing, analyzing, and interpreting the curriculum and instructional program."[11] "A" rationale exists; he will explain it. While its authorship is left unspecified, we could be forgiven for mistaking it for Tyler's, as its genealogy goes unremarked. Tyler encourages readers "to examine other rationales," but these are left unnamed, and he quickly moves on to "the rationale developed here," those "four fundamental questions which must be answered in developing any curriculum and plan of instruction."[12] That verb—"must"—implies that examining other rationales would be a waste of time.

Recall that *Basic Principles of Curriculum and Instruction* is a course syllabus. Strangely, it is a syllabus without readings or references.[13] With no genealogy, the course content would seem to come from the teacher. Tyler may never claim authorship of the rationale he presents, but he never disclaims it. And because the book has one author (Tyler) and no bibliography, readers could be forgiven for assuming that the ideas presented are "conceived" by the author. Are readers alone to be blamed for such an impression?

Not a curriculum theory,[14] the book, Tyler insists, is "not a manual for curriculum construction since it does not describe and outline in detail the steps to be taken."[15] While it is true there is no organizational[16] detail, the book does indeed describe the steps to be taken, and these are listed in numerical order.[17] First one formulates objectives, then "selects" those "educational experiences" likely to lead to the achievement of those objectives. Third is "organization," Tyler's term incorporating both curriculum design and implementation.[18] Fourth is evaluation. A disarmingly simple question—have the objectives been realized?—substitutes for situation-specific professional judgment. In asserting these four questions as "fundamental,"[19] Tyler is using an adjective meaning not only "basic" and "essential" but, in its first definition, "serving as an original or generating source."[20]

Tyler is not the "original" or "generating source" of these four questions. Presenting ideas "without crediting the source"[21] is the definition of plagiarism. After reviewing earlier statements of these "basic[22] principles of curriculum and instruction," it occurred to me why it may not have occurred to Tyler he was committing a crime.[23] While one cannot rule out self-serving motives—namely, that Tyler wanted to claim credit for himself—it could have been the general agreement on the objectives-design-implementation-evaluation sequence—or "interaction"[24] in the Giles et al.[25] graph—as the ruling "paradigm"[26] of curriculum development that encouraged Tyler to present the questions as if they were self-evident truths. In this speculation, Tyler is claiming leadership not authorship of what everybody already knows to be the case. The charge of plagiarism gets reduced to hubris.

The genealogy of the "Tyler Rationale" became a question for me while working on Hilda Taba.[27] At one point—in the preface to her 1962 *Curriculum Development: Theory and Practice*—Taba colludes with Tyler in his deception, although she too knows better.[28] "The idea that there must be a system of thinking about curriculum planning," Taba tell us, "occurred to Dr. R. W. Tyler after a rather confusing meeting on curriculum planning in the 1930s in which conflicting proposals for curriculum designs were being debated."[29] What was confusing about the meeting is left unclear, unless "confusing" is here a synonym for "conflicting." What is clear—in Taba's 1962 preface at least—is that the four questions "solve" the problem of "conflicting proposals for curriculum designs," as all designs must now serve as means to the ends that are the objectives. Sequence substitutes for content.

It was "following" this 1930s meeting, Taba continues, that "Dr. Tyler *and* the writer began to elaborate a scheme for a sequence of questions to be asked and an *order of steps* to be taken in planning curriculum."[30] The first conjunction communicates the collaborative character of this undertaking, registering that she *and* Tyler are co-authors of the questions.[31] Did Tyler ever contradict Taba's claim? Given that it was the association of his name with the "rationale" that ensured his reputation, surely he must have, and perhaps even in court, although I have yet to discover any references to such events. Perhaps Tyler ignored Taba's claim. In his interviews at least, he consigns her to a minor role in his career.[32]

Taba played no minor role, if any part of the 1962 recollection is accurate. In that preface Taba registers the passage of time—not a moment of "conception" noted on a napkin—as the two of them "began" to "elaborate" the "scheme"[33] that led to the questions, a "sequence" of questions, an "order of steps to be taken in planning curriculum." Despite Tyler's aside that curriculum developers can "attack"[34] the challenge of curriculum development starting with any one of the four questions, his collaborator Taba claims otherwise. For the Taba of 1962 these questions are "steps" to be followed in "order." What we have is a procedure; the use of "principles" in Tyler's 1949 book is terminologically inflationary.

After initially attributing authorship to Tyler, Taba upgrades her status to that of co-author, then claims credit for the "fieldwork." She "tried these out in the next workshop held by the Eight Year Study."[35] "These" reference the "questions" that "Dr. Tyler *and* the writer *began*[36] to formulate."[37] The field-testing of the four questions hardly ends at that "next workshop" held by the Eight-Year Study. "Over a period of years," Taba tells us, and "working as a curriculum consultant in several school systems"—as well as "teaching courses in curriculum development"—she "continued testing and refining the scheme and building a theoretical rationale for it."[38] That gerund—"building"—seems exactly right, as Taba's 1962 book constructs an elaborate, systematic, conceptual edifice from the simple four-question scheme she claims Tyler and she *began* to elaborate in the 1930s.

In 1949 Tyler covers his tracks by including no bibliography;[39] readers are left with the impression he is the sole author of these "basic principles of curriculum and instruction." In 1962 Taba calls his bluff by asserting co-authorship and extensive field-testing, the latter absent in Tyler's pity pronouncement. Taba's tracks are not so easily covered, however. How collaborative their relationship remains for me an open question, but the dating is dubious, as in her 1932 *The Dynamics of Education*, Taba[40] references the *Twenty-Sixth Yearbook* (Part II) when listing the four points of procedure Tyler, seventeen years later, converts to interrogatives:

> [T]hat part of the curriculum [that] should be planned in advance . . . includes, (1) a statement of objectives, (2) a sequence of experiences shown by analysis to be reasonably uniform in value in achieving the objectives, (3) subject matter found to be reasonably uniform as the best means of engaging in the experiences, (4) statements of the immediate outcomes of achievements to be derived from the experiences.[41]

Except for step three, these are almost identical to the four questions listed in Tyler's syllabus. And the third is close enough: rather than asking how "learning experiences" can be "organized" for "effective instruction," in this 1926 version "subject matter" is made "uniform" so as to provide "the best means" of "engaging in the [selected] experiences." This is not a difference that makes a difference.

Earlier in *The Dynamics of Education*, while discussing the concept of "purposive learning," Taba[42] quotes Kilpatrick's[43] *Foundations of Method* in which appears the same, if differently worded, sequential scheme. "Purposive learning," Taba tells us, "usually comprises learning which occurs in connection with the pursuit of definite 'ends-in-view,' the acts of learning which follow the scheme of 'Purposing, planning, executing and judging'."[44] Tyler's 1949 questions restate these "ends-in-views" but do not revise their intentions.

These quoted passages confirm that the "Tyler Rationale" is a misnomer. Recall that Daniel Tanner and Laurel Tanner acknowledge "the error," but their point is not plagiarism but "paradigm,"[45] namely that the four questions constitute one.[46] The point they fail to make is that by refusing to reference the 1926 *Yearbook*, the 1932 and 1945[47] publications of his colleague Hilda Taba, and that of their collaborators in the Eight-Year Study—most prominently the 1942 report *Exploring the Curriculum: The Work of the Thirty Schools from the Viewpoint of Curriculum Consultants*—Tyler engineers the illusion that he himself is the author of "the Bible of curriculum making."[48]

In its authority and sole authorship,[49] *Basic Principles of Curriculum and Instruction* has indeed appeared to be the "Bible" of the U.S. field. On occasion, Tyler has even been treated like a god.[50] Is it an illusion the absence of a bibliography creates? Chronology requires us to acknowledge that Taba listed the four steps in 1932, quoting from the *Twenty-Sixth Yearbook*. Given the collaborative character of progressive curriculum development, the genesis of the four questions may not be determinable. What is indisputable, however, is that Tyler presented ideas "without crediting the source" (*Webster's* 1975, 877). They were not "conceived" on a napkin in the 1930s. Nor did Taba and Tyler compose them together. "Everybody" knew these questions by the mid-1920s. They were the "paradigm" of curriculum development. Never again should any student or scholar reference the "Tyler Rationale" without qualifying the phrase in quote marks—as Daniel Tanner and Laurel Tanner do[51]—or without the modifier "so-called." The "Tyler Rationale" is indeed "one man's version" of a decades-old widely shared scheme.[52]

How could Tyler—and Taba later—imagine these ideas as their own? My speculation is that in their "paradigmatic" status these questions seemed to belong to everyone. Consensus conferred anonymity upon them. Only fifteen years after Tyler associates them with his own name does Taba (in that preface to her 1962 book) attempt to establish a genealogy. Hers is a metaphorically gender-confused history, with Tyler "conceiving" the questions but the two of them bringing the "scheme" to term, after which Taba takes their "child" into the world where it becomes extended and operationalized. But the two of them had not worked alone. Many progressives had accepted proceduralism as paradigmatic in curriculum development, as the *Twenty-Sixty Yearbook* demonstrates and Daniel Tanner and Laurel Tanner remind.

Not only the consensus concerning the questions may have rendered the problem of plagiarism remote. It may have also been their nature, that they are steps in a procedure. By definition, procedure—"an established way of doing things"[53]—obscures individual agency and creativity as it forefronts "a series of steps followed in a regular definite order."[54] The noun, then, obscures the verb from which it is derived. To "proceed" is defined as "to come forth from a source" and "to begin and carry on an action, process, or movement," and "to move along a course," as in "advance."[55] No doubt Ralph Tyler—and evidently many others—judged he had achieved an "advance" in his 1949 *Basic Principles of Curriculum and Instruction*. In claiming co-authorship, Hilda Taba would "advance" the paradigm to its systematized conclusion in her 1962 *Curriculum Development: Theory and Practice*.[56] In her theory of curriculum development, Taba acknowledges the past. Should not we?

Notes

1 Tyler 1949.
2 Benjamin, quoted in Eiland and Jennings 2014, 66.
3 Eiland and Jennings 2014, 66.
4 Eiland and Jennings 2014, 66.
5 Block 1995, 169.
6 1932, 244. Several sentences later Taba (1932, 244) adds:

> [K]eeping in mind the conception of the curriculum given above—while everybody who is participating in the educational process contributes to the generation of ideas and meanings, to the reorganization and application of knowledge, they actually contribute to the building of the curriculum.

Taba's conception is one antecedent of curriculum as complicated conversation.
7 2007, 94.
8 Whipple 1926.
9 As do Daniel Tanner and Laurel Tanner (1988), José María García Garduño (1995) also acknowledges Tyler's predecessors, including Dewey, Thorndike, Bobbitt, and Charters. I question the association with Dewey, but that is analysis for another day.
10 1988, 54.
11 1949, 1. Recall that in response to Kliebard's critique Tyler insisted that the Rationale was not a curriculum theory (see Pinar 2011, 83), but surely providing a "a rationale for viewing, analyzing, and interpreting the curriculum" qualifies. It is a theory of procedure not content, as the canonical curriculum question—what knowledge is of

most worth?—is replaced by the organizational question of how shall the curriculum be developed. The curriculum is thereby demoted to the status of "means" to other "ends," in Tyler's (1949, 1) phrase, "a functioning instrument of education."

12 1949, 1.

13 In a 1990 interview with Graciela Cordero Arroyo, Tyler repeats that "my little book" . . . "was developed not as a book, it was developed as a guide for a class that I taught at the University of Chicago." Cordero and García Garduño (see 2004, 3) accept the syllabus story as justification for the absence of references. Then Tyler tells them: "And I discovered that the University of Chicago Press had picked it up as a book when I didn't even know it was made into a book. I started it out as a mimeograph and it became published" (quoted passages in Cordero and García Garduño 2004, 11). If not legal issues, would not professional courtesy obligate the University of Chicago Press to consult Professor Tyler before publication? Tyler is fabricating here.

14 "In a little-known 1970 interview after the release of 'The Tyler Rationale: A Reappraisal' by Herbert Kliebard," Kridel and Bullough (2007, 94) report, "Tyler maintained that he never sought to develop a curriculum theory or 'theoretical formulation of what a curriculum should be' but merely wished to pose an outline of kinds of questions that should be asked."

15 1949, 1.

16 While curriculum organization by school subjects is, Taba (1962, 384) points out, "the oldest and still prevailing form of organizing a curriculum, especially in the high school," it is hardly the only one. So is the "broad fields curriculum" (Taba 1962, 393) as well as curriculum based on "social processes and functions" (1962, 396; see 1962, 398 for an illustration; see also Giles et al. 1942, 23). The "broad fields" organization is also discussed in Giles, McCutchen, and Zechiel (1942, 23). The four questions represent a methodology of curriculum organization, one that relegates academic knowledge to "means" to an "end."

17 Listed as chapters in the table of contents, Tyler's questions are: "1. What educational purposes should the school seek to attain? 2. What educational experiences can be provided that are likely to attain these purposes? 3. How can these educational experiences be effectively organized? 4. How can we determine whether these purposes are being attained?" (Tyler 1949, 1). In the book's final sentence Tyler backs off his sequencing by allowing that "the program may be improved by attacks beginning at any point, providing the resulting modifications are followed through the related elements until eventually all aspects of the curriculum have been studied and revised" (1949, 128). Numbering the questions establishes a sequence, however "flexible" Tyler insists (in the final sentence) the sequence is.

18 "Teaching" disappears into "implementation."

19 1949, 1.

20 *Webster's New Collegiate Dictionary* 1975, 465.

21 *Webster's* 1975, 877.

22 It should go without saying these are *not* "basic principles of curriculum and instruction" but instead entirely arbitrary questions, however consensually shared they once were. That they were widely shared could account for them seeming self-evident, perhaps explaining in part Tyler's failure to attribute them to his predecessors and colleagues. But Taba—who states the questions in her 1945 essay and, as noted, in her 1932 book—manages to reference antecedent formulations, so the question of Tyler's culpability cannot be discarded.

23 It is not that Tyler didn't know how to cite the work of others. On page 42, for instance, he references Thorndike, Judd, and Freeman, although without dates or page numbers. On page 28 there is a probable reference to Louise Rosenblatt, although he fails to mention her name. Whom he does not reference is Taba or Giles and McCutchen or the various contributors to the Twenty-Sixth NSSE Yearbook, all of whom present what Tyler's lists in 1949 as "his" four questions. It is possible—as

the reviewers suggested—that "plagiarism" is too strong a term to depict Tyler's perhaps inadvertent misrepresentation of the four questions. So in this reprinting of the article I will substitute that term for the other.

24 In the graph on p. 2 "objectives" and "subject matter" and "methods and organization" and "evaluation" are portrayed as equally significant and interactive with each other. While I dispute these categories—I question the value of "objectives," regard "evaluation" as inflated, and endorse "complicated conversation," not implementation—their equality and interactivity creates a very different (Taba might say "dynamic") comprehension of curriculum construction. True, it remains organizational rather than intellectual. Despite the authors' enthusiastic embrace of functionalism (see 1942, 5), its proceduralism is defused. Clearly, this 1942 statement is an improvement on 1949 Tyler's numerical sequencing.

25 1942, 2.

26 See Tanner and Tanner 1988, 55, 57. The Tanners acknowledge that the questions appeared in Giles, McCutchen, and Zechiel (1942) and Taba (1945); indeed, they even trace them back to Dewey (1902), surely a stretch but one Garduño (2013) also endorses. Null (2008, 480) tells us that "Tyler's (1949) *Basic Principles of Curriculum and Instruction* put curriculum development on the map," an entirely ahistorical assertion that ignores that it was the topic of the *Twenty-Sixth Yearbook of the National Society for the Study of Education* (Whipple 1926).

27 I prepared "The Achievement of Hilda Taba" as a keynote presentation to the Conference on Hilda Taba in commemoration of her one-hundred-tenth birthday on 7 December 2012. The conference opened that afternoon in Tallinn, Estonia.

28 Taba references the four questions in her 1932 book, as I will document momentarily.

29 1962, vi.

30 Ibid., emphasis added.

31 As the phrase "order of the steps to be taken" makes unmistakable, the Taba-Tyler "scheme" is a procedure, not an interchangeable listing of options to be exercised in any order, as Daniel Tanner and Laurel Tanner (1988, 53) point out that it is in Giles, McCutchen and Zechiel (1942, 2): "As with Dewey, Giles et al. stressed that the process is not linear, and they modeled the questions diagramatically as four interactive determinants encompassing objectives, subject matter, methods and organization, and evaluation." While Tyler (1949, 128) tries to wiggle out of the lock-step sequence he has presented, the deed is done.

32 See Ridings 1982, 256. In his longest interview, Tyler tells Malca Chall:

> In February of 1936 I found Hilda teaching German in the Dalton School, which is one of the schools in the study. She was an Estonian, who had come on a student visa to Bryn Mawr to get a master's in philosophy. Bryn Mawr was involved with international exchanges. When she finished that, she wanted to go on for a Ph.D. and she got a Ph.D. under William Heard Kilpatrick at Columbia. Without changing her student visa she continued to stay and, finally, the immigration authorities caught up with her. They were about to deport her; she did not want to go back to Estonia which had been taken over by the Russians. Since I found her an extremely intelligent person who *knew nothing about testing or curriculum* but she could learn I signed up with the immigration authorities to take her. I began in February of 1936 to teach her, and she became quite an authority. She was at San Francisco State College when she died of an unexpected tetanus which she got in the hospital in the summer of 1967, here in this area. (Regents 1987, 77, emphasis added)

Taba concluded her 1932 *The Dynamics of Education* with a chapter on "Curriculum Thinking." That book was published in a distinguished book series which included volumes by G.E. Moore, Ludwig Wittgenstein, C.G. Jung, I.A. Richards, and Otto Rank, among others. Evidently it was Tyler who knew "nothing" about curriculum.

33 In both Taba and Tyler this "scheme" seems to hinge on an expansive concept of behavior that the purpose of education is to change. "Education," Tyler (1949, 5–6) tells us, "is a process of changing the behavior patterns of people. This is using behavior in the broad sense to include thinking and feeling as well as overt action." As a concept, "behavior" dominates both Tyler's 1949 and Taba's 1962 book. But in her 1932 *The Dynamics of Education*, behavior becomes totalizing. At one point Taba (1932, 13) writes:

> All the major problems of human behavior—those of organism and environmental relations, relations of mind and body, intelligence, consciousness, stimulus and reaction, and the role of meaning—can be adequately studied only from such a dynamic standpoint. They must be regarded first and foremost as parts of a dynamic, ongoing process of life, which we call experience, and of which the behavior act is a unit.

Despite demarcating her view from Thorndike and S-R psychology, in this sentence everything slides into the "unit" which is "the behavior act." Behavior becomes the bottom line, not meaning or experience.

34 1949, 128.

35 1962, vi.

36 This choice of verbs suggests Taba too is rewriting history. Can she have forgotten that she has already quoted the four questions from the *Twenty-Sixth Yearbook* in her 1932 book (see pp. 172, 246)?

37 1962, vi.

38 Ibid. After the decades of consulting and the teaching, Taba (1962, vi) judges her directorship of the project on Intergroup Education as providing "a real chance at a large-scale application of the idea." One article appears in 1945; a book in 1949, antedating or coinciding with the publication of Tyler's *Principles* (1949).

39 How does a university press continue to publish a scholarly book without a bibliography?

40 1932, 246.

41 See Whipple (1926, 19–20). In various but always recognizable forms, the four steps are referenced throughout both volumes. Contradicting Tyler and herself (in her 1962 formulation), Taba (1932, 247, emphasis added) insists that objectives "should be translated into forms of concrete experience that are *ever unique* and therefore different . . . [as] concrete experience tends to evolve objectives *not foreseen* in the predetermined outline." She also contests step three:

> Still more danger of an arbitrary limitation through the curriculum is involved in the proposal of the committee to outline those experiences and subject matter which are of a "reasonably" uniform in achieving objectives. As no two experiences are exactly alike, so no two educational situations, when not artificially controlled, are exactly alike; nor do they hold uniform educative possibilities for everyone participating. Consequently, any attempt to chart the educational situation and its experiences in advance will inevitably become inhibitive to the full educational utilization of the factors and possibilities evolving during the process of learning. (1932, 248)

Given Taba's appreciation of the unique and unpredictable character of educational experience, why did she retain any concept of "objective"?

42 1932, 172.

43 William Heard Kilpatrick served as Taba's Ph.D. supervisor; he composed the foreword to Taba's 1932 book. There her ambivalence over the "project method" is noticeable (see pp. 170–171, 183–184, 187, 253).

44 After citing Kilpatrick's *Foundations of Method*, pp. 200ff., a volume not listed in her bibliography, Taba (1932, 172 n. 1) points out:

> Dr. Kilpatrick has since modified his position on purposive learning considerably, but the scheme of purposive learning as analyzed in *Foundations of Method* still influences educational circles and schools profoundly. The present discussion refers to these prevalent ideas as influenced by Dr. Kilpatrick's *Foundations of Method* rather than to the position that authority holds at present.

Her interest here is to affirm the significance of learning that is not purposive but "indirect" (1932, 172).

45 Tanner and Tanner 1988, 57.

46 There have been three paradigmatic moments in the history of curriculum studies in the United States: (1) curriculum development, (2) understanding curriculum, and—just underway—(3) internationalization and the engagement with alterity (Pinar 2013, 2014).

47 The four questions Tyler lists in 1949 were already elaborated in 1945 by Hilda Taba, no surprise given her 1932 references discussed earlier.

48 Jackson 1992, 24.

49 Recall that the Bible is also comprised of material composed by multiple authors, if retrospectively fused into one presumably omniscient Author.

50 See, for instance, Kridel and Bullough 2007, 75.

51 See 1988, 54.

52 "In essence," Daniel Tanner and Laurel Tanner (1988, 54) emphasize,

> Tyler's syllabus proved to be an orchestration and systematic elaboration of the key elements, sources, determinants, processes, and principles that had been advanced for curriculum development and evaluation by leading experimentalists during the first half of the 20th century.

Orchestration seems the right word: "the arrangement of a musical composition for performance by an orchestra" (*Webster's* 1975, 807). While there is nothing melodious about the four questions, the point is that they existed long before Tyler arranged his version of them in 1949. Rather than author he is an arranger of an extant composition crafted by numerous individuals and groups over several decades. By failing to provide an intellectual history of these "basic principles" Tyler in effect claims them as his own creation, committing plagiarism.

53 *Webster's* 1975, 917.

54 Ibid.

55 Ibid.

56 Taba's 1962 exposition represents the final gasp of the U.S. field's founding paradigmatic moment, as the Kennedy Administration's national curriculum reform meant institutional curriculum development—as Tyler and Taba and their colleagues and predecessors conceived it—could no longer occur. Fifty years on, the four questions fade as accountability collapses the four into one: what's your test score? As a concept and practice, curriculum development has not disappeared; it has been reconceptualized (Pinar 2006).

Bibliography

Cordero, Graciela Cordero and Garduño, José María García. 2004. The Tylerian Curriculum Model and the Reconceptualists: Interview with Ralph W. Tyler (1902–1994). *Revista Electrónica de Investigación Educativa* 6 (2). Retrieved January 19, 2013, http://redie.uabc.mx/vol6no2/contenido-cordero.html

Garduño, José María García. 1995. La Consolidación de la Teoría Curricular en Los Estados Unidos (1912–1949). *Revista Latinoamericana de Estudios Educativos* (México) XXV (2), 57–81.

Garduño, José María García. 2013 February 7. Personal communication.

Giles, H. H., McCutchen, S. P., and Zechiel, A. N. 1942. *Exploring the Curriculum: The Work of the Thirty Schools from the Viewpoint of Curriculum Consultants*. New York: Harper & Brothers.

Jackson, Philip W. 1992. Conceptions of Curriculum and Curriculum Specialists. In the *Handbook of Research on Curriculum*, edited by Philip W. Jackson (3–40). New York: Macmillan.

Kilpatrick, William Heard. 1925. *Foundations of Method: Informal Talks on Teaching*. New York: Macmillan.

Kridel, Craig, and Robert V. Bullough, Jr. 2007. *Stories of the Eight-Year Study: Reexamining Secondary Education in America*. [Foreword by John I. Goodlad.] Albany: State University of New York Press.

Null, J. Wesley. 2008. Curriculum Development in Historical Perspective. In *The Sage Handbook of Curriculum and Instruction*, edited by F. Michael Connelly, Ming Fang He, and JoAnn Phillion (478–490). Los Angeles: Sage.

Pinar, William F. 2006. *The Synoptic Text Today and Other Essays. Curriculum Development after the Reconceptualization*. New York: Peter Lang.

Pinar, William F. 2011. *The Character of Curriculum Studies: Bildung, Currere, and the Recurring Question of the Subject*. New York: Palgrave Macmillan.

Pinar, William F. 2013. *Curriculum Studies in the United States. Intellectual Histories, Present Circumstances*. New York: Palgrave Macmillan.

Pinar, William F. 2014. Curriculum Research in the United States. Crisis, Reconceptualization, Internationalization. In the International *Handbook of Curriculum Research*, edited by William F. Pinar (521–532). [Second edition.] New York: Routledge.

Regents of the University of California. 1987. Ralph W. Tyler. Education: Curriculum Development and Evaluation. [With an Introduction by Carl Tjerandsen.] An Interview Conducted by Malca Chall in 1985, 1986, 1987. Archived in the Regional Oral History Office, the University of California, the Bancroft Library, Berkeley, California. Copyright 1987 by The Regents of the University of California. www.archive.org/stream/educationcurric00tylerich/educationcurric00tylerich_djvu.txt, accessed 19 January 2013.

Ridings, Jeri. 1982. A 1981 Interview with Ralph W. Tyler. In *Educational Evaluation: Classic Works of Ralph W. Tyler*, edited by George F. Madaus and Daniel Stufflebean (243–272). Boston, MA: Kluwer-Nijhoff.

Taba, Hilda. 1932. *The Dynamics of Education. A Methodology of Progressive Educational Thought*. [With a foreword by William Heard Kilpatrick.] New York: Harcourt, Brace and Company.

Taba, Hilda. 1945. General Techniques of Curriculum Planning. In the National Society for the Study of Education, *American Education in the Post War Period: Curriculum Reconstruction*. Forty-fourth Yearbook, Pt. 1 (1945), Ch. 5, 80–115.

Taba, Hilda. 1949. *Curriculum in Intergroup Relations*. Washington, DC: American Council on Education.

Taba, Hilda. 1962. *Curriculum Development: Theory and Practice*. New York: Harcourt, Brace & World,.

Tanner, Daniel and Tanner, Laurel N. 1988. The Emergence of a Paradigm in the Curriculum Field: A Reply to Jickling. *Interchange* 19 (2), 50–58.

Tyler, Ralph W. 1949. *Basic Principles of Curriculum and Instruction*. Chicago: University of Chicago Press.

Webster's New Collegiate Dictionary. 1975. Springfield, MA: G. & C. Merriam Company.

Whipple, Guy Montrose. Ed. 1926. *The Twenty-Sixth Yearbook of the National Society for the Study of Education. The Foundations and Technique of Curriculum-Construction*. Part II: *The Foundations of Curriculum-Making*. [Prepared by the Society's Committee Under the Direction of Harold Rugg.] Bloomington, IL: Public School Publishing Company

CHAPTER 8

CONVERSATION

Commentary

Curriculum is a complicated conversation. This fundamental fact acknowledges not only the individuality and situatedness of students and teachers, but also of those whose work they study. It implies, as education did for Walter Benjamin, "the immanent unity of knowledge," as well as "non-hierarchal relations between teachers and students and between males and females in the university community and in the community at large."[1] Not only organizational, such a conception called for students' commitment to "unceasing spiritual revolution"[2] as well as to "radical doubt"[3] that could create "the culture of conversation."[4] At stake for Benjamin, Eiland and Jennings[5] point out, was "to prevent the degeneration of study into an accumulation of information but also to prepare the way for basic changes in the conduct of everyday life in society."[6] Through such complicated conversation Benjamin aspired to "liberate the future from its deformation in the present."[7]

The sense of possibility Benjamin felt during the summer of 1914 had, after the First World War and just before the Second, evaporated, so that Harold Innis, in 1936, inveighed "against the assumption that more open public discussion of various policy options would facilitate a solution of the problems of the Depression."[8] Watson tells us that Innis had come to regard "the increased level of discussion as partially the cause of, rather than a solution to, the Depression."[9] Secularization and industrialization had, Innis concluded, "confused the role of discussion and the role of contemplation in the advancement of knowledge."[10] Silence can contradict the cacophony of the cellphone present.[11]

Innis would acknowledge that there is no confusion now, as contemplation is almost completely discredited; knowledge utilization is what matters. To the extent one person can influence our conversation, I work to direct it backward, to the past, "to the question," as Roger Simon appreciated, "of what it could mean to live historically, to live within an upright attentiveness to traces of those who have inhabited times and places other than one's own."[12] It is in the past—and the subjective and social reconstruction attentiveness to it can stimulate—that we might find our way to that future effaced by the present.

Bibliography

Archibald, Jo-ann (Q'um Q'um Xiiem). 2008. *Indigenous Storywork: Educating the Heart, Mind, Body, and Spirit*. Vancouver: University of British Columbia Press.

Eiland, Howard and Jennings, Michael W. 2014. *Walter Benjamin. A Critical Life*. Cambridge, MA: Belknap Press of Harvard University Press.
Pinar, William F. 2011. *The Character of Curriculum Studies. Bildung, Currere, and the Recurring Question of the Subject* (1–21). New York: Palgrave Macmillan.
Simon, Roger I. 2005. *The Touch of the Past. Remembrance, Learning, and Ethics*. New York: Palgrave Macmillan.
Watson, Alexander John. 2007. *Marginal Man: The Dark Vision of Harold Innis*. Toronto: University of Toronto Press.
Williamson, Ben. 2013. *The Future of the Curriculum. School Knowledge in the Digital Age*. Cambridge, MA: The MIT Press.

> Inasmuch as understanding involves individualizing rather than normalizing, interpreting rather than objectifying, pluralizing rather than encompassing—in short, radically dialogic processes—we can free ourselves from our own potentially power-determined preunderstanding through an understanding of the other.
>
> Hans-Herbert Kögler[13]

Curriculum is a complicated *conversation*. Structured by guidelines, focused by objectives, overdetermined by outcomes, the school curriculum struggles to remain conversation. It is conversation—efforts at understanding through communication—among students and teachers, actually existing individuals in certain places on certain days, simultaneously personal and public. The fact that students and teachers are individuals complicates conversation considerably, and often in welcomed ways, as each person brings to whatever is being studied his or her own prior knowledge, present circumstances, interest, and, yes, disinterest. Student speech and writing enable teachers to assess where the classroom conversation is, what might happen next, what needs to be reviewed or sometimes sidestepped. Add to these the locale or region where the curriculum is enacted, the nation (its history and present circumstances), the state of the planet, expressed as specifically and mundanely as the weather (with catastrophic climate change threatening us all), and one begins to appreciate just how complicated the conversation the school curriculum is, can be, and must become. There is as well the fact of the individual school, although that institution has often been overemphasized in efforts to improve the curriculum. It is the lived experience of curriculum—*currere*, the running of the course—wherein the curriculum is experienced and enacted.

The verb form is preferable became it emphasizes the lived rather than the planned curriculum, although the two are often intertwined. The verb emphasizes action, process, and experience, in contrast to the noun, which can convey completion. While every course ends, the consequences of study are ongoing, as they are social and subjective as well as intellectual and always specific to course content. The running of the course—*currere*—occurs through conversation, not only classroom discourse, but dialogue among specific students and teachers, and within oneself in solitude. Because the running of the course occurs socially and subjectively through academic study, the concept of *currere* forefronts the meaning of the curriculum as complicated conversation encouraging educational experience. Indeed, *currere* emphasizes the everyday experience of the individual and his or her capacity to learn from that experience, to reconstruct experience through thought and dialogue to enable understanding. Such understanding, achieved through working through History and lived experience, can help us reconstruct our own subjective and social lives. We can be changed by what we study, but the pronoun is relevant, as the "I" is a "we," and "we" are a series of "I's."[14] For Michael Uljens,

> [T]he pedagogical paradox is related to the *subjectivity* of the individual: for learning to be possible there must not only *be* a *somebody* whose reflection is stimulated but also a *somebody* whom the individual *becomes*—that is, there must be the idea that the person in some sense *comes into being* through education.[15]

Educational experience enables subjective and social reconstruction.

Curriculum conceived as a verb—*currere*—privileges the concept of *the individual* in curriculum studies. It is a complicated concept in itself. Each of us is different, meaning we each have a different make-up, genetically as well as different upbringings, families and caretakers, significant others, and, more broadly still, in terms of race, class, and gender, themselves de-individuating concepts inflected by place, time, and circumstances. Informed by culture and by other often homogenizing forces, each of us is, or can be, distinctive. Indeed, we can cultivate that distinctiveness. We can become individualists, committed to actualizing whatever independence we experience and can muster in order to pursue courses of action (including thinking) that we choose as significant.

While distinctive, the individual is comprised of material shared with others. Flesh and blood most materially, but ideas and emotion also come from others, however they are reconstructed through our individual and socially mediated experience of them. We seek clarification of these domains of imprinting, influence, and resemblance through reflection upon them and through conversation with others. That conversation with others is complicated by the fact of our, and their, individuality, their differing generational, genetic, and cultural locations. It seems we share experience but that experience is always altered by these separate locations, in historical time and geographical place, and by our distinctive experience of these. The reverberating fact that we are each individuals—however differently—separates from each other, but it is also what connects us to each other. What have in common, Kaja Silverman suggests, is this shared experience of "finitude."[16] Each of us has a life; each of us dies.

Death provides focus for living. If it seems near-at-hand, death can provide urgency. That sense that each of us has a life, that it is of limited duration, is a fact we share not only with every other human being, but with every living creature. As Silverman appreciates, "finitude is the most capacious and enabling of the attributes we share with others, because . . . it connects us to *every* other being."[17] This is, in William E. Doll, Jr.'s terms, the relationality of life, and this realization characterizes the relationality of curriculum.[18] While we usually think of the curriculum as divided into different courses and concepts, we can also think of it as a "totality," as a "vast, unauthorized book"[19] still being written, including ourselves. Studying the curriculum, then, connects us to everyone else, "not *in spite of* the particularities of their lives but rather *through* them."[20] The fact that conversation is, then, complicated, is not only a pedagogical problem but an educational opportunity to understand difference within resemblance, and not only across our species but life on earth, as well as within our own individuality, as subjectivity itself is an ongoing conversation.[21]

The school subjects themselves codify *conversation*, especially when they are summarized in linear logical fashion in textbooks. The curriculum is a conversation complicated by the singularity of teachers and students, and necessarily so. Teachers cannot teach unless they express themselves through the school subjects they love, and feel committed to explain to those often not eager to leave the confines of what they know already. It is this psychological resistance built into the core of study and learning that positions as primary the relationship teachers can forge with students. Only if class size is sufficiently small and only if the curriculum enables teachers to incorporate their subjective investments and encourage those of their students can such relationships—threaded through the school subjects—form and be expressed. This suggests the educational significance of orality.[22]

Even when they are avowedly interdisciplinary, the school subjects draw upon the academic disciplines as they are advanced at universities. The academic disciplines represent ongoing conversation among scholars and researchers working with concepts and problems discovered and created by their predecessors, prompted by present circumstances, perhaps even governmental priorities. Often considered to be a series of disciplines separate from human interests, even science is structured by these. Moreover, each academic discipline—like biology or chemistry, to which the school subjects correspond—itself represents an interdisciplinary configuration that changes over time. As Anderson and Valente remind, "disciplinarity was always interdisciplinarity."[23] There is no "pure" school subject to be transmitted uncontaminated by those who study and participate in it. That does not mean there are no essential facts in each discipline—what we can call "canonicity"[24]—but it does mean that these are to be engaged, even translated, if they are to be understood.

While not necessarily its outcome, *understanding* is the *raison d'être* of the curriculum. Understanding is intellectual and we work toward it through our minds. These days we are reminded regularly that those minds are housed in our brains and our brains are in our bodies, so we are quite clear that understanding is simultaneously intellectual and emotional, and that it is always embodied, the latter not only conceived as biological and neurological but as immanent. That means that understanding is individual and social, directed to the present as it is informed by the past. In the simultaneity of its sources and the multiplicity of its aspirations, understanding becomes allegorical, "an emotional writing," Rauch explains, "that transforms the signs into a mentality or spirit in the effect of the historic remnants on the individual mind."[25] Emotion is not sufficient, of course, as one cannot experience one's historicity without factual knowledge of the past, but, Rauch continues,

> What the allegorical intends is not the static knowledge of things but the productive imagination of the individual which can associate and create new ideas about a different and better historical setting. The impact of allegory on cognition causes a constant transformation of attitudes and thoughts about reality.[26]

Coupling facts and lived experience in creative tensionality—in part because "allegory expresses the impossibility of a perfect unity between image and concept"[27]—can trigger that constant transformation. Study recasts intellectual, psychological, and physical structures as allegorical. The world is simultaneously empirical and poetical, phenomenological and historical.

The complicated character of understanding has meant that at different times and places we have conceived of communication as only cognitive and at other times as primarily emotional, but each is always historical. It is, of course, all these at once, if in varying degrees according to subject matter, again understood as a double entendre. In a letter written to his wife in June 1909, Gustav Mahler depicted "reason"—the means of the intellect—as "the limited but necessary means for communicating with the phenomenal world."[28] He wrote:

> The rational, that is to say, that which can be analyzed by the understanding, is almost always the inessential and actually a veil which disguises the form. But insofar as a soul needs a body—there is nothing that can be said against that—the artist must pick out his means for presentation from the rational world.[29]

As William McGrath[30] points out, Mahler aspired to express "metaphysical concepts in musical terms," but reason was required not only for such complex composition, but also for expressing in language the content of his music.

In our time this dualism—between mind and body[31]—seems to have been settled in the body's favor. We are, it seems, our bodies. Is it capitalism that has made materialists of us all, or is capitalism materialism's relatively recent manifestation? Ocularcentrism is in play here of course, although its association with science—and racism—complicates speculations regarding its role in the present cultural privileging of objects. While there may be no homunculus inside the body, no separate soul imprisoned in the flesh, the body does not coincide with itself. This structural non-coincidence is the space and time of subjectivity.[32] In that time and space, structured by the body and its being-in-the-world, one knows one is alive. One becomes aware that one is undergoing experience in all its multidimensionality and elusiveness.[33] It is the structural non-coincidence of the alive body—the time and space of subjectivity—that invites us to experience *experience*, e.g. to remember what we have undergone, to forget what we cannot bear to remember, to understand what we can recall and must comprehend. It is subjectivity wherein we begin to know ourselves and the world we inhabit and which inhabits us, e.g. "the historicity of understanding."[34]

Self-knowledge—know thyself—is the ancient educational injunction. Such knowledge implies self-reflection, a process enabled by the fact of structural non-coincidence. In different conceptual systems different terminology applies—in phenomenology there is the transcendental ego—but the general conclusion is that we are able to distance ourselves from our experience and the world wherein it occurs, that we can remember what we undergo, and that we can exercise some choice in affirming those elements we want to emphasize (and in de-emphasizing those elements we prefer to ignore). In certain systems—psychoanalysis most prominently—the sphere of freedom is modest, as it becomes clear that who we imagine ourselves to be may represent a defensive reconfiguration of what we are in fact. "The more we think about the 'I'," George Grant reminds, "the more mysterious this subjectivity will appear to us."[35] Knowing oneself is, then, no simple matter of paying attention to what happens—although it depends on that—and it requires retrieving what has happened already and remains only as residue, and sometimes not readily accessible. This ongoing sense of mystery in fact impels self-study and haunts the formation of the subject.

The Recurring Question of the Subject

> Do we still have the strength . . . to oppose the scientific-deterministic worldview with a self that is grounded in creative freedom?
>
> Gottfried Benn[36]

The idea that there is an individual who can participate in the ongoing reformulation of his or her own character is summarized in the concept of the subject. Often associated with the Enlightenment in Europe—the marker for modernity, that substitution of science for religion as the governing mythology of life—*the subject*, as we have designated the person, emphasizing one's capacity for agency, can learn to exercise reason. Through reason one might ascertain his or her self-interest and distinguish it from the public interest, although on occasion these have been seen to be closely related. Adjudicating the tensions between the private and public spheres, and those tensions within one's own psychic life, was appreciated as prerequisite for the subject to achieve emancipation—freedom—from servitude its several forms, ranging from social conformity to physical enslavement. That latter practice was dependent upon the denial of subjectivity to those enslaved; they were bodies monetized, sometimes sexualized, always commodified.

Converting subjects to numbers has proved pivotal to not only the sophistication of science but to its application to practical life in technology. Evidently we are so enthusiastic about the consequences that we have applied quantification to almost all aspects of life, not only its practical aspects.[37] In the last one hundred years we have applied it to the education of the child, previously imagined in philosophical, then in psychological and social terms. Today we understand education as a series of numerals, as test scores on standardized examinations, to be supplemented, if the Obama Administration succeeds, by rates of graduation.[38] Not only philosophy, but subjectivity itself becomes bleached from schooling, itself reduced to test preparation. In the United States educational institutions have been deformed; they are now cram schools. Dewey's coupling of democracy and education has been superseded by business and schooling.

Certainly that is the trajectory of U.S. school "reform" since 1968. Something remains, however, if only the school's non-coincidence with itself. Despite the repression that is school deform, students squirm, and teachers still try to find opportunities to teach. This has been my life: I remember how the present came to be; I can testify to what has been lost in the rush to reduce students and teachers to numbers. Critique is possible, and *critique* is one crucial practice of curriculum studies. Critique implies not only non-coincidence but reconstruction as questioning, skepticism, forming finally conviction. In such understanding there is created the domain of determination, originating perhaps in passion, subjected to evidence, refashioned as ethics or morality, invoked when present circumstances violate these, or others. Critique is informed by lived experience juxtaposed with academic knowledge and compelled by conviction; it is offered as part of an ongoing conversation (or in order to restart one, or even to end one).

The teacher—the key participant in the conversation that is the curriculum—is a communicant, knowledgeable and committed to explain and assist students to understand the subject at hand, including themselves as they struggle, perhaps revel, in what they read and write and say and hear. Communication incorporates, as James Carey[39] points out, ancient "religious attitudes," now secularized—and naturalized[40]—but still structured by our faith that language can carry us beyond the world we know now, not only to futures foretold (and yet to be told) but also back to the past whose injustices might somehow (through our remembrance of them) stimulate reparation. This "historic religious undercurrent," Carey continues, "has never been eliminated from our thought."[41] Nor should it, I say, as the embrace of the common good constitutes professional ethics for educators of the public. Neither transparent sieves nor accomplices of the state, teachers not only have knowledge: they have, develop, communicate character.

In our time "moral excellence" is not necessarily associated with the Word of God, but with the specificities of situation and subjectivity. In *Webster's*, in fact, most of the eight definitions offered for "character" emphasize its singularity, whether this follows from a "complex of mental and ethical traits and individualizing a person, group or nation (as in assessing a person's character)" or from a "main or essential nature, especially as strongly marked and serving to distinguish." While the former definition acknowledges the internally differentiated complexity of individuality, the latter invites us to associate singularity with culture or nationality or animality, with something essential that is more basic than our ephemeral and shifting subjectivity, with nature's and culture's and history's imprinting of us, and our imprinting of them.

As constructed, the character of the subject is in a sense fictional. However constructed—as persona or avatar—its fictional character does not imply its insubstantiality. I am a subject, subject to my own life history, reconstructed according to my own dreams and internalized demands, called into question by those around me. My subjectivity—the personal possessive implies the subject's non-coincidence with itself—is imprinted by culture, nationality, by historicality itself. There have been those who have been so mesmerized by such internal multiplicity and outer connectivity that they have declared the concept of the subject dead, deconstructed into various often contradictory elements. Instead of a coherent person, today many celebrate prostheses, post-human forms of connectivity, relays of energy and animation that take momentary form then disappear, sometimes forever, reappearing in different not always recognizable forms. In such a postmodern condition the subject fragments, withdraws, becomes a talking head perhaps, images (photos), text without context, registering what remains of the private on public websites, chronicling the sequence of once private (if only because one kept them to oneself) events evidently now everyone undergoes and or at least everyone knows. Such public information can be categorized by businesses that target customers, not subjects. That conversion points to another and more prominent (it's number 1) definition of character that *Webster's* offers. Character is defined as a "cipher that represents information, also a representation of such character that may be accepted by a computer." A "cipher," *Webster's* explains, is a "zero," a "nonentity." Does the question of the subject recur because the subject has vanished?

Subjects seem absent in cram schools, where so-called skills replace academic knowledge, decontextualized puzzles preparing for employment in jobs without meaning, itself a casualty of capitalism's compulsion to profit no matter what it takes. No longer subjects, students become "ciphers" in cram schools. In these deformed institutions—once sites of complicated conversation, now devolving into test prep centers—human subjects become numbers, e.g. test scores. There can be no structural non-coincidence in ciphers. *Just do it* becomes the anthem of our time, action now, suspending judgment, ignoring ethics: only outcomes matter, and outcomes are numbers, only. Representation evaporates, except for the numeral. The subject—the double entendre of the curriculum—becomes subjugated to its reign. We are its subjects. As an academic field committed to subjects not numbers, the circumstances supportive of curriculum studies fade.

There is another definition—indeed, it is also listed among the first series of definitions in *Webster's*—of *character*. In this definition character is not a numeral but a "graphic symbol (as a hieroglyph or alphabet letter) used in writing or printing." This is a definition that reinstalls representation as primary in communication, explicit in an antecedent definition: character is a "conventional graphic device placed on an object as an indication of ownership, origin, or relationship." Indeed, character—also acknowledged by *Webster's* as "magical"—can denote a "style of writing or printing," the definition listed just before its computerization (noted above). Writing or printing denotes self-expression, public testimony, collective remembrance, and these expressive forms and genealogical traces of experience require subjectivity, invoke, in fact, a "person," in this line (it's 6a if you're checking) of *Webster's* list of definitions for character, "marked by notable or conspicuous traits: personage." The hieroglyph inspires this series of associations as well, when, as Rauch suggests, hieroglyph becomes "a metaphor for the remnants of experience that need to be read, put together, instead of interpreted."[42] Reading *is* interpretation, but Rauch is emphasizing here the archeological demand to which reconstruction responds.

Reconstruction means reassembling the remains of what was, as in the United States after the Civil War. Reestablishing the past is in principle impossible, but in the effort to reconstruct what was—understanding it on its own terms—one reconstructs what is now. Finding the future, then, means returning to the past, not instrumentalizing the present. Especially in an epoch defined by its presentism—a state of mind in which everything is now—we cannot escape the constraints of capitalism (and its educational equivalent: the cram school) from where we are now. Nor can improving what we do now—the ameliorative orientation that has so accented curriculum studies in the United States[43]—enable the future to unfold. Because it works within the structures of the present, amelioration risks only reorganizing, not reconstructing, what is. Regression to the past—re-experiencing prior, even archaic, forms of life—opens paths to the future reorganizing the present occludes.

The educational significance of the past positions History, not mathematics or science, as central to the education of the public. Of course, mathematics and science[44] are historical subjects as well, and these histories might be emphasized in the coursework, in part as a corrective to misconceptions that these subjects are independent of time, place, and circumstance, including politics. And corrective as well to the assumption that mathematics and science constitute contemporary versions of nineteenth-century Latin and ancient Greek: difficult subjects whose mastery muscles the mind, preparing it for any eventuality. History also discloses the shifting character of culture, a concept too often misconstrued as timeless, as somehow separate from politics and economics, and in our day ordained as definitive, as "difference." History includes sexuality, which when contained within biology may be misconstrued as ahistorical or non-cultural, leaving students with the misconception that sexual practices are only "natural" and ahistorical. History makes clear that we are ourselves are historical, that what we experience is in part a function of time, and that we are both different and similar to those who have preceded us and from those who will follow. The recognition and reconstruction of such difference enables understanding of our—which becomes, then, educational—experience.

The primacy of the temporal in the curriculum—one among several breakthroughs made by the canonical curriculum theorist Dwayne Huebner[45]—means that it matters who said what when. That phrase can conjure up cross-examination in a courtroom, but only the aspirations of attentiveness, civility, and argumentation associated with litigation are pertinent to the open-ended, often judgment-free, ongoing effort to express oneself, understand the other, and communicate with everyone that characterizes the complicated conversation of the school curriculum. The temporal, then, animates what is spoken and studied as it underscores how memory structures what we experience in the present, and how new experience enables us to reconstruct what we remember and can foresee. We say we learn from experience, but unless there is experience—embodied, temporally structured—there is nothing to learn from. In the curriculum, temporality structures *orality*.

Orality is not necessarily speech, not necessarily behavioral at all. Certainly it is not chatter, saying whatever comes to mind without rhyme or reason. Nor is it clever talk designed to impress the teacher or another classmate or oneself. It is not simply the right answer to a question posed by a teacher confined to a lesson plan or exhibiting a "best practice." Orality references the temporally structured—and structuring—expression of subjectivity through text, a physical text and/or, more broadly, the text that constitutes the ongoing class discussion. It is saying what you think and/or feel, preferably after you've thought about it, although spontaneity can disclose something unforeseen, enabling the speaker to know more about herself and/or her academic subject. Orality is an ongoing and reconstructed form of self-conscious intertextuality, acknowledging that one's statements have antecedents, public and private, past and present.

Even without knowing the details of one's students' lives—in most publicly-funded schools this isn't possible given the excessive size of classes—the teacher can hear the multi-referentiality of the students' statements, provided she is attuned to this variegated temporal character of conversation. On many occasions statements are simple and straightforward, but as memory and openness allow, one can register the past when it is heard in the present. Simple exchange of information is no instance of orality, even when that occurs through speech, unless there is intertextuality or intentionality. Simply saying stuff is simply saying stuff; it is not conversation.

It is tempting to confine such chatter to the Internet, but clearly it occurs everywhere, even in families where personal histories are often in members' faces, as we say. While the Internet is no friend of orality, it does not preclude it either. Face-to-face speech lacks orality when it is amounts to the anonymous exchange of facts, or is a medium of seduction or exploitation, and when it is reduced to giving instructions or obtaining "feedback." Orality requires the articulation of embodiment, of personification, acknowledgement, and engagement, so that the distinctiveness of those present becomes audible in what they say, discernible in how they act, not as an ornamental flourish to an already full act (expressing one's "style"), but as registering the originality and creativity that subjectivity can convey when s/he is embodied in the present moment.

On occasions playful and on others utterly serious, such complicated conversation enables students to experience social democracy, mocked by politicians who are polarized by ideology.

Social democracy is not personal posturing or group-think but, rather, the engagement of others in deciphering the intersubjective reality in which all are embedded and participating, even when they are withdrawn. Such discernment occurs in solitude as well, but among others one hears first-hand, with the "first-hand" of the other (e.g. his or her distinctiveness), how things (or one thing, an idea or a fact or a feeling) look or feel to him or her, what they seem to those assembled. Codes of conduct, rules of civility, questions of conformity, performance, ulterior motives, and social sincerity: all these require the physical presence of others so you can sense what's going on. You can sometimes tell when someone is pulling your leg online, but the body gives off more than odors as so-called nonverbal communication nestles words as they are uttered.

Organizing such conversation goes only so far. No format forms forever, even the relative absence of formats as in the encounter groups in which I participated forty years ago. Sharing a circle with twelve (or so) others, one waited for someone to speak, and so it began. Unguided—on occasion there were interventions from the group leader, often in the form of questions, but infrequently as prohibition or reprimand—the conversation became a projective screen for the preoccupations of those present. Without a shared history or an assigned task, group members made it up, as it quickly became clear to everyone. There was nowhere to hide, as those who had spoken and felt exposed sometimes demanded reciprocity. There was a point to these often unnerving exercises, of course. Not only did group process becomes visible—how what one said produced that response, becoming a crescendo or ensuring silence—but this produced no nomological law, as the particularity of individuals was inescapable, and what became summarized as "social constructivism" was irremediably concrete and personal. No one could deny people were making *this* up.

Its constructed character hardly rendered this speech false, however. What became clear is that social reality is comprised of falsehood as well as factuality, as well as all points in-between. Over time groups acknowledged past events internal to the group, began referencing new statements in terms of previous ones, noting differences and repetitions. Often there was an appetite for new material; other times there was determination to work through puzzles left over from the past. Sometimes the former depended on the latter, and vice versa. The rules of engagement were few, precisely because the ongoing character of group encounter meant that judgments must be made in the moment, to which other judgments would be added. The direction any stream of conversation was headed could be changed by the wave of a wand—a word spoken, a gesture, a sense of something not yet articulated—and the content of conversation could change as well. There was a quality of adventure—and danger—in a process where some safety was assured but the destination was unknown.

That—the loss of adventure—is the catastrophe of objectives, especially when their "implementation" is assessed by tests. The creativity, spontaneity, and originality of conversation are converted to puzzle-solving, task completion, and what is left of group process is funneled toward a predetermined end. The curriculum becomes a tax audit. Receipts are always necessary, as no one takes your word for anything. Professional judgment is replaced by regulation, playfulness by wisecracks, sincerity by cynicism: just do it. Working to find out "what works" we converted the classroom to cram school, the contemporary version of the factory, an assembly line wherein mechanical behavior and efficiency replace inventiveness and memory. Regulation is now internalized, through objectives whose implementation will be assessed later, over and over. Teachers and students still talk, but now as if in prison, exchanging information while walking to the next station, always under surveillance, even if that panopticon is now internally installed. Doing time can be an adventure, but its destination takes the tension out of the unknown and attaches it to others, against whom one aggresses for the sake of a fantasized placidity always extrinsic to the "empty stare,"[46] of the cram curriculum.

The excitement of education may have been excised by "reform," but curriculum studies scholars have kept up appearances. Without jurisdiction—for many heartbreaking, for the field castrating, for the schools devastating—we encouraged enactment of orality through the elaboration of concepts—such as "complicated conversation"—knowing these would be kept out of schools, themselves shut down, sometimes physically, always intellectually, as the adventure of the unknown journey is replaced by the proceduralism of the tax audit, wherein test-item completion substitutes for thinking, especially for the critical and creative kinds. Not immobilized by their severance from the schools, U.S. curriculum studies scholars kept hope alive by remembering the past, reworking the present, and imagining the future. Forced to the sidelines by government intervention, curriculum studies scholars switched from supervising curriculum development in schools to understanding the curriculum in schools, often providing occasions for critique and demanding testimonies to possibility. Nowhere is the latter louder than in the still reverberating work of Maxine Greene. In her Lincoln Center lectures[47] you can hear the frustration of being sidelined, the dignity required for carrying on despite this incomprehensible calamity, the affirmation of action possible through the imagination.

Action inspired by the imagination is one consequence of complicated conversation. "Aesthetics," Mosès asserts, "provides the language through which the fundamentally political nature of history is revealed."[48] Working through the imagination enables us to work creatively within and through constraints. Those constraints are external and political, but they are also internal, emanating from our psychic (what Freud called primary) processes, visceral and unconscious. Despite the weight of the past and the power of the present, breakthroughs are possible. "Each moment of time," Mosès tells us, "bears judgment on moments that precede it."[49] Breakthrough, what for Walter Benjamin was "redemption,"[50] can occur at any moment, breaking the inertia of the present, bringing a new insight, a new reality into the world. This is no quantitative or cumulative conception of historical time, but an idea, as Mosès explains, "borrowed from Jewish messianism, of a utopia appearing in the very heart of the present, of a hope lived in the mode of today."[51] For me, "determination" is sturdier than "hope" but each is attuned to the immanence of worldliness.

While a fact of life—however obscured it becomes in instructional schemes sequencing so-called skills in some grand Ponzi scheme wherein investments now presumably lead to payoffs later—the possibility located in each and every moment can be activated through juxtaposing the past with the present. Such juxtaposition and the creative tension it can install can lead to what gets called a third space, as Hongyu Wang has explained.[52] This third space does not subsume the past and present into some third common category, as in dialectics, but preserves the distinctiveness of each as a new reality struggles to be born. It requires us to enact the non-coincidence of subjectivity with reality through the cultivation of distance, of even estrangement and exile.

Distance has gotten a bad rap in recent decades, as the identity politics of the women's movement and African American affirmations of heritage insisted that experience is the primary prerequisite to knowledge. Only a woman or a black man could know what sexism or racism is, what whiteness communicates. While acknowledging an important fact, such insistence also overstates the authority of experience as it understates the significance of study. While it can—often does—provide invaluable knowledge, experience can also provincialize and even mislead: experience is not always reliable. Men can understand sexism and its institutional and psychic structuration as masculinity through academic study, if they distance themselves from—indeed question—their own self-evident experience and listen to the testimonies of others' first-hand experience. Those of European descent can understand racism and whiteness as well, despite cultural predispositions to substitute identification for empathy,[53] reiterating the arrogance of cultures whose science encouraged them to imagine their knowledge was applicable everywhere.

While experience is invaluable, understanding also takes, as Maxine Greene[54] knew, "a kind of distancing," and for her such distantiation was always infused with the immediacy of the aesthetic moment. Others—like Jane Roland Martin[55]—have been even more confident, asserting that "the greater one's distance from one's object of study, the better one can understand it." In his letters to his wife, Bruford[56] tells us, Humboldt too spoke "repeatedly" of "the need" he felt for "cultivating detachment." Obviously Humbolt was not "completely detached," Bruford comments, "or he would not have become one of Prussia's leading statesmen . . . offered so important and congenial a task as the reorganization of the Prussian educational system."[57] It was through the imagination, Humboldt said, that reality affected him.[58]

For Pasolini, it was indirect discourse—the "contamination" of public aesthetic forms with private passion[59]—that installed distance while preserving identification. Such aesthetic formulation of lived experience—what Thomas Gabriel[60] terms "objectification"—represents "our being-in-the-world," so that "we recognize ourselves." Aesthetic creation is also "capable of rendering the 'spirit' of a life-form, of an epoch, of a typical life in our century, of an atmosphere."[61] In contrast, reification splits off knowledge from subjectivity, installing it as independent of those persons and processes constructing it. Scientism is one familiar form of reification, as it—in Gabriel's language—"denies the paradoxes and antinomies which lie at the basis of determinacy and accredits itself the capacity to investigate into the conditions of possibility of determinacy (of meaning, truth, etc.)."[62] Distance and engagement are two intertwined if tensioned modalities of study, always altering their forms and intensities according to the project at hand, its historical situatedness, its subjective meaning, its social significance.

Rather than the silence produced by the self-segregating smugness of identity politics—with its inverted reinscription of stereotypes—the character of curriculum studies is communicative, committed to dialogical encounter across difference. In what James Carey[63] calls a "ritual view," communication becomes less a transmission of messages, an "act of imparting information," as it is the "representation of shared beliefs." Such communication is associated with concepts of "sharing," "participation," "association," "fellowship," and "the possession of a common faith," as it recalls the etymological roots of the terms "commonness," "communion," "community," and "communication."[64] Rather than "the extension of messages across geography for the purpose of control," Carey (1992, 18) continues, this "archetypal" conception of communication is as "the sacred ceremony that draws persons together in fellowship and commonality." Communication, then, is an ongoing social ceremony aspiring to shared understanding while engaging difference and protecting dissent. It contributes to the creation of community.

Not every classroom matches that description nor should it. There is no formula for "what works," nor should there be. If there is to be communication characterized by the concepts listed above, the forms it will take will differ, even among the same participants on different days on different topics. The vitality of conversation depends in part on its momentariness, how it communicates what is felt or heard or remembered and in ways aligned with the texts and talks that have (re)structured the class thus far. Certain forms of talk—hate speech, for instance—are excluded from classroom conversation. An ongoing aspiration to authenticity is mediated by commitments to civility, personified in individual teachers who regulate—at the beginning of the year and on any particular day—what the range of possible expression can be. Not only the character of conversation is contextualized so specifically, so, I suggest, should be the syllabi.

While I no longer oppose governmental curriculum guidelines—they are preferable to contentless curriculum organized around skill-based standardized tests—I insist on institutional support for teachers' academic freedom to teach the material teachers deem appropriate and in the manner suitable to that material and to those studying it; these judgments should be made by individual teachers, if in consultation with colleagues and others (including colleagues at the university) and with students themselves. From large and heterogeneous to small specialized schools emphasizing curricular themes and serving specific populations, schools' organizational structures ought to be as malleable as teachers and students request them to be. Emphasizing organizational structures over intellectual content risks undermining the vitality of the curriculum, even when reorganization is undertaken in the name of curricular reconstruction.

While democracy depends on citizens and other residents capable of dialogical encounter with the difference they personify, experience, and express, demanding such encounter by forcing students from all backgrounds to enroll in the same classes is not only politically impossible in a democracy but, in practical terms, pedagogically Sisyphean. Still, some schools could be established—I am endorsing here a model of largely self-governed publicly-funded independent schools—that forefront dialogical encounter across social difference, just as others could cultivate the internal differentiation of shared identity, religious or cultural or political.

There can be no Nazi schools, however, just as there can be in a democracy no accommodation for non-democratic, intolerant religious schools either. The protection of religious freedom is limited to worship, not to be extended to publicly funded instruction where secularity must be—in general, with specific and relative exceptions—institutionalized if democracy is to prevail. In a time of terrorism sometimes stimulated by religious zeal, it is appropriate to err on the side of secularism, even though religious expression, when not politically intemperate, ought not be totally repressed in public. In a different era—not our own, but one marked by religious quietism rather than politicization—more exclusive and experimental religious schools could be encouraged. This same temporally tempered—avowedly historical—view of what is educationally appropriate obtains in questions of multiculturalism.[65]

A cosmopolitan curriculum, then, incorporates difference in efforts to understand reality, as it was, is now, and might be. The verb is crucial, as the promotion of difference, or particularism, is a provincialism. Like education itself, cosmopolitanism is imperfect, as Sharon Todd notes. Like multiculturalism—as Sneja Gunew[66] explains—cosmopolitanism is also situated, to be invoked when affirmations of difference become politically and educationally appropriate, that is, during times of trouble. It is no eleventh commandment, no transcendent ethical demand for human holiness. On the contrary, to be cosmopolitan commands contempt for intolerance, as, for instance, Pasolini personified.[67] And it can be expressed in quiet concern for one's neighbors, however local and global one's neighborhood is conceived to be, as in Jane Addams' case.[68] In occurs, then, in the world, not in some split-sphere of (postmodern) abstraction where self-righteousness gets smuggled in, passing for cultural critique and ethical judgment.

The character of curriculum studies is cosmopolitan, encouraging the ongoing understanding of the world as historical, as always changing and different, always unchanging and the same. Allegory conveys this simultaneity of the mythological and the historical, the cultural and the individual, the abstract and the concrete. When I teach the character of the curriculum studies I am also communicating what History expresses through me, as my professionalism as an educator laboring in the public interest requires not only disciplinary expertise but also the commitment to communicate that understanding in variable and always changing social settings. In teaching, then, we are not implementing objectives or preparing students for tests but testifying every day in every way to the human capacity—to the moral obligation—to understand the world and its personification in our subjectivity, its history, its present structurings (in culture, politics, science, as the various disciplines aspire). In teaching, through the past, it is the planetary future that faces us, that constitutes the recurring question of the subject today.

Notes

1 2014, 66–67. I documented the incorporation of such language by corporations intent on moving curriculum online. When and where Benjamin issued his call it constituted a politically progressive move, as it does in China today. Not so when Williamson (2013) colludes with corporations' privatization of public servants.
2 Benjamin, quoted in Eiland and Jennings 2014, 67.
3 Ibid.
4 Ibid.
5 2014, 67.
6 Ibid.
7 Benjamin, quoted in Eiland and Jennings 2014, 66.
8 Watson 2007, 188.
9 Ibid.
10 Ibid.
11 "Many of the Elders kept saying," Archibald (2008, 76) reports, "that it was and is important to learn how to listen." She adds: "Silence is respectful and can create good thinking" (Archibald 2008, 89).

12 Simon 2005, 133.
13 1999, 109.
14 Winch 2008, 295.
15 2003, 46.
16 2009, 4.
17 Ibid.
18 Trueit 2012, 111, 158.
19 Silverman 2009, 9.
20 Ibid.
21 Reichenbach 2003, 101.
22 Pinar 2012, 175.
23 2002, 4.
24 Anderson and Valente 2002, 13.
25 2000, 129.
26 2000, 130.
27 Jay 1993, 112.
28 McGrath 1974, 124.
29 Quoted in McGrath 1974, 124.
30 1974, 120.
31 See, for example, Bordo 1993.
32 "The critical practice of self-distanciation," Kögler (1999, 252) explains, "is to bring about a heightened sense of self-understanding, an enlightened insight into usually hidden linkages between symbolic relations and social networks of power."
33 See Jay 2005.
34 Rauch 2000, 129.
35 1966 (1959), 69.
36 1932, in Kaes, Jay, and Dimendberg 1995, 380.
37 "Numbers on a large enough scale may well come to substitute for an idea of God," Fletcher (2012, 390) suggests, "and in relation to such a sea change we may fear an addictive compulsion to believe only *in the numbers*, whose combinations are capable of infinite modulation."
38 Dillon 2011, March 10, A22.
39 1992, 15.
40 Garrison 2008, 99.
41 1992, 18.
42 2000, 15.
43 See Kliebard 1970.
44 See, for instance, Shapin 2010.
45 1999, 131–142.
46 Grumet 1988, 116.
47 Greene 2001.
48 2009 (1992), 104.
49 2009 (1992), 108.
50 Silverman 2009, 179.
51 2009 (1992), 108.
52 2004.
53 Hartman 1997, 18.
54 2001, 53.
55 2008, 126.
56 2009 (1975), 23.
57 Ibid.
58 Bruford 2009 (1975), 26.
59 Pinar 2009, 185 n. 32.
60 In Gabriel and Žižek 2009, 76.
61 Ibid.

62 In Gabriel and Žižek 2009, 77.
63 1992, 18.
64 Ibid.
65 See Pinar 2011.
66 2004, 1.
67 Pinar 2009, 99–142.
68 Pinar 2009, 59–82.

Bibliography

Anderson, Amanda and Valente, Joseph. 2002. Introduction: Discipline and Freedom. In *Disciplinarity at the Fin de Siècle*, edited by Amanda Anderson and Joseph Valente (1–15). Princeton, NJ: Princeton University Press.

Bordo, Susan. 1993. *Unbearable Weight: Feminism, Western Culture, and the Body*. Berkeley: University of California Press.

Bruford, W.H. 2009 (1975). *The German Tradition of Self-cultivation*: "*Bildung*" *from Humboldt to Thomas Mann*. Cambridge: Cambridge University Press.

Carey, James W. 1992. *Communication as Culture: Essays on Media and Society*. New York: Routledge.

Dewey, John. 1916. *Democracy and Education*. New York: Macmillan.

Dillon, Sam. 2011, March 10. Most public schools may miss targets, education secretary says. *New York Times*, A16, A22.

Fletcher, Angus. 2012. *Allegory: The Theory of a Symbolic Model*. [With a foreword by Harold Bloom and a new afterword by the author.] Princeton, NJ: Princeton University Press.

Gabriel, Markus and Žižek, Slavoj. 2009. *Mythology, Madness and Laughter: Subjectivity in German Idealism*. New York: Continuum.

Garrison, Jim. 2008. The Education of One Philosopher's Eros. In *Leaders in Philosophy of Education: Intellectual Self-portraits*, edited by Leonard J. Waks (93–100). [With a Foreword by Israel Scheffler.] Rotterdam and Tapei: Sense Publishers.

Grant, George P. 1966 (1959). *Philosophy in the Mass Age*. Toronto: Copp Clark Publishing.

Greene, Maxine. 2001. *Variations on a Blue Guitar. The Lincoln Center Institute Lectures on Aesthetic Education*. New York: Teachers College Press.

Grumet, Madeleine R. 1988. *Bitter Milk: Women and Teaching*. Amherst: University of Massachusetts Press.

Gunew, Sneja. 2004. *Haunted Nations: The Colonial Dimensions of Multiculturalisms*. London: Routledge.

Hartman, Saidiya V. 1997. *Scenes of Subjection: Terror, Slavery, and Self-Making in Nineteenth Century America*. New York: Oxford University Press.

Huebner, Dwayne E. 1999. *The Lure of the Transcendent*. Mahwah, NJ: Lawrence Erlbaum.

Jay, Martin. 1993. *Force Fields: Between Intellectual History and Cultural Critique*. New York: Routledge.

Jay, Martin. 2005. *Songs of Experience: Modern American and European Variations on a Universal Theme*. Berkeley: University of California Press.

Kaes, Anton, Jay, Martin, and Dimendberg, Edward. eds. 1995. *The Weimar Sourcebook*. Berkeley: University of California Press.

Kliebard, Herbert M. 2000 (1970). Persistent Issues in Historical Perspective. In *Curriculum Theorizing: The Reconceptualization*, edited by William F. Pinar (39–50). Troy, NY: Educator's International Press. First printed in *Educational Comment* (1970), 31–41.

Kögler, Hans-Herbert. 1999. *The Power of Dialogue: Critical Hermeneutics after Gadamer and Foucault*. Cambridge, MA: MIT Press.

Levine, Donald N. 2007. *Powers of the Mind: The Reinvention of Liberal Learning in America*. Chicago: University of Chicago Press.

Martin, Jane Roland. 2008. It's Not on the List. In *Leaders in Philosophy of Education: Intellectual Self-Portraits*, edited by Leonard J. Waks (125–134). [With a Foreword by Israel Scheffler.] Rotterdam and Tapei: Sense Publishers.

McGrath, William J. 1974. *Dionysian Art and Populist Politics in Austria*. New Haven, CT: Yale University Press.

Mosès, Stéphane. 2009 (1992). *The Angel of History: Rosenzweig, Benjamin, Scholem*. [Trans. Barbara Harshav] Stanford, CA: Stanford University Press.

Pinar, William F. 2009. *The Worldliness of a Cosmopolitan Education: Passionate Lives in Public Service*. New York: Routledge.

Pinar, William F. 2012. *What Is Curriculum Theory?* [Second edition.] New York: Routledge.

Rauch, Angelika. 2000. *The Hieroglyph of Tradition: Freud, Benjamin, Gadamer, Novalis, Kant*. Madison, NJ: Fairleigh Dickinson University Press.

Reichenbach, Roland. 2003. On Irritation and Transformation: A-teleological *Bildung* and its Significance for the Democratic Form of Living. In *Educating Humanity: Bildung in Postmodernity*, edited by Lars Løvlie, Klaus Peter Mortensen, and Sven Erik Nordenbo (93–103). Oxford: Blackwell.

Shapin, Steven. 2010. *Never Pure: Historical Studies of Science as if It Was Produced by People with Bodies, Situated in Time, Space, Culture, and Society, Struggling for Credibility and Authority*. Baltimore, MD: The Johns Hopkins University Press.

Silverman, Kaja. 2009. *Flesh of My Flesh*. Stanford, CA: Stanford University Press.

Todd, Sharon. 2009. *Toward an Imperfect Education: Facing Humanity, Rethinking Cosmopolitanism*. Boulder, CO: Paradigm.

Trueit, Donna. ed. 2012. *Pragmatism, Postmodernism, Complexity Theory: The Fascinating Imaginative Realm of William E. Doll, Jr*. New York: Routledge.

Uljens, Michael. 2003. The Idea of a Universal Theory of Education—An Impossible but Necessary Project? In *Educating Humanity: Bildung in Postmodernity*, edited by Lars Løvlie, Klaus Peter Mortensen and Sven Erik Nordenbo (37–59). Oxford: Blackwell.

Wang, Hongyu. 2004. *The Call from the Stranger on a Journey Home: Curriculum in a Third Space*. New York: Peter Lang.

Webster's New Collegiate Dictionary. 1975. Springfield, MA: G. & C. Merriam Company.

Winch, Christopher. 2008. Complexity, Contestation and Engagement. In *Leaders in Philosophy of Education: Intellectual Self-Portraits*, edited by Leonard J. Waks (289–300). [With a Foreword by Israel Scheffler.] Rotterdam and Tapei: Sense Publishers.

CHAPTER 9

PLACE

Commentary

Through this remembrance of Joe L. Kincheloe I chart the genesis of the concept of "place" in curriculum studies, a concept I formulated after moving in 1985 from upstate New York to the Deep South. After arriving in Louisiana I met Joe Kincheloe who joined me in elaborating the significance of *that* place in understanding curriculum. I trace his intellectual history during the years of our collaboration, specifying the key concepts and intellectual traditions that informed them, concluding with his embrace of critical pedagogy.

Bibliography

Pinar, William F. 2010. A Southern Treasure. *Journal of the American Association for the Advancement of Curriculum Studies* online. Volume 6, 13. www.uwstout.edu/soe/jaaacs/vol6-2.cfm

> Place becomes an important means of linking particularity to the social concerns of curriculum theory.
>
> Joe L. Kincheloe[1]

Joe L. Kincheloe died suddenly on December 19, 2008, cutting short an astonishing career that traversed the history of education to curriculum studies and critical pedagogy. It is a body of work that merits our sustained and critical attention, as it articulates the key concepts and issues with which many of us have grappled during the decades. One place to begin the study of Kincheloe's work is Shreveport, Louisiana, where I met Joe in 1989. At that time I was chair of the Department of Curriculum and Instruction at LSU–Baton Rouge with jurisdiction (technically, not practically) over teacher education at LSU–Shreveport, where Kincheloe taught courses in the history of education. Joe and I hit it off from the start, deciding to collaborate first over doctoral course offerings at Shreveport[2] and then over the concept of "place." Still in shock over the move from Rochester, New York (where I had taught from 1972 to 1985), I was relieved to find a receptive and engaging Joe Kincheloe. Even with his East

Tennessee upbringing and doctorate from the University of Tennessee–Knoxville, Joe agreed with me that Louisiana demanded, well, explanation. The uniqueness of Louisiana not only pointed to its own peculiar history and distinctive multi-culture, it underscored the particularity—including the historicity[3]—of every place, however muted some places seem.

The concept of "place" enabled us to appreciate that even disinterested curriculum inquiry bore some meaningful relation—perhaps "should" bear some meaningful relation—to the place where it occurs. We were hardly interested in affirming provincialism, but, rather, in cultivating cosmopolitanism by working through the local. We began working on a collection that linked the concept of "place" in curriculum theory to the social psychoanalysis of critical theory.[4]

Seeking a "deeper reading of the word and the world,"[5] we fastened upon social psychoanalysis in order to denote the order of inquiry "place" required. Understanding the particularity of place meant understanding subjectivity's reciprocal relation to reality, simultaneously constructed by and contributing to the creation of place. Joe wrote: "Human beings emerge as active agents who, due to their awareness of historical forces and the effects of such forces on individuals, help shape the future expression of these historical forces."[6] Understanding the past's presence functions as a midwife to the birth of the future by enabling agency. No historical teleology or overdetermined structuralism here, Kincheloe's conception is grounded in subjectivity's capacity to extricate itself from the forces which construct it through awareness and understanding. Citing not only the Frankfurt School, but also the early Marx and Paulo Freire,[7] Kincheloe affirmed the "power of humans as creative, meaning-seeking actors."[8] To put the matter almost psychoanalytically: "remembrance" of a repressed past supports "emancipation."[9] Today these formulations sound so *optimistic,*[10] but in that earlier era of "resistance"[11] we were representing less an empirical reality than confirming contestation.

"Remembrance"—now associated with pedagogies of testimony[12] and curricula for reparation[13]—was to be focused on feeling, also forefronted subsequently.[14] Linking feeling to place, Joe referenced Eudora Welty:[15]

> Feelings, Eudora Welty wrote, are bound up in place. Knowing where one started allows one to understand where he or she is. This relationship between place and feeling is central to curriculum theory's study of place.[16]

Bringing the particular into focus, place renders the abstract concrete, including in research.[17]

Like Martha Nussbaum,[18] Kincheloe endorsed "literary understanding"—specifically fiction—as potentially progressive, permitting us to move into "unexplored realms of consciousness, in some cases altered states of consciousness."[19] Also like Nussbaum,[20] Joe suggested that the "imagination" is in fact "unleashed" by "place."[21]

Changing metaphors, Kincheloe characterizes "place" as "a window to the *Lebenswelt*, a vehicle to self-knowledge, and a crack in the structure that allows the archeologist of self to discover the etymology of one's research act."[22] At one point he links sensuality with politicization:[23]

> The appreciation of individual sensation can be the genesis of larger political awareness—the refusal to deny restlessness, discomfort, moral ambiguity,

> and the impulse to reject. As one struggles with the problematic nature of the lived world, he or she begins to sense the unity of self and situation.[24]

Heightened sensation may animate individuals to "struggle and endure . . . emerging as poetry and politics,"[25] a reference to Dwayne Huebner's inspiring call-to-arms.[26] It is not an entirely phenomenological conception of place Kincheloe describes,[27] however, as he insists on the primacy of history: "Place is place only if accompanied by a history."[28]

Certainly the American South is "accompanied by a history." In the South, Kincheloe[29] noted, "place" has been "under attack" at least since the Civil War. Defensively, then, the uniqueness of the South is not only an empirical reality, but, as well, a political counter-attack, an ongoing refusal to be integrated into the Union. The flash-point of this refusal was racial integration, experienced, Joe tells us, as "an invasion of their [Southerners'] parlors."[30] For Southern whites, the public sphere was co-extensive with the private. This affirmation of distinctiveness is expressed in the very structures of knowing, structures, he suggests, of particularity.[31] He cites southern fundamentalism[32] and country music[33] as forms of this cultural preoccupation with detail and specificity.

Kincheloe chooses the Mississippi journalist, novelist, and editor Willie Morris as personifying the white southerner's dilemma. Criticized by some as embracing the local, others dismissed him as scalawag.[34] Morris was, perhaps, Joe's alter ego, enabling him to represent his loyalty to as well as his critical distance from the South that was his home.

Place is the concept wherein the particularities of history, culture, and subjectivity become entwined. Kincheloe endorses the concept of "totality"—foreshadowing his later turn toward the Marxism[35] that is embedded in conceptions of critical pedagogy[36]—in an effort to bridge "particularity" and "generalized socioeconomic structure."[37] In the "totality" of place, he suggests, "economic and individual-focused curriculum theorists might reunite."[38] While the individual-as-agent almost disappears in his later work (except as "produced" by culture and society),[39] this early effort to incorporate subjectivity and sociality gets represented later in his characteristic and totalizing lists.[40] Also a pedagogical device, these lists—in his chapter, as we will soon see, he lists both southern ghosts and southern treasures—constituted "an appreciation of the dialectical interplay between them, e.g. social, economic, and political force [and] particularistic anecdotes."[41] In the early 1990s, Joe Kincheloe associated totality with emancipation: "Indeed, the essence of liberation is attached to the notion of totality, of epistemological synthesis."[42] This dialectical view, I suggest, is the animating aspiration of Kincheloe's life-long scholarly project; it informs his reconstruction of southern ghosts and treasures.

Kincheloe first introduces these concepts in his chapter focused on Willie Morris. This chapter[43] is first and foremost about Morris, but it is also about the social psychoanalysis of place and, indirectly, about Joe's own dilemma as a politically progressive Southerner. Kincheloe starts by underscoring that Morris' work is "primarily autobiographical, constantly relating his personal story to the story of his place . . . to come to terms with those traditions in his or her own life."[44] While that place is Mississippi not Tennessee, it is a South that "is lost to him."[45] That experience of loss, tinged, perhaps, with regret, is qualified, however, as Joe acknowledges that place inhabits subjectivity, even when one is displaced. "Morris," he confides, "writes of structures of feelings that are no longer his."[46] No longer identical to the person he was brought up to be, Morris—and Joe Kincheloe—I am suggesting, are haunted by the loss of who they once were as they are simultaneously sustained by the "treasures" internalized and later synthesized into a reconstructed subjectivity.

How does such subjective reconstruction proceed? In his chapter Kincheloe not only outlines the process; he specifies its content. First is "invalidation" of what he calls "myth," those collective fantasies of what the South was.[47] It becomes clear that this is not only a cognitive affair, but a corporeal one as well. Connecting subjective with social reconstruction, Kincheloe asserts that such invalidation constitutes an "important step toward social progress."[48] So conceived, he posits this step as a key "concern of the reconceptualized southern curriculum—to demystify southern experience in such a manner that distortions are confronted."[49] Without such confrontation and consequent demystification, "individuals lose the memory of that things were once made."[50] Joe lists the myths[51], among them the "Lost Cause," "Southern Womanhood," the "Happy Darkie," and the "Honor Myth."[52] These myths inform the "ghosts" that haunt Southerners today, among them "mindless racism,"[53] "religious tyranny,"[54] "male bonding rituals."[55]

What animates the labor of subjective reconstruction? Writing of Morris, Kincheloe postulates the second step in the process, noting that Morris' "desire to remove himself from his deepest loyalties" he ascribed to the "imagination."[56] It is the imagination that enables Morris—and, presumably, Southerners generally—to envision life beyond what is and what has been.[57] A "deeper level of understanding" is possible as the imagination[58] propels the search for "*Lebenswelt*."[59] The medium of distortion in the past, lived experience becomes now the promise of truth in the future. That Kincheloe's view was no naïvely phenomenological one is indicated by his acknowledgement of the power of language, that, in fact, it is language that makes "accessible" the "world."[60]

Referencing Freud, Fromm, and Barthes, Joe positions demystification as key to laying bare "social distortion, its genesis, its nature, and its effects."[61] From demystification he moves to liberation, referencing Freire's work as extending "our thinking about the relationship between these psychic mutilations, historical location, anthropological context, and liberation."[62] This list specifies the scope of Joe's aspiration. In a key passage Kincheloe claims his Southern heritage as he describes his pedagogical aspiration to understand it:

> I am a child of the South, one who has sought to understand the rhythms of southern life and their effects on me. For many reasons, my first exposure to Willie Morris about twenty years ago provided much insight into my own *southern* consciousness. So profound was the effect that I adopted Morris's *North Toward Home* for my introduction to education classes when I came to Louisiana to teach. An excellent educational autobiography, I hoped that the work would touch the consciousness of my students. I hoped that it would promote an introspective analysis of personal educational experience that might lead to a better understanding of the social forces that shaped southern students.[63]

I shared Joe's conviction that preparing to be a teacher requires reflection on where teaching takes place, if today a planetary as well as regional concept.

Twenty years ago Joe—and I—were teaching in the Deep South. Despite its destruction by industrialization,[64] there remained resources—Joe called them "treasures"—on which Southerners could draw. While he cautioned these "powerful virtues" were not to be "romanticized,"[65] the very concept comes close enough to doing so. To his credit, Kincheloe insisted these "treasures" be juxtaposed with the "ghosts" that haunt the South.[66]

"Closeness to the land" and "a feel for the rhythms of nature" comprise the first of the treasures Joe identifies, followed by "the importance of friendship" and an appreciation for "the aesthetic of sport."[67] Given slavery, the Civil War, racial segregation, and the ongoing struggle for civil rights, the fourth treasure seems delicately worded indeed: "The South is a place where people gain a special sensitivity to the struggle of our national experience through the medium of strained racial relations."[68] This statement is followed by praise of the South as a place where African- and European-Americans "actually know each other."[69] The violent historical content of that "struggle" goes unremarked.

Joe names instrumentalism in the fifth treasure: "time is a precious entity that an individual controls by not letting it be filed with other-directed and organized activity."[70] Suspending my skepticism that time is ever in any sense controllable, this treasure must derive from Joe's childhood, as the Southerners around me worked long and hard (and for less compensation) than any regional grouping in the United States I had known. But no skepticism surfaced when he named the sixth treasure: "The South is a place where people love storytelling and believe that this tradition builds community by linking us to our past."[71] Joe cites his own childhood as filled with such stories, and his cousins, aunts, and uncles (the subjects of these stories) remain, he tells us, "more familiar to me in my mind's eye than some of the people I have called *close friends* in my life in the America of the late twentieth century."[72]

Given the character of fiction, then, one is not surprised that the next treasure is the imagination: "The South is a place where people revere the impulses of the imagination that shape our speech, our music, our literature, our love of place, and our potential."[73] Joe insists his listing of "treasures" does not constitute another moment in the century-long tradition of a romanticized and nostalgic "southern tradition."[74] Indeed, Kincheloe insists that these treasures must be juxtaposed with ghosts.[75]

Despite having moved from critical theory (and its social psychoanalysis) to critical pedagogy (with its emphasis on collective struggle and political analysis), Kincheloe remained committed to culture, history, and subjectivity. In his call for "new phase of critical pedagogy,"[76] he reminded us that "culture shapes the political"[77] as he called for "attention" on "questions of identity and the production of the individual,"[78] even on "self-realization."[79] "What is the relationship," he asked, "between the macro-power and the subjectivity of individual human beings?"[80] In asking this question Joe was once again confronting the collision between private and public life, between the "treasures" of his southern upbringing and the "alienation" he faced in the United States of America.

The last time I saw Joe Kincheloe was over lunch at 2007 meeting of the American Educational Research Association. Sitting between Shirley Steinberg and me, Joe was, as usual, humorous in his bitter, sometimes self-deprecating, way. While he seemed energetic and upbeat, Joe had been working too hard for too long; he took to heart issues others seem to shed like water on a duck's back. Maybe those dead people were calling to him. Despite my ambivalence over the concept of southern treasures, it is clear to me that Joe was one of them.

Notes

1 1991, 21.
2 LSU had hired me to strengthen its Ph.D. program in curriculum and instruction. By the early 1990s, students at Shreveport became able to complete a significant portion of their coursework at LSU–Shreveport, after which they moved to Baton Rouge for a year of residence to complete the degree. Joe was one of two instructors who met eligibility requirements to teach doctoral courses; Ph.D. students took so many courses with him we renamed LSU–Shreveport "the University of Kincheloe." Joe stayed with his students when they came to Baton Rouge to work with me and/or my colleagues, among them Jacques Daignault, William E. Doll, Jr., Cameron McCarthy, Leslie Roman, Tony Whitson. The reference to Shreveport in Joe's Critical Pedagogy Primer is not, then, fortuitous (2004, 8).
3 Roberts 1995, 64.
4 Joe wrote the introduction and recruited all the contributors—Clinton B. Allison (1991), Kathleen P. Bennett (1991), Susan Huddleston Edgerton (1991), Joseph W. Newman (1991)—save Louis A. Castenell, Jr. (1991), whom I had met on a doctoral student-recruiting trip to Xavier University in New Orleans. At that time Castenell was Dean of the Xavier Graduate School; soon after he departed New Orleans to become Dean of the College of Education first at the University of Cincinnati, then at the University of Georgia. Louis and I co-edited *Understanding Curriculum as Racial Text* (1993). Joe reports that he was first introduced to the idea of place by "Manny" Pridgen (1991, 154).
5 1991, 1. Joe would repeat these words, inflected with Freirean concepts, to define critical pedagogy: "Critical pedagogy is enacted through the use of generative themes to read the word and the world and the process of problem posing" (2004, 15).
6 1991, 3.
7 Freire would remain a major inspiration for Kincheloe's prodigious scholarship (see, for instance, 2004, 3, 17, 21; 2007, 11). After accepting a Canada Research Chair at the McGill University, Kincheloe—with his partner Shirley Steinberg—established the Paulo and Nita Freire International Project for Critical Pedagogy.
8 1991, 3.
9 Ibid.
10 In his embrace of critical pedagogy, Kincheloe seemed to me almost abandon his earlier faith in human agency and action, despite agency's prominent appearance in the 2004 primer (see p. 2). (Even I found his definition of agency there—as "a person's ability to shape and control their own lives, freeing self from the oppression of power" (p. 2)—voluntarist, even subjectivist.) In his introduction to the 2007 collection, such "agency" disappears; he reiterates the so-called "repressive hypothesis" (Chow 2002, 4; Silverman 1988, 149) and construes "power" as only oppressive and as almost as a superstructure in its production of subjectivity (2007, 36). While he embraced "self-knowledge (p. 24) and "self-realization" (p. 36), it's not clear what these phrases can mean in a scenario wherein power predominates.
11 See Pinar et al. 1995, 252ff.
12 See Simon, Rosenberg, and Eppert 2000.
13 See Pinar 2006.
14 See Boler 1999.
15 Another scholar who found Welty an inspiration is Mary Aswell Doll (2000, 31, 112, 167–9), if to different theoretical ends.
16 1991, 4.
17 On research Kincheloe cites Giroux's critique of positivism that I, too, knew first-hand (Giroux, Penna, and Pinar 1981). Like Freire and McLaren, Giroux would become central to Joe's later formulation of critical pedagogy (Kincheloe 2004, 10; Giroux 2007). Twenty years ago, however, phenomenological elements predominated: "The

subjectivity of place informs our understanding of the subjectivity of social research in general" (1991, 6).

18 1995, 92.

19 1991, 6. The centrality of the concept of consciousness in curriculum research had been established by Maxine Greene (1971; see also Macdonald 1995, 153ff.). I introduced "heightened consciousness" in my 1973 address to the University of Rochester conference (1974), and returned to it (if in a different form) thirty years later (2006, 43ff.). Recent collections affirm the concept's continuing relevance and not only in the field of education (Mansbridge and Morris 2001; Seixas 2004).

20 1997, 14.

21 1991, 7.

22 1991, 6.

23 This corporeal conception of political engagement had been broached by another figure (dis)associated with the Frankfurt School: Wilhelm Reich. Born in Galicia in 1897 to an assimilated Jewish family, Reich initially associated neuroses with poverty, asserting that political action as well as therapeutic intervention was appropriate to address these subjective sources of social problems (see Zaretsky 2004, 171). Later he would emphasize the role of sexual liberation in socialist revolution (2004, 220), an issue now, if stated negatively. Because U.S. political conservatives have seized the issue—adult demands for abstinence, I have always thought, constitute, at least in part, a restatement of the incest taboo—one is obligated to contest it (see Pinar 2009, 7).

24 1991, 21.

25 Ibid.

26 1999 (1975), 231ff.

27 See 1991, 21.

28 1991, 8.

29 1991, 9.

30 1991, 14.

31 1991, 16.

32 Ibid. In historical terms, Joel Williamson argues, the idea of the South as "the Bible belt" is a twentieth-century phenomenon. It occurred to no one to describe the South as a Bible belt before the Civil War. Perhaps the War was the turning point:

> The modern retreat of the South into the City of God might have had its beginnings on the bloody battlefields of the Civil War. That war brought southerners from high to low very suddenly, perhaps, that they are as yet unable fully to absorb the fact of their defeat. . . . The retreat of the South from reality might have been furthered by the seizure by the Yankee barbarians and the black defectors of the bodies of the southern states during Reconstruction. . . . When southern life recrystallized again after 1915, religion was at stage center. (Williamson 1984, 316)

33 1991, 18.

34 A postbellum Southerner who betrays his fellow Southerners to Yankees for personal gain, "scalawag" (along with carpetbaggers, e.g. Yankees who went South to profit from its military defeat) remains a slur in the contemporary South. Joe Kincheloe demonstrates he was no scalawag, as he lists among the dangers even progressive Southerners face is betrayal of the South. As if anticipating his future sojourn in the North (after leaving Louisiana, Joe moved first to Clemson in South Carolina, Florida International in Miami, then Penn State, followed by Brooklyn College and the City University of New York, and, finally, to McGill University in Montreal, Canada), he states: "The exiled Southerner in search of liberation is ever vulnerable to the temptation to turn one's back on his or her own past in the pursuit of some convenient or trendy sophistication" (1991, 142–3). Not only theories may seduce

the Southerner, apparently any "outsider" is also a risk: "The attempts of outsiders to dictate what a Southerner ought to feel about the South must be resisted" (1991, 143). Perhaps Joe was addressing that line to me specifically, as I complained about "the South" almost constantly during those initial years in Louisiana.

35 Despite its formative influence in critical theory, Kincheloe bleaches Marxism from his expansive (almost totalizing) conception of critical pedagogy: he lists Marx as one influence (along with Weber!), but his primary citation is negative (2004, 51). In his 1991 essay the only reference to Marxism is also critical, e.g. to an "ossified" Marxism that "disregarded the particularistic" (1991, 22), a charge I emphasize in my critique of reproduction theory (2011, 25–38).

36 Kincheloe 2004, 46ff. While Joe came to the party late, he played hard. From its outset, critical pedagogy seemed to me a subspecies of that "academic Marxism that became depressingly familiar after 1968, in which theoretical postures were adopted, according to the dictates of intellectual fashion, by scholars without the means or often the desire to intervene in the world," in contrast, Davidson (2011, 153) is noting here, to the Marxism of Alasdair MacIntyre.

37 1991, 22.

38 Ibid.

39 See 2007, 32.

40 See 2004, 6ff., 50ff.; 2007, 21ff.

41 1991, 22.

42 Ibid.

43 1991, 123–154.

44 1991, 124.

45 1991, 125.

46 1991, 124.

47 1991, 126.

48 Ibid.

49 Ibid.

50 1991, 127.

51 See 1991, 128.

52 Ibid.

53 1991, 134.

54 Ibid.

55 1991, 135.

56 1991, 140.

57 While the South lost the Civil War militarily, it did "rise again" in the form of political conservatism, as a map of electoral results of presidential elections since the 1964 Civil Rights Bill was passed by Democrats shows (2004, 233ff.; 2009, 54). Racial politics and violence are gendered (Pinar 2001), as Joe's list of "ghosts" makes clear. While race receives minimal attention here, it becomes central to a reconstructed canon of critical pedagogy: among "important figures in the emergence of critical pedagogy," Kincheloe (2004, p. 59) lists Du Bois first (if for alphabetical reasons).

58 Here Kincheloe anticipates the later emphases on the imagination importantly advanced (if differently) by Kieran Egan and Maxine Greene. The imagination, Maxine Greene (2001, 30) asserts, is "the most focal" of our "concerns." Imagination is perhaps the central concept in Greene's *oeuvre*, and not only in her 2001 collection of talks to teachers. Recall that her 1995 book is entitled *Releasing the Imagination.* "Without the release of imagination," Greene (2001, 65) asserts, "human beings may be trapped in literalism, in blind factuality." While the imagination may enable distantiation, humor helps as well: "humor must cultivate a fidelity as well as irreverence to place" (1991, 5). Joe Kincheloe's irreverent humor was widely appreciated.

59 1991, 140.

60 1991, 141.

61 1991, 128.

62 1991, 131.
63 1991, 131–132.
64 The "Southern Agrarians" of the 1930s—Allen Tate, John Crowe Ransom, Robert Penn Warren, Donald Davidson, John Gould Fletcher, and Andrew Lytle—bemoaned the loss of traditional Southern life to industrialization. These intellectuals were self-consciously conservative (Genovese 1994, 5); while present-day southern conservatism is linked to them, it seems to me to be a horse of another color (see Pinar 2004, 236). Like his agrarian predecessors, Kincheloe complains about the industrialization of the South, naming social alienation as its social consequence. "The Southerner who seeks authenticity," Kincheloe (1991, 144) cautions,

> must be aware of modern industrial alienation, the nature of it southern manifestation, and its effect on the soul of the individual. The instrumental rationality that accompanies this alienation precipitates a dishonesty with the most distinctive things about one's self; indeed, this destruction of self-knowledge may be its most insidious aspect.

I confess I have always suspected that Southerners' suspicions regarding industrialization were informed by industrialization's association with the North. After all, it was the North's superior industrialization—not its military prowess—that ensured victory over the South one hundred fifty years ago.
65 1991, 145.
66 Ibid.
67 1991, 145–146. Sport, Joe implies, has in the South escaped the commercialization it has suffered in the North. While I was ready to grant him the first two treasures—although I resisted that these were somehow special to the South—this third claim has always seemed strange to me, surrounded as I was by the sometimes outrageously aggressive promotion of LSU sports, especially LSU football.
68 1991, 148.
69 Ibid.
70 1991, 149.
71 Ibid.
72 1991, 150. "Some folks see dead people," Kincheloe (2007, 11) confided, "I write to them."
73 1991, 150.
74 1991, 151.
75 See 1991, 134–135. In overemphasizing Southern treasures and assigning ongoing Southern injustice to the past (as implied by the term "ghosts"), Joe suspected (I think) he was guilty of projecting his own childhood onto the present-day South. Consider this admonition (to himself): "The innocent country boy (who lives inside me) who played happily and carelessly in the mountains of East Tennessee must not impose his happy images of his South upon my present attempt to garner a mature understanding of the region" (1991, 151). To this Yankee living in the same state (although residents acknowledged North and South Louisianans as worlds apart) as was he, it seemed to me that that was exactly what he had done. At one point he characterizes these "treasures" as providing "fullness" and "possibility" (1991, 151) for the South, comprising "something of great value for America" (1991, 152), even a "utopian vision of community" (1991, 152), and certainly an "antidote to the alienation of modern America" (1991, 152). For Joe Kincheloe as an individual, these legacies of the South provided sustenance: "I revere the southern treasures; their humanity, authenticity, and ethical orientation make me confront who I really am and the relationship between that person and who I would really like to be" (1991, 153). As my title implies, understanding Joe Kincheloe requires situating him in "place."
76 2007, 16.

77 2007, 31.
78 2007, 32.
79 2007, 36.
80 2007, 26.

Bibliography

Allison, Clinton B. 1991. Farragut School: A Case Study of Southern Progressivism in the Upper South. In *Curriculum as Social Psychoanalysis: The Significance of Place*, edited by Joe L. Kincheloe and William F. Pinar (27–43). Albany: State University of New York Press.

Boler, Megan. 1999. *Feeling Power: Emotions and Education*. New York: Routledge.

Bennett, Kathleen P. 1991. Wrenched from the Earth: Appalachian Women in Conflict. In *Curriculum as Social Psychoanalysis: The Significance of Place*, edited by Joe L. Kincheloe and William F. Pinar (99–120). Albany: State University of New York Press.

Castenell, Jr., Louis A. 1993. The New South as Curriculum: Implications for Understanding Southern Race Relations. In *Curriculum as Social Psychoanalysis: The Significance of Place*, edited by Joe L. Kincheloe and William F. Pinar (155–163). Albany: State University of New York Press.

Castenell, Jr., Louis A. and Pinar, William F. eds. 1993. *Understanding Curriculum as Racial Text: Representations of Identity and Difference in Education*. Albany: State University of New York Press.

Chow, Rey. 2002. *The Protestant Ethnic & the Spirit of Capitalism*. New York: Columbia University Press.

Davidson, Neil. 2011. Alasdair MacIntyre and Trotskyism. In *Virtue and Politics: Alasdair MacIntyre's Revolutionary Aristotelianism* (152–176), edited by Paul Blackledge and Kevin Knight. Notre Dame, Indiana: University of Notre Dame Press.

Doll, Mary Aswell. 2000. *Like Letters in Running Water: A Mythopoetics of Curriculum*. Mahwah, NJ: Lawrence Erlbaum.

Edgerton, Susan Huddleston. 1991. Particularities of "Otherness": Autobiography, Maya Angelou, and Me. In *Curriculum as Social Psychoanalysis: The Significance of Place*, edited by Joe L. Kincheloe and William F. Pinar (77–97). Albany: State University of New York Press.

Egan, Kieran. 1992. *Imagination in Teaching and Learning*. Chicago: University of Chicago Press.

Genovese, Eugene D. 1994. *The Southern Tradition: The Achievements and Limitations of American Conservatism*. Cambridge, MA: Harvard University Press.

Giroux, Henry A. 2007. Introduction: Democracy, Education, and the Politics of Critical Pedagogy. In *Critical Pedagogy: Where Are We Now?*, edited by Joe L. Kincheloe and Peter McLaren (1–5). New York: Peter Lang.

Giroux, Henry A., Penna, Anthony, and Pinar, William F. Eds. 1981. *Curriculum and Instruction: Alternatives in Education*. Berkeley, CA: McCutchan.

Greene, Maxine. 1971. Curriculum and Consciousness. *Teachers College Record* 73 (2), 253–269.

Greene, Maxine. 1995. *Releasing the Imagination*. San Francisco: Jossey-Bass.

Greene, Maxine. 2001. *Variations on a Blue Guitar: The Lincoln Center Institute Lectures on Aesthetic Education*. New York: Teachers College Press.

Huebner, Dwayne. 1999. *The Lure of the Transcendent: Collected Essays*. Mahwah, NJ: Lawrence Erlbaum.

Kincheloe, Joe L. 1991. Willis Morris and the Southern Curriculum: Emancipating the Southern Ghosts. In *Curriculum as Social Psychoanalysis: The Significance of Place*, edited by Joe L. Kincheloe and William F. Pinar (123–154). Albany: State University of New York Press.

Kincheloe, Joe L. 2004. *Critical Pedagogy*. New York: Peter Lang.
Kincheloe, Joe L. 2007. Critical Pedagogy in the Twentieth-First Century: Evolution for Survival. In *Critical Pedagogy: Where Are We Now?*, edited by Joe L. Kincheloe and Peter McLaren (9–42). New York: Peter Lang.
Kincheloe, Joe L. and Pinar, William F. 1991. Introduction to *Curriculum as Social Psychoanalysis: The Significance of Place*, edited by Joe L. Kincheloe and William F. Pinar (1–23). Albany: State University of New York Press.
Kincheloe, Joe L., Pinar, William F., and Slattery, Patrick. 1994, Winter. A Last Dying Chord? Toward Cultural and Educational Renewal in the South. *Curriculum Inquiry* 24 (4), 407–436.
Macdonald, James B. 1995. *Theory as a Prayerful Act*. New York: Peter Lang.
Mansbridge, Jane and Morris, Aldon. Eds. 2001. *Oppositional Consciousness: The Subjective Roots of Social Protest*. Chicago: University of Chicago Press.
Newman, Joseph W. 1991. Organized Prayer and Secular Humanism in Mobile, Alabama's Public Schools. In *Curriculum as Social Psychoanalysis: The Significance of Place*, edited by Joe L. Kincheloe and William F. Pinar (45–74). Albany: State University of New York Press.
Nussbaum, Martha C. 1995. *Poetic Justice*. Boston: Beacon Press.
Pinar, William F. ed. 1974. *Heightened Consciousness, Cultural Revolution and Curriculum Theory*. Berkeley, CA: McCutchan.
Pinar, William F. 2009. *The Worldliness of a Cosmopolitan Education: Passionate Lives in Public Service*. New York: Routledge.
Pinar, William F., Reynolds, William M., Slattery, Patrick, and Taubman, Peter M. 1995. *Understanding Curriculum: An Introduction to Historical and Contemporary Curriculum Discourses*. New York: Peter Lang.
Roberts, David D. 1995. *Nothing but History: Reconstruction and Extremity after Metaphysics*. Berkeley and Los Angeles: University of California Press.
Seixas, Peter. ed. 2004. *Theorizing Historical Consciousness*. Toronto: University of Toronto Press.
Silverman, Kaja. 1988. *The Acoustic Mirror: The Female Voice in Psychoanalysis and Cinema*. Bloomington: Indiana University Press.
Simon, Roger I., Rosenberg, Sharon, and Eppert, Claudia. eds. 2000. *Between Hope and Despair: Pedagogy and the Remembrance of Historical Trauma*. Lanham, MD: Rowman & Littlefield.
Williamson, Joel. 1984. *The Crucible of Race: Black-White Relations in the American South since Emancipation*. New York: Oxford University Press.
Zaretsky, Eli. 2004. *Secrets of the Soul: A Social and Cultural History of Psychoanalysis*. New York: Alfred A. Knopf.

CHAPTER 10

EMERGENCE[1]

Commentary

In this chapter I chart the emergence of the great anti-lynching activist and public pedagogue Ida B. Wells, providing details of her early life, her teaching and journalistic careers, the infamous lynching "at the curve," and her brilliant lectures in Great Britain, where she managed to mobilize the British public against lynching in America. Linking gender and race in her analysis of racial violence and politics, Wells was able to cast white—not black—men as barbaric, and white—not black—women as sexually promiscuous. Wells' pedagogical acumen remains memorable today.

Bibliography

Pinar, William F. 2001. *The Gender of Racial Politics and Violence in American: Lynching, Prison Rape, and the Crisis of Masculinity*. New York: Peter Lang.

> Perhaps one of the more interesting aspects of biography—if not one of its greatest attributes—is the actual burring of genres.
>
> Craig Kridel[2]

No description of anti-lynching activism in the United States is complete without serious attention to Ida B. Wells. A larger-than-life figure in the civil rights movement from the 1890s until her death in 1931, Wells was the chief architect of the anti-lynching movement in the nineteenth century, a cause to which she came after a brief but memorable career of militant journalism in the black community. Before working as a journalist, Wells had been a schoolteacher. In my view, Wells remained a teacher, if imagining her classroom more expansively to include the American and British publics. Through her pedagogical manipulation of contemporary white assumptions regarding gender, race, and civilization, Wells taught European-Americans that lynching was barbaric. No small accomplishment for a Memphis schoolteacher who had to battle not only white racism, but misogyny and envy from her fellow black reformers. John Hope Franklin summarized her accomplishment this way:

> Her zeal and energy were matched by her uncompromising and unequivocal stand on every cause that she espoused. She did not hesitate to criticize southern whites even before she left the South, or northern liberals, or members of her own race when she was convinced that their positions were not in the best interests of all mankind. She did not hesitate to go to the scene of racial disturbances, including riots and lynchings, in order to get an accurate picture of what actually occurred. She did not hesitate to summon to the cause of human dignity anybody and everybody she believed could serve the cause.[3]

That cause calls us to teach.[4]

Born a slave in Holly Springs, Mississippi, in 1862, Wells was the eldest daughter in a family of eight children. Her father was a skilled carpenter, a man of "considerable ability and much civic concern."[5] He served as a member of the first board of trustees of Rust College. At first named Shaw University, Rust was founded in 1866 by Rev. A. C. McDonald, a minister from the North who served as its first president. Rust College offered curricula for students at all levels and grades, including the basic elementary subjects. Wells' parents stressed the importance of securing an education. At Rust, the young Wells enjoyed the guidance and instruction of dedicated missionaries and teachers who had come to Holly Springs to help the newly freed people. Her teachers regarded her as an exceedingly able student. On Sundays, her religious parents would permit only the Bible to be read, so Wells read it several times before leaving home to teach in the rural schools of Shelby County, where she worked while studying for the teacher's examination for the city schools of Memphis.[6]

After losing her lawsuit against the Chesapeake, Ohio and Southwestern Railroad,[7] Ida B. Wells continued to teach in the Memphis schools for several years, but poor working conditions left her frustrated. In 1887 she began writing for a church paper, in her first article telling the story of her case against the Chesapeake & Ohio railroad and its discouraging results. Soon her articles appeared in other church papers and then in several of the black weeklies. Increasingly secure in her journalistic abilities, she invested her savings in a small newspaper in Memphis, the *Free Speech and Headlight*. Now part owner as well as editor, Wells did not hesitate to tell the truth as she saw it; her articles criticizing the Memphis board of education for poor conditions in segregated black schools led to her dismissal as a teacher in 1891.[8]

Undaunted, Wells threw herself into workings of the newspaper. She abbreviated its name to the *Free Speech*, and was very much engaged with her work and travels for the paper when, on March 9, 1892, "at the curve" (where streetcars turned off Mississippi onto Walker Avenue in Memphis), three young black businessmen—Thomas Moss, Calvin McDowell, and Henry Stewart—were lynched. Wells gives a detailed account of this incident in her autobiography; it was an event that would change her life. The facts were these: three black businessmen—"[t]hree of the best specimens of young since-the-war Afro-American manhood"[9]—were arrested after several white men were wounded in a street fight. Fearing violence, the black community organized protection for the prisoners; a group camped for two nights just outside the jail where they were being held. On the third night, armed white men walked into the jail, took the three prisoners out and lynched them a mile outside town. One of the Memphis daily newspapers delayed its publication so that it might give a detailed report of the lynching.[10]

During the lynching at least one of the men's bodies was mutilated: "the fingers of McDowell's right hand had been shot to pieces and his eyes gouged out."[11] The lynching shocked, horrified, then outraged Wells; it proved to be a key event in her transformation from teacher-journalist to activist.[12] Her close friend, Thomas Moss, had pleaded with the murderers to spare him for the sake of his wife and unborn child. Realizing that his pleas would be ignored, he made his last words these: "Tell my people to go West—there is no justice for them here."[13] In the *Free Speech*, Wells urged readers to take his advice, noting that there was no protection for black people in Memphis. Within weeks a number of black families departed. Those white businesses which relied on blacks suffered. Even the transport system was affected, as those who remained preferred to walk in order to save their money for the move West. Distressed executives from the City Railway Company came to the offices of *Free Speech* and demanded that the black paper use its influence to restore the status quo. Wells published the conversation, then urged her readers to continue to withhold their business. Wells herself traveled West, spending three weeks in Oklahoma. Afterward she reported on the successes of those who had moved West, contradicting fabricated "news" reported in Memphis' white newspapers, stories made up to scare blacks into staying in town.[14]

Two months later Wells wrote a scathing editorial on the lynching. While the motive for this lynching was probably economic—whites were furious that these black businessmen were opening a grocery store in a black district previously served only by whites—Wells, in her May editorial, implied non-economic motives. The headline read: "Eight Negroes Lynched Since the Last Issue of the *Free Speech*." "Three were charged," she wrote, "with killing white men and five with raping white women. If southern white men are not careful . . . a conclusion will be reached which will be very dangerous to the moral reputation of their women."[15] It was then unthinkable to suggest that white women might be sexually interested in black men.

After writing the editorial, Wells traveled North to cover a conference of the African Methodist Church in Philadelphia. From there she made a short trip to New York before she was to return to Memphis. When Wells arrived in New York she was told that the white establishment in Memphis wanted her dead. Several prominent white businessmen had gathered at the Memphis Cotton Exchange Building to discuss Wells' lynching. They had closed her newspaper; anyone who tried to resume its publication would be killed. The offices of the *Free Speech* were sacked, creditors took possession of what was left, "and the Free Speech was as if it had never been," Ida B. Wells wrote from New York City five months later.[16] There could be no thought of returning to Memphis, as white men were watching every train. They had been ordered to kill Wells on sight.

While her support of the economic boycott had alarmed the white establishment, it had been that May editorial, which appeared while she was in Philadelphia, that had provoked the mob to destroy her offices, that had enraged the white men of Memphis so thoroughly that they published their interest in lynching "her" as well.[17] I enclose "her" in quotation marks because white men assumed that such a response could have come only from a man, an assumption evident in the pronouns in the following editorial, first printed in the Memphis *Commercial*, then reprinted in *The Evening Scimitar* of same date, which copied the *Commercial*'s editorial with these words added:

> Patience under such circumstances is not a virtue. If the negroes themselves do not apply the remedy without delay it will be the duty of those whom he has attacked to tie the wretch who utters these calumnies to a stake at the intersection of Main and Madison Sts., brand him in the forehead with a hot iron and perform upon him a surgical operation with a pair of tailor's shears.[18]

In response, Wells bought and carried a pistol, vowing "[i]f I could take one lyncher with me, this would even up the score a little bit."[19] Clearly, as Mary Helen Washington observed, "in an era of growing Jim Crow despotism and black conservatism, Wells was one of the most defiantly militant voices by any standard."[20]

This terrible trauma—the lynching "at the curve" followed by the destruction of her newspaper and threats upon her life—dissuaded Ida B. Wells not at all from challenging white fantasies around lynching. Indeed, it only seemed to intensify her resolve. She continued her antilynching efforts at the *New York Age*: "Because I saw the chance to be of more service to the cause by staying in New York than by returning to Memphis, I accepted their advice, took a position on the *New York Age*, and continued my fight against lynching and lynchers."[21] It was at this time that she began to lecture. It was from the North that Wells launched what was to become an international crusade against lynching. As news of her "crusade for justice" spread, she would receive an invitation to speak in England, Scotland, and Wales. In April and May of 1893 she visited England for the first time.[22]

While there, Ida B. Wells was heartened by the progressive activities of English women reformers and their various civic groups. After returning to the United States, Wells praised the activities of British reformers to New England audiences, urging her American female listeners to become more active in the affairs of their community, city, and nation by organizing civic clubs. Her idea was well received; the first civic club, the Women's Era Club, was organized in Boston. Wells inspired the formation of other clubs in New England and in Chicago, where she herself organized the first civic club for Chicago's black women. When Wells returned to England in 1894, this Chicago group named itself in honor of her.[23]

Indignation, courage, journalistic competence, pedagogical acumen, and political zeal brought Ida B. Wells to international prominence. Convinced that lynching had little to do with black crime, Wells resolved to reveal the exact details of all lynchings which came to her attention. She wrote scores of articles, and a half dozen pamphlets, among them *Southern Horrors*, *A Red Record*, and *Mob Rule in New Orleans*. She would focus on exposing the black-man-as-rapist fantasy. This fantasy was more than false; the truth was (she argued to the horror of most white readers) that some white women preferred the sexual company of black men. If you want to talk rape, let's talk about the white man, who, since slavery's inception had systematically and repeatedly raped black women (and, she did not add, as we suspect now, men). Performing one of her pedagogical reversals of whites' assumptions, Wells suggested that it was white—not black—men who were the rapists in America.

The lynching at the curve and her consequent conversion from journalist to full-time crusader against lynching strengthened her sense of herself as a black woman, Joanne M. Braxton suggests.[24] Braxton characterizes Wells a black woman who did her Christian duty by decrying the evils of lynching and the moral decay at its root. Wells reported that blacks were lynched for wife beating, hog stealing, quarreling, "sassiness," and even for no offense whatsoever. And, Wells learned, white women who had been consensually involved with black men cried rape when confronted by white men. Whatever loyalty these white women might have felt toward their black lovers incinerated in the company of outraged white men.

One of the cases Wells cites—in *Southern Horrors, A Red Record*, and in *Mob Rule in New Orleans*—illustrates this point exactly. It is the case of Edward Coy (or McCoy, as it is also spelled), who was burned alive in Texarkana, Arkansas, on January 1, 1882, after having been accused of assaulting a white woman. Wells writes: "He was tied to a tree, the flesh cut from his body by men and boys, and after coal oil was poured over him, the woman he assaulted gladly set fire to him, and 15,000 persons saw him burn to death." In this case, the woman who started the lynching pyre was known to have been involved with the man for "more than a year previous." As she lighted the blaze, Coy "asked her if she would burn him after they had 'been sweethearting' so long." That was hardly the end of white hypocrisy in the case, Wells writes, as a "large majority of the 'superior' white men" responsible for the lynching were "reputed fathers of mulatto children."[25] "These are not pleasant facts," Wells acknowledges, but facts all the same.

In the lynching story white men told they fantasized about what black men wanted to do to white women; black women were not present in that scenario. Lynching was, it would seem, an affair between men. Of course, black women were involved; there were cases in which black women were lynched, and by virtue of being daughters, mothers, sisters, and wives of men who were lynched, black women were very much involved. Was it because back women were marginal to the lynching scenario in the imagination of white men that Wells was able to point out that the emperor had no clothes? While the heterosexism of the time would not permit her to see that lynching was a mangled version of homosexual rape,[26] Ida B. Wells was never fooled by the white male fantasy of big black bucks raping innocent white ladies. Free of white men's imagination (at least in terms of lynching), Ida B. Wells became lynching's most articulate and daring public critic.[27]

Ida B. Wells' initiatives against the white male practice require one to position as central the role of educated black women in the antilynching protest movement. True, millions of African Americans engaged in indirect protest against lynching, as Fitzhugh Brundage[28] points out. But that significant fact must not obscure another significant fact, namely that Wells' critique of the racial-sexual regime in which lynching made sense was pathbreaking. It was pathbreaking intellectually, politically, and pedagogically. Her international campaign to teach European-Americans through British citizens' indignation represented not only a new departure in black women's public activity, but a dazzling display of pedagogical acumen. The campaign inspired countless numbers of American women to join local efforts at racial and social reform, where their more radical impulses were rerouted from more domesticated forms of "women's work."[29]

In 1892, Wells had been forced into northern exile by her editorial against lynching, printed in her soon-to-be-destroyed *Memphis Free Speech*. Only thirty, she was already an experienced teacher and journalist. As a young black single woman in Memphis, Wells had declined to accept conventional views of a woman's destiny, i.e., to marry and have children. She would later have four children after marrying Chicago attorney Ferdinand L. Barnett, and she would then suffer criticism by others—most prominently Susan B. Anthony—for abandoning public for private life. For her ambition and independence the young Wells had paid a high price, including isolation within and criticism from the larger black community. Wounded men and jealous women accused her of being "a silly flirt and a heartless coquette"[30] who toyed with men's affections. She became the subject of vicious rumors, among them that, as a girl of sixteen, she had been sexually involved with a white man in Mississippi, that she and a male teacher were fired for "immoral conduct," and that her sister Lily was in fact her daughter.[31] Wells was hurt but undeterred.[32]

Exiled in the North, Wells devised new tactics appropriate for her new circumstances. While she continued to urge African Americans to boycott, vote, and agitate against white injustice, she knew these tactics by themselves would not stop lynching. Somehow white people, especially northerners, must be persuaded to intervene in white barbarism. She decided, she later recalled, to focus her efforts on "the white press, since it was the medium through which I hoped to reach the white people of the country, who alone could mold public sentiment."[33] Yet white newspapers declined to hire African American writers. To gain a hearing in the white press, Wells realized that she must devise new arguments. Accordingly, Wells began to reflect upon the white middle-class's conflation of manly authority and white racial dominance.[34]

In *Southern Horrors*, Wells attacked lynching by simple but dramatic inversion. Where whites had depicted black men as unmanly passion incarnate, Wells declared they were the opposite: manliness personified. Those black men who had been lynched for "rape" were innocent victims, often paying with their lives for having been seduced into consensual sexual relations with rapacious white women. In Wells' words these innocent victims were "poor blind Afro-American Samsons who suffer themselves to be betrayed by white Delilahs."[35] White men and women were shocked, then enraged.

Like the Biblical Samson, Wells argued, these innocent men had been manly towers of strength until they were trapped then destroyed by wicked white women. After using them sexually, these white Delilahs falsely cried "rape" in order to protect their reputations. The truth was, Wells asserted, that it was these white women, not their black male victims, who were the real criminals of lust and carnality. To document her claim, Wells named several white women who had willingly pursued sexual relationships with black men. Only upon the public discovery of these interracial love affairs were they then recoded as "rapes." Several of these women worked as prostitutes; Wells had commented with disgust: "'The leading citizens' of Memphis are fending the 'honor' of all white women, *demi-monde* included."[36]

In contrast, then, to white characterizations of white male lynchers as disciplined, manly, and restrained, Wells depicted them as vile, unmanly cowards, disguising their own licentiousness with sanctimonious calls for chastity. They rationalized their savage murders by invoking the honor of white ladies, ladies who were, in some cases, prostitutes. In contrast to whites' characterization of lynchers as righteous defenders of the Christian faith and European civilization, Wells argued that it was white southern men, especially those who lynched black men, who were compelled to rape and sexually assault—as long as the victims were black. Far from suppressing lust, "the white man" wallowed in it. Miscegenation laws, Wells declared, "only operate against the legitimate union of the races: they leave the white man free to seduce all the colored girls he can," knowing he need neither marry nor support the victims of his sexual aggression.[37]

Southern white men, Wells continued, were "not so desirous of punishing rapists as they pretend." If they were truly committed to protecting women from rape, they would not so readily ignore or forgive the countless white men who raped black women. Here too Wells named names and gave dates, overwhelming her readers with numerous cases of black women and girls brutally raped by white men, with no effort from their white neighbors to intervene or punish the offenders afterward. Yet these upstanding white citizens of the South—rapists and accessories to rape—mutilated and murdered black men, the vast majority of whom had not even had sex with white women. They, she asked, should proclaim themselves defenders of chastity?

Wells also went after the illusion that lynching demonstrated the potency of white manliness. The only way northern men could demonstrate their manliness would be by stopping lynching. This argumentative strategy, Gail Bederman[38] explains, echoed old antislavery debates: just as abolitionists had warned that the slave trade would spread North and undermine free labor, so Wells now warned that southern men's unbridled lust would spread and corrupt northern men's manliness. In fact, she suggested, northern white men had already abrogated their manly duty to restrain vice by allowing white southern men to rape and lynch; such tolerance of vice had already rotted their manly character. Throughout the nation, Wells declared, "men who stand high in the esteem of the public for Christian character, for moral and physical courage, for devotion to the principles of equal and exact justice to all, and for great sagacity, stand as cowards who fear to open their mouths before this great outrage."[39]

This was, Bederman observes, not just rhetoric. By refuting the discourse that conflated whiteness and gender in the concept of civilization, Wells was refuting white male rationalizations for lynching. Moreover, she was formulating an alternative discourse of race and manhood. Heretofore the dominant discourse of "civilization" had positioned black men as unmanly savages, unable to control their passions through manly will. Accepting this conflation of whiteness, civilization, and manhood, northern whites assumed that black men were in fact rapists and they therefore tolerated the southern tradition of lynching.[40] By inverting this logic, Wells, as Hazel Carby[41] points out, also reformulated the prevailing ideologies of gender to produce an alternative discourse of womanhood. In so doing Wells' antilynching arguments reformulated dominant discourses of manhood, too, implying connections among lynching, sexuality, and women's rights.

Even after a year of writing and speaking in the North, Wells remained unable to find journalistic work in the white world. She still had no access to the white press, no way to reach northern white readers. When invited to tour England, Wells eagerly accepted, understanding at once that while the white American press could ignore her, they might not so easily ignore an indignant British public. Although her first tour—in 1893—received almost no American press coverage, it laid the foundation for her 1894 tour. That tour received all the publicity she could have wanted. "When Wells returned," Bederman tells us, "she had become notorious; and white Americans had discovered that, due to their tolerance and practice of lynching, the rest of the world's Anglo-Saxons doubted whether white Americans were either manly or civilized."[42] How did Wells accomplish this remarkable turn-around?

Wells planned both campaigns focused on the concept of "civilization." She would demonstrate, by her performance, that is, by her speeches, her writings, and her demeanor, that she represented a civilized race. Wells framed her mission as an appeal from one civilized people to another for protection from a violent and barbaric race gone mad. She did not hesitate to flatter her listeners and readers in Britain, appealing to their own sense of cultural superiority. Moreover, Americans, she said seductively, revered the British; whatever the British thought would be most influential in her former colonies. She told one British journalist that if Britain told white America that "the roasting of men alive on unproved charges and by a furious mob was a disgrace to the civilization of the United States, then every criminal in America, white or black, would soon be assured of a trial under the proper form of law."[43] Wells was quite conscious, Bederman argues, that she was using her British audiences to convince European Americans that their tolerance of lynching left them perceived as savages in the eyes of the civilized world.

It was true, and Wells was well aware, that many European Americans felt a prideful sense of kinship with the British. This identification was "racial" as well, especially in the late nineteenth century, when pseudo-scientific theories of racial superiority were circulating widely. Presumably Anglo-Saxons were, on both sides of the Atlantic, the most manly and civilized of all races. Wells was determined to form an alliance with British reformers which would destroy this smug and imaginary racial solidarity. She played her cards with precision, telling, for instance, an audience in Birmingham (England):

> America cannot and will not ignore the voice of a nation that is her superior in civilization. . . . I believe that the silent indifference with which [Great Britain] has received the intelligence that human beings are burned alive in a "Christian" country, and by "civilized" Anglo-Saxon communities is born of ignorance of the true situation; and that if she really knew she would make the protest long and loud.[44]

Many British already knew or had suspected what Wells was telling them, namely that their former colonists were unmanly and uncivilized and very much in need of instruction from their civilized British superiors.[45] A black woman in Britain would persuade the public that white men in America were, well, neither "white" nor "men."

As the volume of British indignation increased, Wells finally got her hearing in the European-American press. No longer could she be ignored, not now that she had stirred up the British. After all, the British were fellow Anglo-Saxons, racial equals who understood, perhaps better than anyone, what civilization and manliness were. European-American men felt no choice but reply to their accusations.[46] Heads filled with fantasies of an Old South "gone with the wind," southern white men were especially unhappy with this turn of events. They were, in fact, beside themselves with rage.

The *Memphis Daily Commercial* tried to discredit Wells by libeling her character. Playing on longstanding racist fantasies in which black women were figured as licentious (thereby unwomanly and uncivilized), it accused Wells of being a "negro adventuress" with an unsavory past. When these stories reached Wells in England, she calmly turned them to her advantage. She not only demanded proof of these allegations . . . she sued. Her rebuttal, reported in newspapers throughout Great Britain, observed that "so hardened is the [white] southern public mind that it does not object to the coarsest language and most obscene vulgarity in its leading journals so long as it is directed against a negro." Since the *Daily Commercial* was unable to deny the South's frequent lynchings, they were, she pointed out, reduced to smearing her character. British papers were as shocked as Wells wanted them to be. Scandalized by these examples of American journalism, the *Liverpool Daily Post* judged the articles as "very coarse in tone, and some of the language is such as could not possibly be reproduced in an English journal."[47] The British knew and reminded each other that it was neither manly nor civilized to libel a lady's character; the episode functioned only to reaffirm British opinions of American barbarism.[48]

White southerners were dumbfounded; they responded as if there had been a miscommunication. Southern newspapers reiterated that rape justified lynching and that it was of course "the negro" who was uncivilized. The *Atlanta Constitution* declared that British indignation was pointless and futile, since "the negroes themselves are the only people who can suppress the evil, and the way for them to get rid of it is to cease committing" rape.[49] The New Orleans *Times-Democrat* pointed out that once Wells left Britain she would no longer be credible, for Americans "know well that the Negro is not a model of virtue and the white man a cruel, bloodthirsty tyrant, as the Wells woman pretends." A Southern educator complained that "stigmatizing [southern men] as savages and barbarians" was simply unbelievable; everyone knew that the real problem lay with the Negro, who was "still a semi-savage far below the white man in the science and practice of civilization."[50] Imprisoned within their own fantasies, white southerners sputtered, unable to defend themselves.

Northerners tended to be less defensive, as they were less traumatized. They tended to experience the event not as a psychotic break with reality but as simply another instance of British smugness and self-delusion. And so they accused the British of hypocrisy, pointing out firmly that British colonists had abused blacks at least as, if not more brutally than, white southerners had. In response to the British Unitarian Association's condemnations, the Democratic *Philadelphia Daily Record* snorted: "John Bull looks at America with one eye and Africa with the other. His hands are bloody with recent African butcheries."[51] Of course this criticism was accurate—the British *had* behaved in barbaric fashion in Africa—but the Americans' motive had nothing to do with genuine concern for Africans. Northerners were simply irritated at this latest instance of the meddlesome and "superior" British.[52]

British anti-lynchers were undeterred by European-American indignation. In September 1894 the London Anti-Lynching Committee sent a small fact-finding delegation to the South. Governor O'Ferrall of Virginia complained, "Things have come to a pretty pass in this country when we are to have a lot of English moralists sticking their noses into our national affairs." Fourteen other governors, North and South, said much the same. Georgia Governor Northen accused the British of unmanly hypocrisy and directed the antilynching committee to return to England immediately, where they were needed to "prevent by law the inhuman sale of virtuous girls to lustful men in high places. Hang all such demons as 'Jack, the Ripper'; punish as it deserves the barbarous, wholesale slaughter of negroes in Africa by Englishmen who go there to steal their gold." Governor Turney of Tennessee agreed: "I think they had better purify their own morals before coming among a better people."[53]

Governor Turney's self-righteous indignation turned to embarrassment when just several days later six black men were lynched near Memphis. This time he condemned the murders and even offered a reward of $5,000 for the lynchers' capture. The editors of the *Independent* observed: "It is very unfortunate . . . that just after Miss Wells' charges had been loudly pronounced false, other such atrocious cases should have occurred, as if to justify all that she had said."[54] In Memphis, where only two years earlier white leaders had destroyed Wells' newspaper and driven her North for protesting the lynchings of three black businessmen, Wells' British campaign saw success. Suddenly, Memphis' white leaders reversed themselves; now they piously proclaimed their disapproval of lynch law. The *Memphis Scimitar*—the same newspaper that two years earlier had called for Wells' lynching—now editorialized: "Every one of us is touched with blood-guiltiness in this matter, unless we prove ourselves ready to do our duty as civilized men and citizens who love their country and are jealous of its good name."[55] White merchants now demonstrated their "civilized manliness" by meeting to protest lynchings; they even collected $1,000 for the murdered men's widows and orphans. Thirteen white men were indicted for the lynchings, although never convicted. The Memphis press never again condoned lynch law; no new lynchings occurred there until 1917 when Ell Persons was burned alive, his head severed and left on Beale Street.[56]

Not only some southerners were moved to oppose lynching as a result of Wells' British campaign. Now many white northerners objected to lynching more often and more aggressively. In Chicago, Brooklyn, and Santa Cruz, whites organized antilynching societies, although these organizations played no discernable roles in ending the practice. While a few northern papers still defended lynching as necessary to deter black rapists, the majority appeared to agree with the *Cleveland Leader* that "[a]cts of barbarism have been committed in this country within the last twenty years by people claiming to be civilized which would scarcely have been credited to the cruelest and most bloodthirsty savages in Africa."[57]

Wells' British campaign, in Bederman's phrase, "had hit a nerve."[58] With applause still ringing in their ears for the 1893 Columbian Exposition,[59] European-Americans were shocked to discover that prominent British reformers were describing them as unmanly barbarians. To their astonishment, their United States—surely the zenith of the civilized world, the epitome of evolutionary progress—was now the destination of British "missionaries"! Now, finally, Ida B. Wells had the attention of the white American public. By sparking the indignation of British reformers, Wells had forced indifferent, defensive, racist whites to confront the fact of lynching. The *Indianapolis Freeman* was not alone in declaring that Wells' campaign had put an end to white complacency. "For the first time since the commencement of its long debauch of crime, the South has been jerked up to a sudden standstill; it is on the defensive. . . . The North has at last realized that the so-called race problem is a matter that concerns not only the South, but the nation."[60] While she had not persuaded the majority of European Americans to actively oppose lynching, she had, by 1894, taught them that lynching was unacceptable.[61]

As real and important as Wells' success was, in the long run it was but a step. A large step but still a step: after all, her British campaign did not stop lynching.

White men in the South continued to mutilate black men until the Civil Rights movement of the 1960s signaled a new era. The frequency of lynchings did decrease after 1892, although many historians credit factors other than Wells' own efforts. Overwhelmed by the vehemence of white Americans' complaints about the London committee's visit, the British antilynching committees canceled further fact-finding tours, limiting their efforts to outraged letter-writing campaigns. In the short term, southern lynchings continued, and Wells continued her struggle against them.[62]

While Wells' campaign had not stopped mob violence, her success in putting American whites on the defensive did, Bederman argues, force long-lasting shifts in whites' characterization of lynch law. European Americans could not tolerate being called unmanly and uncivilized by the British. After 1894, most northern newspapers and periodicals stopped treating lynching as if it were a colorful southern folk custom. They dropped the jokes and now piously condemned lynching as "barbarous," although they still pretended to be powerless to intervene.[63] Now few doubted that lynching damaged the country in the eyes of the "civilized world." And Wells' statistics forced the northern press to acknowledge that most lynching victims had *not* been accused of rape, let alone been found guilty of it. Southern states even began to pass antilynching legislation, legislation which, however, was almost never enforced. Did these small changes actually deter any prospective lynchers? Given the intensification of white racism during the 1890s, it is, as Bederman acknowledges, difficult to know how far-reaching the influence of these changes were. Still, as Bederman writes, "they must be seen as modest but definite victories."[64]

To appreciate how shrewdly Ida B. Wells conducted her antilynching campaign, one needs to understand, as Bederman points out, how completely Wells understood the conflation of race, gender, and class in the 1890s. Social, economic, and cultural shifts appeared to threaten white middle-class male dominance. Fearful and uneasy, middle-class white men worried that their identity—their manhood—was imperiled. As a compensatory move to fortify faltering traditional manly power, white men turned (hardly for the first time, but with renewed intensity) to race. By characterizing themselves as "the white man," whose superior manliness distinguished him from more primitive even savage dark-skinned races, middle-class white men reassured themselves that their identity—their manliness—remained intact. The concept of "civilization" naturalized this conflation of manliness and racial dominance by linking it to human evolutionary progress. Now that they represented "civilization," they celebrated the fact, most visibly at the 1893 Chicago Exposition. There, with African Americans excluded, white women positioned appropriately (in "gracious submission"), and the rest of the world located deferentially, middle-class white men reassured themselves that they were the most powerful creatures ever to inhabit the planet.[65]

Ida B. Wells was fooled by none of it. She knew how fragile this constructed identity was, how easily it might unravel if she only inverted the link between manhood and white supremacy. Whereas whites in the North had imagined that lynching demonstrated white men's superior manliness and civilization by protecting the threatened white lady, Wells inverted the terms of the fantasy. By her logic lynching proved the opposite; black men were far more manly than whites who tolerated lynching. Whites had labored long and hard to construct elaborate pageants like the Columbian Exposition to dramatize their superior manliness and civilization in contrast to the primitive, even savage, nature of the dark-skinned races. Wells pointed out that the emperor had no clothes. Using the term "civilization" to demonstrate that the opposite was true, Wells made it clear that it was "the white man" who was neither manly nor civilized.[66]

Let us review briefly Wells' pedagogical moves. By inverting "civilization" and thereby severing the link between white supremacy and manliness, Wells created an antiracist notion of manhood. She understood that behind middle-class gender lay a fundamental assumption that "pure" women and "manly" men were white. To focus upon that one point, as Wells did, was to undermine the entire edifice of white middle-class identity and gender. As Gail Bederman so well explains, Victorian ideologies of womanhood marginalized black women by construing them as unwomanly harlots. In sharp contrast were white women. But these were "unreal" women, pedestalized as high-minded and sexually pure. Repudiating these links by insisting on black women's pure womanliness, Wells and other black women reconceptualized womanhood.[67]

Likewise, middle-class formulations of manliness marginalized black men by fantasizing them as unmanly and lust-driven, rapists whose uncontrolled and wanton sexuality contrasted sharply with the equally imaginary restrained self-mastery and manliness of "the white man." By insisting that it was "the white man," and not the black man, who was lustful and uncivilized, Wells engendered a fundamental "cognitive dissonance" which threatened a restructuring of the European-American male self.[68] And she understood that none of this could be pulled off without the cultural authority of the British:

> Since the crusade against lynching was started, however, governors of states, newspapers, senators and representatives and bishops of churches have all been compelled to take cognizance of the prevalence of this crime and to speak in one way or another in the defense of the charge against this barbarism in the United States. This has not been because there was any latent spirit of justice voluntarily asserting itself, especially in those who do the lynching, but because the entire American people now feel, both North and South, that they are objects in the gaze of the civilized world and that for every lynching humanity asks that America render its account to civilization and itself.[69]

The white middle-class conflation of race with gender may seem to some "merely" ideological, but as Bederman points out and Wells recognized, it had crushing material repercussions. White middle-class notions of racialized manliness legitimized both the sexual victimization of black women and the brutal, often sexualized, mutilation of black men. Wells' insistence upon the womanliness of black women and the manliness of black men functioned to dismantle the ideological structure that supported white male violence. By inverting key concepts of whites' racialized discourses of gender, Wells hoped to teach her fellow American citizens how intolerably barbaric racial violence was.[70]

Ida B. Wells stands today as one of America's greatest teachers. Not a great schoolteacher perhaps, as she disliked teaching in school: "I never cared for teaching."[71] But while using all her tactical skills and all her knowledge of the white psyche to end lynching, she was at the same time teaching all Americans to question taken-for-granted assumptions about men, women, race, about "civilization" itself. By disentangling the complexities of middle-class America's race/class/gender system she taught for profound social change. Sensitive to the subtle dynamics of this system, she was able to invert them to her political and pedagogical ends. Helped by her British friends, her rearticulation of the race/class/gender system shocked middle-class whites out of their denial and forced them to focus upon the fact of racial violence in America. By adeptly reading and decoding conflated discourses of class, race, and gender, Wells was able to teach some of the most resistant students—the white American public—on record. Gail Bederman concludes by suggesting that Wells' accomplishment makes clear that the deconstruction of dominant discourses of race, gender, and class is not merely an academic exercise. It is an important practical and political—I would add "pedagogical"—tactic for those committed to the education of the public.

Notes

1 Foucault defines "emergence" as "the entry of forces; it is their eruption, the leap from the wings to center stage, each in its youthful strength." Koopman (2013, 39) points out that the term "is conceptually central for any history written in terms of 'substitutions, displacements, disguised conquests, and systematic reversals'." Quoted passages from Foucault's 1971 essay on "Nietzsche, Genealogy, History," quoted in Koopman 2013, 39.
2 1998, 10.
3 1970 x.
4 See Kemp in press.
5 Duster 1970, xv.
6 See Duster 1970.
7 Wells had been forcibly ejected from the train for failing to take a seat in the "colored" section.
8 See Duster 1970.
9 Wells 1892a/1969, 18.
10 See Ware 1992.
11 Wells 1970, 51.
12 See Tucker 1971.
13 Quoted in Wells 1970, 51.
14 See Ware 1992.
15 Wells 1892a/1969, 4.
16 Quoted in Aptheker 1977, 15.
17 Ware 1992.
18 Quoted in Wells 1892a/1969, 5; Wells 1970, 66.
19 Wells 1970, 62.
20 1995, xvii.
21 Wells 1970, 62.
22 See Duster 1970.
23 Ibid.
24 See Braxton 1989.
25 Quoted passages from Braxton 1989, 121; Wells 1892a/1969, 10.
26 As I argued in Pinar 2001.
27 See Schechter 1997.
28 1993.
29 The former Texas suffragist Jessie Daniel Ames is a prominent example of a white woman whose domestic energies were rerouted to the public sphere. During the 1920s, Ames headed what was probably the most effective of state interracial councils, councils organized throughout the country in order to improve "race relations." In 1929 she became director of women's work for the region-wide Commission on

Interracial Cooperation, and on 1 November 1930, Ames rewrote what had been an amorphous women's program of the Interracial Commission into a well-organized, single-issue crusade against lynching (Hall 1979). This became the Association of Southern Women for the Prevention of Lynching (see Pinar 2001, 145).

30 DeCosta-Willis 1995, 10.
31 See DeCosta-Willis 1995.
32 See Bederman 1995b.
33 Quoted in Bederman 1995b, 414.
34 See Bederman 1995b.
35 Quoted in Bederman 1995b, 415.
36 1892a/1969, 8.
37 1892a/1969, 6.
38 1995b.
39 Quoted in Bederman 1995b, 416.
40 See Bederman 1995b.
41 1987.
42 1995b, 417.
43 Quoted in Bederman 1995b, 417.
44 Ibid.
45 See Bederman 1995b.
46 Ibid.
47 Quoted passages in Bederman 1995b, 420.
48 See Bederman 1995b.
49 Quoted in Bederman 1995b, 420.
50 Quoted passages in Bederman 1995b, 421.
51 Quoted in Bederman 1995b, 421.
52 See Bederman 1995b.
53 Quoted passages in Bederman 1995b, 421.
54 Quoted in Bederman 1995b, 421.
55 Ibid.
56 See Tucker 1971; Bederman 1995b.
57 Quoted in Bederman 1995b, 422.
58 1995b, 422.
59 See Pinar 2001.
60 Quoted in Bederman 1995b, 422.
61 See Bederman 1995b.
62 Ibid.
63 Bederman 1995b, 422–423.
64 1995b, 422.
65 See Bederman 1995b.
66 Ibid.
67 See Carby 1987; Bederman 1995a, 1995b.
68 See Bederman 1995b.
69 Wells 1892b/1969, 72.
70 See Bederman 1995b.
71 Wells 1970, 31.

Bibliography

Aptheker, Bettina. 1977. Introduction to Jane Addams and Ida B. Wells' *Lynching and Rape: An Exchange of Views*. Chicago: University of Illinois, Occasional Paper No. 25.

Bederman, Gail. 1995a. *Manliness and Civilization: A Cultural History of Gender and Race in the United States, 1880–1917*. Chicago: University of Chicago Press.

Bederman, Gail. 1995b. "Civilization," the Decline of Middle-Class Manliness, and Ida B. Wells' Antilynching Campaign (1892–94). In *"We Specialize in the Wholly Impossible": A Reader in Black Women's History*, edited by D.C. Hine, W. King, and L. Reed (407–432). Brooklyn, NY: Carlson.

Braxton, Joanne M. 1989. *Black Women Writing Autobiography: A Tradition Within a Tradition*. Philadelphia, PA: Temple University Press.

Brundage, W. Fitzhugh. 1993. *Lynching in the New South: Georgia and Virginia, 1880–1930*. Urbana: University of Illinois Press.

Carby, Hazel V. 1987. *Reconstructing Womanhood: The Emergence of the Afro-American Novelist*. New York: Oxford University Press.

DeCosta-Willis, Miriam. 1995. Introduction. *The Memphis Diary of Ida B. Wells* (1–16). Boston: Beacon Press.

Duster, Alfreda M. 1970. Introduction to Ida B. Wells's *Crusade for Justice* (xiii–xxxii). Chicago: University of Chicago Press.

Franklin, John Hope. 1970. Foreword to Ida B. Wells' *Crusade for Justice* (ix–xi). Chicago: University of Chicago Press.

Hall, Jacquelyn Dowd. 1979. *Revolt against Chivalry: Jessie Daniel Ames and the Women's Campaign against Lynching*. New York: Columbia University Press.

Hartman, Saidiya V. 1997. *Scenes of Subjection: Terror, Slavery, and Self-Making in Nineteenth Century America*. New York: Oxford University Press.

Koopman, Colin. 2013. *Genealogy as Critique: Foucault and the Problems of Modernity*. Bloomington: Indiana University Press.

Kridel, Craig. 1998. Introduction to *Writing Educational Biography* (3–12). New York: Garland.

Pinar, William F. 2001. *The Gender of Racial Politics and Violence in America*. New York: Peter Lang.

Schechter, Patricia A. 1997. Unsettled Business: Ida B. Wells against Lynching; or, How Antilynching Got Its Gender. In *Under Sentence of Death: Lynching in the South*, edited by W. Fitzhugh Brundage (292–317). Chapel Hill: University of North Carolina Press.

Tucker, David M. 1971, Summer. Miss Ida B. Wells and the Memphis Lynching. *Phylon*, 32, 112–122.

Ware, Vron. 1992. *Beyond the Pale: White Women, Racism and History*. London: Verso.

Washington, Mary Helen. 1995. Foreword to the *Memphis Diary of Ida B. Wells* (ix–xvii). [Edited by Miriam Decosta-Willis. Afterward by Dorothy Sterling.] Boston, MA: Beacon Press.

Wells, Ida B. 1892a (1969). *Southern Horrors: Lynch Law in All Its Phases*. New York: Arno Press/New York Times.

Wells, Ida B. 1892b (1969). *A Red Record. Tabulated Statistics and Alleged Causes of Lynchings in the United States, 1892–1893–1894*. New York: Arno Press/New York Times.

Wells, Ida B. 1970. *Crusade for Justice: The Autobiography of Ida B. Wells*. [Edited by Alfreda Duster.] Chicago: University of Chicago Press.

CHAPTER 11

ALTERITY

Commentary

To demonstrate that curriculum development is intellectual, not procedural, I composed a textbook as complicated conversation among concepts, in methodological terms, an "act of collage: the citation and arraignment of a finite set of testamentary texts and images in juxtaposition."[1] That textbook was a study of whiteness.

Slave-owners and racial segregationists pointed to Genesis 9:23 as providing divine endorsement of their practices. What happened that night in Noah's tent that had legitimated racialized subjugation? I examined two answers to that question, juxtaposing them and that mythic event to analyses of the mental breakdown of the late nineteenth-century German judge Daniel Paul Schreber. What the juxtaposition revealed is the genesis of race in gender, specifically within the convoluted sexual politics between father and son. Such a queered understanding of alterity contributes to teachers' education in a multicultural society.

Bibliography

Pinar, William F. 2006. *Race, Religion and a Curriculum of Reparation*. New York: Palgrave Macmillan.

Pinar, William F. 2009. *The Worldliness of a Cosmopolitan Education: Passionate Lives in Public Service*. New York: Routledge.

Simon, Roger I. 2005. *The Touch of the Past. Remembrance, Learning, and Ethics*. New York: Palgrave Macmillan.

> [T]he study of racism is dirty business. It unveils things about ourselves that we may prefer not to know.
>
> Lewis R. Gordon[2]

> [O]ur deepest cultural assumptions are biblical.
>
> Regina M. Schwartz[3]

Curriculum development after the Reconceptualizaton is intellectual, not bureaucratic, concerned with concepts not objectives. To illustrate, I describe here a textbook[4] for teachers I have composed, a synoptic text summarizing and juxtaposing research that enables teachers to complicate the curricular conversation in which they and their students are engaged. The book is a form of curriculum research, performing pedagogy through academic knowledge. As in intellectual history, this form of curriculum research appreciates that "understanding always therefore entails what might be called . . . proleptic paraphrase or anticipatory synopsis."[5] By juxtaposing fragments from various disciplinary traditions, I support students' study of race from vantage points anticipated perhaps by no one discipline.

I continue to work on understanding race, in particular, whiteness. I seek its genesis. Slaveholders and the segregationists who followed them justified their practices by references to the Bible, a practice not uncommon in the American South today, although gender, not race, is the salient subject of biblical injunction today. The substitution is no accident.

For racists past and present, God Himself ordained the "Great Chain of Being" at which "whites" are secured at the top. In the United States, this racial hierarchy is not only social and economic, it is gendered, indeed, sexualized. Bleached of race (conservatives insist that racism is past), the civic sphere is specularized and sexualized. Until the conflation of "race" and "sex" becomes unknotted, we educators cannot teach "tolerance." To untie that knot, I return to the primal scene of race, Genesis 9:24.

What happened that mythic night in Noah's tent?[6] The main points are these: Noah (of flood fame) plants a vineyard, makes wine, gets drunk, and passes out, naked, in his tent. His son Ham—Noah has two other sons (Shem and Japheth)—goes into the tent and, later, leaves. After time passes, Noah emerges: "And Noah awoke from his wine, and knew what his younger son had done unto him."[7] Noah curses not Ham, but Ham's son Canaan: "a servant of servants shall he be unto his brethren."[8] There is no explicit reference to "race" in these passages. It would seem that slaveholders and segregationists' fabricated the association of race with Noah's rage. Why?

To answer that question, we must return to the provocation of Noah's rage. What could his son have done to prompt him to curse his grandson and his progeny to perpetual enslavement? Exegetes have proposed two main answers.[9] The first and primary one is that Ham violated the ancient Israelite prohibition against looking at the body of the father. The secondary answer is that Ham violated his father sexually. These are intersecting speculations, I suggest, as each involves a symbolic "castration" of the father, an "unmanning" that the patriarch repudiates by cursing the son's son to servitude. In his defensive rejection of the son's desire—Noah, the second Adam, almost "replants" the Garden in his marriage tent or Chuppah—Noah curses Ham's progeny to servitude.

The "Noah Complex" is Regina M. Schwartz's[10] phrase, devised to depict the dynamics of the Curse of Ham. Schwartz points out that son's incestuous desire for the father[11] produces an "intolerable guilt"[12] that is projected heavenward. God-the-Father (or his emissary, in this instance Noah) punishes the son (or a grandson here) by turning him into a "reviled Other." Schwartz invokes the notion of "scarcity" to account for this curse, scarcity referring to a "shortage of parental blessings and love."[13] "Scarcity imposes hierarchy"; she continues, it "imposes patriarchy."[14]

Scarcity is a misleading term to depict the genesis of hierarchy, of patriarchy, of "race." It is not "scarcity" but a surplus of desire that provokes the father to sacrifice his son for the sake of the social order. True, scarcity describes the emotional poverty of Yahweh, a demanding and unforgiving Father who commands his son to cut his penis in order to demonstrate his piety. "The son's desire for his father," Schwartz[15] understands, is expressed in efforts to become like the father (in his image), in yearnings to

> build heavenward, yearnings to become "as the gods," yearnings not only for the father's blessing but for the father's mantle, yearnings to enter the presence of God as Moses does and to be transformed by his glory, and even yearnings to *be* God, as in the case of Christ.

As Schwartz notes, desire structures such yearning.

Servitude severs the self, now split and abjected, an "other." "In other words," David Marriott[16] writes (in a different but related context), "the violated body of the black man comes to be used as a defense against the anxiety, or hatred, that the body appears to generate." To trace white racism to its genesis in gender, specifically in the repudiation of father-son desire, promises, I submit, to subvert its curse; it risks but does not achieve an "evacuation" of the "significance" of race, as Robyn Wiegman[17] worries. Rather, it implies a shattering of white (especially male) subjectivity.

It was the racialization of gendered alterity that enabled Europeans to rationalize the slave trade. Europeans re-mythologized Genesis in racial terms, positioning Africans at the bottom of the Great Chain of Being, a metaphysical, "scientific," and sexualized hierarchy at its peak of acceptance during the eighteenth century.[18] In their exploitation of alterity through the slave trade, Europeans imagined they were justified by religion and, later, science. Forgotten was the genesis of race in the disavowal of desire. What followed was the structuration of the Other through specularization, rendered rational through scientific observation. Forgotten in the triumph of "ocularcentrism" in the presentism of modernity was the prehistory of race in incestuous desire disavowed.

The ancient Israelite taboo against looking at the naked body of the father represented a ritualized repudiation of incestuous desire. Through the son's eyes the father experienced his nakedness, his vulnerability, his desire, a "lack" Noah denied. Converted to a curse, lack denied became alterity, first gendered, later racialized. In this sequence, gender is the father of race. Racialization becomes formulated through a sexually sublimated specularization: Africans and their descendants were characterized by what Europeans and their descendants "saw" when they "looked" upon the naked bodies of those who had become "Other." It was Noah's revenge; now "he" looks at the naked body of the son, a body safely enslaved, enabling him as the "viewing subject," Kaja Silverman[19] points out (in a different but relevant context), to protect himself from the "perception of lack by putting a surrogate in place of the absent real. The surrogate becomes the precondition for pleasure."

For me, the reasons for reconstructing the primal scene of race in the West are curricular. What can the study of this primal scene provide us who teach in the present? What can be the pedagogical point of recovering a lost origin, except to enable us to more fully understand who we have already become? How we can understand the continuing and mutating forms of white racism unless we appreciate that, at its genesis (in the white imagination), it was an incestuous "aboriginal event" between men, a sexual struggle between father and son recoded by subsequent generations as racialized. The father repudiated his son's desire (expressed genitally and/or visually) because it violated his status as a "man," a category that, in its patriarchal formation, requires those who claim it to assert agency, power, possession. As an object of the male son's desire (and we cannot rule out: as the subject desiring his son), the patriarchal edifice threatens to shatter, stimulating a process of regression to an earlier psycho-sexual stage in which the infant son, like his sister, is identified with the maternal body.

We can study this psycho-sexual shattering and its racialization in the infamous case of the late nineteenth-century German judge Daniel Paul Schreber. Schreber's psychotic breakdown—recorded in his *Memoirs*[20]—provided Freud with his original theorization of paranoia as an effect of repressed homosexual desire, a theorization no longer taken seriously by most practicing psychoanalysts, but an idea that echoes in the psycho-politics of whiteness. Like Noah, Schreber claims direct contact with God-the-Father, contact Schreber finds, against his will, sexually stimulating, and which turns him into a "woman." Like Ham, this son, too, was cursed by God-the-Father, leaving him wounded and enslaved, in Schreber's case, within his hallucinations.

This sexualized and specular structure of white racism fantasizes blackness on the surface of the body, a "colored" surface of skin organized, in the white mind, genitally. In late nineteenth-century America, white southerners (and many whites in the north) "saw" young black men as rapists or potential rapists. One hundred years later, and not just in the South, the "rapist" has morphed into the "stud," and black hypermasculinity appeals not only to gay white men, but to white men who imagine themselves "straight" and are also obsessed with black men: with hip-hop performers, with athletes, with the "thug" mystique. Whether rapist or stud, white (including straight male) attention remains fixed on the surface of black body, and, especially, the (imagined) black phallus. Almost five hundred years later, whites remain mesmerized by the black body, remained deformed by that desire's disavowal: paranoid, predatory, possessive. Black subjectivity remains effaced and, by black critics'[21] accounts, too many young black men believe they are primarily their bodies and, specifically, their phallus.

Desire disavowed does not disappear; the repressed "returns" in mutated form, and not only in the fetishization of the black male body. "One of the most consistent medical characterizations of the anatomy of both African American women and lesbians," Siobhan Somerville[22] points out, "was the myth of an unusually large clitoris."

In late nineteenth-century Europe, it was a circumcised phallus that provided the fetish for white fantasies of vulnerability, desire, and emasculation. These were fastened to the body of the Jew.[23] (Unfortunately, the Jewish body did not escape the attention of European-Americans, as the lynching of Leo Frank testifies.) In contrast to European Americans' hypermasculinization of the African American male body, Europeans feminized Jews. Like African Americans, Jews were imagined a race apart: sexually rapacious, ethically nefarious, culturally contaminating. As they did in the U.S. version,[24] misogyny and homosexual panic (they are interrelated, of course) structured the European crisis of masculinity, a crisis animating the creative strategies of artists such as Frank Wedekind, Thomas Mann, and Wassily Kandinsky.[25] It was a crisis theorized theologically and performed sexually by Daniel Paul Schreber.

The curse of Ham becomes "deferred and displaced" in various rituals of servitude, in which the "grandson"—the young male body—is branded by the father, signifying its status as property of the patriarch, a status codified genealogically, subjectively interpellated, and anatomically marked as circumcised.[26] The son not repudiated becomes genealogical property: a member of the "family." The father's repudiation of his son's desire (and of his own incestuous desire for his son) is signified by circumcision. Unlike Schreber, Noah rejects his own "castration"—as men have tended to characterize negatively what they experience as their "femininity"—by projecting it onto the possessed son, whose penis is then marked to document the interpellating event. Circumcision signifies the sublimated son's "covenant"[27] with his father, with God-the-Father, images of paternity with, as we will see, blurred boundaries.

The father's preoccupation with the son—convoluted as it wavers between the sexual and the sublimated—is not, however, restricted to the West, as studies of coming of age rituals worldwide suggest.[28] Those coming-of-age rituals in which semen is exchanged between older and younger men implies the apparently universality of this sexualized, often sadistic, interest of fathers in sons. Whether "giving head" in New Guinea or "becoming head" of household in the West, the son is relegated to servitude, sublimated, or sexualized. Black servitude, of course, was not confined to a specific coming-of-age phase; it was a life sentence without parole: eternal life.

With Thomas DiPiero,[29] I challenge the assumption that (hetero)sexual difference constitutes the "founding" or "fundamental difference" in "human subjectivity." I argue that *self-same* sexual difference is the founding or fundamental difference in subjectivity in the West. Its repudiation and projection condemned women and Africans to sometimes conflated positions of sexualized servitude. In Genesis, the splitting off of self-same desire by God-the-Father created (wo)man from the rib of "man," presumably an "opposite sex" who, for men, has tended to function as a displaced and symbolic extension of what he himself is missing. In this patriarchal fantasy, "woman is man minus the phallus."[30] The fundamental difference within male subjectivity in the West is this splitting off of self-same desire, and its consequent abjection as an "abomination," a refusal to know (performed perversely through specularized observation), an insistence on genealogical possession, an obsession to enslave.

In the West, incestuous desire disavowed mutates into epistemology, as Louis Sass' scholarship on Schreber makes concrete, and which David Levin's[31] and Martin Jay's[32] studies of the hegemony of visuality in the West make abstract and general. Louis Sass[33] employs Foucault's notion of panopticism to characterize Schreber's hyperconsciousness, casting Schreber's "rays of God" not as libidinal cathexes but, rather, as "symbolic representations" of Schreber's own "consciousness," a consciousness both "rent" and "joined" by an internalized "panopticism." In this view, the nerves represent those elements of subjectivity that are observed—"self-as-object"—and the rays represent those (especially mental) elements that do the observing, i.e. "self-as-subject."[34] The God who "lies behind" the rays, Eric Santner[35] points out, "corresponds" to that "invisible, potentially omniscient," but "only half-internalized Other" who is the "source" and "grounding" of Schreber's specific form of "introversion." It is, as it turns out, an introversion that produces "inversion."

While the hegemony of ocularcentrism in modernity—in particular its political expression as panopticism and surveillance—cannot be attributed directly to that mythic night in Noah's tent, the scholarship does suggest that the disavowal of self-same sexual desire structures alterity through specularity. In the beginning was the word, a "speech act . . . finally less verbal than libidinal," Kaja Silverman[36] explains, in which self-same sexual desire splits off into "opposite" sexes, a self-division that multiples "others," including "opposite" races. The racialization of alterity through a sexualized specularity produces a paranoid fear of "difference" associated with "others," including the Big Other, but rarely with oneself.

Split off from the self-same body into "opposite" sexes and races, self-same sexual desire is no longer auditory and tactile, but systematically specular, a disembodied, de-individuated mode of visual perception and relation that commodifies and quantifies.[37] The "scientific" systematization of the Europeans' sexualized racial commodification of the Other becomes structured by the epistemology of observation, itself an institutionalization of knowledge production displaced from that interiority self-same difference and desire denied relocated to the exteriority of the bodies of others.

The color of sex, Mason Stokes[38] asserts, is black. For many whites, the character of "black" is sexual. While the phenomenon of "race" is hardly as simple as that sentence suggests, it cannot, I believe, be grasped or historically surpassed without understanding the relations among alterity, specularity, and the disavowal of incestuous desire between father and son. I am suggesting that the first two follow from the third, that they represent, in part, symbolic wounds of the father (once a son) as he curses the son's son (one day a father, perhaps, who shall carry on the curse). The covenant, requiring filial obedience and generational reproduction, institutionalized the repudiation of that incestuous desire visuality threatened to expose. The injuries it inflicts do not originate in a literal event, of course, but in a mythic one; nor are they contained there. They are restimulated and given aggressive, indeed, vicious social and political form during specific moments in the history of the Western imagination.[39] That vicious social form is the Curse, not only that of Ham, but the other Curse, the servitude of those sons who sublimate (who do not look, who pretend he is not naked) and who are rewarded with the Kingdom of God: that racialized patriarchal system wherein not only women constitute "units of currency"[40] in "gracious" submission to men who imagine themselves white.

How can we educators work to make whiteness conscious of itself, and in so doing, help dissolve it? Teaching for tolerance is not enough. The concept of "citizenship" functions, Russ Castronovo[41] observes, to "dehistorize historical conditions." Anti-racist education cannot be only attitudinal; it must be historical and theoretical. We must theorize the sediments of experience visible today by devising new interpretations of ancient attitudes and practices. Present experience is, as Pier Paolo Pasolini understood, a palimpsest. If "the world . . . was, at first, a pure source of sensations expressed by means of a ratiocinative and precious irrationalism," Pasolini speculated, and "has now become an object of ideological, if not philosophical, awareness," then, "as such, it demands stylistic experiments of a radically new type."[42] For those teachers who appreciate the centrality of academic knowledge in the cultivation of self-reflexive and ethical intelligence, I provide summaries of scholarship whose juxtaposition might make those civilizational sediments discernible.

It is through the Law of the Father and the law of castration, as Lee Edelman[43] and David Eng[44] have pointed out, that the (re)construction of the primal scene is retroactively structured as a project of heterosexual identification. The traumatizing knowledge of the primal scene for the heterosexual male viewing it in (be)hindsight is precisely the memory of its sodomitical uncertainty, that, like Schreber, he, too, may have been the apple of his Father's eye. The genealogical descendants of Shem and Japheth—"straight," especially "white" men—decline to see the naked truth. Enslaved and lynched black bodies populate the "material history of the [white] unconscious."[45]

Sexual and gender difference imagined as coinciding with anatomical differences—between, presumably, "opposite" sexes, that is, between "men" and "women"—requires an specific "economy of visibility."[46] It is an economy, recalling the curse of Ham, that "casts social subjectivity as constitutive of the flesh."[47] In the binary signification of "sex" as "colored" and "race" as "sexual," social and human subjectivities were segregated within European cultures. Moreover, in the disciplinary technologies associated with modernity, as these became systematized as classifications, the body's "race" and "gender" were employed, Wiegman points out, as "indexes" of "psychic interiority" itself.[48]

Specularity replaces subjectivity. The "visible" serves as the "signifying structure," Wiegman notes, for the black body's apparently "evacuated interior domain."[49] Specularity precipitates and subjectively restructures in servitude the son's evacuation from the body of the father, inside the father's tent. This paternal repudiation of the son, Wiegman continues (speaking of Harriet Beecher Stowe but making my point as well), constitutes the "radical negation" compelled by "domination."[50] The abjection of self-same desire becomes alterity, racialized, materialized in the body of the son in servitude. Subjectivity becomes invisible as alterity is visualized. The body of the father becomes the race of the son.

The curse of the covenant will not be dispelled in one lifetime, let alone one semester. Our calling is to study it. I have no hope,[51] only resolve. There seems a certain inevitability to the "covenant" between father and son, across culture, religion, and historical moment. Is circumcision the sublimated substitute for semen transfer which expresses, in ritualized form, Noah's repudiation of the desire Sambian men[52] performed? Among the ancient Israelites, this repudiation is strident, constructed by a curse legislated by the Leviticus Laws. Among Christians, the cursed and sacrificed son is hung nearly naked upon a cross, his death enabling him to become conjoined with the Father, back inside that Chuppah now fantasized as "heaven."

For Schreber, the feminized male body, abjected as the body of the Jew, internalized the curse of the covenant, enabling him to disidentify with the father and experience his desire. In the crisis of late nineteenth-century European masculinity, the figure of the Jew came to represent the disavowed desire of Christian fathers and their abject sons, a desire that was transgendered and culturally transposed. Was it fortuitous that the clitoris was known at this time in Viennese slang as the *Jude* or Jew?[53] In the crisis of late nineteenth-century European-American masculinity,[54] African Americans represented the desire that must be segregated, contained, castrated, its origins in Genesis 9:23 obscured. Rather than feminized, black men were hypermasculinized, the other side of the same queer coin.

Stephen Haynes[55] asks us to reimagine the Curse of Ham so that the dynamics of blame are "subverted." Such subversion can be accomplished, he suggests, "only when the story is read in the context of the biblical canon and its message of redemption."[56] My curricular agenda shares Haynes' interest in subversion but is, obviously, more secular and more aggressive. For me, reparation, not "redemption," is what is ethically and erotically[57] required. Payments to make amends, the "work of reparation" requires the "affirmation of the ineluctability of difference and deferral."[58] Reparation requires what Kaja Silverman[59] characterizes as the shattering or dissolution of hegemonic white masculinity, as it is that series of subject positions that has underwritten and continues to underwrite racism. Hegemonic—racist, misogynistic, homophobic—white masculinity is, for me, the horrific legacy of that mythic drunken night inside Noah's tent.

Whether Ham's transgression was sexually penetrating his father or "merely" looking at the naked body of the father, in both instances he saw his "lack," an embodied state of "castration," which the father then denied in the curse. Schreber performed his gendered and racialized lack, as he succumbed to God-the-Father's desire. In Noah, lack denied displaced alterity from within the self-same body; projected it onto an "other" specularized as "difference" doomed to servitude. In Schreber, alterity introjected shattered his subjective structures, rendering him unable to re-enter the world as, in Fanon's[60] utopic phrase, a "new man."

We want neither Noah nor Schreber; like Fanon, we want a "new man." The curriculum I have sketched here will not midwife the birth of a "new man," but it asks students to encounter their own alterity, specularity, and lack. It invites students to re-experience what Freud characterized as the "negative" oedipal complex, enabling a restructuring of internal object relations in which binaries are mixed and merged in the self-same (now simultaneously the "opposite" sexed) body. "When identification is non-identical," Regina Schwartz[61] has observed, "there is no motive to replace." There is no genealogical impulse, no compulsion to replicate oneself in future generations, indeed, no future in Lee Edelman's[62] sense, in which the present is sacrificed for what never will be.

Such an educational undertaking hardly promises (although teachers may be tempted by the ambition) that white students can "deconstruct their own whiteness and decolonize their Eurocentrism in order to abolish or transcend their racial significance."[63] Whiteness and, in particular, hegemonic masculinity are too pervasive, too unconscious for white men to be so confident. Nor will the racialized self-understanding of whiteness to which I hope *Race, Religion and a Curriculum of Reparation* contributes be the "if only" the technology of education always promises (and always fails to deliver). There can be no predictable "outcomes" of serious study; there can be no science of education. What is possible is study.

Challenging the hegemony of ocularcentrism in Western (white) culture does not threaten blindness. Let us all look, then, at ourselves, as the palimpsest we personify. Like W.J.T. Mitchell,[64] I have assembled *Race, Religion and a Curriculum of Reparation* as one might fashion a "photograph album," a "collection" of "snapshots" of whiteness, a textbook addressed, especially, to white men who wish to study the stereotypical in themselves. After Mitchell, I ask, what if we thought of whiteness, itself a form of representation,

> not as a homogeneous field or grid of relationships governed by a single principle, but as a multi-dimensional and heterogeneous terrain, a collage

> or patchwork quilt assembled over time out of fragments. Suppose further that this quilt was torn, folded, wrinkled, covered with accidental stains, traces of the bodies it has enfolded.[65]

These stains are not, of course, accidental; they are traces of enslaved and mutilated black bodies.

Such a model of whiteness might make materially visible the genesis of racism, whiteness as deferred and displaced incestuous desire. Stripped from its originary setting, whiteness becomes intelligible as an "ongoing process of assemblage, of stitching in and tearing out," mutating into a "multi-dimensional and heterogeneous terrain," disguised even as interracial homosocial friendship. Still following Mitchell,[66] I ask what if we thought about whiteness, not as a noun but as a verb, structuring a set of relationships? "Suppose," he continues, "we de-reified the *thing* that seems to 'stand' before us, 'standing for' something else," and thought of whiteness "as a process in which the thing is a participant, like a pawn on a chessboard or a coin in a system of exchange?" Like this expansive and dynamic notion of representation, such a conceptual move would construe whiteness as "roughly commensurate with the totality of cultural activity," including

> that aspect of political culture which is structured around the transfer, displacement, or alienation of power—from "the people" to "the sovereign," the state, or the representative, from God to father to son in a particular system, from slave to master in an absolutist polity.[67]

Such "cultural activity" is the sea in which we white men swim, taken for a ride on an ark by an odd old man who, after the waters have receded, is about to plant a vineyard. This time we do not accept our servitude; this time we will articulate our "language of desire."[68]

When we speak this language, Silverman[69] tells us, we come to "understand" that the "past is not yet fully written" . . . thereby releasing us from the "paralysis of being" into the "mobility of becoming." So released, will we become other than our Father cursed us to be? What will study engender?

Notes

1 Simon 2005, 149.
2 1995, ix.
3 1997, x.
4 Pinar 2006.
5 Jay 1988a, 59.
6 For an introduction, see Mottram 1937.
7 Genesis 9:24.
8 Genesis 9:25.
9 See Cohen 1974.
10 1997, 115.
11 See also Eilberg-Schwartz 1994.
12 Ibid.
13 Ibid.
14 1997, 115–116.
15 1997, 114.

16 2000, 12.
17 1995, 163.
18 See Wahrman 2004, 131.
19 1988, 5.
20 1903.
21 See, for instance, West 1993.
22 2000, 27.
23 See Boyarin 1997, 1998.
24 See Pinar 2001, chapter 6.
25 See Izenberg 2000.
26 See Gollaher 2000.
27 See Hoffman 1996.
28 See Gilmore 1990.
29 2002, 15.
30 Grosz 1994, 277.
31 1993.
32 1988; 1993a, 1993b.
33 1992, 253–254; see Santner 1996, 173–174, n. 35.
34 Santner 1996, 174.
35 1996, 175.
36 2000, 16.
37 See Silverman 2000.
38 2001.
39 See Haynes 2002.
40 Rubin 1975.
41 2001, 212.
42 Quoted in Greene 1990, 37.
43 1994.
44 2001, 128.
45 Castronovo 2001, 20–21.
46 Wiegman 1995, 195.
47 Ibid.
48 Ibid.
49 Ibid.
50 Ibid.
51 See Morris 2001.
52 Herdt 1982.
53 See Boyarin 1997, 211; DiPiero 2002, 139.
54 For a summary of scholarship, see Pinar 2001.
55 2002, 203.
56 Ibid.
57 See Silverman 2000, 47.
58 Lukacher 1986, 44.
59 1992.
60 1968, 316.
61 1997, 117.
62 2004.
63 Cohen 1997, 245.
64 1994, 417.
65 Mitchell 1994, 419.
66 See 1994, 410.
67 Ibid.
68 Silverman 2000, 67.
69 Ibid.

Bibliography

Boyarin, Daniel. 1997. *Unheroic Conduct: The Rise of Heterosexuality and the Invention of the Jewish Man*. Berkeley: University of California Press.

Boyarin, Daniel. 1998. What Does a Jew Want?; or, The Political Meaning of the Phallus. In *The Psychoanalysis of Race*, edited by Christopher Lane (211–240). New York: Columbia University Press.

Castronovo, Russ. 2001. *Necro Citizenship: Death, Eroticism, and the Public Sphere in the Nineteenth-century United States*. Durham, NC: Duke University Press.

Cohen, H. Hirsch. 1974. *The Drunkenness of Noah*. Tuscaloosa, AL: University of Alabama Press.

Cohen, Phil. 1997. Laboring under Whiteness. In *Displacing Whiteness: Essays in Social and Cultural Criticism*, edited by Ruth Frankenberg (242–282). Durham, NC: Duke University Press.

DiPiero, Thomas. 2002. *White Men Aren't*. Durham, NC: Duke University Press.

Edelman, Lee. 1994. *Homographesis: Essays in Gay Literary and Cultural History*. New York: Routledge.

Edelman, Lee. 2004. *No Future: Queer Theory and the Death Drive*. Durham, NC: Duke University Press.

Eilberg-Schwartz, Howard. 1994. *God's Phallus: And Other Problems for Men and Monotheism*. Boston: Beacon Press.

Eng, David L. 2001. *Racial Castration: Managing Masculinity in Asian America*. Durham, NC: Duke University Press.

Fanon, Frantz. 1968. *The Wretched of the Earth*. [Preface by Jean-Paul Sartre. Trans. Constance Farrington.] New York: Grove Press.

Gilmore, David. 1990. *Manhood in the Making*. New Haven: Yale University Press.

Gollaher, David L. 2000. *Circumcision: A History of the World's Most Controversial Surgery*. New York: Basic Books.

Greene, Naomi. 1990. *Pier Paolo Pasolini: Cinema as Heresy*. Princeton: Princeton University Press.

Grosz, Elizabeth. 1994. The Labors of Love. Analyzing Perverse Desire: An Interrogation of Teresa de Lauretis's *The Practice of Love*. *Differences* 6 (2+3), 274–295.

Haynes, Stephen R. 2002. *Noah's Curse: The Biblical Justification of American Slavery*. New York: Oxford University Press.

Herdt, Gilbert H. 1982. Fetish and Fantasy in Sambia Initiation. In *Rituals of Manhood*, edited by Gilbert H. Herdt (44–98). Berkeley: University of California Press.

Hoffman, Lawrence A. 1996. *Covenant of Blood: Circumcision and Gender in Rabbinic Judaism*. Chicago: University of Chicago Press.

Izenberg, Gerald N. 2000. *Modernism and Masculinity: Mann, Wedekind, Kandinsky through World War I*. Chicago: University of Chicago Press.

Jay, Martin. 1988. Scopic Regimes of Modernity. In *Vision and Visuality*, edited by Hal Foster (3–23). Seattle: Bay Press.

Jay, Martin. 1993a. *Downcast Eyes: The Denigration of Vision in Twentieth-century French Thought*. Berkeley: University of California Press.

Jay, Martin. 1993b. Sartre, Merleau-Ponty, and the Search for a New Ontology of Sight. In *Modernity and the Hegemony of Vision*, edited by David Michael Levin (143–185). Berkeley: University of California Press.

Levin, David Michael. Ed. 1993. *Modernity and the Hegemony of Vision*. Berkeley: University of California Press.

Lukacher, Ned. 1986. *Primal Scenes: Literature, Philosophy, Psychoanalysis*. Ithaca, NY: Cornell University Press.

Mitchell, W.J.T. 1994. *Picture Theory: Essays on Verbal and Visual Representation*. Chicago: University of Chicago Press.

Morris, Marla. 2001. *Holocaust and Curriculum*. Mahwah, NJ: Lawrence Erlbaum.

Mottram, R.H. 1937. *Noah*. London: Rich & Cowan.

Pinar, William F. 2006. *Race, Religion, and a Curriculum of Reparation*. New York: Palgrave Macmillan.

Rubin, Gayle. 1975. The Traffic in Women: Notes on the "Political Economy" of Sex. In *Toward an Anthropology of Women*, edited by Rayna Reiter (157–210). New York: Monthly Review Press.

Santner, Eric L. 1996. *My Own Private Germany: Daniel Paul Schreber's Secret History of Modernity*. Princeton, NJ: Princeton University Press.

Sass, Louis A. 1994. *The Paradoxes of Delusion: Wittgenstein, Schreber, and the Schizophrenic Mind*. Ithaca, NY: Cornell University Press.

Schreber, Daniel Paul. 2000 (1903). *Memoirs of My Nervous Illness*. [Introduction by Rosemary Dinnage. Trans. and edited by Id Macalpine and Richard A. Hunter.] New York: New York Review Books.

Schwartz, Regina M. 1997. *The Curse of Cain: The Violent Legacy of Monotheism*. Chicago: University of Chicago Press.

Silverman, Kaja. 1988. *The Acoustic Mirror: The Female Voice in Psychoanalysis and Cinema*. Bloomington: Indiana University Press.

Silverman, Kaja. 1992. *Male Subjectivity at the Margins*. New York: Routledge.

Silverman, Kaja. 2000. *World Spectators*. Stanford, CA: Stanford University Press.

Stokes, Mason. 2001. *The Color of Sex: Whiteness, Heterosexuality, & the Fictions of White Supremacy*. Durham, NC: Duke University Press.

Wahrman, Dror. 2004. *The Making of the Modern Self: Identity and Culture in Eighteenth-century England*. New Haven, CT: Yale University Press.

West, Cornel. 1993. *Race Matters*. Boston: Beacon Press.

Wiegman, Robyn. 1995. *American Anatomies: Theorizing Race and Gender*. Durham, NC: Duke University Press.

CHAPTER 12

DISCIPLINE

Commentary

Not only race is queer, so is education, at least when it enacts practices that appear to be in the service of desire, not the cultivation of the human subject. Here I juxtapose two accounts of discipline in the medieval teaching of Latin to show the sexual subtext of teacher-student relationships. In so doing I demonstrate queer theory's questioning of identity as a stable category of self-definition and social practice.

Bibliography

Pinar, William F. 2013. Strict Discipline. *International Journal for the Historiography of Education* 3 (1), 94–101.

> [T]he lack of individuality is a mark of medieval culture.
>
> Karl Joachim Weintraub[1]

In our time, sexual desire has been minoritized, rendered an identity, safely segregating what had before been feared as a potential sin anybody could commit. Imprisoned by its social recognition, homosexual desire no longer circulates secretly, certainly not on "pride" day, where it caricatures itself as a distinct "culture." Questioning the coherence of culture and concomitant concepts of identity, queer theory[2] enables us to discern desire in multifarious forms, even in forms of teaching and learning. To illustrate, I present an example of strict discipline—flogging (or whipping)—dedicated to punish students who have failed to progress in their studies or who have behaved inappropriately in the classroom. In this example the concept of "discipline" becomes queer(ed), as it no longer denotes punishment or self-control or the school subject but (also) sexual stimulation. To portray this "perversion," I juxtapose[3] the scholarship of Walter Ong, Jesuit scholar and English professor, and David Savran, literary scholar, on the practice of flogging (or whipping) students, inviting readers to comment and critique this instance of the concept of queer in education, or enact whatever form of "discipline" they deem appropriate.

In focusing on the teaching of Latin in Renaissance Europe, Walter Ong[4] notes that the role of the preceptor was dominant, "for the puberty rites are essentially didactic." Ong likens the Renaissance Latin preceptor to those "didactitians" among the Bechuans,[5] who require their boys to dance nude before them as they pummel them with long, whip-like rods while demanding to know: "Will you guard the chief well?" or "Will you herd the cattle well?"[6] "Needless to say," Ong[7] notes, as if in an aside, "because they incorporate youth into the tribe rather than into the family, puberty rites involve sexual segregation. The rites for boys are for boys alone." Whatever its social function or cultural rationale, the rite is specifically gendered: older men are observing naked younger men.

Ong[8] focuses on the significance[9] of what he terms "chastisement" in puberty rites. Since the early Greek and Roman periods through the Renaissance, Ong[10] summarizes, "chastisement was definitely involved." He is thinking not only of the punitive actions of preceptors, but the various forms of hazing associated with schooling. Among late nineteenth-century British educators and parents, hazing was associated with a pervasive masturbation fear, a fear, given that boys often masturbated with other boys, of the socially identifying set of sexual practices that became known as "homosexuality."[11]

Although there were general associations between schooling and puberty rites during the Renaissance, Ong's[12] point is that "the status of Latin encouraged in a special way the development of a puberty-rite setting and puberty-rite attitudes in the educational activity of the time." The rationale of the Renaissance school was not, Ong continues, to teach reading and writing in vernacular, but the Latin language. He suggests that this medieval and Renaissance situation lingers in school terms, at least where elementary schools are called not reading and writing schools but grammar schools. He suggests that the term "grammar" in the phrase "grammar schools" refers to the teaching of Latin grammar.

Closed to girls and to women, schools, including universities with their own "schools" (*scholae* or classrooms), were, Ong[13] suggests, sites of "male rendezvous," not unlike those segregated and isolated huts where boys' underwent initiation in "primitive" societies.[14] Not only were *only* men in schools, but in the universities, with the exception of doctors of medicine (who at the University of Paris, Ong reports, were allowed, after the year 1452, to marry), teachers during the Middle Ages and the Renaissance (and in many universities much later than the Renaissance) were required to remain unmarried if they were to teach.

Latin played, Ong[15] argues, a key psychological role in the maintenance of this "closed male environment." Latin was the language of those on the "inside," and thus learning Latin at any level constituted a first step toward initiation into the closed and gendered world of learning. What threatened this initiation was the presence of women:

> The difficulty was that if there were too many women around, the child would speak English, not Latin. He would slip back into the vernacular family circle instead of being forced out already at this tender age into the world of the "tribe," of men. We are faced here with a rather precocious appearance of the puberty-rite situation around the age of seven, but the humanists favored precociousness and promoted it when they could.[16]

Latin was not the only puberty rite in schools it seems. Or shall we say that while Latin was the medium, the message was "Roman," but not exactly in a strictly semantic sense.

While hardly gay pride parades, Renaissance schools, in Ong's depiction of them, also seemed at cross-purposes. By segregating boys and men to avoid distraction (by girls), these schools seemed to have, however inadvertently, provided opportunities for boys to become distracted by each other. In the next two sections, this "perversion" dynamic—discipline attracting its dissolution—becomes perfectly clear (or should I say queer) in the practices and controversies of those who ruled by the rod, that phallic symbol of masculine power. In the final section I will query what we have learned from these lessons in "Latin."

"Rule by the Rod"[17]

As Ong points out, whipping or flogging was a practice common since antiquity. "The fact that school pupils were all boys," Ong[18] writes, "*of course* encouraged rule by the rod." I suppose the "of course" implies that male masters would have been kinder to the "fairer sex." The *double entendre* of the word "rod" implies a homoerotic element at work, an element that becomes explicit in David Savran's commentary on anti-flogging treatises, as we will see momentarily.

In the Middle Ages not only does "rule by the rod" persist, but, Ong[19] reports, "there is evidence that the specifically initiatory cast of the punishment grew more intense and evident." He cites stories by Leach, who reported on the flogging in school of boys aspiring to life in the monasteries. He quotes from Aelfric's[20] Colloquy the "highly characteristic" question which Aelfric has his typical master put to his typical pupils: "Are you willing to be flogged while learning?"[21] To this question the boys answered at once that they prefer flogging to ignorance. From what ignorance did flogging protect?

The question, the answer, and the setting remind Ong[22] of the initiation practices among the Bechuans (noted earlier). Returning to Europe, Ong[23] concludes: "The boy must acknowledge the equation of learning and flogging, and thereby face courageously into learning as into an initiation, something of itself taxing and fearsome." A rose is a rose, Gertrude Stein insisted, but there is another—could it be queerer?—"flower" here, one suggested by the reaction to flogging. Can it be that the experience of flogging was knowledge in itself, a knowledge of pleasure in male-male physical intimacy, a knowledge disavowed through pain as it was secretly enjoyed?

Renaissance educators did not, Ong[24] informs us, "abate the ferocity of medieval or ancient school punishment." He notes that pictorial representations of Renaissance classroom activity (such as Pieter Brueghel the Elder's engraving "The Ass at School") reveal bundles of switches as "regular classroom equipment."[25] Nor did "advanced" ideas on education reduce the frequency and ferocity of physical punishment, Ong suggests. To support this claim, Ong notes that Nicolas de Nancel, Peter Ramus' biographer and student and secretary, reports that Ramus (who was a highly regarded educator with presumably "advanced" ideas) often punished his pupils in "savage outbursts of temper,"[26] not only whipping but also kicking them until they were "half dead" (*semineces*) although—and, Nancel adds apologetically, "for this he must praised"—during the violence he never swore.[27]

"Invigorating Lashes"[28]

[T]he pain of the whip is obsessively ghosted by sexual pleasure.

David Savran[29]

While, as Ong notes, it was the secretive, non-feminine use of Latin as a passage out of the maternal home into the masculinized world of ideas and public life that qualified Latin as a rite of passage, it was flogging that made the language "come alive" in homosociality.[30] While flogging was, presumably, justified only as "chastisement," it was clear to Ong[31] "that, whether it should be or not, punishment is felt by some masters as advisable for reasons other than the encouragement of formal learning."

What could these other reasons be? Ong declines to pursue this point, but he seems subliminally aware of the homoerotic dynamic in flogging, noting: "Nor does it seem entirely irrelevant to this dialectic that corporal punishment and the stress on Latin in school have, pretty generally, been disappearing in modern times with the emergence of coeducation."[32] If Latin and flogging were employed "for reasons other than the encouragement of formal learning," and if those "reasons" were in some way homoerotic, would not one predict their disappearance in co-educational settings? If we take seriously David Savran's review of the medieval and Renaissance practice of flogging, the "if" in the preceding sentence disappears.

Savran begins with the 1629 treatise by German physician Johann Heinrich Meibom, entitled, *De Flagrorum Usu in Re Veneria & Lumborum Renumque Officio* (*On the Use of Rods in Venereal Matters: Also of the Office of the Loins and Reins*), which immediately became an authoritative text and was widely cited for two hundred years. Meibom[33] reports the scandalous finding that "that there are persons who are stimulated to *Venery by Strokes of Rods, and Worked up into a Flame of Lust by Blows*; and that the *Part*, which distinguishes us to be *Men*, should be raised by the Charm of invigorating Lashes" (quoted in Savran 1998, 11–12). Flagellation that produced erections and other erotic effects was, for Meibom, "an abominable Crime," the product of "a perverse and frenzical Appetite" as it ran the risk of feminizing the male subject, rendering him passive, submissive, even impotent.[34] Should the boy resist flogging's erotic lures and, to recall the title of Savran's provocative study, "take it like a man," he might traverse apparently feminine ground to become a "man."

The second major treatise on flagellation was published in 1700, Savran reports. It is the Abbé Boileau's *Historia Flagellantium, de recto e perverso flagrorum usu apud Christiano* (*The History of the Flagellants, and of the Correct and Perverse Use of Rods among Christians*). In this more extensive volume, the Abbé condemns the use of the rod, focusing on self-flagellation (or performance of "*Disciplines*") which were, he argued, "unknown in the happy periods of the primitive Church" and contrary to the will of God.[35] There is in this early eighteenth-century volume a distinction made between flogging on "the bare back or shoulders," which the Abbé calls the "*upper*" discipline, and "the posteriors," which he names "the *lower* discipline."[36]

Drawing on Meibom's anatomical studies, the Abbé Boileau judges 'the lower discipline" as the area of danger, the area wherein he finds the "perverse use of rods" noted in the title of his book. The 1777 English edition (whose translation and annotation are attributed to John Lois Delolme) describes flagellatory practices that date back to antiquity. The erotic potential of flagellation is condemned in both editions, Savran observes.

The next volume Savran discusses was published in 1788 by François-Amedée Doppet and is entitled the *Aphrodisiaque externe, ou Traité due fouet et de ses effects sur le physique de l'amour* (*The Exterior Aphrodisiac, or Treatise on the Whip and its Effects on the Physics of Love*). Unlike the Abbé Boileau, Doppet focused on pedagogical rather than ecclesiastic flagellation, and recommended that, Savran[37] writes, "flogging the naked buttocks of children be curtailed because it functions, dangerously and prematurely, a sexual stimulant." Doppet argued flogging threatened to be erotically stimulating due to the proximity of the buttocks to the genitals. Doppet deplored the flogging of boys because the "interest in the buttocks often leads to children whipping each other, to fondling and masturbation."[38] Like Ong, suspecting that (male) teachers had extracurricular reasons for flogging, Doppet alleged that some teachers' "sodomitic inclinations" lead them "positively [to] enjoy whipping their pupils on the buttocks."[39]

It was during the nineteenth century, Savran argues, that erotic flagellation became recast as masochism. Savran notes that the modern notion of sexuality—as opposed to sex—is predicated on two assumptions: first, upon the eighteenth-century characterization of sexuality as the matrix of physiological and psychological mechanisms governing the individual's genital functions, and second, upon the nineteenth-century interpretation of sexuality as "instinct" or "drive." As "instinct" or "drive," sexuality becomes a "force" that structures, albeit in ways not always known to us, our conscious life, indeed, our character and personality. By Freud's time, sexuality had been elevated to metaphysical status, as somehow *the truth* about, not only the individual, but also "races" and genders.

As nineteenth-century physicians brought the sexuality of children under particularly close scrutiny, they associated the flogging of children, especially the flogging of boys, with masturbation. Indeed, the end of the nineteenth century saw a pandemic fear of masturbation in the United States and Great Britain, especially masturbation among boys, and this fear was linked to the fear of homosexuality.[40] Savran[41] quotes William Acton who was sure that "whipping children [i.e. boys] on the nates . . . has a great influences in exciting ejaculation." Savran[42] quotes Rousseau as well, who worried that flogging was the "first incitement to masturbation," which, he warns, is extremely hazardous, leading inevitably to the failure of the boy's health and the dimming of his "intellectual powers."

While flogging in medieval and Renaissance schools may have had a pedagogical purpose, the practice taught more than Latin. From Savran's review of the major treatises on the subject dating back to the mid-seventeenth century, it is clear that the application of rods had, for many, an erotic lesson to teach. Indeed, evidently many employed rods deliberately to incite erection in their young charges. While some writers, like the Abbé Boileau, labor (as the title of his treatise suggests) to demarcate the "correct" from the "perverse" use of rods, the distinction becomes, as Savran[43] points out, "more and more inadvertently problematized." In attempting to distinguish the dangers of "the lower discipline" from the "upper," the Abbé's text discloses slippage between the two, discloses that the "perverse" is already inscribed within its presumed opposite, the "correct." The "perverse" threatens and taunts the correct: as the schoolmaster whips the bare buttocks of pubescent boys, he unleashes sexual excitement in the name of discipline. As Savran[44] observes, the "pain of the whip is obsessively ghosted by sexual pleasure."

"Perhaps," Savran[45] allows (cautiously, I should say), "there is a connection between the flogging of children and erotic flagellation." He notes that in his *Three Essays on the Theory of Sexuality* (1905), Freud suggested that they are causally linked. Recalling Rousseau, Freud characterized "the painful stimulation of the skin of the buttocks" as "one of the erotogenic roots of the *passive* instinct of cruelty (masochism)." Because flogging in childhood surfaces over and over again in the etiologies of masochism, Savran[46] suggests that "perhaps the two practices are connected, both ontogenetically and culturally." Just as the abused child may grow up to be a masochist, so may a culture of flagellation evolve into a culture of masochism and, even more sweepingly, voluntary self-subjugation. "Perhaps," Savran[47] continues,

> the flagellant is the shadow lurking behind the bourgeois subject as it is being consolidated in diaries, fictions, and philosophical traits. And perhaps sparing the rod does not so much spoil the child as prepare it to take its own self-regulating place in a self-disciplining society.

Up through the seventeenth century, Savran suggests, flogging was the standard method in Europe for punishing unruly children (especially boys). In early modern England, both in homes and schools, across the boundaries of social class, the birch rod—as administered by parents, servants, nurses, tutors, or teachers—became the means of conventional "chastisement" (to recall Ong's term). Contrary to Ong's account, possibly because he is reviewing flogging practices in the home and church as well as the school, Savran[48] asserts that "both boys and girls" were required to be deferential to their elders.[49] They were, Savran[50] continues, "beaten routinely" for a wide range of offenses, among them "disobedience, obstinacy, laziness, a missed stitch, a flubbed Latin conjugation."

Not only did the provocations for flogging vary; so did the severity of the punishment, from "a gentle hand slap to prolonged, violent whippings that sometimes resulted in the death of the child."[51] In addition to the buttocks (either naked or clothed), the child's hand, mouth, face were considered appropriate sites for beating. In addition to the birch rod, a ferula—a wooden slat with a large rounded end and a hole in its middle—was used. Savran draws on the research of Lawrence Stone to note that in English grammar schools, the standard method of administering the rod required one active and two passive participants: a boy would be beaten "with a birch" by his master "on the naked buttocks while bent over and horsed on the back of another boy."[52] Even in the universities, young men were regularly submitted to public whippings, flogged while stretched over a barrel.[53]

Toward the close of the seventeenth century, Savran[54] suggests, "a concerted and widespread campaign" emerged to intervene in corporal punishment. Anonymous pamphleteers condemned flogging in schools while John Aubrey denounced "the ordinary schoolmaster's tyrannicall beating and dispiriting of children [from] which many tender ingeniose children doe never recover again."[55] Hundreds of years of flogging, Savran[56] concludes, "superseded by a much more discreet, subtle, and insidious means of control."

Savran goes on to Locke but perhaps enough has been said to raise the question: when is a rose not only a rose? Is education always also a rite of passage—and not only among the Bechuans—in which not so subtle erotic (and hardly only homoerotic) dynamics between the aging and youth animate more rational and institutional obligations? Rather than a recognized but segregated identity, is homosexual desire an omnipresent potential even (especially?) where it is most prohibited?

Conclusion

> Queer, then, is an identity category that has no interest in consolidating or even stabilizing itself.
>
> Annamarie Jagose[57]

The project of queer theory, Jagose (1996, 130) emphasizes, questions the coherence of identity, including sexual identity. It could even be said to advance an "anti-identity" politics, one wary of "foundations" or "essentialisms." Influenced first by Foucault[58]—who argued that the contemporary concept of homosexual *identity* could be dated (to "around" 1870),[59] was not "natural" but, rather, political—queer theory followed the institutionalization of gay and lesbian studies during the 1970s in North America. That there *is* a lesbian and gay community—celebrated in the annual "pride" parades—was yet another category queer theory questioned.[60]

The concept of "queer" declines to reduce gender to sexuality. Boys can be girls, queer theory asserts, and vice-versa, and, moreover, there are many living "in-between"[61] what is not a continuum but a montage, no static state but sexuality in motion, historically, culturally, politically. The binary upon contemporary sexual identity depends—heterosexual vs. homosexual—is itself questioned. Socially inscribing such a sharp distinction requires "strict discipline," because, Judith Butler[62] points out, "gender itself is internally unstable, [and] . . . transgendered lives are evidence of the breakdown of any lines of causal determinism between sexuality and gender." Once sexuality and gender are separated, the former can be noticed circulating within the latter. Indeed, "opposite" sexes can occur within one gender, polarizing subject positions not in opposition but attraction.

To make matters perfectly queer, "discipline" as depicted by Ong and Savran seems to be sex by another name. That's not all it is—it is, after all, still "discipline" in the service of learning Latin—but it cannot be contained by what claims. If that suggestion seems unsavory, that is unsurprising, as Lee Edelman[63] notices: "Queer theory's . . . proper task [is] the ceaseless disappropriation of every propriety." Well, to disappropriate *every* propriety seems an inversion that is not so very queer, as universalization itself demands a strict discipline that produces unwanted erections, in this instance conceptual rigidities that lacerate the lesson, Latin or queer.

Notes

1 1978, 74.
2 Queer theory represented a radicalization of gay and lesbian studies. Teresa de Lauretis, the theorist often credited with introducing the phrase "queer theory,"

abandoned it later, complaining it had been co-opted by forces of normalization (see Jagose 1996, 127). For an introduction to queer theory see Jagose 1996; Pinar 1998.

3 A common practice, juxtaposition can become a concept in curriculum design, reposing the question of sequence not as always linear (from concrete to abstract for instance) but as elements of a montage (see Pinar 2009, 185 n. 32; 187 n. 36). Discussing the recontextualization of medieval culture in contemporary queer theory (citing the work of Carolyn Dinshaw), Cvetkovich (2003, 49) implies that "histories can 'touch' one another, that there are resonant juxtapositions between past and present whose explanatory power is not causal or teleological; instead, the affective charge of investment, of being 'touched,' brings the past forward into the present." Does my juxtaposition of Ong and Savran "touch" the present, one wherein standardized test scores stand in for flogging?

4 1971, 117.

5 In the nineteenth century in what is now Botswana was Bechuana, and its inhabitants—the Tswana people—were then termed Bechuans.

6 Quoted in Ong 1971, 117.

7 1971, 117.

8 1971, 118.

9 Intergenerationally, such chastisement represented a form of discipline designed to form boys into men, providing tests of endurance and self-control that forced boys to disavow the femininity their childhood intimacy with mothers and other women had inadvertently installed. As David Gilmore's (1990) summary of cross-cultural anthropological research shows, such "discipline" threatens to dissolve these gendered categories in its determination to imprint the distinction between them.

10 1971, 118.

11 See Hunt 1998.

12 1971, 119.

13 Ibid.

14 See Gilmore 1990.

15 1971, 121.

16 1971, 123.

17 1971, 124.

18 1971, 124, emphasis added.

19 1971, 124.

20 Aelfric of Eynsham (955–1010) was a monk known for his hagiography, homilies, and biblical commentaries.

21 Quoted in Ong 1971, 124.

22 See 1971, 117.

23 1971, 124.

24 1971, 125.

25 Ibid.

26 Ong's phrase: see 1971, 125.

27 Quoted in Ong 1971, 125.

28 Quoted in Savran 1998, 12.

29 1998, 15.

30 See Sedgwick 1985.

31 1971, 135.

32 1971, 138.

33 Meibom also published "*Epistel über die Nützlichkeit der Geißelhiebe beim Liebesspiel*" ("Epistle on the Utility of Whipping in Games of Love"), a title that would seem to acknowledge flogging's flexibility along the continuum of pain and pleasure.

34 Quoted in Savran 1998, 12.

35 Ibid.

36 Ibid.

37 1998, 13.

38 Quoted in Savran 1998, 13.
39 Ibid.
40 See Hunt 1998.
41 See 1998, 14.
42 Ibid.
43 Ibid.
44 1998, 15.
45 1998, 17.
46 Ibid.
47 Ibid.
48 Ibid.
49 "Masters" is Rousseau's term; see Baker 2001, 283. In a different context, Fletcher (2012, 385) recalls that for C. S. Peirce, "the most striking characteristic of medieval thought is the importance attributed to authority."
50 1998, 17.
51 Ibid.
52 Quoted in Savran 1998, 18.
53 See Savran 1998.
54 1998, 18.
55 Quoted in Savran 1998, 18.
56 1998, 19.
57 1996, 132.
58 Jagose 1996, 80.
59 See Jagose 1996, 11.
60 See Jagose 1996, 111.
61 That "in-between" is not only psychological. In his study of circumcision, David Gollaher (2000, 203) discusses the involuntary gender reassignment of sexually ambiguous infants by physicians, a practice that during the 1980s and 1990 in the United States became public:

> Based on the diagnosis of ambiguous genitalia, or "intersexuality," doctors perform surgeries on some 2,000 children each year. Nine out of ten of these are classified as female, though this sex assignment may reflect little more than the surgeon's choice. Using the traditional techniques of plastic surgery, they endeavor to make a child look natural. This is where the trouble lies, with some activists accusing surgeons of operating far too aggressively with little sense of the lasting damage such procedures may do to women's lives. Depending on the extent of surgery, women may be left with scars, numbness, and loss of sensation in their sexual organs, as well as with an abiding shame and embarrassment.

Rolling Stone published an account of "The True Story of John/Joan," a male baby who was "maimed" in a "botched" circumcision and was, as a consequence, "reassigned" to the female sex, as physicians performed plastic surgery to fashion female genitalia, followed by hormone treatments to transform John into Joan (Gollaher 2000, 203–204).
62 2004, 54.
63 2004, 24.

Bibliography

Baker, Bernadette M. 2001. *In Perpetual Motion: Theories of Power, Educational History, and the Child*. New York: Peter Lang.
Butler, Judith. 2004. *Undoing Gender*. New York: Routledge.

Cvetkovich, Ann. 2003. *An Archive of Feelings: Trauma, Sexuality, and Lesbian Public Cultures*. Durham, NC: Duke University Press.
Edelman, Lee. 2004. *No Future: Queer Theory and the Death Drive*. Durham, NC: Duke University Press.
Fletcher, Angus. 2012. *Allegory. The Theory of a Symbolic Model*. [With a foreword by Harold Bloom and a new afterword by the author.] Princeton, NJ: Princeton University Press.
Gilmore, David. 1990. *Manhood in the Making*. New Haven: Yale University Press.
Gollaher, David L. 2000. *Circumcision: A History of the World's Most Controversial Surgery*. New York: Basic Books.
Hunt, Alan. 1998. The Great Masturbation Panic and the Discourses of Moral Regulation in Nineteenth-and Early Twentieth-Century Britain. *Journal of the History of Sexuality* 8 (4), 575–615.
Jagose, Annamarie. 1996. *Queer Theory: An Introduction*. New York: New York University Press.
Ong, Walter J. 1971. *Rhetoric, Romance, and Technology*. Ithaca, NY: Cornell University Press.
Pinar, William F. ed. 1998. *Queer Theory in Education*. Mahwah, NJ: Lawrence Erlbaum.
Pinar, William F. 2009. *The Worldliness of a Cosmopolitan Education: Passionate Lives in Public Service*. New York: Routledge.
Savran, David. 1998. *Taking It a Like a Man: White Masculinity, Masochism, and Contemporary American Culture*. Princeton, NJ: Princeton University Press.
Sedgwick, Eve Kosofsky. 1985. *Between Men: English Literature and Male Homosocial Desire*. New York: Columbia University Press.
Stone, Lawrence. 1977. *The Family, Sex and Marriage in England, 1500–1800*. New York: Harper & Row.
Weintraub, Karl Joachim. 1978. *The Value of the Individual: Self and Circumstance in Autobiography*. Chicago: University of Chicago Press.

CHAPTER 13

IDENTITY

Commentary

Contemporary identity politics privileges collective over individual forms of identity,[1] inadvertently reinscribing the totalizing generalizations those of European descent too often used to stereotype and demonize peoples different from themselves, among them "Indians," "Negroes," and "Queer." Misrepresenting their ancestors through self-righteous declarations of victimhood and moral superiority, contemporary politicians of identity extol the virtues of "indigeneity," "blackness," and "queerness" as they condemn those "others"—often "straight white males"—who are, I remind, not abstractions but persons.

Zitkala-Ša lived through the cultural catastrophe Europeans brought, witnessing—indeed living through, as did the Crow chief Plenty Coups—the cultural death of the indigenous subject. "Only if one acknowledges that there is no longer a genuine way of going on *like that*," Lear[2] notes, "might there arise new genuine ways of going on *like that*." The "subjective catastrophe"[3] of cultural devastation requires subjective reconstruction, "coming back to life in a form that is not yet intelligible,"[4] "aiming for a subjectivity that is [in Plenty Coups' case] at once Crow and does not yet exist."[5] That scale and specificity of challenge is what Zitkala-Ša faced as well. Confronting it, I suggest, points to the decolonizing politics of individuating identity.

Bibliography

Lear, Jonathan. 2006. *Radical Hope: Ethics in the Face of Cultural Devastation*. Cambridge, MA: Harvard University Press.

Pinar, William F. 2009. *The Worldliness of a Cosmopolitan Education: Passionate Lives in Public Service* (21–26). New York: Routledge.

Simon, Roger I. 2005. *The Touch of the Past. Remembrance, Learning, and Ethics*. New York: Palgrave Macmillan.

> There is nothing inherently liberating about the recognition of difference. In fact, Orientalism feeds on it.
>
> Mitsuhiro Yoshimoto[6]

I would supplement Yoshimoto's second sentence: it is, after all, the misrecognition of difference that feeds fantasies like Orientalism. And it is fantasy that feeds misrecognition. Not only the colonists and their descendants misapprehend the Other. The colonized and their descendants, Frantz Fanon predicted, would misapprehend themselves, and in so doing, usher in—Fanon was, of course, thinking of Africa, not Asia—a period of neocolonialism in which indigenous peoples would replay the genocidal roles assumed by European invaders. That prediction has been realized in post-colonial African genocides. In his study of Fanon, Ayo Sekyi-Otu[7] notes that in the "postcolonial world . . . the agony and ecstasy of the particular—became the nightmare of absolutism." For Fanon, a "dying colonialism" foreshadowed the reinscription of black skin with white masks.

The binaries structuring colonialism's cultural cannibalism and genocide can, have, become reinscribed within postcolonial cultures. In the North American academy, such reinscription has been achieved through the establishment—and visible in the excesses—of identity politics. "What . . . are the political and ethical consequences of attributing centrality to race?" Sekyi-Otu[8] asks. He continues:

> Does it result in an indiscriminate and genocidal antagonism toward the Other on the one hand, and, on the other, the tyrannizing protectionism of racial confraternity, a separatist chorus so mystified by its own chant of togetherness that it stifles the anguished cries of other languages of separation and subjugation, old and new—class, gender, ethnicity?[9]

The separatist chorus that is North American identity politics threatens to subsume the particular into "absolutes," including totalizing phrases such as "indigenous perspectives." In such a phrase, where is acknowledgement of the diversity of indigenous cultures? Where is the recognition of internal differences? These disappear into generalizing claims such as, for instance, indigenous cultures respect elders[10] or that African Americans (regardless of class or gender or region or historical moment) and "other ethnic groups of color" require for academic achievement so-called "culturally-responsive teaching,"[11] itself a totalizing instrumentalism.[12]

Through the self-righteous indignation of contemporary identity politics, the concrete "culture" one claims to represent disappears into abstractions, totalized into generalizations recapitulating, if through reversal, the stereotypes fabricated by the colonizers. Moreover, in the totalizing, nostalgic abstraction of "culture" the capacity for self-critique fades. I think, for instance, of the 1930s *négritude* movement in France[13] or more contemporary invocations of a pre-colonial African identity,[14] the former of which fantasized blackness as an unchanging cultural core of intuition, rhythm, sentiment, and creativity, the latter emphasizing manhood and morality. In both, blackness is always and everywhere beautifully and self-righteously non-European, non-rationalistic, non-technological, non-imperial. Having dismissed European cultures as monolithic and as only evil, there are descendants of the colonized—some of whom are our colleagues—who become trapped in a hall of mirrors, projecting onto the European-American Other the bifurcating elements they themselves have internalized through colonization. Speaking of this curse of colonialism, Masao Miyoshi[15] points out:

> Once survival and self-defense cease to be a desperate necessity, however, identity politics often turns into a policy of self-promotion, or, more exactly, a self-serving sales policy in which a history of victimization becomes a commodity that demands payment. It can pervert itself into opportunism and cannibalism. . . . In the name of multiculturalism, one privileges one's own identity, while making merely a token acknowledgement of the other's whom one proceeds to disregard when an occasion for help arrives.

As a member of a victimized group claiming floor-space in the exhibition hall of multiculturalism, I know first-hand such temptations.

For many of us queers, it is the "straight world" that kills us, or, at least, makes us over in its image. "Queer" and "straight" are, of course, abstractions and binaries queer theory itself claims to deconstruct. Never mind, "it is as if self-identity were an article of private property, which the group—but more likely its elite leadership—claims to own and guard exclusively."[16] Never able to shed the suspicion that my work has sometimes been dismissed due to homophobia and heterosexism, I have often felt, still feel, victimized, a strange self-pity, I remind myself, given Matthew Shepard and the daily assaults queers suffer worldwide. Almost any provocation scrapes off the scar of my social wound, and my vision is refracted through the pain of the old, ongoing injury. Identity politics is the privilege claimed by the academic elite to represent absent victimized others, justified in the name of suffering and social justice. As Jean Elshtain[17] points out (in a different but related context), "victimization does not confer moral rightness or political acuity."

The testimonial—indeed, political—labor of identity politics is, I think, more responsibly and convincingly conducted by autobiography. Rather than claiming for oneself a collective identity, in which one presumes to be the representative absent Other, one might refocus one's moral obligation and pedagogical opportunity toward one's own decolonization, wherein those internalized binaries structured by colonialism might be reconstructed as multiple and linked identities, traversing the divides history and politics cut in our psychic terrain. These self-representations are singular—yes, even hybrid[18]—and they testify to cultural as well as personal survival and rejuvenation.

Consider the case of Zitkala-Ša (1876–1938). A Sioux educated in a boarding school, Zitkala-Ša taught briefly at the Carlisle Indian Industrial School, founded in Pennsylvania in 1879 by Richard Henry Pratt, an army officer. Carlisle became the model for federal Indian boarding schools designed to destroy tribal nations and strip Native children of their cultures, languages, and religions. A century ago, even those European-Americans who claimed to take a "pro-Indian" side in the national debate over how to solve "the Indian problem" assumed that the educational project was one of assimilation: the eventual elimination of tribal culture and identity. These white, usually Christian policymakers and philanthropists were convinced that Indians must finally disappear into the European-American population. They were considered "friends" because they opposed the complete physical extermination of native peoples, a position advocated by many.[19]

At Carlisle, Indian students were forbidden to speak native languages, wear traditional clothing, or practice ancestral religions. Because the student body was Pan-Indian, because the children had been taken away from their families when they were very young and kept away for years at a time, Indian students were, it was hoped by Pratt and others, severed from their tribal traditions.[20] The case of Zitkala-Ša demonstrates the disappointment of this hope. Her case speaks to the educational potential of autobiography, including its capacity to alert readers to and engage them in one's political cause. Because it portrays that cause not in abstract and totalizing terms, but, rather, through vivid narratives of lived experience, potentially autobiography can traverse the divide between writer and reader.

After leaving her teaching position at Carlisle, Zitkala-Ša published three important autobiographical essays. Appearing in *The Atlantic Monthly* in 1900, Zitkala-Ša recalled her early childhood on the reservation, followed by her experiences as a student at a Quaker off-reservation boarding school, then her brief stint as a teacher at Carlisle.[21] Zitkala-Ša's autobiographical narrative makes plain the genocidal character of the boarding schools, documenting specifically the tension between the representative Indian and the self-representing Indian. Exploiting the politics of self-representation by representing herself in different terms in different settings, Zitkala-Ša described herself as orator, musician, poet, storyteller, political activist, Dakota, half-blood, Indian, pagan, and Catholic.[22]

This variable and singular set of identities not only testified to her specific accomplishments (and accommodations), it advanced her political agenda of self-representation, contesting specifically the reductionism of the term "Indian." Contrary to contemporary identity politics in which the individual disappears into the victimized category (now valorized positively as "indigenous"), Zitkala-Ša emphasized her agency as an individual, reconstructing the self-annihilating process of assimilation as, in fact, for her, self-enhancing. Unlike Paul Willis' "lads," this "victim" resisted "resistance" as well as assimilation. Contradicting Audre Lorde's warning,[23] Zitkala-Ša employed the master's tools to dismantle the master's house. As would both black revolutionaries and lesbian activists sixty years later, Zitkala-Ša rejected her given surname. In a simple but significant act of agency, Gertrude Simmons became Zitkala-Ša, a Lakota name that translates as Red Bird.[24]

This self-naming is significant in its testimony to and identification with her Indian ancestry, but Zitkala-Ša did not disappear into that collective identity. She continued to use her name Gertrude Simmons (later Gertrude Simmons Bonnin) in her private life. As a public intellectual and political activist, however, Simmons used her self-given Lakota name as a literary *nom de plume*, claiming in "School Days of an Indian Girl" that her muse, indeed her very voice, derived from her "Indian nature."[25] Zitkala-Ša never mentions that her father was white, emphasizing in that essay her Dakota roots. Through her choice of a Lakota name after years as a student and teacher in schools dedicated to the extinction of Indian cultures, and through her ascription of her authorial success to her Sioux heritage, Zitkala-Ša reverses the boarding-school teachers' practice of providing "savage" students with "civilized" English names, emphasizing that for her, education is no linear or bifurcated process of assimilation or resistance,[26] but a particular, in her case multicultural, reconstruction of who she was born to be and educated to become.

As her autobiographical essays make clear, Zitkala-Ša was hardly uneducated when she was taken to the boarding school. She was already a young woman in the process of being educated in the culture of her tribe. By testifying to her indigenous education, Zitkala-Ša negates Pratt's assertion that Indian students arrived at Carlisle like a blank slate, ready for imprinting with the text of civilization.

Nor, however, does Zitkala-Ša represent her Dakota education as occurring in a pristine, pre-colonial past. She makes clear that her education—even at home with her mother—always occurred through accommodation to white encroachment.[27] Although Dakota-identified during her childhood, Zitkala-Ša proclaims her multiplying adult identities: indeed, she affirms self-difference[28] through the articulation of her multiple and linked identities, listed earlier. These situated and singular identities constituting her multivariate individuality do not disappear into collective identifications like "Indian" or "Indigenous." Nor does her criticism of whites become diffused by projection; she makes her criticism concrete and specific through autobiography, explaining in narrative detail, for instance, why she is a pagan. Through her defiant and creative autobiographical reconstruction of the colonial culture she had internalized, Zitkala-Ša traversed the trauma of "cultural devastation."[29]

Autobiography, then, not identity politics, testifies to injustice and injury, providing particular referents for totalizing abstractions that otherwise risk recapitulation of colonist binaries, if with reversed valences. Articulating subjective experience keeps a string on these conceptual kites that, in their distance from the everyday, enable more panoramic views of our location in the world. If unconnected to those to whom they bear witness, however, such totalizing phrases threaten to function as fatuous free-floating signifiers, scraping the scars off injuries ancient and ongoing, injuries at once individual and collective. That recognition of self-difference to which an autobiography of alterity testifies is prerequisite to the representation of the multivariate complexity of experience and identity. In so doing, autobiography makes plain that the Other is another person.

Notes

1 "The principle of general equivalence," Simon (2005, 141) reminds, "cannibalizes the particular into an abstraction (identity), which then becomes suitable for (undifferentiated) exchange."
2 2006, 51.
3 Lear 2006, 96.
4 2006, 95.
5 2006, 104.
6 2002, 387.
7 1996, 20.
8 1996, 13–14.
9 Ibid.
10 See Grant 1995, 212.
11 See Gay 2000, 13, 25.
12 See, for instance, Gay 2000, 111.
13 See Young-Bruehl 1996, 492; Kesteloot 1991.
14 See, for instance, Pinar 2001, 861ff.
15 2002, 45.
16 Miyoshi 2002, 45.
17 2002, 201.
18 The excess of this discourse, usually associated with the work of Homi Bhabha, was definitively critiqued a decade ago: see Parry 2002.
19 Katanski 2005, 3
20 Katanski 2005, 4.
21 Katanski 2005, 96.

22 Katanski 2005, 113.
23 See De Veaux 2004, 248.
24 Katanski 2005, 113, 114.
25 Katanski 2005, 114.
26 Katanski 2005, 115.
27 Katanski 2005, 116.
28 Katanski 2005, 118–119.
29 Lear traces the struggles of Plenty Coups (1847–1932), "the last great chief of the Crow nation" (Lear 2006, 1; see also Krupat 1994, 241), who "lived through a period in which the Crow abandoned their traditional nomadic-hunting way of life. But he seems to have become a spokesman from inside that way of life for the death of that way of life" (Lear 2006, 6–7). To live through this cultural devastation, Lear (2006, 141) suggests, "Plenty Coups drew on traditional tribal resources—the chickadee—to formulate an *ego-ideal of radical hope*. That is, he gave the tribe the possibility of drawing on a traditional ideal that would help them endure a loss of concepts." Such "living through" historical trauma discloses not only fidelity to culture lost but an apparent openness to what can be reconstructed from the ruins.

Bibliography

De Veaux, Alexis. 2004. *Warrior Poet: A Biography of Audre Lorde*. New York: Norton.

Elshtain, Jean Bethke. 2002. *Jane Addams and the Dream of American Democracy*. New York: Basic Books.

Gay, Geneva. 2000. *Culturally Responsive Teaching: Theory, Research, and Practice*. New York: Teachers College Press.

Grant, Agnes. 1995. The Challenge for Universities. In *First Nations Education in Canada: The Circle Unfolds*, edited by Marie Battiste and Jean Barman (208–223). Vancouver: University of British Columbia Press.

Katanski, Amelia V. 2005. *Learning to Write "Indian": The Boarding-School Experience and American Indian Literature*. Norman: University of Oklahoma Press.

Kesteloot, Lilyan. 1991. *Black Writers in French: A Literary History of Négritude*. Washington, DC: Howard University Press.

Krupat, Arnold. 1994. *Native American Autobiography: An Anthology*. Madison: University of Wisconsin Press.

Lear, Jonathan. 2006. *Radical Hope: Ethics in the Face of Cultural Devastation*. Cambridge, MA: Harvard University Press.

Miyoshi, Masao. 2002. Ivory Tower in Escrow. In *Learning Places: The Afterlives of Area Studies*, edited by Masao Miyoshi and D.H. Harootunian (19–60). Durham, NC: Duke University Press.

Parry, Benita. 2002. Signs of Our Times: A Discussion of Homi Bhabha's *The Location of Culture*. In *Learning Places: The Afterlives of Area Studies*, edited by Masao Miyoshi and D.H. Harootunian (119–149). Durham, NC: Duke University Press.

Pinar, William F. 2001. *The Gender of Racial Politics and Violence in American: Lynching, Prison Rape, and the Crisis of Masculinity*. New York: Peter Lang.

Sekyi-Otu, Ato. 1996. *Fanon's Dialectic of Experience*. Cambridge, MA: Harvard University Press.

Willis, Paul. 1981. *Learning to Labour*. Hampshire, England: Gower.

Young-Bruehl, Elisabeth. 1996. *The Anatomy of Prejudices*. Cambridge, MA: Harvard University Press.

Yoshimoto, Mitsuhiro. 2002. Questions of Japanese Cinema: Disciplinary Boundaries and the Invention of the Scholarly Object. In *Learning Places: The Afterlives of Area Studies*, edited by Masao Miyoshi and D.H. Harootunian (368–401). Durham, NC: Duke University Press.

CHAPTER 14

RESOLVE

Commentary

What exists between hope and despair? With that resounding question Roger Simon structured his pedagogy of remembrance, witness, and testimony. No set of skills promising employability in a "global marketplace," Simon's pedagogy reactivates knowledge of the traumatic past. Contrary to arrest,[1] to activate means to vitalize, to breathe life into, and to be breathed into life. Reactivating the past means engagement with alterity—in this instance the singularity of the past in its distinctive complexity—that sets in motion, well, we can't know. In such inner motion can form resolve, that which, I suggest, exists between hope and despair.

Bibliography

Pinar, William F. 1994. *Autobiography, Politics, and Sexuality: Essays in Curriculum Theory 1972–1992*. New York: Peter Lang.

Pinar, William F. 2014. Between Hope and Despair is Resolve: Remembering Roger Simon. *Journal of the Canadian Association for Curriculum Studies* 11 (2), 6–20.

> Can there be a more hopeful way to live historically?[2]
>
> Roger Simon

"[H]ow might remembrance," Roger Simon[3] asked, "be understood as a praxis creating the possibilities of new histories and altered subjectivities?" That is a loaded question, reverberating with echoes of Simon's earlier commitments to "empowerment,"[4] teaching against the grain,[5] and counter-commemoration.[6] Rather than remembrance as intrusion—being reminded of something one might prefer to forget—remembrance is in Simon's question an expression of agency.[7] No voluntaristic action by a socially severed self, remembrance becomes in Simon's sentence a praxis in which thought and action are enacted reciprocally. And it is not self-enclosed, as what is remembered is reconstructed and she or he who remembers is also reconstructed by the encounter. That education is "self-formation," Simon was sure.[8] "[E]ducation is, for me," Simon[9] asserted, "a basic resource for the task of self-constitution."

To act in remembrance within the amnesia of the present—in a culture of narcissism there is no memory[10]—means the reactivation of the past. Reactivation is my term; in Simon's language, it becomes two-pronged: thought and "pedagogic action"[11] that cultivate "historical consciousness."[12] The canonical curriculum question—what knowledge is of most worth?—cannot be answered definitively—that is in part why it is an ongoing pedagogic provocation—but in remembrance knowledge matters. Knowledge cannot be replaced with a skill set standardized tests measure and the "global marketplace" presumably employs. In retrospect, it is painfully clear that our progressive predecessors were too eager to replace knowledge as the center of the curriculum.[13] Knowledge enables remembrance and the reactivation of the past.[14]

The opposite of arrest,[15] to activate means to vitalize, to breathe life into, and be breathed into life. Reactivating the past is engagement with alterity—in this instance the singularity of the past in its distinctive complexity—that sets in motion, well, we can't know.[16] The history Simon and his colleagues emphasize is savage: massacres, mutilation, misery, each episode beyond endurance. Unlike its function for the "history boys," remembrance is no means to upward mobility.[17] Simon's is a more dangerous game than saying something interesting, as those who remember—not just recall for an entrance exam—can be consumed by what is remembered. Perhaps its state as apparently past misleads us into mistaking the present moment as still, even safe. That innocence (or denial) renders the present moment potentially ruthless.

Why, then, this fantasy of "new history"? Sure there will be new smart phones but history's not going to get any better. Is Simon enticing us with that phrase—the "possibilities of new histories"—to make the risk seem worth taking, the risk of remembrance that promises to unleash what is repressed?[18] Perhaps Simon risked remembrance in part because he knew there can be no future—no reparation—without reactivating the past. In remembrance—then at the least we know we are its progeny—there are no innocents only victims, however sweet the deal we've inherited. (With the planet imperiled, no deal will prove sweet enough.) Did Simon risk remembrance to change the subject from identity politics[19] to the victims from whom we cannot profit, even when we are their descendants? Changing the subject means subjective reconstruction, and for me that requires regression to a past occluded in the present, perhaps in autobiographical acts of subjective dissolution.[20]

Ethical engagement with that alterity that is within subjectivity carries its own risks. "It may be objected," Simon[21] knew, "that the reflexivity I suggest as being necessary to the formation of a public memory is a narcissism that turns an engagement with history toward a concern with oneself rather than the concerns of others." Because remembrance—I use regression[22] to emphasize returning to the past rather than recalling it from the present—means self-dissolution, subjectivity becomes the site for social reconstruction, not its substitute. Becoming "deceased,"[23] descendants engage with the legacies they have been bequeathed by accidents of birth, self-shattering as also debt to the dead.

Simon, Rosenberg, and Eppert[24] emphasize the former when they construe "remembrance . . . as a *strategic practice* in which memorial pedagogies are deployed for their sociopolitical value and promise." For the sake of social reconstruction one engages in the self-shattering remembrance regression engenders. This is no one-way street from the present to the past, as "remembrance," Simon, Rosenberg and Eppert point out, is "a *difficult return*, a psychic and social responsibility to bring the dead into presence, a responsibility that concurrently involves learning to live with, and in relation to, loss."[25] The presence of the past—most prominently its causalities disinterred through remembrance—restructures the present[26] as temporal, as inhabited by what we have lost not only by what we hope to gain. Not only the dead live again, but we the living die, dissolved among the dead, returning not unharmed but alive, as we could not have been before.[27]

Remembrance, then, means regression, living with/in loss, returning to what was past, returning to a present we might not now recognize because we are different. Because the present now slips past, we become historical, conscious of our situatedness in what has happened and is happening still. Becoming dated breaks the spell of the screen in front of which we may have forgotten what time it is, what time is, as the endless now of technoculture renders everything eternal in its virtuality.[28] Becoming actual means becoming historical, becoming attuned to the distinctiveness of historical moments, as John Toews[29] details. For both Kierkegaard and Marx, Toews[30] points out, becoming historical meant subjective reconstruction:

> Becoming historical involved a historical reconstruction of the current forms of self-identification—in this case, the reflective egoism of postrevolutionary bourgeois society—as a specific product of human practices in time. The goal was to experience the self that was simply given as a self that was historically particular and contingent. Implicit in this reconstructive activity was a conception of the self as not only product but also producer. . . . Experiencing one's own individual identity as a historical product implied an act, or series of acts, that brought this existing self into being.

Reconstruction, then, enacts agency as it engages the specificities of historical determination.[31] Remembrance *is* agency, enabling understanding of how our—their—determination occurred, understanding that initiates non-coincidence with it. "A response is expected," Simon[32] knew, "everything must be taken into account." We must understand how history happened, and that understanding presents us with our next move.

True, the presence of the past can leave one entranced by what cannot be undone, but Toews' analysis implies that engaging with what our descendants did and what was done to them can make contingent what might have seemed set in stone. The world may not change but its capacity to reproduce itself through us can. Racism remains but its forms mutate; in certain places (psychic[33] and social[34]) it's on the run. In other places it's dug in deep. Subjectively speaking, the circuit starting with Ham (or so the slaveholders and segregationists imagined) can get rerouted—yes even defused in certain spheres—as our soft wiring splinters.[35] In acts of subjective reconstruction one moves between hope—in *Teaching Against the Grain* Simon[36] defines it as "the acknowledgement of more openness in a situation than the situations easily reveals; openness above all to possibilities"—and despair—succumbing to what was as what must be.[37] Resolve is not a strategy; it is ethical conviction.[38] It is, I suggest, the "synthesis" to which "regression" can lead.

No resolution of atrocities, no redistribution of suffering or of ill-gotten gains, resolve registers defiance by remembering contingency. There's no profit in resolve, no return on investment, no "social justice," as if it—like "culturally responsive pedagogy"—could, in one fell swoop, set things right. History—humanity—fantasizes such redemption but admits it is always futural. Like the virtual, the futural isn't actual. Remembrance knows that it is the past that is real. The present is made of it. Begrudging the present requires becoming historical and that means living in the past. Which we can't do, stuck in the mud of the moment we are. So loss is our gain. Remembrance means, Simon, Rosenberg, and Eppert[39] remind, "learning to live with loss, a learning to live with a return of a memory that inevitably instantiates loss and thus bears no ultimate consolation, a learning to live with a disquieting remembrance." Such disquiet—that non-coincidence with what is—can engender resolve, that which is in-between hope and despair.

Notes

1 Pinar 1994, 38–40.
2 Surely this is the crucial question: given its power and horror, how can the past not ruin the future? Can remembering the murdered resurrect hope for a future denied them but etched into our remembrance of them? Simon's sentence leaves the question open, offering us passage between hope and despair: see 2000, 18.
3 2004, 186–187.
4 Simon 1987.
5 Simon 1992.
6 Simon 1993. These concepts and practices anticipate his final magisterial work, *The Touch of the Past*.
7 "The hopeful person," Simon (1992, 3, italics added) emphasized, "does not merely envisage this possibility as a wish; the hopeful person *acts* upon it now by loosening and refusing the hold that taken-for-granted realities and routines have over imagination."
8 1992, 17. "I am working from the assumption," Simon acknowledged, "that education is but one initiative in relation to the process of self-formation, the means through which people attempt to constitute themselves as subjects of their own experience" (1992, 17). That "self" is social and historical, as "there can be no 'fully realized' person beyond and outside the history within which the forms of everyday life have been constructed" (1992, 21).
9 1992, 22. But never only self-constitution, as Simon (2005, 10) emphasizes that "the study of remembrance [is] integral to the possibilities of social transformation." For me the two are interrelated, a fact that at one point Simon (2005, 153) also acknowledges: "This work, this poesis, is the foundation of remembrance as both a personal and social practice."
10 Walter Benjamin, Simon (2005, 137) points out, appreciated that

> the link between memory and experience was being threatened within what he termed a "phantasmagoric" flow of information that resulted in an age well informed about itself but, at the same time knowing very little. Missing was the 'wisdom' of experience, its non-indifference, its transitivity.

11 1992, 82. Here Simon (1992, 98, n. 7) associates "pedagogical action" with "symbolic violence" but his reflection upon the pedagogue's implicatedness in students' "fear of theory" underscores his resolve to reconstruct—Simon uses "transcend"—such violence as a "pedagogy of possibility."
12 "The historical consciousness we refer to here," Simon, Rosenberg, and Eppert (2000, 2) explain, "is not simply a 'state of mind,' the cognitive accumulation that comprises one's knowledge of the past." Not "simply," of course, but it is, they

acknowledge, both "state of mind" and "knowledge." While starting points for Simon, Rosenberg, and Eppert, they are central points for me. Simon, Rosenberg, and Eppert (2000, 2) emphasize its social nature: "[w]e view historical consciousness as always requiring another as an indelibly social praxis, a very determinate set of commitments and actions held and enacted by members of collectivities."

13 "If the curriculum of our schools is to serve its true function," Harold Rugg (1926, 3–4) wrote,

> it must be reconstructed on a two-fold basis. Adequate provision must be made for creative personal development, and tolerant understanding of American life must be erected as the great guiding intellectual goal of education. Its reconstruction, therefore, must concentrate upon two foci—child growth and the dynamic content of American civilization.

While Dewey and many of his colleagues appreciated the interrelatedness of these two foci, here Rugg ignores that it is academic knowledge that enables their reciprocal cultivation.

14 At one point Simon (2000, 10) seems to devalue knowledge:

> What must be signaled at the outset then, is that "historical memory" is not to be conceived singularly as a practice of retention, as the recollection of expressed experiences or grounded narrations of past events. Quite differently, historical memory also includes the potential for a fertile commingling between present consciousness and the staging of evidentiary traces of past presence.

The use of "includes" shows Simon has not discarded "knowledge," but it is the "juxtaposition" (see Simon 2000, 21, 23)—a concept of interest to me as well (2009, 154 n. 13) and others (see Strong-Wilson 2008, 63)—of "evidentiary traces of past and present"—Benjamin's "dialectical images" (Simon 1992, 140)—wherein remembrance's pedagogical potential lies.

15 See Pinar 1994, 38.

16 See Simon 2005, 112.

17 I am thinking of the movie, an adaptation of Alan Bennett's play (2006). Groping aside, Hector is my hero. For the students, it is the juxtaposition of Hector, Irwin, and Dorothy that makes their study of history so stimulating.

18 "Remembrance does not ensure anything," Simon (2005, 110) admits at one point, "least of all justice and compassion."

19 "This essentialization of experience within a form of relationship called identity politics," Simon (1992, 68) knew, "needs careful scrutiny." It needs criticism, as I supplied in the chapter preceding this one.

20 This is, of course, the first step in the autobiographical method of *currere*, but not the last, as futural fantasy (progression), analysis, and synthesis follow in my "praxis" of educational experience (Pinar 1994, 19–27). I theorize its racial enactment in regression to the so-called Curse of Ham (2006; see chapter 11, this volume). While Simon never uses this term—he emphasizes instead history's return to the present rather than our return to the past (see, for instance, Simon, Rosenberg, and Eppert 2000, 3, 4)—he does suggest that "zakhor requires a particular mode of attendance, a particular embodied cognizance necessary to support its pedagogy. What is at issue here is the sensibility with which one engages the stories of others" (Simon 2000, 17). It is that sensibility regression shatters, enabling its reconstruction. Simon (2005, 149) affirms that

> the work of a historiographic poetics will not be "about something," but rather that it will *be* something, a form of remembrance that attempts to clear the way for the arrival of the new, and emergent. This requires a focused conversation

> within which one is enabled to work with and through the dialogical and transferential relations evoked by the transitive demands of testimony.

LaCapra (2009, 124) references "Walter Benjamin's notion of historiography as returning to unrealized possibilities of the past that are worth reactivating in the present." To do so, I suggest, requires reactivating the past by "returning" to it.

21 2004, 197.

22 Regression means reconstruction in its historiographic sense, as laboring to understand the past on—in—its own terms, supplemented by subjective engagement of varying intensities as one grapples with what that distinctive past was. When Simon, Rosenberg, and Eppert (2000, 2) speak of "engagement with the traces of traumatic history" they imply the intensity "regression" allows, but they seem to want memory to "return" to the present (see 2000, 3), rather than us to "return" to the past, as regression encourages. In the third stage of the method of *currere*—analysis (following regression and progression)—there is "mindful attentiveness to, learning from, and participation in the memory of the traces of traumatic history," for Simon, Rosenberg, and Eppert (2000, 3) a matter requiring understanding.

23 Here such "departure from life" means departing the subjective sites presentism installs, thereby "becoming historical," e.g. engaged in the historical present through reactivating the past that is forgotten or repressed within it, including what is forgotten or repressed within oneself.

24 2000, 3.

25 Ibid.

26 It is a matter, Simon, Rosenberg, and Eppert (2000, 5) suggest, of "reopening the present."

27 Will the "the future will be better if one remembers"? Simon, Rosenberg, and Eppert (2000, 4–5) acknowledge "the limits of a consolatory assurance that the past can be discursively integrated into coherent—and pragmatic—contemporary frames of social memory." Limits indeed.

28 "If 'being touched' amounts to a negation of the fragmentation and isolation of experiences," Simon (2005, 136) explains,

> then also redemptive is the contiguity and causality supplied by the historiographic impulse that seeks human continuity within historical narratives. Likewise, connectedness of experience is possible in the context of allegorical or emblematic readings wherein one set of experiences is understood through the representation of another.

I emphasize this point in chapter 2, this volume.

29 2008, 281, 303, 371.

30 2008, 438.

31 Acknowledging the power of determination that reproduction theory proclaimed (for my critique see Pinar 2011, 25–38), Simon (1992, 10) affirmed agency:

> While I do not wish to contest the outlines of this rather bleak picture nor diminish the need for structural change, this view of schools cedes too much. The current hegemony over how schooling is to be done remains a project, not an accomplishment. Within the spaces that do exist in certain schools, courses of study, and classrooms, this hegemony has been and is being contested by students, teachers, and parents who remain genuinely hopeful that pedagogies which support social transformation can be realized.

That agency is not individualistic but formed and expressed in solidarity (see 1992, 66–69). But, he noted, "it makes little sense to consider the notion of social forms abstractly, outside the context of history" (1992, 21). While not using the word, "reconstruction" seems to me to be what Simon (1992, 139) has in mind in his pedagogy of possibility, which he links to the work of Walter Benjamin:

> He [Benjamin] begins to formulate the epistemological outlines of one aspect of what might be recognized as a pedagogy of possibility. This was a practice that did not require the obliteration of the past and its replacement with a new "truth," but rather a fundamental reconfiguration [reconstruction] and rereading of the documents of tradition in a way that might help "reveal the present as a revolutionary moment."

32 2004, 184.
33 "The possibility of hope," Simon (2000, 17) argues, "depends on our capacities for providing a psychic locus of such stories, a locus that requires we take up the stories of others with in the pedagogical dynamics of zakhor."
34 See McCarthy, Bulut, and Patel 2014.
35 Mica Nava (2007) shows how racism can mutate into eroticism even cosmopolitanism. Racism remains but surely sex is to preferable to violence (even though the two are hardly mutually exclusive).
36 1992, 3.
37 In his study of the cultural catastrophe European settlement of North America precipitated, Lear (2006, 152) focuses on Plenty Coups, the last great chief of the Crow nation:

> Plenty Coups had to acknowledge the destruction of a *telos*—that the old ways of living a good life were gone. And that acknowledgement involved the stark recognition that the traditional ways of structuring significance—of recognizing something as happening—had been devastated. For Plenty Coups, this recognition was not an expression of despair; it was the only way to avoid it.

Plenty Coups required no regression; he was immersed in the past and lived its self-shattering destruction. What was required of him, and what he achieved (as Lear makes plain) was facing up to this crushing historical reality and somehow working it through psychically and culturally: subjective reconstruction provided the only path to move through the ruins. That undertaking—between hope and despair—requires the courage that congeals into resolve.

38 "At stake," Simon (2005, 5) reminds, "is whether one is able to realize the responsibilities of an ethical relation to past lives, traced through that testament of disaster that does not efface its own historical disfiguration."
39 2000, 4.

Bibliography

Bennett, Alan. 2006. *The History Boys*. London: Faber & Faber.

LaCapra, Dominick. 2009. *History and Its Limits: Human, Animal, Violence*. Ithaca, NY: Cornell University Press.

Lear, Jonathan. 2006. *Radical Hope: Ethics in the Face of Cultural Devastation*. Cambridge, MA: Harvard University Press.

McCarthy, Cameron, Bulut, Ergin, and Patel, Rushika. 2014. Race and Education in the Age of Digital Capitalism. In *The International Handbook of Curriculum Research*, edited by William F. Pinar (32–44). [Second edition.] New York: Routledge.

Nava, Mica. 2007. *Visceral Cosmopolitanism: Gender, Culture and the Normalization of Difference*. Oxford and New York: Berg.

Pinar, William F. 1994. *Autobiography, Politics, and Sexuality: Essays in Curriculum Theory, 1972–1992*. New York: Peter Lang.

Pinar, William F. 2006. *Race, Religion, and a Curriculum of Reparation*. New York: Palgrave.
Pinar, William F. 2009. *The Worldliness of a Cosmopolitan Education: Passionate Lives in Public Service*. New York: Routledge.
Pinar, William F. 2011. *The Character of Curriculum Studies: Bildung, Currere, and the Recurring Question of the Subject*. New York: Palgrave Macmillan.
Rugg, Harold. 1926. The School Curriculum and the Drama of American Life. In *The Twenty-Sixth Yearbook of the National Society for the Study of Education. The Foundations and Technique of Curriculum-Construction.* Part I: *Curriculum-Making: Past and Present*, edited by Guy Montrose Whipple (3–16). Bloomington, IL: Public School Publishing Company.
Simon, Roger. 1987, April. Empowerment as a Pedagogy of Possibility. *Language Arts* 64 (4).
Simon, Roger. 1992. *Teaching Against the Grain*. South Hadley, MA: Bergin & Garvey.
Simon, Roger. 1993. Forms of Insurgency in the Production of Popular Memories: The Columbus Quincentenary and the Pedagogy of Counter Commemoration. In *Between Borders: Pedagogy and the Politics of Cultural Studies*, edited by Henry A. Giroux and Peter McLaren (127–142). New York: Routledge.
Simon, Roger. 1998, June. The Contribution of Holocaust Audio-Video Testimony to Remembrance, Learning and Hope. *International Journal of Audio-Visual Testimony*, 141–152.
Simon, Roger I. 2000. The Paradoxical Practice of Zakhor: Memories of "What Has Never Been My Fault or My Deed. In *Between Hope and Despair: Pedagogy and the Remembrance of Historical Trauma*, edited by Roger I. Simon, Sharon Rosenberg, and Claudia Eppert (9–25). Lanham, MD: Rowman & Littlefield.
Simon, Roger. 2004. The Pedagogical Insistence of Public Memory. In *Theorizing Historical Consciousness,* edited by Peter Seixas, (183–201). Toronto: University of Toronto Press.
Simon, Roger I. 2005. *The Touch of the Past: Remembrance, Learning, and Ethics*. New York: Palgrave Macmillan.
Simon, Roger and Dippo, Don. 1980. Dramatic Analysis: Interpretive Inquiry for the Transformation of Social Settings. *JCT* 2 (1), 109–134.
Simon, Roger and Dippo, Don. 1986. On Critical Ethnographic Work. *Anthropology and Education Quarterly* 17 (4), 195–202.
Simon, Roger, Rosenberg, Sharon, and Eppert, Claudia. (eds.) 2000. *Between Hope and Despair: Pedagogy and the Remembrance of Historical Trauma*. Lanham, MD: Rowman & Littlefield.
Strong-Wilson, Teresa. 2007. *Bringing Memory Forward*. New York: Peter Lang.
Toews, John. 2004. *Becoming Historical: Cultural Reformation and Public Memory in Early Nineteenth-Century Berlin*. New York: Cambridge University Press.

CHAPTER 15

DECOLONIZATION

Commentary

There are those who have testified—who testify today—to what is at stake in the subjective and social reconstruction decolonization requires. To engage in decolonization, Frantz Fanon appreciated that one must not only politically repudiate the colonizing regime, one must also participate in the subjective and social challenge of constructing a postcolonial civil society. Through the self-conscious reconstruction of his own interpellation, Fanon understood that the political, social, and the subjective were inextricably interrelated.

Bibliography

Pinar, William F. 2011. *The Character of Curriculum Studies. Bildung, Currere, and the Recurring Question of the Subject* (39–48). New York: Palgrave Macmillan.

> Fanon's current fascination for us has something to do with the convergence of the problematic of colonialism with that of subject-formation.
>
> Henry Louis Gates, Jr.[1]

> The time has indeed come to remember Fanon.
>
> Ato Sekyi-Otu[2]

Minus self-knowledge, resistance to power risks becoming a repetition compulsion. Stripped of subjectivity and historicity, power becomes a projection that only reproduces itself. There is something "there" all right, but without addressing the apparatus that experiences the "something" and the "there," reality reduces to social currents that only sweep one away. Floundering in a sea of sociality, action becomes quixotic, as one's voice becomes increasingly shrill as one moves farther away from shore. That shore is self-knowledge, never a completed project, always retrospective if a provocation of a painful present. It is never self-identical, however intimate and singular its contents and structures, and it is never still, as new knowledge, experience, and the pull of the present require ongoing reconstruction. In such reconstruction—simultaneously subjective and social—one activates agency, as one commits to the ongoing study of the past, a "regression" that enables one's entry into the future. In becoming subjective, one becomes historical. One develops character, one becomes a subject, and the canonical curriculum question—*what knowledge is of most worth?*—recurs.

That question is washed away in preoccupations with "the social" that devalue the specificity of historical experience, its lived and genealogical character, its political and personal meanings. Self-knowledge requires social knowledge, requires attending to what is happening around as well as in one, knowledge that is simultaneously subjective and historical, as the present is itself never identical with itself, is always the latest wave washed ashore, carrying us away, miles from where we began, miles away from where the wave began. Such images become concrete in specific lives, in all lives that are necessarily specific, however standardized the molds others construct. Molds never stay outside the skin, but seep through, and so resistance to power requires self-conscious scrutiny of one's inner life as the "enemy" is also within. There are heroic individuals who have testified—who testify today—to what is at stake in such subjective reconstruction, one form of which is decolonization.

One such heroic individual was Frantz Fanon. Coming-of-age in French colonized Martinique, Fanon knew firsthand the psychological trauma of "being objectified, stigmatized, and thus humiliated into consciousness."[3] To engage in decolonization, Fanon appreciated that one must not only politically repudiate the colonizing regime, but also one must participate in an ongoing process of self-negation.[4] Political resistance, even when victorious in collective terms, is insufficient: what is also necessary is subjective reconstruction, extricating oneself psychologically from interpellation by the colonizing regime. And that interpellation may have occurred for generations of indigenous peoples, installing at the deepest psychic levels tendencies toward mimesis that portend self-contradiction, even self-destruction. Through the self-conscious recovery of his own interpellation—accomplished initially through academic study in France—Fanon understood that the political and the psychological, the subjective and the social, were inextricably interrelated. No reproduction theory for Fanon.

Autobiography—the regressive-progressive-analytic-synthetic method of *currere*[5]—can be political when it disables, through remembrance and reconstruction, colonization through interpellation. By affirming the capacity to restructure one's subjectivity, autobiography disentangles us from absorption into collectives—even when presumably these are self-affirming cultural identities. Indeed, I share Edward Said's[6] lament over the narcissism of identity politics: "Identity, always identity, over and above knowing about others." Contradicting autobiography's association with the U.S. cult of individualism, I have invoked the method of *currere* to perform a collective autobiography, a process of intersubjective negation (through self-criticism) and reconstruction (toward political mobilization), tracing the history of the nightmare that is the present for U.S. schoolteachers and education professors. Continuing to emphasize the centrality of academic knowledge in self-formation, I work from intellectual history to restructure the autobiographical demand as curriculum development[7] conceived as allegories of the present.[8] The juxtaposition of the past and the present, the subjective and the social, can produce the shock of self-engagement that Weimar critic Siegfried Kracauer associated with progressive film.[9]

In "teaching the postcolonial,"[10] we study, then, not only the social forces that structure reality, as these confine us to the surface of the present, itself consuming through dispersing our subjective coherence. To escape the present and its disintegrative presentism, we must flee to the past; from there we can find the future. In the lives and work of those heroic individuals who struggled for freedom and independence against colonial regimes, we can engage in the subjective and social reconstruction of the subjects we have been interpellated to be. In the struggles of postcolonial artists and intellectuals, Greg Dimitriadis and Cameron McCarthy[11] found that "there is always an effort to link individual will and fortune to collective possibility." Surely the three are inextricably intertwined. For Fanon, there could be no collective possibility without subjective and social reconstruction.

The Revolutionary

> The liberation of the individual does not follow national liberation. An authentic national liberation exists only to the precise degree to which the individual has irreversibly begun his own liberation.
>
> Frantz Fanon[12]

> To repair oneself, burdened with an identity that has been constructed (in proslavery language, black = "slave"), is to *dis-identify* with it.
>
> Françoise Verges[13]

On December 6, 1961, Frantz Fanon died in the United States. Born on July 20, 1925, on Martinique, educated in France to become a psychiatrist, Fanon became a militant during the Algerian Revolution of 1954–1962. It was in colonized Algeria, where he had been assigned to a psychiatric hospital, that he experienced his political awakening, and it was through the Algerian Revolution that he came to theorize the meaning of such subjective and political struggle for liberation. Such struggle was allegorical, simultaneously specific and universal. "The battle of Algeria," Irene Gendzier[14] suggests, "became for him the battle for man." The war for Algerian independence required decolonization, restructuring Algerians' social (including gender) relations with one another and with France.

Fanon maintained his conviction, Gendzier tells us, that the struggle for self-understanding and reconstitution is integral to if not identical with the struggle for a people's political independence. In a hectic, violent, and brief lifetime, Frantz Fanon wrote four books that serve as a powerful record of the psychological and materials costs of colonization and decolonization.[15]

Fanon's writings were first appreciated within the European civilization that he so cogently criticized.[16] These writings become testaments for U.S. black revolutionaries (among them, the Black Panthers)[17] who considered African Americans members of the Third World.[18] The white middle class, including conservatives who read Fanon from their own racial anxiety, studied him carefully. *Time Magazine* listed Fanon's last book, *The Wretched of the Earth*, as one of the five most important books of the 1960s.[19] "More than any other thinker," bell hooks[20] reports, "he [Fanon] provided me with a model for insurgent black intellectual life that has shaped my work."[21]

Strongly influenced by Nietzsche and Freud,[22] and like his contemporaries Sartre and Camus, Fanon was par excellence the organic intellectual *engagé*, a "great philosopher," in Lewis Gordon's judgment.[23] The duty of the revolutionary intellectual, Fanon believed, is to integrate oneself into the interior of, through working dialogically with, the people. Speeches to the masses are insufficient, he judged. The peasantry is quite capable, he insisted,[24] of progressive political activity if the proper questions are posed to them: "[P]olitical education means opening their minds, awakening them, and allowing the birth of their intelligence; as Césaire said, it is to 'invent souls.'"[25]

Fanon has been acclaimed as the "prophet of revolution," an original thinker who "is to Africa what Lenin is to Europe, or Mao to Asia." Others[26] compared him to Ché Guevara; many pronounced him a contemporary Karl Marx. Some declare he was a "humanist," a "socialist," and a "passionate internationalist," and others denounced him as a "nihilist," "an apostle of violence," and a "prisoner of hate," as did the April 30, 1965, issue of *Time Magazine*. *The Wretched of the Earth* has been likened to both Marx and Engels's *The Communist Manifesto* and Hitler's *Mein Kampf* (*Time*, same issue); the book was, some said, the black man's "Revolutionary Bible."[27] While many philosophers would dispute the claim that Fanon was a great philosopher, few would contest that he was, also in Lewis Gordon's[28] judgment, "one of the most influential [intellectuals] of the twentieth century."

Early in his life, Gendzier suggests, Fanon concluded that he needed to understand himself as he was. Self-knowledge included grasping how the world looked at him: his interpellation. To change the world required understanding the world. Only through such understanding, Fanon realized, might he grasp the world's absurdities as well as the possibilities of its transformation. To write could become a form of action, Fanon knew. In its subjective origins, writing is self-focused and reflexive, but in its social expression, writing becomes outward-reaching, engaging the world. By its very nature, writing is, Fanon appreciated, an effort to communicate, to teach.[29] As he frankly faced his situation—a Martiniquean whitened by colonization but always black in the eyes of the colonizer—Fanon testified to his subjective experience of racialization, experience he knew he shared with others. While theoretical in character, his works are strongly autobiographical. Like U.S. slaves who wrote narrative histories,[30] Fanon wrote to understand himself and mobilize others. These are intersecting projects.

Subjective Struggle as Revolutionary Activity

> To Fanon, there is a continuity between individual and political freedom.
>
> Françoise Verges[31]

> For Fanon, true liberation is the achievement of subjectivity.
>
> Terry Goldie[32]

Fanon employed psychiatric research into the incidence and forms of personality disorders to understand certain cultural and political elements of the historical process.[33] Only through the medium of human personality, Fanon thought, could one understand the colonial experience. By conceiving psychiatry as a political action, his psychology of colonialism departed sharply from practice common at that time. Many psychiatrists rejected the possibility that mental illness could follow from class position or social experience, that individuals could become ill *because* they are politically powerless and racially loathed.[34]

In contrast to most Europeans, many North Africans did not regard the pathological person as responsible for his illness. The patient was taken to be an innocent victim of spirits (genies) over which she or he had no control.[35] To grasp Algerians' experience of mental illness, Fanon began to study the basic features of Algerian life, including the centrality of religion and family in Algerian culture. Fanon studied Arabic; by the end of 1956, he could understand most of what patients were telling him. Fanon's respect for traditional cultural beliefs ended, however, when they interfered with what he regarded as responsible psychiatric methods.[36]

In his resignation letter to Robert Lacoste, resident minister of Algeria, Fanon complained that the Algerian had become an "alien" in his own country, driven to "desperate" acts due to the "absolute depersonalization" French governance had inflicted.[37] Fanon's letter of resignation was answered by an order of expulsion. Within two days, Fanon and his close associates departed what would later (after 1962) be named the Frantz Fanon Hospital.[38]

Fanon integrated the roles of the intellectual and the political activist in the Algerian cause. The reflective "I" that had animated *Black Skin, White Masks* became the committed "we" of identification with the Algerians. Fanon's singular contribution to the cause of the Algerian independence at this time was, Emmanuel Hansen[39] believes, the internationalization of the Algerian struggle. Through his journalistic and theoretical writings, Fanon characterized the war not only as an Arab nationalist movement; it was also, he insisted, a catalytic event in the liberation of Africa. At the time of his death, however, Fanon concluded that there had been no effective liberation because there had been no decolonization: internalized psychic colonial structures had not been destroyed. What happened at independence, he lamented, was simply the Africanization of colonialism.[40]

To destroy colonialism, Fanon concluded that violence was necessary. Violence destroys not only the formal institutional structures of colonial rule but, as well, the alienated consciousness—what William J. McGrath,[41] in another context, terms the "psychic polity"—that colonial rule had implanted in the native.[42] For Fanon, violence was morally justified because it transformed the colonized psychically as well as politically. "Decolonization destroys both colonizer and colonized," in Samira Kawash's[43] paraphrase of Fanon, "in its wake, something altogether different and unknown, a 'new humanity,' will rise up." Without such destruction, colonialism would reappear in the political and social life of the newly independent nations.

To address psychic alienation required political action *and* a restructuring of the colonized character of the individual. What was necessary was the eradication of those noneconomic—psychic, mythological—mechanisms that sustained racism.[44] In addition to destroying the economic foundations of colonialism, Fanon insisted, it was imperative to demolish the cultural and subjective residues of that history.[45] Unsurprisingly, then, Fanon was interested in the role of schooling in racism. He argued that in the cultural matrix of white society—he was referring specifically to the French and Martiniquean societies of his lifetime—schooling channeled racial aggression into socially acceptable forms. Children's games, psychodramas, some folktales, and other school activities provided, he thought, forms of racial catharsis, the social expulsion of collective anxieties. In many stories written for white children, the characters symbolizing fear and evil were represented by Indians or blacks. Racism infiltrates everything, Fanon knew. The destruction of racism was not possible as long as schools simply rechanneled it.[46]

Decolonization meant, then, not only fundamental social, cultural, and economic restructuring, but political education as well.[47] Fanon rejected Marxism; it reduced psychology to economics. He had no faith that shifts in the spheres of production and ownership would lead to shifts in consciousness. For Fanon, Zahar[48] points out, the political process of decolonization can be realized only when the psychological mechanisms produced by colonialism are destroyed. Fanon linked decolonization to processes of self-immersion and Dionysian descent, McCulloch argues, forms of self-understanding achieved through self-negation and consequent subjective restructuring. Only through such self-shattering can internalized racism be destroyed.

Fanon worked through image and fantasy—"those orders that figure transgressively on the borders of history and the unconscious"[49]—in order to contest colonial conditions. He articulated the problems of colonialism in the psychoanalytic language of demand and desire. In so doing, Bhabha explains, Fanon radically questioned the formation of both individual and social authority as they appear in Western discourses of sovereignty. In Bhabha's[50] words: "[F]ebrile, phantasmatic images of racial hatred . . . come to be absorbed and acted out in the wisdom of the West. These [are] interpositions, indeed collaborations of political and psychic violence within civic virtue, alienation within identity." This intrapsychic violence of civic self-formation was evident not only in colonized regions, but in the colonizing nation-states themselves.

Fanon argued that colonialism produced reverberations the colonial powers could not escape. These were "boomerang" effects, the importation of those violent practices, attitudes, and institutions exported by the colonizing bourgeois ruling classes. For Fanon, Fascism and Nazism were internalized—self-directed—expressions of Europe's colonial violence.[51] These boomerang effects disclosed that racism was, finally, a form of masochism, political as well as psychic. Indeed, Fanon equated racism with masochism.[52] The boomerang effects of colonialism's masochism constitute "blowback," a term employed by some to characterize the terrorist attacks of September 11, 2001.[53] Like reproduction and resistance, "blowback" is insufficient an explanation, as it obscures religious and subjective sources of violence. Specific individuals committed to jihad undertook this violence against humanity.

The Here and Now

> Fanon's postcolonial imagination is a challenge: an insistence that one confront the here and now.
>
> Nigel Gibson[54]

> Fanon's contemporary urgency is thoroughly bound up with the way his memory—precisely in its menaced and even contested character—represents for us the state of specifically cultural emergency in which we find ourselves.
>
> John Mowitt[55]

Rather than trying to capture the authentic Fanon, Stuart Hall[56] admonishes us to "engage in the after-life of Frantz Fanon." For Hall, that means (after Derrida) dwelling in Fanon's "spectral effect," facing the present in its "moment of danger."[57] While that danger remains associated with terrorism, for me that "moment of danger" is the political present in the United States, a period like interwar Germany riddled by antidemocratic movements, among them political "conservatism" and Christian fundamentalism, not always intersecting phenomena.[58] The "boomerang effects" of imperialism abroad include continuing assaults on democracy at home.

In the ongoing political crisis of the (dis)United States, the nation's originary tendencies toward unregulated capitalism and religious extremism now take the form of "preemptive strikes," aimed at both domestic and foreign targets. This predatory America has now become politically polarized, thanks to the intensification of right-wing reaction, including aggressive disinformation[59] campaigns of so-called conservatives. While its aggressive foreign policy has been moderated under President Barack Obama, the nation's economic instability intensifies as the effects—high unemployment, an unsustainable national debt, and increasing economic inequality—of the Great Recession (itself the result of mass violence: the invasion of Iraq and a deregulated financial industry free to fleece not only the general public but investors as well) intensify. "We are living," Peck[60] warns, "through a slow-motion catastrophe, one that could stain our culture and weaken our nation for many, many years to come."

Memories are short, however, as the intensification of daily life, the psychically disintegrative effects of the information technologies, and pervasive standardized testing in the schools erases the capacity to situate subjectivity historically. The three-decades-long federal government's assault on public schools continues by emphasizing standardized tests that measure intellectually vacuous "skills," devoid of intellectual content, thereby institutionalizing historical amnesia, eviscerating creativity and critical thinking, as both require subjective attunement to the historical moment.[61] The American Federation of Teachers' proposal of a common curriculum[62] is, in my view, a desperate if reasonable effort to blunt the anti-intellectual, neo-fascist authoritarianism of U.S. school deform.

Perhaps future generations will judge my generation with contempt. Perhaps, after Fanon, we should take up armed struggle against the neo-fascists in our midst. In confessing my disinclination to take up arms—except rhetorically—am I acknowledging my moral failure and lack of political courage? Or am I expressing my commitment to nonviolence? What I do know is that I feel keenly—as did Bhabha[63] —that "remembering Fanon is a process of intense discovery and disorientation. It is painful re-membering, a putting together of the dismembered past to make sense of the trauma of the present." To make sense of the present historical moment—political polarization, economic destabilization, and the impending climate crisis—I study and teach the past, determined to find there a passage to a future forced from factuality by neoconservative colonists of the homeland. "For Fanon shows us," Kawash[64] points out, "decolonization is not an event that happens in history; it is rather the shattering of that history and the opening to an otherwise that cannot be given in advance, but that is always, like justice, to come." Staring at screens, can we discern what is to come?

Notes

1 1991, 458.
2 1996, 10.
3 Chow 2002, 183.
4 Even self-shattering: Pinar 2006b, 180–183.
5 These subjectively restructuring temporal phases are, I am suggesting, also political practices that enact Fanon's emphasis upon the subjective reconstitution of the social in his revolutionary thought.
6 1993, 299.
7 Pinar 2006a, 180 n. 3.
8 Pinar 2012, 49.
9 Levin 1995, 26.
10 See Dimitriadis and McCarthy 2001.
11 2001, 21.
12 1967b, 103.
13 1999, 267.
14 1973, vi.
15 These four books—listed in the references—remain influential today. "The current engagement with issues of coloniality/postcoloniality is," Teresa Ebert (1995, 220 n. 1) emphasizes, "deeply indebted to the work of Fanon although Fanon often becomes the 'unsaid' of these discourses." I trust this chapter contributes to rendering Frantz Fanon "said" in postcolonial discourses in North American curriculum studies.
16 Among those Europeans who took Fanon seriously was Roland Barthes, whose 1957 *Mythologies* theorized how "innocent" or well-intentioned citizens reproduce those forms-of-being that support colonialism. Barthes constructed an inventory of the psychosocial forms around which consciousness becomes constituted as "white," middle class, and, especially, racially supremacist (see Sandoval 1997, 86). Sandoval (1997, 88) positions Barthes as "one of the first white Western critical theorists to develop an analytical apparatus for theorizing white consciousness in a postcolonial world." In my genealogical study of whiteness, I labor to contribute to this very project (2006b).
17 See, for example, Haymes 1995, 16.
18 Influence did not travel only one way. Fanon was also influenced by African American writers, among them Richard Wright, to whom he wrote expressing his admiration for Wright's work and his interest in conducting an in-depth study of it, requesting titles he might have missed (see Fabre 1991, 191).
19 See Geismar 1971.
20 1996, 85.
21 Due to the polemical character of his writing, Fanon has sometimes been dismissed as a writer of only political consequence. Some cite the political character of his work in order to forgive even the most obvious problems that plague his most popular writings. McCulloch (1983, 205) positions himself in-between: "Unfortunately Fanon's style has encouraged a preoccupation with his biography and with specific aspects of his theory, to the detriment of a recognition of his major intellectual achievement." For me, it is the relations *among* his life history, intellectual activism, and accomplishment that render Fanon such an intriguing figure.
22 See Bhabha 1989.
23 1995, 2. While a medical student at Lyons, Fanon somehow found time to study philosophy and literature. He attended the lectures of philosophers Jean Lacroix and Maurice Merleau-Ponty while he studied Kierkegaard, Nietzsche, Hegel, Marx and Lenin, Husserl, Heidegger, and Sartre (see Zahar 1974, ix).
24 As would Freire: see 1968.
25 Fanon 1968, 197. Like Foucault, Ewa Plonowska Ziarek (2001, 38) points out, "Fanon associates political action with the invention of new modes of life," arguing

that "aesthetic self-relation does not close the circle of self-reflexivity of the knowing subject but intensifies the force of dispersion and discordance within the subject." Indeed, such dispersed and discordant self-reflexivity—both the prerequisite and consequence of subjective reconstruction—"opens the passage to pure exteriority," as "the self-relation is at the same time an interruption of all relatedness." Simply said, without subjective reconstruction, decolonization cannot occur and vice versa. Ato Sekyi-Otu (see 1996, 6), however, disputes this formulation of a reciprocal relation between the two, insisting that, for Fanon, "the psychic and the psychological deserve in the 'colonial context' the status of dependent rather than determining realities." In this view, only after political liberation does self-decolonization matter. Without it, liberation cannot be institutionalized. I do not doubt that subjective reconstruction matters differently at different historical conjunctures in different revolutionary situations. Whenever it most usefully occurs—before or after or during political liberation—my point is that it must occur. Otherwise—as Fanon predicted—we suffer the reinscription of colonialism disguised by black masks. Contemporary Uganda and Zimbabwe are among the many contemporary examples of the catastrophic failure of Africans to decolonize subjectively after political independence.

26 See, for example, Caute 1970.

27 Geismar 1971, 2; other passages quoted in Bulhan 1985, 5–6.

28 1995, ix.

29 Fanon was preoccupied, Irene Gendzier (1973, 29–30) tells us, with "two questions," both centered on communication. One was the question of communication between men, and second was the question of communication between men of "different color." Communication was undermined by objectification and possession, ideas elaborated by Sartre, whose work Fanon studied and admired. Part of Fanon's contribution is his racialization of those philosophical concepts. There are controversies over Fanon's gendering of such communication (see Sharpley-Whiting 1998).

30 See, for instance, Butterfield 1974.

31 1996, 49.

32 1999, 79.

33 In McCulloch's view (1983, 131), Fanon was never entirely successful in integrating his practice as a clinical psychiatrist with his commitment to African socialism.

34 See McCulloch 1983; Verges 1996.

35 See Bulhan 1985.

36 See Geismar 1971; Verges 1996.

37 Quoted in Gendzier 1973, 98.

38 See Gendzier 1973.

39 1977.

40 See Hansen 1977, 50; Sekyi-Otu 1996, 12.

41 1986, 230.

42 See Hansen 1977; Gibson 2003.

43 1999, 237–238.

44 See McCulloch 1983, 84; see also Sandoval 1997, 100.

45 See McCulloch 1983; Gibson 2003.

46 See Gendzier 1973.

47 See Hansen 1977, 119; Sekyi-Otu 1996, 122.

48 See 1974, xxi.

49 Bhabha 1989, 136.

50 1989, 137.

51 See Jinadu 1986, 25.

52 See Young-Bruehl 1996, 497.

53 "Blowback" is a CIA term first used in March 1954 in a recently declassified report on the 1953 operation to overthrow the government of Mohammed Mossadegh in Iran. It is a metaphor for the unintended consequences of the U.S. government's

international interventions that have been kept secret from the American people. Article posted on September 27, 2001 (October 15, 2001, issue): "Blowback by Chalmers Johnson." Retrieved on July 9, 2006, from: www.thenation.com/doc/20011015/johnson

54 2003, 204–205.

55 1999, 96.

56 1996, 14.

57 Ibid.

58 I employ scare quotes around the word to underscore that there is nothing conservative about many U.S. "conservatives," radical revisionists of American history (lying about the founding fathers' religious convictions, for instance), of Christianity as well (replacing the spiritual piety and humility of that tradition with self-righteous intolerance and political aggressivity), and of democracy (now construed as the opportunity to bilk the poor, provide welfare for the rich, and institutionalize a predatory capitalist culture of commodity fetishism). "Conservative" political tactics sacrifice democratic dialogue for political advantage; in their demonizing of politically vulnerable minorities, they are reminiscent of fascists' tactics 80 years ago in Germany. Here they are performed by neo-fascists American-style (John Yoo and Dick Cheney come to mind, but Michelle Bachman and Glenn Beck are examples as well). Many white southern Republican congressmen and senators amount to neo-Confederates. These two anti-American traditions were savagely combined in George W. Bush. Both are now evident in the mob psychology of the Tea Party Movement (Lilla 2010, 53).

59 Fox News is the most conspicuous site of disinformation in North America, but its disregard for facts is surely matched by the pronouncements of school deform fanatics and profiteers, who insist that teachers, not students, are accountable for students' educational achievement, and who convert the complicated conversation that is the school curriculum into cramming for standardized tests measuring intellectually vacuous "skills." As (I write in April 2011) Republican-dominated state legislatures not only strip public school budgets but also limit or eliminate historically established rights to collective bargaining—could a more explicit assault on teachers be made?—officials continue to lie. "This is in no way, shape or form an attack on teachers; it is a comprehensive effort to reform a system," offered Tony Bennett, the superintendent of public instruction in Indiana. There, in Indianapolis, demonstrators besieged the Capitol in opposition to bills supported by Dr. Bennett and Gov. Mitch Daniels, a Republican, that would limit teachers' collective bargaining, allow principals to set class sizes and school hours, and to lay off teachers based on job performance, not years of service (Gabriel 2011, A18). As in colonial servitude, knowledge and experience are irrelevant. A longtime participant—Chester Finn—in school deform predictably blames the victim:

> They are reaping a bitter harvest that they didn't individually plant but their profession has planted over 50 years, going from a respected profession to a mass work force in which everyone is treated as if they are interchangeable, as in the steel mills of yesteryear. (quoted in Gabriel 2011, A18)

The consequence is clear—destruction of a profession that teaches in the public interest—but the cause is glossed. The profession was targeted by the right wing, starting with Richard Nixon's demand that schools go "back to the basics" (see Pinar 2012, chapter 3). Curiously, that "argument" is no relic, as it was invoked by Republican Bob Huff of San Bernadino, who criticized a bill in the California state senate requiring students to learn gay history; "[H]e worried that the bill would water down the state curriculum and distract students from learning the basics" (Medina 2011, A11).

60 2010, 56.

61 The emergency of daily life—wherein experience "[c]an neither be possessed nor internalized . . . too 'large' to be contained within the boundaries of the individual self or ego" (Foster 2005, 176)—is the context of my study of cosmopolitanism (2009).

62 While for decades I have opposed a national curriculum—as at the university, school curriculum, I have argued, should be determined by teachers in consultation with university professors and representatives of the general public—this specific proposal seems defensible in light of the erasure of academic knowledge by standardized testing focused on "skills." Indeed, the statement signed by a bipartisan group (including Randi Weingarten, president of the federation, and prominent Democrats, including Richard W. Riley, secretary of education under President Clinton; several Republicans also signed, including former governor Tom Kean of New Jersey; Chester E. Finn, Jr., an assistant secretary of education under President Ronald Reagan; and Susan B. Neuman, an assistant secretary of education under President George W. Bush) excludes "performance standards, textbook offerings, daily lesson plans or rigid pedagogical prescriptions." A "sequential set of guidelines in the core academic disciplines," the national curriculum guidelines "would account for about 50 to 60 percent of a school's available academic time with the rest added by local communities, districts and states" (quoted in Dillon 2011, A12). This stipulation protects academic—intellectual—freedom. Conspicuously absent from the original signers is former school deformer Diane Ravitch (2010, 231), who has been a strong advocate of a national curriculum.

63 1990, 206.

64 1999, 256.

Bibliography

Bhabha, Homi K. 1989. Remembering Fanon: Self, Psyche, and the Colonial Condition. In *Remaking History*, edited by Barbara Kruger and Phil Mariani (131–148). Seattle, WA: Bay Press.

Bhabha, Homi K. 1990. Interrogating Identity: The Postcolonial Prerogative. In *Anatomy of Racism*, edited by David Theo Goldberg (183–209). Minneapolis: University of Minnesota Press.

Bulhan, Hussein Abdilahi. 1985. *Frantz Fanon and the Psychology of Oppression*. New York: Plenum Press.

Butterfield, Stephen. 1974. *Black Autobiography in America*. Amherst: University of Massachusetts Press.

Caute, David. 1970. *Frantz Fanon*. New York: Viking.

Chow, Rey. 2002. *The Protestant Ethnic & the Spirit of Capitalism*. New York: Columbia University Press.

Dillon, Sam. 2011, March 7. Bipartisan Group Backs Common School Curriculum. *New York Times*, A12.

Dimitriadis, Greg and McCarthy, Cameron. 2001. *Reading & Teaching the Postcolonial: From Baldwin to Basquiat and Beyond*. New York: Teachers College Press.

Ebert, Teresa L. 1995. Subalterity and Feminism in the Moment of the (Post) Modern: The Materialist Return. In *Order and Partialities: Theory, Pedagogy, and the "Postcolonial,"* edited by Kostas Myrsiades and Jerry McGuire (203–227). Albany: State University of New York Press.

Fabre, Michel. 1991. *From Harlem to Paris: Black American Writers in France, 1840–1980*. Urbana: University of Illinois Press.

Fanon, Frantz. 1967a. *Black Skin, White Masks*. [Trans. Charles Lam Markmann.] New York: Grove Weidenfeld. [Originally published in French under the title *Peau Noire, Masques Blancs*, copyright 1952 by Editions du Seuil, Paris.]

Fanon, Frantz. 1967b. *Toward the African Revolution*. [Trans. Hakkon Chevalier.] New York: Grove Press. [Originally published in France under the title *Pour la Revolution Africaine*, 1964, by François Maspero.]

Fanon, Frantz. 1967c. *A Dying Colonialism*. [Trans. Haakon Chevalier.] New York: Grove Press.

Fanon, Frantz. 1968. *The Wretched of the Earth*. [Preface by Jean-Paul Sartre. Trans. Constance Farrington.] New York: Grove Press. [Originally published by François Maspero éditeur, Paris, France, under the title *Les damnés de la terre*, 1961.]

Foster, Thomas. 2005. *The Souls of Cyberfolk: Posthumanism as Vernacular Theory*. Minneapolis: University of Minnesota Press.

Freire, Paulo. 1968. *Pedagogy of the Oppressed*. New York: Seabury.

Gabriel, Trip. 2011, March 3. Teachers Wonder, Why the Heapings of Scorn? *New York Times*, A1, A18.

Gates, Henry Louis, Jr. 1991. Critical Fanonism. *Critical Inquiry* 17 (3), 457–470.

Geismar, Peter. 1971. *Fanon*. New York: The Dial Press.

Gendzier, Irene L. 1973. *Frantz Fanon: A Critical Study*. New York: Pantheon Books.

Gibson, Nigel C. 2003. *Fanon: The Postcolonial Imagination*. Cambridge: Polity.

Goldie, Terry. 1999. Saint Fanon and Homosexual Territory. In *Frantz Fanon: Critical Perspectives*, edited by Anthony C. Alessandrini (75–86). London: Routledge.

Gordon, Lewis R. 1995. *Fanon and the Crisis of European Man*. New York: Routledge.

Hall, Stuart. 1996. The After-Life of Frantz Fanon: Why Fanon? Why Now? Why Black Skin, White Masks? In *The Fact of Blackness: Frantz Fanon and Visual Representation*, edited by Alan Read (12–37). Seattle, WA: Bay Press.

Hansen, Emmanuel. 1977. *Frantz Fanon: Social and Political Thought*. Columbus: Ohio State University Press.

hooks, bell. 1996. Feminism as a Persistent Critique of History: What's Love Got to Do with It? In *The Fact of Blackness: Frantz Fanon and Visual Representation*, edited by Alan Read (76–85). Seattle, WA: Bay Press.

Haymes, Stephen Nathan. 1995. *Race, Culture, and the City: A Pedagogy for Black Urban Struggle*. Albany: State University Of New York.

Jinadu, Adele. 1986. *Fanon: In Search of the African Revolution*. London and New York: KPI.

Kawash, Samira. 1999. Terrorists and Vampires: Fanon's Spectral Violence of Decolonization. In *Frantz Fanon: Critical Perspectives*, edited by Anthony C. Alessandrini (235–257). London: Routledge.

Levin, Thomas Y. 1995. Introduction to Siegfried Kracauer. In *The Mass Ornament: Weimar Essays*, edited by Thomas Y. Leven (1–30). Cambridge, MA: Harvard University Press.

Lilla, Mark. 2010, May 27. The Tea Party Jacobins. *New York Review of Books* LVII (9), 53–56.

McCulloch, Jock. 1983. *Black Soul White Artifact: Fanon's Clinical Psychology and Social Theory*. Cambridge: Cambridge University Press.

McGrath, William J. 1986. *Freud's Discovery of Psychoanalysis: The Politics of Hysteria*. Ithaca, NY: Cornell University Press.

Medina, Jennifer. 2011, April 16. California May Require Teaching of Gay History. *New York Times*, A11.

Mowitt, John. 1999. Breaking Up Fanon's Voice. In *Frantz Fanon: Critical Perspectives*, edited by Anthony C. Alessandrini (89–98). London: Routledge.

Peck, Don. 2010. How a New Jobless Era Will Transform America. *Atlantic* 305 (2), 42–56.

Pinar, William F. 2006a. *The Synoptic Text Today and Other Essays: Curriculum Development after the Reconceptualization*. New York: Peter Lang.

Pinar, William F. 2006b. *Race, Religion and a Curriculum of Reparation*. New York: Palgrave Macmillan.

Pinar, William F. 2012. *What Is Curriculum Theory?* [Second edition.] New York: Routledge.

Ravitch, Diane. 2000. *Left Back: A Century of Battles Over School Reform*. New York: Simon and Schuster.

Said, Edward W. 1989. *Yeats and Decolonization*. In *Remaking History*, edited by Barbara Kruger and Phil Mariani (3–29). Seattle, WA: Bay Press.

Said, Edward W. 1993. *Culture and Imperialism*. New York: Alfred A. Knopf.
Sandoval, Chéla. 1997. Theorizing White Consciousness for a Post-Empire World: Barthes, Fanon, and the Rhetoric of Love. In *Displacing Whiteness: Essays in Social and Cultural Criticism*, edited by Ruth Frankenberg (86–106). Durham, NC: Duke University Press.
Sekyi-Otu, Ato. 1996. *Fanon's Dialectic of Experience*. Cambridge, MA: Harvard University Press.
Sharpley-Whiting, T. Denean. 1998. *Frantz Fanon: Conflicts & Feminisms*. Lanham, MD: Rowman & Littlefield.
Verges, Françoise. 1996. Chains of Madness, Chains of Colonialism: Fanon and Freedom. In *The Fact of Blackness: Frantz Fanon and Visual Representation*, edited by Alan Read (48–75). Seattle: Bay Press.
Verges, Françoise. 1999. "I Am Not the Slave of Slavery": The Politics of Reparation in (French) Postslavery Communities. In *Frantz Fanon: Critical Perspectives*, edited by Anthony C. Alessandrini (258–275). London: Routledge.
Young-Bruehl, Elisabeth. 1996. *The Anatomy of Prejudices*. Cambridge, MA: Harvard University Press.
Zahar, Renate. 1974. *Frantz Fanon: Colonialism and Alienation. Concerning Frantz Fanon's Political Theory.* [Trans. Willfried F. Feuser.] New York: Monthly Review Press.
Ziarek, Ewa Plonowska. 2001. *An Ethics of Dissensus: Postmodernity, Feminism, and the Politics of Radical Democracy*. Stanford, CA: Stanford University Press.

CHAPTER 16

INWARDNESS

Commentary

The First World War, Robert Musil concluded, had become possible because the dominant ideologies of the day—Marxism, Christianity, and Liberalism—no longer articulated the inwardness, the lived experience, of Europeans. What had been—what was—needed, Musil discerned, were more subtle ways of thinking that dissolved rigidities in thought and feeling, enabling Europeans to imagine the possibility of a profoundly committed life. Prerequisite to such a life, Musil knew, was a language that could articulate the inner life. Composing that language comprised Musil's all-consuming challenge.

Bibliography

Pinar, William F. 2010. On the Privacy of Public Pedagogy: The Essayism of Robert Musil. In *Handbook of Public Pedagogy*, edited by Jennifer A. Sandlin, Brian Schultz, and Steven Burdick (45–55). New York: Routledge.

> The parallels between our time and Musil's are so striking that it is no longer possible *not* to read his writings historically and politically.
>
> Stefan Jonsson[1]

Robert Musil (1880–1942) achieved fame in Germany and Austria for a few years after 1930 and then disappeared from the public eye until 1949, when an article in the *Times Literary Supplement* named him as the most important writer in German of his time.[2] "Probably," David Luft[3] suggests, Musil is "the equal of anyone since Nietzsche in his intelligence and insight in the realm of the soul." Musil may still be, in the words of Frank Kermode, "the least read of the great twentieth-century novelists."[4] Musil is also an exemplary example of a public-and-private intellectual, that is, one who draws upon subjective resources to address the pressing issues of the day.

Born in Klagenfurt, Musil studied mechanical engineering in Stuttgart, receiving a degree in 1901. After completing his military service and working as an engineer for a year, he began to study philosophy and experimental psychology in Berlin, where he moved in 1903. Musil then took a degree in philosophy at the University of Berlin, training with Carl Stumpf, who (like Freud and Edmund Husserl) had studied with Franz Brentano.[5] His Ph.D. dissertation (1908) examined the epistemology of physicist and philosopher Ernst Mach (1838–1916).[6] During this time he wrote his first novel, *Young Torless*, published in 1906. Afterward, he resolved to pursue philosophy through fiction, to live as a writer rather than to become an academic philosopher. In 1911 he was married to Martha Marcovaldi (née Heimann) the daughter of a Jewish businessman and a student of the impressionist painter Lovis Corinth.[7]

From 1914 to 1918 Musil served as an officer with the Austrian army. After the war he worked as a press liaison officer for the Foreign Ministry, then as a scientific adviser to the Ministry of War. From 1922 on he supported himself as a freelance writer, contributing to various literary journals while participating in the rich café and literary life of Vienna during the postwar years. It was during these years he began work on the novel *The Man Without Qualities*, a project that would occupy him for the rest of his life. In December 1930, Musil presented to the reading public the first installment of this, his main work. Although two volumes appeared during his lifetime, this classic portrait of "Kakania"[8] remained unfinished at his death.

Coetzee[9] points out that Robert Musil, like others of his generation, experienced firsthand the successive phases of the collapse of nineteenth-century European civilization:

> first, the premonitory crisis in the arts, giving rise to the various Modernist reactions; then the war and the revolutions spawned by the war, which destroyed both traditional and liberal institutions; and finally the rudderless post-war years, culminating in the Fascist seizure of power.

In *The Man Without Qualities*, Coetzee continues, Musil set out to comprehend this collapse, which he came to understand as the historical inadequacy of the Enlightenment, an inadequacy presciently depicted in *Young Torless* (1906). There, in a residential military school, the Austrian compartmentalization of intellect and emotion enables reason to devolve into a device of homosexual subjugation.

To Musil, fascism was the logical if catastrophic consequence a fundamentally problematic European civilization. More appropriate pedagogically than a knee-jerk demands for action, Musil offered, was a careful reexamination of European humanistic values. For him, the freedom of the creative individual was the paramount value. In the alarmed atmosphere of 1935, such a contemplative view seemed self-involved and politically reactionary. Against his intentions, Musil maneuvered himself, as Bernd Hüppauf phrased it, into the position of an "outsider among the outsiders."[10]

H. Stuart Hughes called Musil's "the generation of 1905."[11] For the leading intellectuals of this generation, history seemed no longer to hold hope for humankind, as the nineteenth century (in the shadow of Marx) had believed. Indeed, many took history seriously only in times of crisis, abandoning everyday reality to custom and clichés.[12] Accepting the uncertainty of experience and knowledge as well as the inadequacy of every form of dogmatism, the intellectuals of Musil's generation were painfully conscious of the fragility and brevity of human life. Although they often dealt with social and ideological matters after the First World War, their central concerns were psychological, ethical, and aesthetic, all focused on the inner crisis of European culture.[13]

One of Musil's notebooks (No. 4) from his early years contains a series of sketches entitled *Monsieur le vivisecteur*. The title is noteworthy: the term vivisection is used in that sense of psychological investigation associated with Nietzsche, Dostoevsky, and Strindberg (whose work Musil knew). The original ambitious plan was for a book showing the figure *M. le vivisecteur* in family and society. In this passage we glimpse possible titles as well as two revealing statements: "To stylize is to see and teach others to see," and "paradoxes: let us for once turn everything back to front."[14] Both these statements foreshadow key elements of Musil's writing. In the first we see an intensifying appreciation for form, and in the second his preference for paradox, evident in all his work.[15] This section of Musil's *Notebook 4* shows him examining his historical and cultural situation, suggesting that "the riddle of the age has for each a private solution."[16]

Musil's mixing of Nietzsche with Emerson is not, Hickman suggests, as idiosyncratic as it might appear; there is evidence that Nietzsche, too, was influenced by Emerson. Musil studied Husserl as well. During Musil's student days in Berlin he came to know several men who became what would be known as Gestalt psychologists. During this time he read widely, concentrating, however, on Nietzsche, Emerson, and Dostoyevsky.[17]

After his marriage, Musil returned to Vienna, where he worked as an archivist at the Technical Institute. Just before the War broke out in 1914, the couple returned to Berlin, where he assumed his new post as an editor of Samuel Fischer's *Die neue Rundschau*, the most important literary publication in German-speaking world.[18] While working in Berlin, Musil came into contact with some of the leading artistic and intellectual figures of the period, among them Rainer Maria Rilke and Franz Kafka. The War and the ensuing political, economic, and social catastrophes disrupted Musil's already interrupted literary career. Partly due to History and partly due to his psychology, a gap of ten years punctuated the publication of Musil's second and third books.[19]

In the 1920s, although he lived in Vienna, Berlin was the center of intellectual life for Musil. His sympathy for modern science made him unusual in the intellectual world of the Weimar Republic, where both the Left and Right were critical of liberal rationalism, influenced as they were by German idealism. These were years of intense politicization, economic crisis, and cultural polarization in Germany.[20] Like other writers of his generation, Musil was profoundly affected by the War itself and later by the political, social, and economic crises in Germany and Austria, which began in 1917 and intensified during the 1920s. After the War, many of Musil's essays addressed contemporary political themes, such as the Treaty of Versailles or *Anschluss*[21] with Germany, but these were also contextualized in a broader concern for what he regarded as the crisis of European culture and the catastrophe that had been the First World War.[22]

Musil emphasized the elasticity and interrelatedness of human nature and culture. He opposed those aspects of liberalism that reflected and supported the bureaucratization of the modern state. It is clear that he found value in the religious atmosphere of prewar intellectual culture. Like Nietzsche, Musil focused on the spiritual value of truth. Knowledge and truth, he thought, ought to give

> new and bold directions to the feelings, even if these distinctions were to remain only mere plausibilities; a rationality, in other words, for which

thinking would exist only to give an intellectual armature to some still problematic way of being human: such a rationality is incomprehensible today even as a need.[23]

Close to Musil's heart was the idiosyncratic individual.[24] Perhaps the appropriate philosophy for his time, he thought, was no philosophy at all. Those who engaged him were mainly modern, mainly empirical, and at the "experiential" margin of academic philosophy, especially Ernst Mach, Nietzsche, and Emerson, three diverse but lasting influences on him.[25]

Musil was not convinced by arguments or doctrines. Musil was drawn to those ideas and that thinking embedded in lived experience. It was these orders of thinking he had in mind when he employed the term "essay." Pike and Luft[26] explain: "Musil was constantly absorbing the world as we actually *live* it, and trying to understand a civilization that is just now coming into being." Musil had no interest in the programmatic or prescriptive. Instead, he aspired to explore what it might be possible for human beings to *be*. He wanted to participate in renewals and revolutions of thinking, feeling, sexuality, and politics.[27]

Musil believed neither thought nor thinking kept pace with historical reality. Perhaps important feelings remained the same, he speculated, but he worried that they devolved into ideologies that obfuscated self-understanding. This was the case in 1914, he felt sure, when the dominant ideologies—Marxism, Christianity, Liberalism—all collapsed. Each had failed to make sense of the peace or to deflate enthusiasm for war. Why? Musil thought that these ideologies failed because they no longer articulated the inwardness, or lived experience, of most Europeans. They failed to represent the reality people experienced in their daily lives. What was needed, Musil theorized, was a new, more patient way of thinking that overcame rigidity in thought *and* feeling. He wanted to imagine the possibility of a profoundly committed life. He wanted to imagine a spirituality that acknowledged frankly the conditions of subjective life in modern Europe.[28]

To do so required a new language, Musil knew, in order to articulate the inner life. For Musil, the inner life acknowledges the necessity of both reason and religion (understood as mysticism); they are simultaneously operating functions of the human mind in its efforts to apprehend reality. Both poles of experience and perception possess equal validity; one must resist the temptation of positioning only one at the center of one's life. In practice, however, Musil believed that the process of balancing these poles probably involved a thorough, even dialectical investigation first of the one and then of the other. Their synthesis Musil termed "*das rechte Leben*," the creative or right life. Accordingly, when Musil decided to abandon his career as an engineer in order to study philosophy and psychology at the University of Berlin, his decision did not represent a rejection of science and the scientific attitude. He wanted, rather, to balance his experience by studying those dimensions of human experience that appeared to lie outside the boundaries of strict scientific investigation. For Musil, Peters[29] asserts, "the synthesis of reason and mysticism had to regarded as the most urgent task facing mankind in the twentieth century." The new morality that resulted would be based neither upon social prohibitions nor upon God-given commandments, but rather upon those potentialities latent within the individual himself.

Other critics have explored Musil's interest in bridging reason and emotion, science and literature, appearance and reality. Luft[30] writes: "The central task of Musil's work was to mediate his culture's antagonisms between intellect and feeling, truth and subjectivity, science and art." To do so he explored sexuality, which, in his view, both reflected and precipitated "ecstatic states,"[31] if only when freed of the social conventions and stereotypes in which sexuality was too often locked.[32] Torless' participation in homosexual sadistic practices at his school is one provocative portrait in Musil's art of a crisis of consciousness precipitated by and resolved through sexuality. Through Torless' sadistic, then amorous, relationship with Basini, he experienced a refinement of his personality that contributed to his evolution as a cosmopolitan person. Musil was more interested, Luft notes, in the both the psychic sources and biographic functions of sexuality and less in its particular objects. While Luft is right in emphasizing the "biographic functions" of sexuality, he is mistaken to discount altogether the homosexual theme of the novel. The anatomy of the characters is crucial. Had Basini been a female student, the politics and meaning of the situation—including its biographic significance—would have been quite different.

In *Young Torless*, Musil portrayed the power of "thoughts as moments in the inner life which have not yet frozen into fixed form."[33] Musil emphasized the biographic significance of these "living thoughts," a significance quite apart from their logical value as propositions. Their spiritual significance occurs in lived experience, in their consequences for self-understanding. Luft[34] writes: "*Torless* formulates the possibility of a revolt against bourgeois culture which does not produce something equally rigid and pathological, and stakes out a position of isolation and freedom, marked by Musil's enormous tolerance for ambiguity." The empiricist in Musil appreciated that we never know with certitude or finality that a rigorous openness to experience means subjective reconstruction.

The subtlety of Musil's art distinguishes *Young Torless* from the genre of "school novels." The severe atmosphere of the school makes it no place for either caring or self-realization; the pedagogical inadequacies of the instructors are glaring. Critics have observed that there is, however, no attempt to blame the episode on the school or to idealize the values and experience of the students. The threat to civilization comes from Beineberg and Reiting, whose sadism and manipulation point to the world outside the academy.[35] But only to the world outside? Are critics too quick to absolve the school? Can the rape and psychological subjugation of Basini not also be decoded as a desublimation of the repressive pedagogy of this authoritarian school?

Musil was interested in phenomenological method, Luft suggests, so that he might explore lived experience. Musil's method was not exclusively phenomenological, however; it was also grounded in experimental science as well. Free of the metaphysical certainties espoused by many of his contemporaries, Musil set out to investigate the complexity of love, religion, and the soul as lived. Musil believed that the intellectual despair of his generation had to do with too sharp a distinction drawn between science and mysticism. He regarded the essay as the representational form appropriate to address this polarized situation, a form of thinking poetically in prose that hovered between science and art, between private and public, what Wang[36] might describe as curriculum in a third space. Essayism was a representational form that enabled Musil to remain loyal to the precision[37] of the scientist as he undertook an aesthetic search for beauty and ethical values in the midst of cultural and spiritual degradation. In literature, sexuality, religion, and politics, Musil fought to extricate emotions from archaic and distorting concepts. Essayism supported this search for a new balance—a right distance, as Taubman[38] might describe it—between concept and the flesh, between intellect and soul, the concrete and the abstract. Luft[39] points out:

> The characteristic fault of bourgeois reason was its misapplication of the model of natural science; in its drive for uniformity, bourgeois reason had lost track of the capacity to create value and enhance life. In its yearning for truth, concept and abstraction, it had lost respect for the flesh, for the concrete lives of individual human beings.

In demands for "evidence-based" research, "scientific" education research effaces educational experience. Its political agenda is, indeed, uniformity.

Musil's primary preferences may have been aesthetic, but the collapse of the Habsburg Empire and the resulting crisis of European civilization as "the generation of 1905" had known it required political analysis. Georg Lukács might have had Musil in mind when he wrote: "Many a writer of a basically contemplative type has been drive to participation in the life of the community by the social conditions of his time."[40] Musil had grave doubts about the expressionist style of revolutionary politics prominent in 1919. In the call for the New Man, sounded both by Communists and Fascists, he saw a form of pessimism. Revolutionary politics were finally romantic, and, he believed, would only compound the disaster of the old order they aspired to replace.[41]

Refusing collectivism and systematicity, Musil explored those spheres of lived space and moments of lived time when predictability and regularity disappear. He investigated the unique, the individual: what is, finally, incalculable. What was required for his investigation was neither more emotionality nor historicity but a subtle style of thinking which kept concepts in an explicit if variable relation with the lived experience of everyday life, an exploration "of the reason, connections, limitations, the flowing meanings of human motives and actions—an explication of life."[42] In a somewhat Heideggerian statement, Musil once said: "But the struggle of the soul with its isolated solitude is actually nothing other than its outrage against the false connections among human beings in our society."[43] The enemy of creativity was the disappearance of soul from social life, banished by the conventions of bourgeois culture and under the supervision of the mandarinate. In such circumstances, "immorality" may be a passage to soul, to creativity. Musil said as much: "All my apparently immoral people are 'creative.'"[44]

The search for an intensely subjective relationship to reality was by no means otherworldly, as it hardly represented a negation of world as is. As Musil pointed out, ages of religious awakening were characterized not only by "the intense preoccupation of the human being with God, but also with life, a burning factuality of 'being there.'"[45] Like Kierkegaard, Musil knew that it was the religious individual who had the courage to take oneself, one's actions, and the meaning of one's experience in earnest. After Kierkegaard, Musil understood that ethical experience—love, presentiment, contemplation, humility—was "entirely personal and almost asocial."[46] After the First World War, what remained of authentic ethics, Musil believed, existed in art, in essayism, and within the sphere of private relations.

For Musil, Luft points out, the danger to independence of spirit lay less in specific political, social, or economic forms (such as capitalism or communism) than in their tendency to erase inwardness and, consequently, that freedom the inner life (with its emphasis on lived experience) enabled. From his locations in Vienna and Berlin, it seemed to Musil that German culture had produced the world's most powerful forms of academic study and aesthetic feeling. But it also seemed to him that each had been rigidly compartmentalized in German culture. Musil was neither indifferent to politics nor trapped in the historical specificity of 1914 Vienna; indeed, he was trying to think the meaning of the twentieth century for the history and future of European civilization. In doing so, it is clear that, during his final years in exile, living in Geneva in the midst of the calamity that was the Second World War, he diagnosed the cultural dilemma of European civilization as requiring complementary but self-critical interests in mysticism and politics. It was a set of interests to which another great public pedagogue—Pier Paolo Pasolini—would testify, through various literary, visual, and filmic arts as well as through journalism.

For much of his career Musil, too, worked as a journalist. He composed serious articles and essays on culture, contributing to the literary feuilletons of newspapers. He reviewed books and plays for various periodicals. As in his fiction, Musil insisted that life is no sequential narrative of discrete actions or ideas but a fluid, multi-momented mosaic. For Musil, actions and ideas were inseparable from sensation and emotion. He was committed to theorizing an ethical framework for living, working toward what he termed, simply, the "right life." No standard model was forthcoming, of course, as Musil's aspiration in language as in thought, evident in all his essays and his fiction, was "precision and soul."[47] What is soul? In 1912 he wrote: "Soul is a complex interpenetration of feeling and intellect."[48] Such "interpenetration" of mind and emotion is materialized in flesh, enacted in a state of being I term worldliness. The abstraction of these concepts masks the irreducible specificity of their personification in individual lives; Musil was determined to articulate links between the two domains.

Robert Musil lived in Vienna and Berlin during the most catastrophic period of Europe's twentieth-century history. During this cataclysmic time, he wrote about science and mathematics, capitalism and nationalism, the changing roles of women and writers, sexuality and epistemology, demonstrating a breadth not uncommon to intellectuals in fin de siècle Vienna. While the range of his interests may not have been unusual, the scale of his accomplishment was. Indeed, Musil is regarded one of the great essayists of the twentieth century. His conception of the essay traverses the concrete and the abstract, the private and the public; it provides, I suggest, one exemplar for privately animated pedagogical engagement with the complicated conversation that is knowledge, history, alterity.

Essayism

> Essayism epitomizes the movement of an aesthetic imagination that infuses reality with meaning by means of rigorously singular accounts.
>
> Patrizia C. McBride[49]

Musil defined essayism as an intellectual strategy that extended the methodological rigor of the natural sciences into the sphere of singularity, that domain represented by art (especially fiction) and ethics. Rather than looking for laws and regularities, essayism seeks the understanding of lived experience in individual and particularistic ways that rely on metaphor rather than upon nomological relations among numerically represented variables.[50] Musil's early devotion to the rigorous examination of lived experience led him to oppose what he discerned as the irrationalism and anti-intellectualism that permeated public discourse on art, evident in various movements of the day, among them Impressionism, Symbolism, and Expressionism.[51] While acknowledging the primacy of feeling in aesthetic creation, he declined to abandon rationality. Doing so, he felt sure, severed art from society and history, purloined from purposive human conduct. Retrospectively, Musil believed, this cultural conflagration had helped set the stage for fascism in Germany.

For Musil, McBride[52] points out, a socially engaged aesthetic and ethical practice "is sustained by art's ability to trigger the estrangement and rearrangement of shared narratives of reality." Through the artist's original representation of reality, public perception is challenged. Because this subjectively sourced originality reconstructs social reality, it can provoke dissonance, even instability. Certainly dissonance followed the 1910 London Exhibition of "Manet and the Post-Impressionists."[53] And despite late capitalism's capacity to incorporate (through commodification) all forms of dissonance, it happened during the 1980s over (U.S.) National Endowment for the Arts funding for Robert Mapplethorpe's black-male nudes.[54] If s/he can get under the public's skin (as it were), the artist—specifically, the essayist—has a chance to teach through provocation. In this respect, as McBride[55] notes, "the critique to which [the essay] subjects reality is inherently immanent and contingent, for it remains inextricably entwined with the social system it seeks to scrutinize." Being entwined with social reality (or getting under your skin) means that subjective expression—that originality estrangement sometimes precipitates—can express and result in the reconstruction of "shared narratives of reality." What Musil appreciated, then, was the privacy[56] of public pedagogy.

Musil came to appreciate the primacy and fluidity of subjectivity, the latter an affirmation of Nietzsche's dismissal of any conception of a stable, self-identical subject. Musil's contemporaries, however, fetishized the epiphanal ecstasy that can accompany self-shattering, decrying the allegedly stifling repression of reason as they extolled the presumably regenerative potential of instinct and sensuality. Reason cannot convey, let alone sustain (they insisted), the Dionysian intoxication accompanying (especially sexualized) self-shattering. It was this view of reason as only repressive that Musil disputed. The representation of what Musil termed the "other condition" is not obvious; there is no inevitable verisimilitude between signifier and signified. The point of the essay form, Musil asserted, is to rescue this "shadowy side of the individual"[57] from ineffability, to articulate the private through engagement with the public. The private life does not disappear into its articulation, as in some poststructuralist ruminations, "multiplying its textual pleasures, aporias, and indeterminacies in an atmosphere of wall-to-wall discourse."[58] Indeed, Musil's essay always returns the reader to that private reality representation reconstructs as public.

Like Fanon, Musil called for a new ways of being human, the reinvention of "the inner person,"[59] a "'new human being,' one who would resist assimilation into imperialist, nationalist, or fascist communities."[60] Like art, the Musilian essay demonstrates an antithetical but explicit relationship to lived experience, enabling one to inhabit a subjective sphere that is at once connected to and yet distanced from everyday reality.[61] By its non-coincidence with lived experience, the Musilian essay becomes the "constitutive other" to social reality itself.[62] Like the synoptic text in curriculum studies,[63] the Musilian essay communicates a multiplicity of apparently irreconcilable perspectives,[64] creating fissures through which intellectual breakthrough becomes possible.[65] As apparently paradoxical, the essay bridges[66] incommensurate realities[67] via juxtaposition,[68] creating a "cacophony of rivaling perspectives."[69] "For Musil," McBride[70] points out, "the intellectual mindset of essayism enabled the observer to avoid getting too bogged down in any one ideological quibble and instead made it possible to glimpse the strengths and shortcomings shared by antagonistic ideological positions." Anticipating Pasolini's insistence on ideological dexterity,[71] Musil affirmed the significance of order without systematicity.[72] Musil underscored his own situated particularity by juxtaposing competing points of view.[73]

Essayism's ethical challenge invokes an Apollonian reconstruction of a Dionysian descent into self-shattering otherness into public discourse. This invocation of the private is self-canceling if pragmatic: indeed, for Musil, the contemplation essayism invites occurs only absent instrumental reason. Engaging reality assumes no cohesive thinking subject; it requires a decentered, even democratic, subjectivity embracing "disunity,"[74] the lived and individuated substratum of a public sphere striated by difference. The subjectively existing individual is, then, no homunculus manipulating Archimedes' lever. As Musil appreciated: "appeals for decisive action often mask ineptitude, even panic, testifying to their own stupidity."[75] In order to engage in political action, it was imperative (Musil thought) to represent reality not reduced to race or ideology or as a means of achieving utopia but, instead, relying on this graduate training in physics, as "field[s] of force, which are charged with meaning based on the unique constellation of factors within which they are inscribed."[76] Musil writes out of as he replies to the "non-repeatable moment."[77] It is this precision that enables the public to be reconstructed through the private.[78] Musil worked from within.

Notes

1 2000, x.
2 See Hickman 1984.
3 2003, 3.
4 Quoted in Rogowski 1994, 4.
5 Luft 2003, 94.
6 "Seldom," Janik and Toulmin (1973, 133) assert,

> has a scientist exerted such an influence upon his culture as has Ernst Mach. From poetry to philosophy of law, from physics to social theory, Mach's influence was all-pervasive in Austria and elsewhere. Robert Musil, among others, was very much in Mach's debt.

Probably the most famous of those who came under Mach's spell was the young physicist Albert Einstein, who acknowledged Mach's profound influence upon him in his youth. Indeed, Janik and Toulmin suggest that Einstein's early career was predicated on Mach's view of the nature of the scientific enterprise. After meeting Mach, a dazzled William James called him, simply, a "pure intellectual genius" (quoted in Janik and Toulmin, 133), who had read and was able to discuss nearly everything.

7 Luft 2003, 106; Appignanesi 1973. Luft (2003, 106) suggests that Marcovaldi inspired Musil to think more carefully about women's sexuality as well as about his own; she proved "decisive in helping Musil to become himself and to sustain his creativity." A permanent point of reference for his fiction, Luft continues, she personified the significance of Berlin modernism in his life.

8 Musil invented this name; it conveyed a double meaning. On the surface, it is coined from the initials K.K. or K.u.K., standing for "Imperial-royal" or "Imperial and royal," a couplet that characterized all major institutions of the Habsburg Empire. To anyone familiar with German nursery language, however, it carried a second meaning: "Excrementia" or "Shitland" (Janik and Toulmin 1973, 13). In his portrayal of Kakania, Luft (2003, 96) points out, Musil "was concerned not so much with a particular traditional empire as with general qualities of modernity."
9 2001, ix.
10 Quoted in Rogowski 1994, 16; see Luft 2003, 126.
11 Quoted in Luft 1980, 13.
12 Luft 2003, 124.
13 See Luft 1980.
14 Quoted in Hickman 1984, 8.
15 See Hickman 1984.
16 Quoted in Hickman 1984, 14.
17 See Peters 1978.
18 See Pike and Luft 1990.
19 See Rogowksi 1994.
20 See, for instance, Weitz 2007.
21 As Luft (2003, 97) points out, Musil was "perfectly content" for Austria to be annexed to Germany. Although the *Anschluss* of Austria did not take place until 1938 (and under circumstances Musil abhorred, indeed, which forced him to flee to Switzerland where he died four years later), it had in effect occurred a decade earlier. By the end of the Weimar Republic, Musil observed, so many Viennese lived in Berlin that few creative Austrians remained at home.
22 See Pike and Luft 1990.
23 Quoted in Pike and Luft 1990, xviii.
24 In early twentieth-century Austria, education for individuality was informed by German humanism's ideal of *Bildung*. While later associated with class privilege, gender (masculinity specifically), and even national essence, the eighteenth-century version of *Bildung* as self-cultivation conveyed a religious meaning, quite in contrast to later conceptions in which individuality devolved into competitive individualism (see Luft 2003, 15).
25 See Pike and Luft 1990.
26 1990, xxi.
27 See Pike and Luft 1990.
28 Ibid.
29 1978, 12.
30 1980, 2.
31 Luft 2003, 104.
32 Luft 2003, 128.
33 Luft 1980, 60.
34 1980, 61.
35 See Luft 1980.
36 See Wang 2004.
37 The point of precision for Musil was the articulation (combining style and substance) of specific situations. He was not alone: Samuel Beckett too, as Mary Aswell Doll (1988, 5) points out, sought "precision amidst fluidity." Like Musil, Beckett sought to bridge everyday reality with "the other condition." "More than any other writer of our time," Doll (1988, 3) asserts, Beckett makes this other reality the 'soul' center of his concern."
38 1990.
39 1980, 115.
40 1964, 12; quoted in Luft 1980, 121.
41 Luft 1980.

42 Quoted in Luft 1980, 157.
43 Quoted in Luft 1980, 160.
44 Quoted in Luft 1980, 161.
45 Quoted passages in Luft 1980, 162.
46 Ibid.
47 See Pike and Luft 1990.
48 Musil 1990, 10.
49 2006, 144.
50 Luft 2003, 91.
51 See McBride 2006.
52 2006, 24.
53 Stansky 1996, 2.
54 Dellamora 1995, 152; Mercer 1994, 203.
55 2006, 24.
56 Dating from the fifteenth century, privacy is defined as 1(a): the quality or state of being apart from company or observation: seclusion, and (b): freedom from unauthorized intrusion <one's right to privacy>, and 2 (archaic): a place of seclusion and 3(a): secrecy, and (b): a private matter: secret. While subjectivity is never separate from sociality, it does requires seclusion, understood as solitude and inner freedom. It is a "place" of safety in which subjectivity enjoys "free play" as it takes indirect form through study (Rohdie 1995, 156).
57 McBride 2006, 47.
58 Radhakrishnan 2008, 21.
59 Quoted in McBride 2006, 7.
60 Jonsson 2000, x.
61 McBride 2006, 103.
62 Ibid.
63 As, I trust, this volume testifies.
64 See McBride 2006, 93.
65 In both disciplinary—see Axelrod 1979—and subjective, lived—see Wang 2004—senses.
66 McBride (2006, 162) points that Musil "portrays aesthetic experience as an extensionless bridge connecting ordinary life and the Other Condition." Aoki's (2003 [1995], 318) bridge is not a bridge.
67 McBride 2006, 105.
68 McBride 2006, 111.
69 McBride 2006, 131.
70 2006, 94.
71 Because Pasolini appreciated that every ideology devolves into orthodoxy (Ward 1999, 334), Pasolini's subjectivism was enacted in the service of resistance to ideological rigidification. The assertion of "I think" challenges objective reality constructed by ideologues, referring the artist to his or her reconstruction of lived experience, expressed (possibly) through montage (Liehm 1984, 188).
72 See McBride 2006, 94.
73 McBride 2006, 131.
74 McBride 2006, 111.
75 Quoted in McBride 2006, 121.
76 McBride 2006, 143.
77 Ibid.
78 As the great Polish (if residing in Argentina for 24 years) novelist Witold Gombrowicz (1904–1969) asserted: "True reality is the one that is peculiar to *you*" (quoted in Longinovic 1998, 37). It is through reality's disclosure through subjectivity that the public world can be discerned with precision. "One of the main objects of my writing," Gombrowicz observed, "is to cut a path through Unreality to Reality" (quoted in Longinovic 1998, 36).

Bibliography

Aoki, Ted T. 2003 (1995). In the Midst of Doubled Imaginaries: The Pacific Community as Diversity and as Difference. In *Curriculum in a New Key*, edited by William F. Pinar and Rita L. Irwin (303–319). Mahwah, NJ: Lawrence Erlbaum.

Appignanesi, Lisa. 1973. *Femininity and the Creative Imagination: A Study of Henry James, Robert Musil, and Marcel Proust*. London: Vision Press.

Coetzee, J.M. 2001. Introduction to Robert Musil's *The Confusions of Young Torless*. New York: Penguin.

Coviello, Peter. 2000. Apocalypse From Now On. In *Queer Frontiers: Millennial Geographies, Genders, and Generations*, edited by Joseph A. Boone, Martin Dupuis, Martin Meeker, Karin Quimby, Cindy Sarver, Debra Silverman, and Rosemary Weatherston (39–63). Madison: University of Wisconsin Press.

Dellamora, Richard. 1995. Queer Apocalypse: Framing William Burroughs. In *Postmodern Apocalypse: Theory and Cultural Practice at the End*, edited by Richard Dellamora (136–167). Philadelphia: University of Pennsylvania Press.

Doll, Mary Aswell. 1988. *Beckett and Myth*. Syracuse, NY: Syracuse University Press.

Hickman, Hannah. 1984. *Robert Musil and the Culture of Vienna*. London: Croom Helm.

Janik, Allan and Toulmin, Stephen. 1973. *Wittgenstein's Vienna*. New York: Simon and Schuster.

Jonsson, Stefan. 2000. *Subject without Nation: Robert Musil and the History of Modern Identity*. Durham, NC: Duke University Press.

Liehm, Mira. 1984. *Passion and Defiance: Film in Italy from 1942 to the Present*. Berkeley: University of California Press.

Longinovic, Tomislav Z. 1998. Witold Gombrowicz: Formal Abjection and the Power of Writing in *A Kind of Testament*. In Gombrowicz's *Grimaces: Modernism, Gender, Nationality*, edited by Ewa Plonowska Ziarek (33–50). Albany: State University of New York Press.

Luft, David S. 1980. *Robert Musil and the Crisis of European Culture 1880–1942*. Berkeley: University of California Press.

Luft, David S. 2003. *Eros and Inwardness in Vienna: Weininger, Musil, Doderer*. Chicago: University of Chicago Press.

Lukács, Georg. 1964. *Studies in European Realism*. [Trans. Edith Bone.] London: Merlin Press.

McBride, Patrizia C. 2006. *The Void of Ethics: Robert Musil and the Experience of Modernity*. Evanston, IL: Northwestern University Press.

Mercer, Kobena. 1994. *Welcome to the Jungle: New Positions in Black Cultural Studies*. New York: Routledge.

Musil, Robert. 1908. *Beitrag zur Beurteilung der Lehren Machs*. Berlin: University of Berlin, Ph.D. dissertation.

Musil, Robert. 1955 (1906). *Young Torless*. [Preface by Alan Pryce-Jones.] New York: Pantheon Books.

Musil, Robert. 1990. *Precision and Soul*. [Edited and translated by Burton Pike and David S. Luft.] Chicago: University of Chicago Press.

Musil, Robert. 1995 (1979). *The Man Without Qualities*. [Trans. Sophie Perkins and Burton Pike.] New York: Knopf.

Peters, Frederick G. 1978. *Robert Musil: Master of the Hovering Life*. New York: Columbia University Press.

Pike, Burton. 1961. *Robert Musil*. Ithaca, New York: Cornell University Press.

Pike, Burton and Luft, David S. 1990. Forward and Introduction to Robert Musil 's *Precision and Soul*. Chicago: University of Chicago Press.

Radhakrishnan, R. 2008. *History, the Human, and the World Between*. Durham, NC: Duke University Press.

Rogowski, Christian. 1994. *Distinguished Outsider: Robert Musil and His Critics*. Columbia, SC: Camden House.
Rohdie, Sam. 1995. *The Passion of Pier Paolo Pasolini*. Bloomington: Indiana University Press.
Stansky, Peter. 1996. *On or about December 1910: Early Bloomsbury and its Intimate World*. Cambridge, MA: Harvard University Press.
Taubman, Peter Maas. 1990. Achieving the Right Distance. *Educational Theory* 40 (1), 121–133.
Wang, Hongyu. 2004. *The Call from the Stranger on a Journey Home: Curriculum in a Third Space*. New York: Peter Lang.
Ward, David. 1999. Pier Paolo Pasolini and the Events of May 1968: The "*Manifesto per un Nuovo Teatro*." In *Pasolini Old and New*, edited by Zygmunt G. Baranski (321–344) Dublin: Four Courts Press.
Weitz, Eric D. 2007. *Weimar Germany*. Princeton, NJ: Princeton University Press.

CHAPTER 17

INDIVIDUALITY

Commentary

A person of "marked individuality,"[1] Jane Addams was born in 1860 in Cedarville, Illinois. She died in Chicago in 1935. It is how she traveled from Cedarville to Chicago I consider here, an educational journey that began at home in her father's library, formalized at Rockford Female Seminary (now College), and extended during her two tours of Europe during which she met Leo Tolstoy and visited Toynbee Hall in London. It was there her inchoate conception of public service took specific form. From teaching her neighbors to teaching her fellow human beings, Addams' quietly passionate life became expressed in profound public service.

Bibliography

Pinar, William F. 2009. *The Worldliness of a Cosmopolitan Education: Passionate Lives in Public Service* (59–82). New York: Routledge.

> There is no first or final point of resistance to political power other than in the relationship one has to oneself.
>
> Michel Foucault[2]

Jane Addams was an American social activist and theorist born in 1860 in Cedarville, Illinois. She died in Chicago in 1935. It is how she traveled from Cedarville to Chicago I want to consider, an educational journey that began at home in her father's library, formalized at Rockford Female Seminary (now College), and extended during her two tours of Europe during which she met Leo Tolstoy and visited Toynbee Hall in London. It was there her then inchoate conception of public service took more specific form. As her biographers make clear, Addams sought lived experience to supplement academic study, thereby reconstructing both, transposing her devotion to family into devotion to the world. From teaching her neighbors to teaching her fellow human beings, Addams' quietly passionate life was expressed in profound public service.

In her brief for Jane Addams as canonical in curriculum history, Petra Munro[3] emphasized Addams' courage in defending immigrants, vilified especially during

World War I (as was she, for her pacifism). While immigrants—her neighbors in Chicago's Nineteenth Ward—remained her lifelong concern, African Americans also engaged her ethical commitment to democracy in America.[4] Influenced by her father, by her study at Rockford (Seminary, then College), by her tours abroad (including her momentous visit to Toynbee Hall), Addams arrived at her commitment to democracy quite on her own. Louise Knight[5] underscores Addams' intellectual independence:

> [Addams] was ferociously determined to think through matters on her own. There was intellectual hubris in this position—she was clearly confident of her ability to reason things out for herself and reluctant to consider that her class origins blinded her in any way—but there was moral courage in it, too. Many of the most difficult and defining moments in Jane Addams' life would arise because she insisted on speaking the truth as she saw it. This was one tenet of individualism that she would never abandon.

Jane Addams' experience of academic study was a "snare of preparation." Missing, she felt, was experience in the world, experience outside the claims of family and the confines of institutions. It was, I suggest, her "marked individuality" that she fashioned from her two tours of Europe[6] as well as her emotional (and possibly sexual) engagement with Ellen Gates Starr[7] and Mary Rozet Smith[8] that enabled her to honor what she came to call the "social claim." Her acceptance of that claim resulted in a courageous career of social service and intellectual accomplishment, a passionate life devoted to public service. It is evident in her relationship with John Dewey, her support of W. E. B. Du Bois, and her long-term colleagueship with Ida B. Wells.

Addams was always attentive to the "evolutionary process by which an individual or a social condition came to be," one of her most perceptive biographers—Victoria Bissell Brown[9]—points out. If Addams could know the genesis of a situation, she thought, more likely it was that she could devise interventions precisely appropriate to its resolution. "By tracing the evolution of Addams' own approach from arrogant heroics to democratic process," Brown[10] advises, "we can appreciate why her lived experience convinced her that we learn best about life from life itself." While I think Brown draws too sharp a line between Addams' early embrace of a heroic individualism and her later apparently selfless service, her point about learning from life itself specifies the source of Jane Addams' worldliness.

When the self-centered ego—what Addams called "the great I"—shatters, the specific subjectivity that is oneself hardly disappears. That subjectivity structures as it animates one's engagement with the world, as it is stimulated and reconstructed by that engagement. When, in Christopher Lasch's[11] terms, the "minimal self" (contracted, he argues, by self-protective, survivalist retreat from the world) "expands" into one's lived—and civic—space, it risks dissolution by engaging with the world. Such experience—lived experience, informed by academic study, subjectively reconstructed—is educational.

The two tours of Europe gave Addams a taste for what experience could yield, but her post-graduation period of fidelity to the "family claim" that she would later depict as "the nadir of my nervous depression and sense of maladjustment"[12] seemed to her a suspension of educational experience. Brown, however, emphasizes this period as also one of education. It was during this period, for instance, that Addams began reading Leo Tolstoy's religious and social criticism, affirming her focus on the historical Jesus. Reading Tolstoy confirmed Addams' sense that true Christianity demanded faith in Jesus' message about human salvation on earth, not faith in a supernatural Jesus or promises of life after death.[13] It was Christianity's meaning for *this* world that preoccupied Jane Addams.

Possibly even more crucial in her self-formation was Addams supplementation of her Rockford persona as student leader and intellectual with sustained attention to "women's personal style" and "emotional authenticity."[14] Addams was critical of what she worried was higher education's tendency to engender women's detachment from the world. Education, she felt sure, ought not undermine women's ability to notice people's faces, to be "bread givers," to preserve "the softer graces."[15] This was a period, Brown[16] suggests, of Addams' affirmation of women's culture. Her attachment to her sisters and to other women, among them her teachers Sarah Blaisdell and Sarah Anderson, and fellow alumnae, prominently among them Ellen Gates Starr, signified an "embrace of female culture."[17] It was during this time that Addams realized that, as Brown[18] notes, "any heroism she aspired to would draw upon the connections that women fostered in their relationship." This was no incipient separatism; in fact during her second tour of Europe it was the study of Auguste Comte—specifically "his belief in a supreme 'fellowship' of all humanity based on lived experience rather than metaphysics"[19]—that provided Addams a rationale for extending her embrace of "female culture" to humanity itself.

It was the juxtaposition of study and experience that enabled Addams to imagine opening—with Ellen Gates Starr—a settlement house. Brown[20] tells us that Addams was reading Walter Besant's popular 1882 novel, *All Sorts and Conditions of Men*, the same week (in June 1888) she visited Toynbee Hall. The novel's plot seemed to reproduce the main points of Addams' life: the heroine, Angela Messenger, a wealthy heiress who felt lost after graduation from Newnham College, moves to East London to live and learn (and fall in love) among the working classes. There she builds there a People's Palace as a center for culture. After reading *All Sorts and Conditions of Men*, Addams visited the actual "People's Palace," a new East London youth center built with private and public funds. The Palace's classrooms, meeting rooms, billiard rooms, music and dance rooms, and library were, Brown[21] suggests, "an important model" for Hull-House, a settlement house that would be much more "alive with the sounds of youth than Toynbee Hall." There was to be no simple mimicry: moved by her experience in London, informed by her ongoing academic study, she was able to imagine her future course of action. However shared that course would be, it would be distinctively hers; Hull-House would bear the subjective stamp of the young woman from Cedarville, Illinois.

In her eulogy delivered at the memorial service for Anna Peck Sill (the founder and headmistress of Rockford Female Seminary) a year after her return from Europe, Addams asserted that a college education was nothing more than a "mountain of mere straw and stubble" if it did not give graduates "a moral purpose."[22] From Brown's depiction of her post-Rockford period—she describes it as a "postgraduate education in humanity and humility"[23]—we are reminded it was Addams who restructured the subjectivity her upbringing and education had formed. That subjectivity proved to the sustaining source for her commitment to learn from experience. In one of many beautifully crafted passages,

Brown[24] summarizes the shifts Addams underwent during the period after her undergraduate education but before the founding of Hull-House:

> Those years of "ever-lasting preparation" taught her to value the caring and intimacy fostered by female culture, directed her eye away from the hero on stage and toward the individual on the street, and forced her to realize that in a world of bent backs, dying children, filthy factories, and selfish power, heroism was not a romantic flight of the disembodied but a daily decision to show up and hold on. She knew none of this when she left Rockford, and without the intervening years she could not have grasped, replicated, or—most important—improved upon what she saw at Toynbee Hall.

As this passage (and Brown's biography) makes clear, becoming worldly-wise is part accident of circumstances and part subjective capacity made conscious and articulate through academic and self-study. From lived experience and self-reflective academic study Addams synthesized a coherent self capable of sustained, critical, and creative engagement with the world.

By 1912—when she becomes the first women to second a presidential nomination (at the Progressive Party Convention)—Addams' reputation had grown far beyond Hull-House; she was widely acknowledged as "one of the most articulate voices for progressive reform on the American scene," appreciated for her "prodemocratic" and "promediation" commitments for which she was, by then, "well known" and "widely respected."[25] When Addams confessed, in her 1910 autobiography, that she longed for "a definite social creed," Brown[26] believes that,

> she seriously underestimated her own achievement in fashioning—out of the bits and pieces of a scattered, self-directed education—a coherent, consistent social philosophy of democratic mediation that suited her temperament, caught the spirit of her time, and gave her the authenticity for which she had longed.

This sentence conveys the subjective confluence of lived experience, autobiographical consciousness,[27] and academic study attuned to the historical moment and grounded in "place" that the concept of "study" communicates.

Individuality is no educational "objective" for which teachers can be held "accountable." Juxtaposing autobiographical and academic study, situated socially and attuned historically, is no formula for student success or teaching effectiveness. As Brown's perceptive observation makes explicit, a "marked individuality" forms from an ongoing retrospective judgment on a life already lived, one that Addams felt was, for a time, lost. That she fashioned a progressive selfhood out of what she felt was the provincialism of her late nineteenth-century academic and family experience is a testimony to her genius, but also to that experience and those who figured so prominently in it: her father, Ellen Gates Starr, her teachers, and, later, to fortuitous events.[28] Her genius drew upon her fidelity—her intellectual and emotional honesty—to her lived experience, subjectively reconstructed through study and attuned to the historical moment in which and the place where she lived.[29]

Individuality is not only a function of openness to the world, but, as well, openness to the world of one's interiority. The distinctiveness of one's genetic legacy, individual life history, and present experience is not only one's curse to bear, but one's ongoing opportunity to act. It is the gift of life from one's parents and those who cared for and taught one. That distinctiveness—an individuated sense of dependence on and independence from others, on the biosphere, enmeshed in History, facing one's fate—is, I submit, one's obligation to cultivate. It is also one's ongoing knot to unravel—as Pasolini put it, "the problem of my flesh and life"[30]—tying us to those preceding us, those around us now, finally, if indirectly, to everyone on/and the planet. That Addams appreciated the inextricable relation between subjectivity and sociality is evident in her acknowledgement that "a righteous life cannot be lived in a society that is not righteous."[31] Addams' life contradicted this assertion.

A passionate life in public service among Chicago's working-class poor represented no sacrifice of Addams' life to "the other," nor, Brown suggests, was it any simple expression of duty in expectation of gratitude. Addams' life at Hull-House was "freely chosen and exuberantly embraced."[32] That choice was not immediately obvious; it took years of study at school and experience at home and abroad to provide the knowledge she needed to solve the problem of her "flesh and life." What she discovered was that the knot to be unraveled was simultaneously social and subjective. What "Jane Addams carried out of her education and into her career," Brown[33] tells us, was "the certain knowledge that democracy—as daily practice—was the path to joy, and it was the experience of joy that guided the next forty years of her democratic endeavor." It was a life of passionate public service that brought on the accusation, by the paranoid right-wing,[34] that she was the most "dangerous woman in America."[35]

As Munro points out, Addams' life among Chicago's immigrants forced upon her a keen sense of the limitations of American democracy. While contradicted by political facts, Addams' faith in humanity was, Brown[36] argues, finally spiritual: "it was a hard-won and deeply felt spiritual conviction from which arose all her other convictions." That conviction did not follow from "gracious submission" to others, but from an insistence on thinking things through for herself. "It was," Knight[37] concludes,

> this persistent *rethinking*, and not only the experiences, that produced her profoundest insights and taught her the most about her class, her gender, and herself. Addams' love of abstract theory, of sweeping generality, of uplifting philosophy had almost trapped her in her given life of reading, but it was the same passion for larger meaning that drove her to break free of that life, to struggle to integrate her experiences with her thought, and to change her mind.

Through this independence of mind Addams became engaged with the world, threaded through her own distinctive life history and individual character, placed in the Nineteenth Ward of Chicago. Note that "rethinking" is no technical cognitive process educational researchers are forever attempting to specify; self-reflexively such rumination integrates lived experience of alterity with one's knowledge and in so doing reconstructs subjectivity. As subjective and social reconstruction are reciprocally related, Addams reconstructed not only herself but the world.

Early in the research for her biography, Knight found a passage in Addams' writings that remained one of her favorites: "[W]e are under a moral obligation in choosing our experiences," she wrote, " since the result of those experiences must ultimately determine our understanding of life."[38] "Her experiences"—most of which were not chosen—"along with key books she read" provided the passage from the "individualistic, absolutist, benevolent ethics of her father and her own class in favor of what she perceived to be the working-class ethic of cooperative justice, which she found less selfish and self-righteous."[39] While no doubt idealized, such an ethic enabled Addams to distance herself from the self her upbringing had formed, thereby providing the self-reflective opportunity to restructure her subjectivity according to the commitments she had acquired and cultivated through academic study and lived experience.

The order of moral and intellectual courage individuality requires was an order of courage Addams mustered over and over again. "Addams earns our greatest respect as a profound student of life and as a moral and political philosopher of what it means to be fully human," Knight[40] asserts. As her nephew, Weber Linn, recalled, her "real eagerness" was for understanding. Addams used the word "interpretation" to describe her soul-searching analysis of experience. "Many experiences in those early years," she later wrote, "although vivid, seemed to contain no illumination."[41] It is self-reflection—including social and self-criticism—that enables experience to be illuminated, to be educational. It was illuminated not according to one light—an absolutist ethics, for instance, or by gender or ethnicity—but according to the distinctive kaleidoscopic prism her individual insight permitted. She had "absorbed," Knight[42] observes, a "passionate individualism into her very bones."

For Knight, Addams's "passionate individualism" contained two sides: a "solemn moral earnestness" and a "fascination with the imaginary and mystical."[43] Perhaps the former disposition provided a mooring for the latter. Academic study provided opportunities for the ongoing articulation of these dispositions; without such study they might well have remained silent, inactive, self-enclosed. In addition to her formal study at Rockford, the books the young Jane Addams read in the family library "taught . . . that private passions, nurtured by the flights of one's imagination, brought one closest to spiritual understanding and to happiness."[44] Later, Addams would express those passions through service to others. Through that public service she experienced spiritual understanding and happiness. How? In a vividly imagistic passage, Knight[45] explains:

> Entirely private, it [reading] linked her through her imagination to the world. Its effects, as future developments will show, were various. Sometimes reading flooded her mind like a tide that swept into a shallow inlet and set swirling eddies of confusion in motion; sometimes reading exploded in her mind like a bomb, perhaps when an idea was first met, perhaps later, when it collided with another idea and there was a double explosion; sometimes reading corroded her mind with a steady drip of acidic doubts, tiny "what ifs" that, over the years, would eat away the iron framework of certainty built by her parents, church, and school; eventually, reading would transform her mind from a sponge that absorbed to an engine of initiating, discriminating energy, from a receiver to a transmitter, from an organ of her body to an instrument of her soul. In the 1870s, reading was changing Jane Addams. From then on, because she wished it to, but even when she did not, it would never stop changing her.

I would be hard pressed to produce a more succinct and striking statement of study as lived. Study does not just yield new "information," it restructures one's subjectivity, animating and focusing one's engagement within the world. That potential acknowledged, how study in fact functions cannot be predicted in advance or generalized across individuals. Had she been forced to funnel her attention according to "objectives" and the attainment of "skills" Addams' genius might well have not achieved articulation.

Among the teachers Addams found inspiring was Caroline Potter who taught rhetoric and history. Potter became her favorite teacher. In her second year at Rockford, Addams took Potter's required ancient history and modern history courses. Potter met with each student individually to discuss her essays. Fifty years later Addams recalled that "[t]he hours spent with her . . . are still surrounded with a sort of enchantment."[46] In addition to history and rhetoric, Potter also taught literature and composition, but her "real responsibility," Knight[47] reports,

> was to teach character, the force that, to her mind, shaped history and supplied the central theme in the study of Western civilization. Character was an expansive concept. A man of character was decisive, bold, creative, original, engaged with his times, able to withstand pressures to compromise his integrity, responsible, courageous, and determined. Potter's entire curriculum was an intense and lengthy seminar on the heroic.

How did Addams respond? She was "entranced."[48]

While Knight employs the generic "man" in the above passage, she emphasizes that Potter taught the heroic as a virtue for women. She was always looking for students who showed promise of fulfilling women's "grand potential." Those were students capable of "discipline" and who were willing, "if she found the right course of study for them," could (in Potter's own words) "exhaust [their] strength in [study's] pursuit."[49] She also looked for originality and for the willingness to act "upon the demand of the occasion."[50] Knight tells us that Potter was quite conscious that those students, particularly women who fell in love with learning, might fail to take the ideas "back into the world." For Potter, "learning was not for its own sake."[51] Given the enforced domesticity the separate-spheres ideology rationalized, one appreciates Potter's call for worldly engagement as "progressive." In our time of vulgar vocationalism, however, learning for its own sake is a progressive idea.

"Encouraged by Potter's woman-affirming curriculum," Knight[52] tells us, Addams explored the potential of female power, and began to appreciate "women's feelings as useful in the world of public action." Potter's influence is discernible in an essay Addams wrote in her sophomore year in which she employed George Sand in an argument for women's rights. "This splendid . . . woman," Addams wrote, "declares the social independence and equality of woman [in] her relations to man, society and destiny." Like Sand, she continued, today's woman "wishes not to be a man or like a man but she claims the same right to independent thought and action."[53] While she comes to the suffrage campaign late, these lines leave no doubt that Jane Addams appreciated at age eighteen the injustice of the separate-spheres arrangement. As Knight[54] notes, these lines also convey as well "her confidence in the power of ideas to change the world." Addams' linking of social and intellectual independence with equality is also significant; it presages the gendered character of U.S. teachers' "gracious submission" to scripted curricula, standardized examinations, and to "best practices" they themselves have not devised.

"No list survives of all the books that Jane Addams read at Rockford Seminary," Knight[55] continues, "but she undoubtedly read a great many." Knight suggests Addams had come to Rockford in order to read as "widely and as fruitfully as possible, . . . to pursue culture."[56] The moral significance of such a pursuit was articulated by, among others, Matthew Arnold in his 1869 essay *Culture and Anarchy*, which Addams read at Rockford. By studying "the best which has been thought and said in the world," one strengthened one's commitment to improving society: a "moral and social passion for doing good."[57] In effect, Knight notes, culture was Christianity's replacement, the means by which one redeemed oneself and others. This promise of secular salvation Addams would articulate in two early essays: "The Subjective Necessity for Social Settlements" and "The Objective Value of a Social Settlement" (both dated 1892). For Addams, this conception of culture "both challenged her to escape her class and racial biases and reinforced their claim on her."[58] Significantly, these essays link self-reconstruction to the reconstruction of society. In so doing, it demonstrated culture's—indeed, education's—"deepest appeal: its ability to awaken her profoundest longings and desires."[59]

In addition to Arnold, several other texts were influential in Addams' intellectual formation. The first she read in Baltimore after returning in 1885 from her first trip to Europe; it was Giuseppe Mazzini's *Duties of Man*. Mazzini (1805–1872) was critical of the family's demands on one's loyalty and interests, insisting that "your first duties . . . are . . . towards Humanity."[60] Mazzini reverses the order Addams had learned; for him it was selfish to serve the family and in doing so fail to serve strangers. Reading Mazzini, Knight[61] reports, was for Addams an "unsettling, even shocking, experience." Serving others, Mazzini argued, was a Christian duty because Christ's love was directed toward humanity. It was also a democratic duty because through democracy each person can become "better than he is."[62] For Mazzini, education was also central, but so was the opportunity for people from different social classes to come to know each other. Addams would combine those two ideas.

The Christian element in Mazzini's tract would become amplified for Addams when she read Leo Tolstoy's *My Religion*, which was published in the United States in 1885. Knight[63] tells us that "it touched her as no other book had." Decades later (1927), Addams would identify *My Religion* as "the book that changed my life."[64] What Addams remembered those many years later, Knight suggests, was that at age 50 Tolstoy felt himself a failure; after converting to Christianity he was able to transform his life. That Addams was reading Tolstoy during the depth of her own despair illustrates the "biographic function"[65] of study, the confluence of life history and intellectual interest in stimulating movement in one's life.

While Tolstoy's book was pivotal, others influenced Addams' formation as social theorist and activist as well, among them W.H. Fremantle's *The World as the Subject of Redemption* (1885) and Brooke Foss Westcott's *The Social Aspects of Christianity* (1883). Fremantle wrote that,

> the main object of effort is not . . . either . . . the saving of individual souls out of a ruined world, or . . . the organization of a separate society destined

> always to be held aloof from the world, but . . . the saving of the world itself.

This would be accomplished by abandoning selfishness and "imbu[ing] all human relations with the spirit of Christ's self-renouncing love."[66] Westcott called upon his readers to find fellowship with the poor and thereby learn the significance of duty: "the end of labor is not material well-being but that larger, deeper, more abiding delight which comes from successfully administering to the good of others."[67] Knight observes that Addams found these ideas "consistent"[68] with her own desire to transform the world.

Not only did Tolstoy inspire a discouraged Jane Addams, he introduced her to the concept of nonviolence, or "non-resistance." Addams would make this idea her own. In the introduction to her 1907 *Newer Ideals of Peace*, she declares "non-resistance" to be "too feeble." She prefers a more "aggressive ideal of peace."[69] Tolstoy had written that anger "is an abnormal, pernicious, and morbid state."[70] Knight (2005, 145) reminds us that anger was a familiar experience for Jane Addams, as living with her "willful" and "relentless" stepmother meant living with "Anna's anger and her own." Her practice of non-resistance required, Knight notes, a willingness to undergo suffering. By the time she arrived at Hull-House in 1889, but possibly as early as 1886, Knight tells us that the concept of nonviolence had become central to her theory and practice.[71]

Nonviolence was a feminist issue. Knight[72] reports that during this period two books challenged her thinking about women: John Stuart Mill's *The Subjection of Women* and Leo Tolstoy's *What Shall We Do*? Each undercut those beliefs about gender she had acquired during childhood. Each asked her to question the assumptions she held about gender, including the primacy of the family's claim upon a daughter's life. It was Tolstoy's book that enabled Addams to affirm that an upper-middle-class, educated young woman could not ignore the social problem of poverty.[73] As she read, Knight writes, "her mind, which had earlier been sabotaging her with self-criticism, became her ally."[74]

Almost twenty years later, when members of women's organizations gathered in Washington, D.C. in 1915 to create the Women's Peace Party, they asked Jane Addams to give the keynote address. Then they elected her chair. Not limited to war, the party's platform proclaimed a feminist agenda. When World War I ended in 1918, the Party was absorbed into a new organization, the Women's International League for Peace and Freedom.[75] Jane Addams was elected president. In recognition of her efforts, Jane Addams would be awarded the Nobel Peace Prize in 1931.[76] For Christopher Lasch, "Jane Addams made her greatest contribution to the cause of peace."[77]

Perhaps Addams was overstating her dilemma when she declared herself to be snared by preparation. Despite her confinement in Rockford Female Seminary and in a family who asserted that her significance was limited to service to the family, Addams reconstructed her subjectivity through reading. Perhaps reading alone would have been insufficient: without the experience of the "bullfight" and of Toynbee Hall—without her teachers at Rockford (emphasizing, for instance, the feminine heroic)—Addams would have been unable to mobilize herself and find her way out. Without reading, without study—that intersection of subjective longing with scholarship and theory ("culture")—it is difficult to imagine the bullfight incident provoking the moral crisis to which Toynbee Hall provided a solution. Once again, Louise Knight provides us with an insightful and detailed depiction of Addams' subjective and intellectual passage out of the family into society:

> During the seven years since she had graduated from seminary, culture in the form of books—that is, the humanities—had continued to change her. Books had freed her from a too narrowly defined duty to family, shown her that society's restrictions on women's responsibilities were artificial and cruel, allowed her to examine the responsibilities that accompanied her inherited wealth, deepened her ideas about class, capitalism, and poverty, revised her understanding of Christianity, and helped her reinterpret the meaning of her interest in the poor. These were large gifts. In her childhood, culture—in the broader sense of society's teachings—had placed her in a necessary prison of unexamined assumptions. But as she grew older, culture—in the sense of "higher" learning—also gave her the key to unlock the door. From culture she received the ability to stand back and examine those assumptions and consciously and selectively reject them.[78]

This subjective undergoing of estrangement and exile[79] that study affords enables self-reconstruction,[80] one perquisite to political activism and cultural politics dedicated to social reconstruction.[81]

For Addams, education provided the passage between subjectivity and society. At Hull-House, the first subjects offered—all "academically substantive"[82] were in the humanities. The students who took them were factory workers, teachers, bank tellers, clerks, and others who, Addams' thought, had "some education" and had "kept up an intellectual life and are keen for books" in spite of "adverse circumstances."[83] "Defiant of cultural barriers," Knight[84] suggests, the curriculum was comprised of—after Arnold—the "best" of European civilization. Ellen Gates Starr taught George Eliot's novel *Romola* (and the history of art, in which she specialized) while Addams (who remained the generalist)[85] taught Mazzini's *Duties of Man* in English translation to a group of Italian men, several of whom had fought in Italy's struggle for nationhood. Later these men presented Hull-House with a bust of Mazzini, causing Addams to quip: "perhaps in gratitude that the course was over!"[86] By teaching art, literature, and music, Brown suggests,

> Jane and Ellen accidentally tapped into a feature of immigrant life which too often went unrecognized: that immigrants had not only ambition for their future lives but deep connections to their past lives which were often culturally, if not materially, rich.[87]

Rather than reducing the gap between immigrants' culture and life in Chicago, Addams and Starr provided passages between the two.

As more volunteer teachers joined Addams and Starr, additional offerings—in French, Latin, German, Greek, painting, music, mathematics, rhetoric, and Roman history—were formalized as "College Extension Classes," the first adult college extension courses in Chicago.[88] Indeed, during the early years of Hull-House there developed, Addams[89] suggested, "a cordial cooperation" between settlements and universities, one that Charles Beard described as "as exerting beyond all question a direct and immediate influence on American thinking about industrial questions, and on the course of social practice."[90] Settlement houses were, Munro[91] suggests, "curricular experiments that contested dominant notions of education."

In 1891, Addams launched a working people's summer school, held for four weeks in July on the campus of her alma mater. A liberal arts curriculum was taught to the same working-class women who took college extension classes at Hull-House: factory workers, public school teachers, seamstresses, and others. About ninety women, most of them first-or second-generation Chicagoans of Irish, German, Jewish, or English descent, attended the summer school that first year, staying for two weeks or a month; they paid $2 a week. Taught by Starr, Addams, and several volunteers, the curriculum included Browning, Emerson, Victor Hugo, Ruskin, as well as botany, gymnastics, tennis, singing, and German conversation. Addams and Starr were offering workingwomen intellectual opportunities they had themselves had been offered and at the same place. It was possibly the first time a residential liberal arts college experience had been offered to workingwomen; the school would continue for ten years.[92] As Adams[93] knew, cultural reconstruction "depend[s] upon fresh knowledge and must further be equipped with a wide and familiar acquaintance with the human spirit and its productions." Throughout her life Addams continued to learn; she regarded herself, Brown[94] suggests, as a "reformer ever in need of reform."

The concept of education had a broad meaning for Jane Addams, Lasch[95] points out. While education may have been institutionalized in the form of classroom instruction, it was hardly contained there, for it was Addams' contention (shared by other progressive educators), that education was ongoing and inhered in any situation that required improvisation. For Addams, education was as broad as experience itself, Lasch notes. Experience *was* educational. It was the failure of professional educators to come to grips with this fact, in Addams' view, that accounted for the sterility of what progressives would pillory as *traditional* education. Such education had divorced itself from "life," and the task of educators was to reestablish the connection.[96]

These ideas derived from Addams' judgment that her own college training left her within "the snare of preparation," a self-contained cognitive affair that had kept her from engagement with the world. During her long years of waiting for such engagement—they start during her time at Rockford[97]—Addams reflected on the consequences of acquiring culture without having experience. "I gradually reached a conviction," Addams[98] concluded,

> that the first generation of college women had taken their learning too quickly, had departed too suddenly from the active, emotional life led by their grandmothers and great-grandmothers; that the contemporary education of young women had developed too exclusively the power of acquiring knowledge and of merely receiving impressions; that somewhere in the process of "being educated" they had lost that simple and almost automatic response to the human appeal, that old healthful reaction resulting in activity from the mere presence of suffering or of helplessness; that they are so sheltered and pampered they have no chance even to make "the great refusal."

Such shelter created the "subjective necessity of settlements," Addams would later assert.[99] That subjective necessity required acknowledgement that "the dependence of classes on each other is reciprocal"[100]

What has intrigued me is the movement of Jane Addams from Cedarville to Chicago, from the provincial to the cosmopolitan. There was no simple adoption of "sophisticated" attitudes, no knee-jerk rejection of her past, no fantasies of "us" versus "them," no disappearance into a collective identity. The "marked individuality" of Jane Addams followed from her study at home, at Rockford, abroad, and with friends. Addams incorporated as she reconstructed her lived experience. There was not always a direct open path ahead: given the constraints upon women at that time that path led to an apparent cul-de-sac. The struggle against her confinement within the family was feminist in both intention and result: the affirmation of women's culture, as Brown points out, was an essential consequence of this period of her life. It was a feminism appreciative of men's thought and activism, as her reading and visits to Russia and England confirm. Identity politics would have struck Addams as a phase—as Sartre saw *négritude*—to be moved through swiftly, in part because it sacrifices the individual to the collective, the concrete to the abstract. For Lasch, it is the unique interplay between the two that implies the

> distinctive quality of Jane Addams' intelligence. She loved the concrete, but she was always earnestly seeking the general. She theorized about every subject she ever touched, but without arriving at a general theory of modern society—doubtless because she distrusted the dogmatism with which such theories are often associated.[101]

Doubtless she distrusted dogmatism of any kind.

Addams method was, Lasch[102] asserts, "essentially autobiographical," and the "virtues" and "defects" of her work were those associated with writing from one's experience. He acknowledges that she wrote "superbly" about the revolt of youth, the plight of women, the estrangement immigrants suffered, and the disintegration of family life under the assaults of industrialism. On subjects like prostitution, he continues, Addams' writing was less effective, perhaps because, he suggests, there was no parallel in her experience. Whether writing from experience directly or imaginatively, Addams' writing is often compelling, in part due to the heartfelt—passionate—commitment she obviously felt. The illustrations are vivid; they lend the writing an immediacy that other forms of prose lack. It is her subjective presence—in her writing, in her public service—that sculpts its distinctiveness. Because she was a person of "marked individuality," Addams led a passionate life in public service.

Notes

1 Addams' individuality was "marked." In a newspaper article in June 1894, a reporter described Addams as a "person of marked individuality [;] she strikes one at first as lacking in suavity and graciousness of manner but the impression soon wears away before [her] earnestness and honesty." She was struck, too, by Addams's paleness, her "deep" eyes, her "low and well-trained voice," and how her face was "a window behind which stands her soul" (quoted in Knight 2005, 313–314). Inserted and unquoted words are Knight's.

2 Quoted in Koopman 2013, 173.

3 Now Petra Munro Hendry.

4 Munro 1999, 42–43.

5 2005, 296–297.

6 Like academic study, touring Europe provided Addams with opportunities for acquiring culture, e.g. "high" culture.
7 See Brown 2004, 194; Knight 2005, 218.
8 See Brown 2005, 255–259.
9 2004, 8.
10 Ibid.
11 See 1984.
12 Quoted in Brown 2004, 148.
13 See Brown 2004, 164.
14 Brown 2004, 176.
15 Ibid.
16 2004, 177.
17 Brown 2004, 183.
18 2004, 177.
19 Brown 2004, 195.
20 2004, 203–204.
21 Ibid.
22 Quoted in Brown 2004, 206.
23 2004, 206.
24 2004, 205.
25 Brown 2004, 293.
26 2004, 293.
27 See Earle 1972.
28 Prominent among these was the infamous bullfight: see Lasch 1965, 8; Brown 2004, 7, 198–199; Knight 2005, 163–164.
29 For Kögler (1999, 246), "[t]he 'essence' of individuality consists precisely in projecting itself anew; in developing innovative and different ideas about self, world, and society, in opposing, the prevailing interpretations and practices."
30 Quoted in Greene 1990, 14.
31 Quoted in Brown 2004, 243.
32 Brown 2004, 297.
33 2004, 297.
34 Hofstadter 1996 (1965).
35 Munro 1999, 40.
36 2004, 297.
37 2005, 404, emphasis added.
38 Quoted in 2005, 1.
39 Knight 2005, 4; see Lasch 1965, xxi.
40 2005, 4.
41 Quoted in Knight 2005, 4.
42 2005, 13.
43 2005, 50.
44 Knight 2005, 50.
45 2005, 70.
46 Quoted in Knight 2005, 85.
47 2005, 86.
48 Ibid.
49 Knight 2005, 86.
50 Quoted in Knight 2006, 83.
51 Ibid.
52 2005, 99.
53 Quoted passages in Knight 2005, 87.
54 2005, 87.
55 2005, 88.
56 2005, 88–89.

57 Quoted in Knight 2005, 89.
58 Knight 2005, 90.
59 Knight 2005, 137.
60 Quoted in Appiah 2005, 240.
61 2005, 142.
62 Quoted in Knight 2005, 142–143.
63 2005, 142.
64 Quoted in Knight 2005, 142.
65 Pinar 1994, 46–57.
66 Quoted passages in Knight 2005, 173.
67 Quoted in Knight 2005, 173.
68 2005, 174.
69 Quoted in Lasch 1965, 221, 219.
70 Quoted in Knight 2005, 145.
71 2005, 145. As it is for Hongyu Wang 2014.
72 See 2005, 148.
73 Knight 2004, 149.
74 2005, 148.
75 Brown 2004, 5.
76 Knight 2005, 395; Elshtain 2002, 224.
77 1965, 218.
78 2005, 156.
79 See Wang 2004.
80 Nussbaum 1997, 29.
81 Mansbridge and Morris 2001; Goodwin, Jasper, and Polletta 2001.
82 Knight 2005, 205.
83 Quoted in Knight 2005, 205.
84 2005, 206.
85 Knight 2005, 224.
86 In Lasch 1965, 214.
87 2004, 237.
88 Knight 2005, 206, 223; Brown 2004, 233.
89 In Lasch 1965, 212.
90 Quoted in Lasch 1965, 212.
91 1999, 19.
92 See Knight 2005, 225–226.
93 In Lasch 1965, 201.
94 2004, 6.
95 1965, 175.
96 Ibid.
97 See Knight 2005, 91.
98 In Lasch 1965, 16–17.
99 Lasch 1965, 29.
100 Quoted in Lasch 1965, 29; Siegfried 1996, 225.
101 Lasch 1965, xxv–xxvi.
102 1965, xxvi.

Bibliography

Appiah, Kwame Anthony. 2005. *The Ethics of Identity*. Princeton, NJ: Princeton University Press.

Brown, Victoria Bissell. 2004. *The Education of Jane Addams*. Philadelphia: University of Pennsylvania Press.

Earle, William. 1972. *The Autobiographical Consciousness: A Philosophical Inquiry into Existence*. Chicago: Quadrangle Books.

Elshtain, Jean Bethke. 2002. *Jane Addams and the Dream of American Democracy*. New York: Basic Books.
Goodwin, Jeff, Jasper, James M., and Polletta, Francesca. eds. 2001. *Passionate Politics: Emotions and Social Movements*. Chicago: University of Chicago Press.
Greene, Naomi. 1990. *Pier Paolo Pasolini: Cinema as Heresy*. Princeton, NJ: Princeton University Press.
Hofstadter, Richard. 1996 (1965). *The Paranoid Style in American Politics and Other Essays*. Cambridge, MA: Harvard University Press.
Knight, Louise W. 2005. *Citizen: Jane Addams and the Struggle for Democracy*. Chicago: University of Chicago Press.
Kögler, Hans-Herbert. 1999. *The Power of Dialogue: Critical Hermeneutics after Gadamer and Foucault*. Cambridge, MA: MIT Press.
Koopman, Colin. 2013. *Genealogy as Critique: Foucault and the Problems of Modernity*. Bloomington: Indiana University Press.
Lasch, Christopher. ed. 1965. *The Social Thought of Jane Addams*. Indianapolis, IN: Bobbs-Merrill.
Mansbridge, Jane and Morris, Aldon. eds. 2001. *Oppositional Consciousness: The Subjective Roots of Social Protest*. Chicago: University of Chicago Press.
Munro, Petra. 1999. Political Activism as Teaching: Jane Addams and Ida B. Wells. In *Pedagogies of Resistance: Women Educator Activists, 1880–1960*, edited by Margaret Smith Crocco, Petra Munro, and Kathleen Weiler (19–45). New York: Teachers College Press.
Pinar, William F. 1994. *Autobiography, Politics, and Sexuality: Essays in Curriculum Theory 1972–1992*. New York: Peter Lang.
Wang, Hongyu. 2014. A Nonviolent Perspective on Internationalizing Curriculum Studies. In the *International Handbook of Curriculum Research*, edited by William F. Pinar (67–76). [Second edition.] New York: Routledge.

CHAPTER 18

COSMOPOLITANISM

Commentary

This final chapter[1] addresses the cosmopolitan cause at the core of curriculum studies, referencing concepts and countries depicted in the second edition of *The International Handbook of Curriculum Research*.[2] I review the intellectual histories we have inherited and the present circumstances in which we find ourselves as we strive to comprehend concepts across difference: national, cultural, temporal. To contradict the presentism of the current historical conjuncture I recommend "becoming historical"[3] to encourage non-coincidence with the current regimes of enforced universalization and homogenization. Temporal non-coincidence, I suggest, provides the occasion for cosmopolitanism.

Bibliography

Pinar, William F. 2013, October. The Cosmopolitan Cause of Curriculum Studies. Keynote address presented to the inaugural meeting of the European Association for Curriculum Studies, Braga, Portugal. Copyright William F. Pinar.

Pinar, William F. Ed. 2014a. *The International Handbook of Curriculum Research*. [Second edition.] New York: Routledge.

Toews, John. 2008. *Becoming Historical: Cultural Reformation and Public Memory in Early Nineteenth-Century Berlin*. New York: Cambridge University Press.

> We are attempting to develop each child's individuality, each child's special interests and abilities, as fully as possible, and we are trying to train him in the use of his own particular abilities for the welfare of others, to instill in him a fundamental sense of his dependence upon and responsibility for the group of which he is a part—a group which gradually enlarges until it embraces all mankind.
>
> Carleton Washburne[4]

Contemporary curriculum studies may have originated in the United States, but its recontextualization[5] worldwide in nations with distinctive histories and cultures underline its localized and reconstructed character. The particular remains primary despite globalization and its common denominator: standardization through assessment and technology. Despite this homogenization, the distinctiveness of national history and local cultures continue to inform the curriculum as it is enacted in concrete classrooms in specific nations, regions, and localities.[6] If curriculum is complicated conversation its contextually inflected, phenomenologically animated oral character is crucial in the education of the subject. The contextualization of curriculum is not only an empirical fact to be acknowledged, it is a political position[7] corroding the homogenizing structures globalization installs.

Contextualization is not only geopolitical, it is historical. Indeed, one cannot grasp "place"[8] unless one knows its history. (The more fashionable concept—space—colludes with presentism and virtuality, as it could be anywhere.)[9] Becoming historical means knowing where you and what time it is.[10] It is an expression of professional ethics in this time of "obsessive contemporality," in Ivor F. Goodson's succinct phrase.[11] Intellectual histories—as Goodson himself has famously conducted and inspired—are prerequisite to understanding our present circumstances.

Globalization summarizes our present circumstances, the ruthless promotion of standardized assessment, technology, and through them curricular content. Reactions against globalization testify to the pervasiveness of its psychic and well as political penetration. In contrast to globalization, "internationalization" is a term I reserve for the cosmopolitan cause of curriculum studies, the articulation of difference through democratic dialogue among colleagues within and across national borders. Such dialogue requires clarification through questioning of and by colleagues located elsewhere, as concepts are understood first on their own terms, then recontextualized according to local circumstances.[12]

The internationalization of curriculum studies encourages "postcolonial" networks that ignore bifurcations such as "center-periphery," as we engage each other in conversations complicated not only by multiple languages but by concepts that must be contextualized locally in order to be understood internationally. The institutionalization of this opportunity is already underway in the International Association for the Advancement of Curriculum Studies (www.iaacs.ca), the IAACS journal, triennial IAACS meetings, and with its affiliated organizations.[13] Nothing could be more important now, it seems to me, than nationally distinctive fields engaging in sustained dialogue with each other, forging a "new internationalism"[14] that forefronts professional ethics rather than politics as the bonds that bind.

Informing such dialogical encounter[15] are politics, culture, and history, each of which complicates the conversation, and often in welcomed ways, especially if we construe our "citizenship" as in curriculum studies first, the nations wherein we hold passports second. That allegiance hardly produces peace, as differing theoretical allegiances as well as the shifting historical moment and distinctive national settings can converge to create conflict. Nonviolent conflict is crucial to the internationalization of the field, as Hongyu Wang[16] argues. Clarification of our concepts encourages understanding, a cosmopolitan cause we have in common. Such commitment to understanding constitutes our own form of "internationalism," a term affirming solidarity across difference.

Intellectual Histories

Engaging in academically informed, ethically engaged complicated conversation is our professional calling. The ancient concept of "calling" informs our profession's ethics, our commitment to study and to teach as we engage in academic research to understand curriculum historically, politically, as social, indeed as lived experience. Such a multivariate and situated sense of professional ethics incorporates the concept of the "moral," a term often "atrophied," Tero Autio[17] points out, when translated into English as "moralistic." In his important chapter in the second edition of *The International Handbook of Curriculum Research*, Autio argues that it is the "moral" that "makes education educative," as students and teachers engage in ongoing judgments of what knowledge is of most worth, when, and why." Autio continues: "At best, the moral shifts teaching from transmission to transformation," as the curriculum is then no longer test preparation but a "complicated conversation where all the participants at every level think about the basic curriculum question of the worthwhileness of the content and subject matter just taught and addressed." Autio locates this conception of curriculum within the various *Didaktik* traditions in Europe, suggesting that their aim is "to encourage thinking, to make subjective yet knowledgeable judgments and decisions, to think against the subject matter, to think against oneself, to transcend, to transform."

Such subjective reconstruction requires study of concepts we cannot assume we understand, as their use in singular settings must make us suspicious of our assumptions. Self-suspension seems prerequisite to ethical engagements with others, as listening to our colleagues from elsewhere, appreciating the circumstances in which their work occurs, inevitably invites us to rethink our own circumstances and the concepts that structure the curriculum research with which we are most familiar. Consider the concept of "race."

"This is the [historical] moment in which we live," Cameron McCarthy, Ergin Bulut, and Rushika Patel[18] point out; it is one of "radical reconfiguration and re-narration of the relations between centers of power and their peripheries." Any conception of racial identity restricted to "origins," "ancestry," "linguistic" or "cultural unity" is shattered, disintegrated by "hybridity, disjuncture, and re-narration." Culture is now severed from place, as "migration, electronic mediation, and biometric and information technologies" proliferate and intensify.[19] Given the "existential complexity" of the "lived" experience of "real existing racialized subjects," McCarthy and his colleagues conclude, "our research imaginations on race are in sore need of rebooting."[20]

Such "rebooting" may require setting the machines aside, as they embed us in virtual space, not a material place, submerging us in screens disengaged from actual situations that speak to us from the past. Modernity and its heir apparent, postmodernity, flatten the temporal structure of the present as they install calculation, not contemplation, as the primary means of reason. Instrumental rationality[21] assures us that we can get "there" from "here," that the future will be what we plan, not what follows, however unexpectedly, from the past. Its economistic subspecies—neoliberalism—ensures the end of education, as curriculum becomes "interactive"—not communication among actually existing persons—and is moved online.[22]

For David Geoffrey Smith, the "debacle" of neoliberalism—privatization, standardized tests, instructional technologies, all rationalized by the concept of "development"[23]—leaves us with a resounding pedagogical question: "how can the shape and character of education be re-imagined . . . in the face of the dissipation of its basic operating assumptions?"[24] This crucial question becomes almost inaudible in a culture of *distraction*, a self-disintegrating state compelled by capitalism with its never-ending emphasis on development, accumulation, and consumption.

"Within the operation of capital," Smith[25] explains, "cultivating distraction is foundational to all marketing psychology, and the maintenance of distraction is an absolute requirement for product innovation and production." One such "innovation" is online learning, a presumably "progressive" and "student-centered" recasting of teaching that threatens the very concept of professional identity. Erudition—having something to "profess," Smith[26] reminds, takes years of sustained self-critical study—is replaced with the provision of "simple facilitation" to supporting students' acquisition of "skills" for use in the "global marketplace." Indeed, "if learning means only the acquisition and accumulation of information," Smith[27] points out, "teaching in the traditional sense becomes superfluous."

Ongoing analysis of neoliberalism is imperative, but for David Geoffrey Smith so is the "postcritical" moment when one labors to work through the current crisis, and on a human scale. "It is precisely here," Smith[28] argues,

> that wisdom traditions have the most to say, and their voice is virtually univocal: To heal the world I must engage in the work of healing myself. To the degree that I heal myself, so will my action in the world be of a healing nature.

Such healing means "becoming mindful," what Smith regards as "the ultimate condition of our freedom as human beings." A "turn" to "wisdom," he[29] continues, "is a deeply political act, an act of cultural insurrection, because it refuses to take seriously the seductions of secondary gods."[30] In my phraseology, this is "working from within."[31]

While not always a political undertaking, attentiveness to our "inward freedom" is one lasting legacy of German educational thought, as Daniel Tröhler[32] reminds. Nationally specific genealogies enable understanding curriculum internationally, Tröhler argues, as present-day schools and educational policies become intelligible only when their (sometimes religious) prehistories are excavated. He makes the contrary case as well: "in order to reconstruct the past (as key to self-awareness) comparison is a precondition." Indeed, "probably the most noble effect of learning other systems of reasoning across times and spaces," Tröhler suggests, "is this chance of becoming aware of ourselves as historical and cultural constructions."[33]

It is such awareness Hongyu Wang asks us to cultivate. In her reflection on "nonviolence," Wang[34] reminds us of "our own implication in the logic of control that renders nonviolence unthinkable and unimaginable." It is, she notes, "long overdue" for the field of curriculum studies "to embrace nonviolence as an educational vision." It is a vision that could inform our daily practice as educators, including, Wang notes, our intellectual and organizational work in curriculum studies.[35] Wang[36] addresses the "nonviolent relational dynamics" of the intersecting domains of local, the national, and the international.[37] Like David Geoffrey Smith, Wang draws upon wisdom traditions as well as examples of international nonviolence activism in envisioning "nonviolence as a guiding principle for internationalizing curriculum studies."[38] Central to the conception of nonviolence that Wang elaborates is an embodied sense of "interconnectedness" that affirms "compassionate" and "affiliating" aspects of humanity. Such affirmation of "fellowship" and "shared life" she finds in several philosophical, religious, and ethical traditions, including the Christian principle of "love your enemy," the African notion of *ubuntu,* the Chinese notion of *Tao*, as well as in indigenous peace-making traditions in North America.[39] Referencing the role of gender in violence and nonviolence, Wang cautions that we must not now resort to another mode of "domination" to destroy violence, "but we must work *through* it."[40] Recalling the simultaneity of self-healing and political insurrection Smith invokes, Wang asserts that nonviolent activism is "*both* internal *and* external." It is "fundamentally an educational project." Wang emphasizes that "inner peace is the basis for outer peace."[41] "Ultimately," she notes, "violence and nonviolence are felt by the individual body, and the fundamental task of education is personal cultivation."[42]

What would it mean for us to cultivate ourselves "personally," that is, as human subjects, sometimes silenced by the distractions of daily lives intensified by the institutions apparently incapable of providing conditions supportive of the calm contemplation "cultivation" requires. Becoming historical[43] can encourage us to extricate ourselves from the flat-lined present where even commonplace concepts—like race—require reconsideration. Living in the past—perhaps through the wisdom traditions Smith and Wang invoke—would no longer be certification of irrelevance but transcendence. Being "out-of-date"[44] could become an aspiration, not a lamented sign of aging. Becoming historical becomes, then, an ongoing act of political intransigence.[45]

For me, a nonviolent internationalization of curriculum underscores the significance of clarification. We cannot assume we understand how colleagues are using concepts we ourselves use, or that their referents are identical.[46] Our positioning in particular nations, and within particular localities, informed by different intellectual traditions—not to mention different sometimes competing institutional and intellectual networks—disables us from grasping the particularities of our colleagues' conceptualizations. Once we understand those—through quiet questioning and study—we might well express disagreement, if respectfully, nonviolently. The solidarity that this "new internationalism"—*our* internationalism—expresses acknowledges irreconcilable differences. Understanding is not necessarily agreement in communities without consensus.[47] Dialogical encounter through clarification promises no resolution of conflicting concepts; it is an enactment of professional ethics expressed nonviolently. Given the forces that aggress against us and our colleagues and their students in the schools, the tendency will be—as the great Brazilian educator appreciated[48]—toward horizontal violence, expressing to each other what is properly directed vertically, at those who seem determined, in the United States at least, to end education.[49]

Present Circumstances

That is the state of curriculum research in the United States, struggling to survive extinction given the federal government's collusion with corporations, abetted by the Bill and Melinda Gates Foundation. For-profit schools with curriculum moved online demote teachers to auditors, as children are abandoned to the Internet, with its often deleterious effects on social development, cognitive functioning, and, in very young children, apparently the very biological architecture of the brain.[50] Federally funded research is focused on "what works," often bypassing educational researchers and slipped to economists. The academic field of curriculum studies retreats into preoccupations with social justice and reparation, colluding unwittingly with politicians who displace their responsibilities for social welfare onto the schools.[51]

In Germany, curriculum, evaluation, and control are also interlocking but privatization is perhaps not yet (and may never be) as pervasive as in the U.S. Wolfgang Böttcher summarizes present circumstances there as, like the United States, dominated by "standards"[52] and a new governance structure following participation in PISA[53]—but, importantly, he reminds readers of the past. In the 1960s Saul Benjamin Robinsohn[54] had reintroduced the term "curriculum." Robinsohn acknowledged the worth of ancient thought and languages, but it was the vacuous concept of "change" that drove reform.[55] Böttcher recalls Wolfgang Klafki's emphasis upon "global and epochal key problems," among them peacekeeping and international understanding, human rights, social inequity, technology assessment, equality between men and women, labor, environment protection, and the pursuit of happiness. After PISA, the curriculum debate became "trivial,"[56] Böttcher laments, inadequate to the "complexity" of "global problems to be solved." The test-driven curriculum trivializes indeed contradicts what Böttcher points out is the very rationale for "standards-based reform," namely the reduction of inequality. It is not the students' purposes "reform" serves, "but, rather, the purposes of testers and politicians who can, after Germany has gained a few places in the education rankings, fool an innocent public into believing that this was the effect of smart politics."[57]

In her analysis of "competence-oriented curriculum reform" in Germany, Charlotte Röhner works historically as well. But it is the present that compels her attention, and so it is curriculum debates after TIMMS[58] and PISA that she summarizes. As in Spain,[59] "all efforts," focus on how the "skills" children bring to school can be improved. "In particular," Röhner[60] continues, "the initial language skills of children from families with a migration background . . . have become a focus and have resulted in extended language support measures at the prep-school institutions of all federal states." While enjoying only "average" success, these measures served as the "starting point for a comprehensive reorientation of elementary education." Also referencing Klafki's key contribution and continuing relevance, Röhner points out that contemporary concepts of competence emphasize "cognitive" tasks and problems of "learning," in sharp contrast to Klafki's more sophisticated and multi-modal formulation. Such a constricted conception has been accompanied by curriculum development as "informed arbitrariness" in the service of a "nationwide orientation" and "standardization." A "critical analysis" of "curriculum discourse," Röhner[61] concludes, "must still be developed."

Such critical analysis seems well underway in Finland where education, Antti Saari, Sauli Salmela, and Jarkko Vilkkilä explain, represents a "singular concoction"[62] of *Bildung* from Germany and (after World War II) the Tyler Rationale from the United States. The "challenge" today, Saari, Salmela, and Vilkkilä tell us, is constructing a "new communal and collective public space for free self-expression."[63] The past may provide passage, and they suggest "we might extract from what is still powerful in the *Bildung*—tradition, a vision of an autonomy that is aware of historical traditions, while being able to transform them into something new. This understanding might open up a space for freedom."[64] The liberty that sustained study of the *artes liberales* supports is, Saari, Salmela, and Vilkkilä suggest, an "inner freedom." "An individual controlled and regulated by the economy," they warn, "will never be free, and no educational system governed by the economy can produce freedom."[65]

Everywhere, it seems, freedom is replaced by "choice," technoculture compelling the commodification of curriculum, no longer ideas and facts addressed to actually existing persons in particular places, but interactive exercises on screens that silence the human subject and thereby stunt social democracy, replacing speech with skills, subjective presence with sensorimotor strokes of the keyboard. Even in Italy evidently, as Paula Salvio reports that that nation too has "fallen into step with what is perceived as a global market demand for a unified curriculum that is homogeneous with the rest of the continent, as made evident, to provide one example, by its participation in the PISA program."[66] Salvio is reminded of the *Riforma Gentile* of 1923, set in motion by Mussolini's first Minister of Public Instruction, Giovanni Gentile. Gentile abolished instruction in all languages other than standard Italian: "The belief that the individual practices his or her individuality by merging with the state was, of course, a hallmark of Italian fascism."[67] Invoking the "mythic Roman past," the post–World War II Italian curriculum communicated a "heroic victimhood" that effaced the facts of Italy's invasion of Ethiopia and its imperialist aspirations. Not until the student protests of the 1970s were high-school textbooks revised. In the 1980s, as elsewhere, neoliberalism arrived, embraced by right and center-right political parties. "No one is quite sure what PISA measures," Salvio[68] sagely asserts, "but what we do know is that PISA is a private corporation sponsored by the Organization for Economic Co-Operation and Development (OECD) that supports the OECD's promotion of STEM curricula (science, technology, engineering and mathematics)." What is not valued by such "corporate auditing systems," Salvio continues, is the "art" of "cultivating historical consciousness . . . that would illuminate rather than obscure aspects of Italy's history of colonization."[69] Cultivating historical consciousness—becoming historical—is, I conclude, the cosmopolitan cause of curriculum studies.[70]

The "Obsessive Contemporality" of Our Time[71]

However hounded by globalization, the curriculum remains nationally based, locally enacted and individually experienced. Whether these fundamental facts support tendencies toward cosmopolitanism or provincialism cannot be ascertained apart from studies of our respective national situations.[72] That is why the international handbook of curriculum research as well as my book-length studies of curriculum studies in Brazil, China, India, Mexico, and South Africa have been organized by country[73] and why they emphasize history, the intellectual histories of nationally distinctive fields and the political histories of the nations where curriculum researchers reside. In political as well as intellectual terms, such an emphasis challenges the "obsessive contemporality" that renders globalization "reasonable."

Globalization is rationalized, Stephen Carney, Jeremy Rappleye, and Iveta Silova explain, by technology, science, and the myth of progress. One such rationalization—"world culture theory"—is challenged by the evidence, e.g. the "local enactment" of global demands.[74] The "evidence" cited by world culture theorists does not support claims of a "world culture," Carney, Rappleye, and Silova conclude, instead it tends to "*produce* them."[75] What the evidence makes clear is the "incompleteness, pragmatism, and chaos of so much education reform."[76] These facts represent not failures of implementation but recontextualizations of imported[77] models of "reform." Future research, Carney, Rappleye, and Silova recommend, is better focused on "how" and "under what conditions ideas travel, transfer, and take form as practices."[78]

Articulating "how" and "under what conditions ideas travel, transfer, and take form as practices" is the intellectual labor of internationalization. Such enunciation—a theoretically nuanced term associated with the scholarship of Elizabeth Macedo[79]—involves not only documentation but recontextualization. Examples come from Asia and South America. In China, Zhang Wenjun[80] reports, postmodernism was reconfigured by some as primarily historical—and thus irrelevant, as China remains, these critics insisted, a country not yet in modernity—and by others split into destructive and constructive versions, inspiring some scholars to critique both Chinese and Western cultures. In Brazil, postmodernism merged with critical theory to produce what Alice Casimiro Lopes characterizes as "hybridism."[81]

Not only does recontextualization contradict world culture theory, so does the theory's retrospective historiography. Its "harmonizing" method, Daniel Tröhler[82] points out, starts with the positing of a globalized world, then works from the present to the past: from modernity and secularity backward to Christianity.[83] Another form of "Whig" history, Tröhler[84] notes, this grand narrative displays a "teleological progression" towards ever-increasing "individual liberty" and "enlightenment," formulated as liberal democracy and scientific progress. Modernity is now construed, Tröhler[85] observes, as the "permanent" obligation of "continuous self-development," a national undertaking that (over)relies on the educational system. Although crippling questions remain concerning the alleged link between educational and economic-social-political development,[86] these have not been acknowledged in demands for "development." The one world society, Tröhler[87] argues, "requires both the nation-state and its overcoming in the age of globalization." Perceiving this apparent paradox requires bifocality, conveyed in the concept of "glocal," as do Yehoshua Mathias and Naama Sabar in their insightful study of curriculum research and development in Israel.[88]

The paradox of "glocal" is evident in Hongyu Wang's theorization of the term "international" as "in-between" and as "fluid spaces" wherein "multiplicity" and "differences" are neither "excluded" nor "self-contained."[89] Both "national" and "international" are "relational concepts," Zhang Hua[90] has pointed out, so that "we should understand them based on relational" not "atomized" or "entity thinking." In contrast to "globalization," the "internationalization" of curriculum studies, Wang underscores, "supports the decentering of both the national and the global through a focus on interaction and relationship that leads to the transformation of both locality and globalness."[91] The "shared meaning" world culture theorists project on the actually existing world of endless difference is enunciated locally through academic study, teaching, and research. Shared meaning cannot enforced by standardized testing but constructed in complicated conversation informed by our expertise, animated by our professional ethics.

How might those of us committed to understanding curriculum encourage such meaning, shared but structured by difference? "We believe the study of the genesis and consolidation of an international curriculum field may contribute not only to analyses focused on specific settings," José Augusto Pacecho and Filipa Seabra[92] write, "but also . . . build upon the diversity and the recognition of realities, that, in many ways, are intersected." Here is the hybridism with which several Brazilian scholars work as well as the recontextualization our Chinese colleagues now emphasize.[93] As Pacheco and Seabra appreciate, "the internationalization of curriculum studies represents the contestation of globalization."[94]

That contestation is predicated on the primacy of the particular yes, but not (of course) its adoration, as we are obligated to articulate the relations among them. Implicit is no transcendental set of universals, but an implied, if differently experienced, sense of shared ideals[95] immanent to our experience, in part structured by the emergency of the present and the impending catastrophe that is apparently the future. It *is* time, as Michael F.D. Young knows, to bring knowledge back in, social, historical, indeed academic knowledge, including knowledge of our respective fields, their intellectual histories and present circumstances. These are the particulars we work to articulate. As Pacheco and Seabra[96] know, the "homogenization" of globalization "can never silence the role of the subject in the educational process," a subject simultaneously social and historical as well as subjective, racialized, gendered and classed, but species-identified too, as it is the earth that is now imperiled by climate change, a fact that cannot be comprehended apart from capitalism's consumption of education[97] as well. These bipolar scales of catastrophe—simultaneously personal and planetary—dilate the present moment, but the intensity of immediacy is now associated less with the excitement of existential engagement than it is to an uneasy feeling that time is running out.[98] Despite these crushing circumstances, buoyed by our intellectual histories, let us remain committed to understanding and, through understanding, creating more worthwhile curriculum[99] for children to study.

Notes

1 Keynote Address presented to the meeting of the European Association for Curriculum Studies held in Braga, Portugal, October 2013.
2 See Pinar 2014a.
3 "To become historical," Toews (2008, xix) explains, meant that "recognizing that personal and communal identity were historically constituted was also to take upon oneself the obligation of constituting oneself, personally and collectively, in historical action."
4 1926, 223.
5 In Mexico, for example Díaz Barriga (2014, 329) reports, a "hybridization" occurs as "structures and practices that stem from diverse origins can combine in order to create new entities in a kind of crossbreeding process which is never free from contradictions and exclusions." Such hybridization encourages "cosmopolitanism" that, within the Mexican field, is associated with "multicultural perspectives, openness to diversity and the balance between local and universal values" (2014, 329).
6 In their updated chapter on curriculum research in Israel, Yehoshua Mathias and Naama Sabar (2014, 253) acknowledge that curriculum is often the reflection of power struggles among various groups. But it is not only a "reflection" they note: "curricula are not merely reproductions of what is taking place in other sectors, but are also influenced by autonomous educational factors."
7 Professional ethics requires intransigence, and in a time of forced standardization intransigence means the endorsement of difference. In a different historical moment or in a different region today—say one dominated by parochial localisms—standardization could be cosmopolitan.

8 In the United States, Joe Kincheloe and I (1991) were the first to seize upon the significance of this concept to curriculum studies. For an elaboration of Kincheloe's pre-critical pedagogy phase—for me his most sophisticated—see Pinar 2010.
9 See Pinar 2014b, 526, 528 n. 12.
10 "The separateness and alterity of the past," Simon (2005, 112) explains, is what *faces* me. In this tensive demand of facing, there is a momentary shattering of the hermeneutic horizon on which past and present meet and within which historical interpretation becomes possible. This shattering interrupts the givenness of the present, opening the possibility of learning not just *about*, but *from* the past. In the past, thus, there inheres the possibility of an unforseeability, a *futurity* without predetermined direction."
11 Goodson 2014, 515.
12 For example, in Switzerland, as Rebekka Horlacher and Andrea De Vincenti (2014) explain, the two common terms "*Lehrplan*" (instruction plan) or "*Lehrplanung*" (instruction planning) may not coincide "fully" with their meanings and historical resonance in Germany.
13 The last meeting was held in Rio de Janeiro in July 2012, chaired by Professors Elizabeth Macedo and Alice Casimiro Lopes. In 2015 the meeting moves north to Ottawa—to be chaired by Professor Nicholas Ng-A-Fook—before returning to Asia in 2018.
14 See Wang 2014, 72; Pinar 2011a, 42, 178, 182, 203.
15 As Kögler (1999, 267–268) observes, "The subject is obviously supposed to be both situated and distanced, engaged and critically reflective, immersed in a specific context while analytically observing the structural implications of that very context. As I will argue, this integration of both attitudes is possible if one takes the process of reflexivity, which is indeed constitutive of subjectivity in this model, to be triggered by the other in a dialogical encounter always already embedded in a cultural context."
16 See Wang 2014 and my brief discussion of that work ahead in this text.
17 Autio 2014, 18.
18 McCarthy, Bulut, and Patel 2014, 34.
19 McCarthy, Bulut, and Patel 2014, 39.
20 McCarthy, Bulut, and Patel 2014, 42.
21 "The main expressions of instrumentalism in current educational policy," Michael F. D. Young (2008, 93) notes, "are marketization . . . and regulation."
22 See Pinar 2013.
23 Daniel Tröhler also acknowledges the central role this concept has played in rationalizing neoliberalism (see Tröhler 2011, 184).
24 Smith 2014, 46.
25 Smith 2014, 51.
26 Smith 2014, 48.
27 Ibid.
28 Smith 2014, 49.
29 Smith 2014, 51.
30 For curriculum as meditative inquiry see Kumar 2013.
31 Pinar 1972.
32 Tröhler 2014, 61.
33 Tröhler 2014, 65. As Tröhler (2011, 192–193) writes elsewhere:

> As there seem to be no Archimedean point from which we can perceive the subject of inquiry objectively, the inquiry needs to address the researcher as well—not in order to eliminate the researcher's own worldview and epistemological frame but in order to become aware of it.

34 Wang 2014, 67.

35 "Because curriculum is the heart of education," Wang (2014, 72) explains, "nonviolence needs to be at the center of curriculum studies." If we affirm a "new internationalism," she continues, "then nonviolently mobilizing organic relationships *within* and *across* the local, the national, and the international becomes important." Wang asks us to "envision nonviolent relationality as the central thread of internationalizing curriculum studies."
36 Wang 2014, 67.
37 Indeed, "the simultaneity of the local, the national, and the international dynamics is important for orienting curriculum studies towards nonviolence education," Wang (2014, 75) suggests.
38 Wang 2014, 67.
39 Wang 2014, 67–68.
40 Wang 2014, 68.
41 Wang 2014, 69.
42 Wang 2014, 75. Not only is social justice intertwined with subjectivity, so is history, as Tröhler (2011, 193) appreciates: "I see no other way than to historicize not only a topic but the construer of the topic as well."
43 The phrase is John Toews': "To become historical in the sense of recognizing that personal and communal identity were historically constituted was also to take upon oneself the obligation of constituting oneself, personally and collectively, in historical action" (2008, xix).
44 I am not endorsing the "person whose ideals and outlook would have been appropriate in a previous time or culture, but who cannot or will not change with the changing times" (Lear 2006, 119). "However unfairly," Lear (2006, 119) notes, "such people are stuck in the past." I am endorsing being "out-of-date" as a means not being stuck in the present.
45 Pinar 2012, 238.
46 Even within the nations where we work can we assume that!
47 Janet L. Miller is at work now on thinking through the theoretical issues embedded in this concept, one she phrases in terms of "communities without consensus" (see Pinar 2014b, 529, n. 16.)
48 See Freire 1970, 30, 33, 42, 51
49 In his study of Fanon, Bulhan (1985, 144) summarizes this dynamic: "The oppressors' violence, which has been internalized and institutionalized among the oppressed, is henceforth externalized and redirected in the service of personal and collective liberation. Horizontal violence thus changes into vertical counterviolence."
50 The American Academy of Pediatrics recommends that parents avoid screen media for children under two years of age (Singer 2013, August 8, B8).
51 For details see Pinar 2013.
52 Böttcher 2014, 201.
53 Program for International Student Assessment.
54 Böttcher 2014, 202. See also Tröhler 2014, 61.
55 Böttcher 2014, 202.
56 Böttcher 2014, 206.
57 Böttcher 2014, 207.
58 The Trends in International Mathematics and Science Study (TIMSS) provides (presumably) reliable and timely data on mathematics and science achievement.
59 In Spain, César Coll and Elena Martín explain, what is to be incorporated into the school curriculum is that knowledge that contributes "most" to developing abilities with the "greatest social relevance." This model means a "more open curriculum" offering teachers "greater autonomy" but accompanied by intense assessment.
60 Röhner 2014, 208.
61 Röhner 2014, 214.
62 Saari, Salmela, and Vilkkilä 2014, 184.
63 Saari, Salmela, and Vilkkilä 2014, 196.

64 Saari, Salmela, and Vilkkilä 2014, 196.
65 Ibid.
66 Salvio 2014, 270.
67 Salvio 2014, 271.
68 Salvio 2014, 273.
69 Salvio 2014, 275.
70 "Inasmuch as we elude the contingent familiarity of our thought and action by unmasking their historical-cultural origin," Kögler (1999, 174) clarifies, "we actualize at the same time an element of reason and reflexivity that is not simply bound up with contingent circumstances."
71 The phrase is Ivor Goodson's (2014). My term is "presentism" (2012, 58–58) but both reference the same phenomenon.
72 "Marxists do not find the dissolution of the local and particular that is effected by capitalism to be simply negative and destructive," Callinicos (2011, 75) reminds. "For them, the expansion of human powers and the subversion of tradition it brings are potentially liberating."
73 It is "too early to mourn the Nation-State's demise," Mathias and Sabar (2014, 260) appreciate, "since it is quite often the driving force behind standardization and reforms." Because the State continues to play a "dominant role in defining the educational curriculum, allocating hours, mobilizing pedagogical and organizational reforms, evaluating achievements and training and supplying the educational system's workforce," it is the State, Mathias and Sabar point out, that maintains the power to "interpret" what is meant by "global educational reform."
74 Carney, Rappleye, and Silova 2012, 367.
75 Carney, Rappleye, and Silova 2012, 368. First outlined by John Meyer in the 1970s, world culture theory's central theoretical claim, Carney, Rappleye, and Silova (2012, 368) explain, was that educational "expansion" was not especially responsive to the political, economic, and social structures of individual nation-states, but to global demands for world society. Carney, Rappleye, and Silova (2012, 371–373) outline the intellectual history of world culture theory, working from Weber through Parsons, referencing its revisions and additions (such as globalization as "shared meaning": see 2012, 374). As have Daniel Tröhler (see 2011, 184) and others (including myself: Pinar 2011, 51–52), Carney, Rappleye, and Silova (2012, 377, 379) are critical of the research of Ramirez and his colleagues, not only methodologically but also due to its apparent endorsement of standardization as effective, efficient, and equitable (see Carney, Rappleye, and Silova 2012, 383). Carney, Rappleye, and Silova (2012, 387) advise "all scholars to look inward and question the values embedded in their own science." Interesting, that admonition—"look inward"—coincides with Tröhler (2011, 193) conclusion: "Doing history is essentially the self-discovering of one's own standpoint."
76 Carney, Rappleye, and Silova 2012, 385.
77 Sometimes forcibly so, as in Mexico in the 1960s: see Pinar 2011, 209.
78 Carney, Rappleye, and Silova 2012, 387.
79 See Macedo 2011.
80 2014.
81 In Pinar 2011b, 14.
82 Tröhler 2011, 182.
83 See Tröhler 2011, 188–189.
84 Tröhler 2011, 182.
85 Tröhler 2011, 185.
86 See Coyle 2007, 51.
87 Tröhler 2011, 185.
88 Mathias and Sabar 2014.
89 Wang 2014, 72.
90 Quoted passages in Pinar 2014c.
91 Wang 2014, 72–73.

92 Pacheco and Seabra 2014, 397.
93 See Pinar in press.
94 Pacheco and Seabra 2014, 402.
95 Agathocleous (2011, 147) reminds that for Marx "revolutionary ideals must circulate differently."
96 Pacheco and Seabra 2014, 407.
97 See Pinar 2013 for details for its consumption in the United States by Apple, Pearson, and others.
98 "The postmodern militant," Perreau-Saussine (2011, 145) notes, "yesterday still fascinated by the future to be desired, is today anxious about the danger to be held at bay." Under such circumstances, Agathocleous (2011, 174) notes "the concept of humanity . . . is no longer a [neo]liberal one, for it is based on the notion of survival rather than a shared consciousness or set of ideals."
99 The canonical curriculum question—what knowledge is of most worth?—is embedded in this phrase—"more worthwhile curriculum"—composed by Professor Zhang Hua of Hangzhou Normal University (China) and the former President of the International Association for the Advancement of Curriculum Studies. The concept of "worthwhile"—"being worth the time or effort spent" (*Webster's* 1975, 1353)—reminds us that not only economic gain but subjective and social interest and well-being, historical reparation as well as intrinsic worth are to be considered in answering the ongoing curriculum question.

Bibliography

Agathocleous, Tanya. 2011. *Urban Realism and the Cosmopolitan Imagination in the Nineteenth Century. Visible City, Invisible World.* Cambridge: Cambridge University Press.

Autio, Tero. 2014. The Internationalization of Curriculum Research. In *The International Handbook of Curriculum Research,* edited by William F. Pinar (17–31). [Second edition.] New York: Routledge.

Böttcher, Wolfgang. 2014. Curriculum, Evaluation, and Control in Germany. *In The International Handbook of Curriculum Research*, edited by William F. Pinar (201–207). [Second edition.] New York: Routledge.

Bulhan, Hussein Abdilahi. 1985. *Frantz Fanon and the Psychology of Oppression*. New York: Plenum Press.

Callinicos, Alex. 2011. Two Cheers for Enlightenment Universalism. Or, Why It's Hard to Be an Aristotelian Revolutionary. In *Virtue and Politics*: *Alasdair MacIntyre's Revolutionary Aristotelianism*, edited by Paul Blackledge and Kevin Knight (54–78). Notre Dame, IN: University of Notre Dame Press.

Carney, Stephen, Rappleye, Jeremy, and Silova, Iveta. 2012, August. Between Faith and Science: World Culture Theory and Comparative Education. *Comparative Education Review* 56 (3), 366–393.

Coyle, Diane. 2007. *The Soulful Science: What Economists Really Do and Why It Matters*. Princeton, NJ: Princeton University Press.

Díaz Barriga, Frida. 2014. Curriculum Research in Mexico. In the *International Handbook of Curriculum Research,* edited by William F. Pinar (329–339). [Second edition.] New York: Routledge

Freire, Paulo. 1970. *Pedagogy of the Oppressed*. [Trans. Myra Bergman Ramos.] New York: Herder & Herder.

Garduño, José María García. 2011. Acculturation, Hybridity, Cosmopolitanism in Ibero American Curriculum Studies. In *Curriculum Studies in Mexico: Intellectual Histories, Present Circumstances* (137–163). New York: Palgrave Macmillan.

Goodson, Ivor F. 2014. Developing Curriculum History. A British Perspective. In the *International Handbook of Curriculum Research*, edited by William F. Pinar (515–520). New York: Routledge.

Horlacher, Rebekka and De Vincenti, Andrea 2014. From Rationalist Autonomy to Scientific Empiricism. A History of Curriculum in Switzerland. In *The International Handbook of Curriculum Research*, edited by William F. Pinar (476–492). [Second edition.] New York: Routledge.

Kincheloe, Joe L. and Pinar, William F. eds. 1991. *Curriculum as Social Psychoanalysis: The Significance of Place*. Albany: State University of New York Press.

Kögler, Hans-Herbert. 1999. *The Power of Dialogue: Critical Hermeneutics after Gadamer and Foucault*. Cambridge, MA: MIT Press.

Kumar, Ashwani. 2013. *Curriculum as Meditative Inquiry*. New York: Palgrave Macmillan.

Lear, Jonathan. 2006. *Radical Hope: Ethics in the Face of Cultural Devastation*. Cambridge, MA: Harvard University Press.

Macedo, Elizabeth. 2011. Curriculum as Cultural Enunciation. In *Curriculum Studies in Brazil: Intellectual Histories, Present Circumstances*, edited by William F. Pinar (135–153). New York: Palgrave Macmillan.

Mathias, Yehoshua and Sabar, Naama. 2014. Curriculum Planning from the National to the Glocal. The Israeli Case. In *The International Handbook of Curriculum Research*, edited by William F. Pinar (253–268). [Second edition.] New York: Routledge.

McCarthy, Cameron, Bulut, Ergin, and Patel, Rushika. 2014. Race and Education in the Age of Digital Capitalism. In *The International Handbook of Curriculum Research*, edited by William F. Pinar (32–44). [Second edition.] New York: Routledge.

Pacheco, José Augusto and Seabra, Filipa. 2014. Curriculum Research in Portugal. Emergence, Research, and Europeanization. In *The International Handbook of Curriculum Research*, edited by William F. Pinar (397–410). [Second edition.] New York: Routledge.

Perreau-Saussine, Emile. 2011. The Moral Critique of Stalinism. In *Virtue and Politics: Alasdair MacIntyre's Revolutionary Aristotelianism*, edited by Paul Blackledge and Kevin Knight (134–151). Notre Dame, IN: University of Notre Dame Press.

Pinar, William F. 1972. Working from Within. *Educational Leadership* 29 (4), 329–331. [Reprinted in *Autobiography, Politics, and Sexuality*, Peter Lang Publishing, 1994, 7–11.]

Pinar, William F. Ed. 2003. *International Handbook of Curriculum Research*. Mahwah, NJ: Lawrence Erlbaum.

Pinar, William F. 2010. A Southern Treasure. *Journal of the American Association for the Advancement of Curriculum Studies* online.

Pinar, William F. 2011a. *The Character of Curriculum Studies. Bildung, Currere, and the Recurring Question of the Subject*. New York: Palgrave Macmillan.

Pinar, William F. Ed. 2011b. *Curriculum Studies in Brazil: Intellectual Histories, Present Circumstances*. New York: Palgrave Macmillan.

Pinar, William F. 2011c. Ed. *Curriculum Studies in Mexico: Intellectual Histories, Present Circumstances*. New York: Palgrave Macmillan.

Pinar, William F. 2012. *What Is Curriculum Theory?* [Second edition.] New York: Routledge.

Pinar, William F. 2013. *Curriculum Studies in the United States: Intellectual Histories, Present Circumstances*. New York: Palgrave Macmillan.

Pinar, William F. 2014b. Curriculum Research in the United States. Crisis, Reconceptualization, Internationalization. In *The International Handbook of Curriculum Research*, edited by William F. Pinar (521–532). [Second edition.] New York: Routledge.

Pinar, William F. ed. 2014c. *Curriculum Studies in China. Intellectual Histories, Present Circumstances*. New York: Palgrave Macmillan.

Röhner, Charlotte. 2014. Competence-Oriented Curriculum Reform in the Federal Republic of Germany. In *The International Handbook of Curriculum Research*, edited by William F. Pinar (208–216). [Second edition.] New York: Routledge.

Saari, Antti, Salmela, Sauli, and Vilkkilä, Jarkko. 2014. Governing Autonomy. Subjectivity, Freedom, and Knowledge in Finnish Curriculum Discourse. In *The International Handbook of Curriculum Research*, edited by William F. Pinar (183–200). [Second edition.] New York: Routledge.

Salvio, Paula. 2014. "Cities and Signs." Understanding Curriculum Studies in Italy. In *The International Handbook of Curriculum Research*, edited by William F. Pinar (269–277). [Second edition.] New York: Routledge.

Simon, Roger I. 2005. *The Touch of the Past. Remembrance, Learning, and Ethics*. New York: Palgrave Macmillan.

Singer, Natasha. 2013, August 8. Group Criticizes Learnings Apps for Babies. *New York Times*, B8.

Smith, David Geoffrey. 2003. Curriculum and Teaching Face Globalization. In *The International Handbook of Curriculum Research*, edited by William F. Pinar (35–51). Mahwah, NJ: Lawrence Erlbaum.

Smith, David Geoffrey. 2014. Wisdom Responses to Globalization. In *The International Handbook of Curriculum Research*, edited by William F. Pinar (45–59). [Second edition.] New York: Routledge.

Toews, John. 2008. *Becoming Historical: Cultural Reformation and Public Memory in Early Nineteenth-Century Berlin*. New York: Cambridge University Press.

Tröhler, Daniel. 2011. *Languages of Education. Protestant Legacies, National Identities, and Global Aspirations*. New York: Routledge.

Tröhler, Daniel. 2014. International Curriculum Research. In *The International Handbook of Curriculum Research*, edited by William F. Pinar (60–66). [Second edition.] New York: Routledge.

Wang, Hongyu. 2014. A Nonviolent Perspective on Internationalizing Curriculum Studies. In *The International Handbook of Curriculum Research*, edited by William F. Pinar (67–76). [Second edition.] New York: Routledge.

Washburne, Carleton. 1926. The Philosophy of the Winnetka Curriculum. In *The Twenty-Sixth Yearbook of the National Society for the Study of Education. The Foundations and Technique of Curriculum-Construction*. Part I: *Curriculum-Making: Past and Present*, edited by Guy Montrose Whipple (219–228). Bloomington, IL: Public School Publishing Company.

Webster's New Collegiate Dictionary. 1975. Springfield, MA: G. & C. Merriam Company.

Zhang, Wenjun. 2014. Growing with Postmodernism: A Story of Curriculum Studies in China. In *Curriculum Studies in China*, edited by William F. Pinar (115–128). New York: Palgrave Macmillan.

EPILOGUE

> History, then, is not a single time space: it is a multiplicity of time spans that entangle and envelope one another.
>
> Michel Foucault[1]

What has changed from the days Addams faced, this our own Gilded Age, our not exactly cosmopolitan present? Public schools are now purchased by profiteers posing as reformers. Our cherished concepts are turned against us, as teachers are demoted to facilitators, slated soon to slide into marginality, rehired as auditors, checking online curriculum structured like tax returns that talk back. No pensions to pay teachers then—just short-term, performance-based, contract busywork—but even bigger bonuses for CEOs at Apple, Microsoft, News Corp., Pearson, and the other predators feeding on the anxieties of parents and the innocence of children. We witness the end of curriculum as lived, as knowledge degrades into information, history disappears into presentism, materiality into virtuality, and alterity is incorporated into the homogeneity recognition requires.

I feared such a future when, in 1976, Madeleine Grumet and I called for a "poor" curriculum, e.g. one stripped of technology, structured instead by dialogical encounter, solitude, and sustained study.[2] We weren't alone, and with others we reconceptualized curriculum studies, a field split off from the schools, as entrepreneurship, not expertise, qualified one to exercise jurisdiction over the school curriculum. Distracting the public from their own failures, politicians made sure that the shell game that is U.S. school reform was the only game in town by scapegoating teachers and those of us who teach them.

I've named our home in the woods "Varykino" to invoke the image of a secluded retreat at the end of an era. There is no poem for me to write by candlelight, deep in the exquisite if suffocating snow—how grateful I am that our suffering is so small compared to that recorded in *Dr. Zhivago*—only an epilogue, but a love poem still, if on this occasion to a lifetime of study, to that ongoing ethical engagement with alterity that is educational experience as lived. Thinking, Foucault knew,[3] "must be lived." Submerged in screens, what is "lived" today? Alas, all the terms in my title are now "under erasure":[4] silenced but still audible, if as an echo.

Restructured by technology—indeed we are now post-human—the person remains primary for me, even if as a flickering memory, an image on the screen in an old movie, a character in a novel or poem, the subject of a book chapter. I'm not claiming to be one, only a refugee who remembers. You did meet several actual (if deceased) persons of "marked" individuality in this collection, personifying my conviction that unless it is lived, educational experience empties, devolving into a mental game, a "second life"—an online virtual abstraction, too often reduced to a numeral—not an actual material problem of "my life and flesh,"[5] as Pasolini appreciated. With resolve, focused on the flesh, we can become historical, individuated, even educated. Still.

I am still studying—after 9/11, after 3/11, before calamities to come, political acts and natural disasters made worse by technological means and effects.[6] We are no longer standing, no longer reserve, now spellbound by screens that stare back at us, pretending to please as they consume us. History doesn't repeat itself, but as Twain teased, it rhymes. Now it rings.

Notes

1 Quoted in Koopman 2013, 43. "Genealogy," Koopman comments, "does not aim to substitute space for time, but rather aims to substitute temporal complexity and contingency for historical unity and necessity."
2 Now being reprinted: see Pinar and Grumet in press.
3 See Luxon 2013, 148.
4 Lather 2007, 73, 109.
5 Quoted in Pinar 2009, 108.
6 "[I]t is in study," Block (2007, 47) reminds, "that we mean by the present to change the future and rewrite the past."

Bibliography

Block, Alan A. 2007. *Pedagogy, Religion, and Practice: Reflections on Ethics and Teaching*. New York: Palgrave Macmillan.
Koopman, Colin. 2013. *Genealogy as Critique: Foucault and the Problems of Modernity*. Bloomington: Indiana University Press.
Lather, Patti. 2007. *Getting Lost: Feminist Efforts toward a Double(d) Science*. Albany: State University of New York Press.
Luxon, Nancy. 2013. *Crisis of Authority. Politics, Trust, and Truth-Telling in Freud and Foucault*. Cambridge: Cambridge University Press.
Pinar, William F. 2009. *The Worldliness of a Cosmopolitan Education: Passionate Lives in Public Service*. New York: Routledge.
Pinar, William F. and Grumet, Madeleine R. in press. (1976). *Toward a Poor Curriculum*. Troy, NY: Educator's International Press.

SOURCES AND PERMISSIONS

Introduction: Pinar, William F. 2009. The Primacy of the Particular. In *Leaders in Curriculum Studies: Intellectual Self-Portraits*, edited by Leonard Waks and Edmund C. Short (143–152). Rotterdam and Tapei: Sense Publishers. Used with permission.

Chapter 1 Study: Pinar, William F. 2004, June. The Problem with Curriculum and Pedagogy. *Journal of Curriculum and Pedagogy*, Taylor & Francis. Volume 1, Issue 1, pp. 21–24. Used with permission.

Chapter 2 Allegory: From Pinar, William F. 2012. *What Is Curriculum Theory?* (49–56). [Second edition.] Routledge.

Chapter 3 Internationalization: NA (unpublished).

Chapter 4 Nationalism: Pinar, William F. 2011. Nationalism, Anti-Americanism, Canadian Identity. In *Curriculum in Today's World: Configuring Knowledge, Identities, Work and Politics*, edited by Lyn Yates and Madeleine Grumet (31–43). London: Routledge. Used with permission.

Chapter 5 Technology: Pinar, William F. 2013. The First Task of Thought in Our Time. *Critical Literacy: Theories and Practices* 7 (1), 1–16. © William F. Pinar

Chapter 6 Reform: NA (unpublished).

Chapter 7 Misrepresentation: Pinar, William F. 2013, May. Plagiarism and the Tyler Rationale. *Journal of the American Association for the Advancement of Curriculum Studies* 9 (1), 1–13. Used with permission.

Chapter 8 Conversation: Pinar, William F. 2011. Introduction. *The Character of Curriculum Studies. Bildung, Currere, and the Recurring Question of the Subject* (1–21). New York: Palgrave Macmillan.

Chapter 9 Place: Pinar, William F. 2010. A Southern Treasure. *The Journal of the American Association for the Advancement of Curriculum Studies* online. Used with permission.

Chapter 10 Emergence: Pinar, William F. 2001. *The Gender of Racial Politics and Violence in American: Lynching, Prison Rape, and the Crisis of Masculinity*. New York: Peter Lang. Used with permission.

Chapter 11 Alterity: Pinar, William F. 2006. *Race, Religion and a Curriculum of Reparation*. New York: Palgrave Macmillan. Used with permission.

Chapter 12 Discipline: Pinar, William F. 2013. Strict Discipline. *International Journal for the Historiography of Education* 3 (1), 94–101. Used with permission.

Chapter 13 Identity: Pinar, William F. 2009. *The Worldliness of a Cosmopolitan Education: Passionate Lives in Public Service*. New York: Routledge. Used with permission.

Chapter 14 Resolve: Pinar, William F. 2014. Between Hope and Despair is Resolve: Remembering Roger Simon. *Journal of the Canadian Association for Curriculum Studies* 11 (2), 6–20. Used with permission.

Chapter 15 Decolonization: Pinar, William F. 2011. *The Character of Curriculum Studies. Bildung, Currere, and the Recurring Question of the Subject*. New York: Palgrave Macmillan. Used with permission.

Chapter 16 Inwardness: Pinar, William F. 2010. On the Privacy of Public Pedagogy: The Essayism of Robert Musil. In Jennifer A. Sandlin, Brian Schultz, and Steven Burdick. Eds. *Handbook of Public Pedagogy* (45–55). New York: Routledge. Used with permission.

Chapter 17 Individuality: Pinar, William F. 2009. *The Worldliness of a Cosmopolitan Education: Passionate Lives in Public Service*. New York: Routledge. Used with permission

Chapter 18 Cosmopolitanism: Pinar, William F. 2013, October. The Cosmopolitan Cause of Curriculum Studies. Keynote address presented to the inaugural meeting of the European Association for Curriculum Studies, Braga, Portugal. Unpublished.

INDEX